terra australis 35

Terra Australis reports the results of archaeological and related research within the south and east of Asia, though mainly Australia, New Guinea and island Melanesia — lands that remained terra australis incognita to generations of prehistorians. Its subject is the settlement of the diverse environments in this isolated quarter of the globe by peoples who have maintained their discrete and traditional ways of life into the recent recorded or remembered past and at times into the observable present.

List of volumes in Terra Australis

Volume 1: Burrill Lake and Currarong: Coastal Sites in Southern New South Wales. R.J. Lampert (1971)

Volume 2: Ol Tumbuna: Archaeological Excavations in the Eastern Central Highlands, Papua New Guinea. J.P. White (1972)

Volume 3: New Guinea Stone Age Trade: The Geography and Ecology of Traffic in the Interior. I. Hughes (1977)

Volume 4: Recent Prehistory in Southeast Papua. B. Egloff (1979)

Volume 5: The Great Kartan Mystery. R. Lampert (1981)

Volume 6: Early Man in North Queensland: Art and Archaeology in the Laura Area. A. Rosenfeld, D. Horton and J. Winter (1981)

Volume 7: The Alligator Rivers: Prehistory and Ecology in Western Arnhem Land. C. Schrire (1982)

Volume 8: Hunter Hill, Hunter Island: Archaeological Investigations of a Prehistoric Tasmanian Site. S. Bowdler (1984)

Volume 9: Coastal South-West Tasmania: The Prehistory of Louisa Bay and Maatsuyker Island. R. Vanderwal and D. Horton (1984)

Volume 10: The Emergence of Mailu. G. Irwin (1985)

Volume 11: Archaeology in Eastern Timor, 1966–67. I. Glover (1986)

Volume 12: Early Tongan Prehistory: The Lapita Period on Tongatapu and its Relationships. J. Poulsen (1987)

Volume 13: Coobool Creek. P. Brown (1989)

Volume 14: 30,000 Years of Aboriginal Occupation: Kimberley, North-West Australia. S. O'Connor (1999)

Volume 15: Lapita Interaction. G. Summerhayes (2000)

Volume 16: The Prehistory of Buka: A Stepping Stone Island in the Northern Solomons. S. Wickler (2001)

Volume 17: The Archaeology of Lapita Dispersal in Oceania. G.R. Clark, A.J. Anderson and T. Vunidilo (2001)

Volume 18: An Archaeology of West Polynesian Prehistory. A. Smith (2002)

Volume 19: Phytolith and Starch Research in the Australian-Pacific-Asian Regions: The State of the Art. D. Hart and L. Wallis (2003)

Volume 20: The Sea People: Late-Holocene Maritime Specialisation in the Whitsunday Islands, Central Queensland. B. Barker (2004)

Volume 21: What's Changing: Population Size or Land-Use Patterns? The Archaeology of Upper Mangrove Creek, Sydney Basin. V. Attenbrow (2004)

Volume 22: The Archaeology of the Aru Islands, Eastern Indonesia. S. O'Connor, M. Spriggs and P. Veth (2005)

Volume 23: Pieces of the Vanuatu Puzzle: Archaeology of the North, South and Centre. S. Bedford (2006)

Volume 24: Coastal Themes: An Archaeology of the Southern Curtis Coast, Queensland. S. Ulm (2006)

Volume 25: Lithics in the Land of the Lightning Brothers: The Archaeology of Wardaman Country, Northern Territory. C. Clarkson (2007)

Volume 26: Oceanic Explorations: Lapita and Western Pacific Settlement. S. Bedford, C. Sand and S. P. Connaughton (2007)

Volume 27: Dreamtime Superhighway: Sydney Basin Rock Art and Prehistoric Information Exchange. J. McDonald (2008)

Volume 28: New Directions in Archaeological Science. A. Fairbairn, S. O'Connor and B. Marwick (2008)

Volume 29: Islands of Inquiry: Colonisation, Seafaring and the Archaeology of Maritime Landscapes. G. Clark, F. Leach and S. O'Connor (2008)

Volume 30: Archaeological Science Under a Microscope: Studies in Residue and Ancient DNA Analysis in Honour of Thomas H. Loy. M. Haslam, G. Robertson, A. Crowther, S. Nugent and L. Kirkwood (2009)

Volume 31: The Early Prehistory of Fiji. G. Clark and A. Anderson (2009)

Volume 32: Altered Ecologies: Fire, Climate and Human Influence on Terrestrial Landscapes. S. Haberle, J. Stevenson and M. Prebble (2010)

Volume 33: Man Bac: The Excavation of a Neolithic Site in Northern Vietnam: The Biology. M. Oxenham, H. Matsumura and N. Kim Dung (2011)

Volume 34: Peopled Landscapes: Archaeological and Biogeographic Approaches to Landscapes. S. Haberle and B. David.

terra australis 35

Pacific Island Heritage

ARCHAEOLOGY, IDENTITY & COMMUNITY

**Edited by Jolie Liston, Geoffrey Clark
and Dwight Alexander**

ANU
THE AUSTRALIAN NATIONAL UNIVERSITY

E PRESS

ANU
E PRESS

© 2011 ANU E Press

Published by ANU E Press
The Australian National University
Canberra ACT 0200 Australia
Email: anuepress@anu.edu.au
Web: http://epress.anu.edu.au

National Library of Australia Cataloguing-in-Publication entry

Title:	Pacific island heritage : archaeology, identity and community / edited by Jolie Liston, Geoffrey Clark and Dwight Alexander.
ISBN:	9781921862472 (pbk.) 9781921862489 (ebook)
Series:	Terra Australis ; 35.
Subjects:	Cultural property--Protection--Palau. Historic preservation--Palau. Historic sites--Palau. Archaeology--Palau. Palau.

Other Authors/Contributors:
Liston, Jolie.
Clark, Geoffrey R. (Geoffrey Richard), 1966-
Alexander, Dwight.

Dewey Number: 363.6909966

Series Editor: Sue O'Connor

Typesetting and design: Rachel Lawson

Cover image: Getty Images LPI:72263240, Children fishing on bambo raft, Palau

Back cover map: Hollandia Nova. Thevenot 1663 by courtesy of the National Library of Australia.
Reprinted with permission of the National Library of Australia.

Terra Australis Editorial Board: Sue O'Connor, Jack Golson, Simon Haberle, Sally Brockwell, Geoffrey Clark

Acknowledgements

The *Pacific Island archaeology in the 21st century: Relevance and engagement* conference was sponsored by generous grants from the UNESCO Participation Program, the Guam Preservation Trust, the Richard F. Taitano Micronesian Area Research Center at the University of Guam, the AusAid International Seminar Support Scheme, the AusAid Small Grants Scheme in the Embassy of the Federated States of Micronesia, the Australian Department of the Environment, Water, Heritage and the Arts Asia Pacific Focal Point Program, the World Archaeological Congress, and the US National Park Service. Donations from Palau's businesses and community members also contributed to the conference's success. The event was organised by the Palau Bureau of Arts and Culture, the Belau National Museum, Garcia and Associates: Natural and Cultural Resource Consultants, and Archaeology and Natural History in the School of Culture, History and Language in the Australian National University, with the assistance of the Palau Community Action Agency. The editors thank all the people and institutions who supported the Palau conference and this volume.

The editors gratefully acknowledge publication support from the Micronesian Area Research Centre (MARC, University of Guam), the Guam Preservation Trust (Inangokkon Inadahi Guahan) and Garcia and Associates, Natural and Cultural Resource Consultants.

GUAM
INANGOKKON
PRESERVATION
INADAHI GUAHAN
TRUST

MARC

GANDA

GARCIA and ASSOCIATES
NATURAL & CULTURAL RESOURCE CONSULTANTS

Rita Olsudong
28/04/1965–30/03/2009

The *Pacific Island archaeology in the 21st century* conference and this volume are dedicated to the memory of Rita Olsudong, Palau's National Archaeologist. Rita had a strong commitment and passion to preserve the cultural heritage of Palau and she was an inspiration and good friend to fellow Pacific Islanders and foreign researchers.

Rita began her career in cultural preservation as an archaeological surveyor under Palau's Historic Preservation Program in 1991. After earning her MA in archaeology at La Trobe University in Australia in 1995, she returned to Palau to become the National Archaeologist, overseeing all archaeological work in the Bureau of Arts and Culture and for the Republic of Palau. At the time she was one of a small but steadily growing number of indigenous archaeologists working in the Pacific.

Rita performed a number of key surveys during her tenure as National Archaeologist, identifying hundreds of significant cultural sites, and assisted the National Registrar to collect information for the Palau Historical and Cultural Advisory Board. The archaeological data obtained was vital in protecting significant historical properties and many new sites are known as a result of her detailed recording of cultural properties affected by development projects. Rita also provided invaluable assistance to foreign archaeologists in their academic endeavours and to major infrastructure works such as the Compact Road and Capital Relocation Projects.

Rita was passionate about speaking to Palau's youth, endeavouring to instil in them a desire to safeguard their heritage. She taught at the Palau Community College and encouraged students to serve as the nation's next generation of archaeologists and historic preservation experts. Rita was instrumental in registering four of Palau's cultural sites on the World Heritage Tentative List; Tet el Bad (stone coffin), Beluu er a Imeong (Imeong Traditional Village), Oubalang er a Ngedebech (Ngedebech Terraces), and Uet el Daob ma Uet el Beluu and Chelechol ra Orrak (Yapese Stone Money Quarries).

Rita wanted to showcase Palau's traditional lifeways and unique natural and cultural heritage at the Pacific Island archaeology conference, but tragically passed away just months before the conference. She was a driving force in making cultural heritage a community and national issue. Her enduring contribution is the preservation of Palau's culture, history and prehistoric sites for future generations. Rita is survived by her husband Calvin Taurengel Emesiochel, son Brandon Ngiratong Shiro and daughter Dilreng Emesiochel.

Contents

Introduction

Pacific Island heritage: An overview

Jolie Liston[1], Geoffrey Clark[1] and Dwight Alexander[2]

1. Archaeology and Natural History, College of Asia and the Pacific, The Australian National University, Australia

2. Bureau of Arts and Culture, Ministry of Community and Cultural Affairs, Republic of Palau

The conference *Pacific Island archaeology in the 21st century: Relevance and engagement* was held in the Republic of Palau from 1–3 July in 2009 and was attended by more than 300 local and international participants. The conference assessed how Pacific Islander culture is integral to preserving and protecting the natural and cultural resources of Oceania as both are currently threatened by rapid economic, social and environmental changes. The premier registrar of natural and cultural sites is the UNESCO World Heritage List, which currently consists of 911 properties, of which 77% are cultural, 20% natural and 3% mixed. The tropical Pacific Islands have only a small number of listed properties, with many major islands and archipelagos under-represented. At the national level, cultural properties are often outnumbered by natural parks and protected marine and forest environments. Many prehistoric sites in the Pacific are owned/occupied by local groups with traditional land rights, who have the primary responsibility for managing historically significant sites, prehistoric as well as those of recent age. The focus of the conference was therefore on community engagement in cultural heritage preservation and management. Under rapid economic development, the social effects of globalisation and the nascent impacts of climate change, communities and governments in the Pacific Islands will need to protect their heritage by marshalling specialised resources at home and abroad and increasing community involvement in cultural and natural site preservation. Such an approach reinforces a necessary and productive union between natural and cultural resource management, which allows the views and expertise of community stakeholders to be combined appropriately with the knowledge of academics, scientists and heritage professionals.

The conference was held to facilitate and reinforce these delicate relationships while emphasising the need for groups involved in heritage management to deepen their understanding of each other's methods and perspectives. In the Pacific, for instance, oral history and many aspects of subsistence collection and social activity are culturally prescribed and sanctioned as 'traditional' by long use. In popular thought, and indeed in some public policy, the traditional behaviour of insular societies can be taken as the manifestation of unchanging cultures that are highly vulnerable to contemporary challenges such as climate change, high rates of migration and the societal impacts of globalisation. Yet archaeology and palaeoenvironmental studies demonstrate that not all cultural behaviour in Pacific societies was retained in the past to become 'traditional'. There is extensive evidence that Pacific societies have frequently adapted to a multitude of environmental and social events in the past. It is this historical evidence for continuity, resilience and resourcefulness that is evident today in many Pacific communities where engagement with cultural heritage is increasingly seen as a means of strengthening and retaining group identity and preserving the local environment while allowing many Pacific Islanders to participate effectively in an increasingly globalised economy and society.

As the papers in this volume demonstrate, knowledge of the past is continually used to adjust to cultural and natural changes, and physical sites of tangible heritage frequently act as a focus for community and national identity in a similar way to the performance of traditional chants, songs, oratory and dances. Preservation of archaeological and historic sites assists in the maintenance of community history, therefore, as sites function as a cultural mnemonic and community management of heritage sites often leads to renewed interest in traditional activities, increased local and international tourism, and increased social cohesion. In our view, Pacific societies that are grounded in their tangible and intangible cultural heritage are more likely to be cohesive and able to respond effectively to the environmental and social shifts forecast in the 21st century.

As the first large-scale Pacific heritage meeting held in Micronesia, the conference provided an opportunity to build region-wide networks that could be used to foster sustainable growth and economic development around community management of cultural and natural heritage sites. The personal and professional networks created during the conference will assist in creating a critical mass of expert opinion and on-the-ground management skills that will benefit heritage sites in many Pacific Islands. The conference was organised around a series of concurrent symposia, panel discussions and public lectures, with a day devoted to heritage ecotourism. The sessions examined indigenous, public and scholarly interpretations of cultural sites, island environments and climate change, indigenous heritage research and management, the connections between oral tradition and archaeology, practical approaches to heritage tourism, community involvement in heritage management, the role of museums in developing nations, and strategies for combining natural and cultural resource management.

James Dion, Associate Director of the Centre for Sustainable Destinations, National Geographic Society, gave the keynote address and chaired a session on the use of community-based heritage ecotourism to generate income through sustainable economic development. President of the World Archaeological Congress Professor Claire Smith (Flinders University) spoke on global trends in cultural heritage and how these will affect Pacific Island nations. Dr Rufino Mauricio, Chairman of ICOMOS Pacifica, Director of the FSM National Historic Preservation Office, and Secretary General of the FSM National Commission on UNESCO, gave a second keynote on the relevance of cultural and historical resources, with an example of the merging of oral history and archaeology in Pacific heritage management. An evening presentation was given by Professor Patrick Nunn, Professor of Oceanic Geoscience, University of the South Pacific, followed by a lengthy question and answer session about his presentation on the impact that changing sea levels will have on Pacific Island environments and societies.

More than 300 people attended the conference, with 90 off-island delegates and the remainder from Palauan communities. Represented were academic institutions, government agencies, heritage resource consultants, environmental groups, tourism associations, educators, chiefly councils, museums, NGOs, and construction and tour businesses. Delegates came from 18 nations, including Sweden, Germany, New Zealand, Australia, Fiji, Rapa Nui, the United

States, Samoa, Vanuatu, New Caledonia, Guam, the Commonwealth of the Northern Marianas, the Federated States of Micronesia, the Republic of the Marshall Islands, French Polynesia and the Philippines.

The issues of greatest interest concerned contemporary economic development and climate change, particularly the effects of a rising sea level, the need to merge natural and cultural heritage management rather than treat each separately, and the implementation of community strategies to manage heritage sites. Heritage tourism was seen by many participants as a sustainable form of economic development that could be used by a community to conserve its heritage sites and employ local people. The presentation by the Guampedia Foundation on the use of its website to provide heritage resources was also enthusiastically received and several Pacific nations are now exploring the possibility of creating internet sites dedicated to their national and community heritage. In a peer-reviewed dictionary format, such sites will make information about the culture and traditions of a Pacific Island available to local students, islanders living outside the Pacific, and other interested parties.

The strong public participation by Palauan people through attendance and involvement in sessions was a conference highlight and bridged a long-standing divide between foreign researchers and local communities actively seeking information to manage heritage sites. Too often, the science of archaeology has been separated from the practical realities of site management, and although there are several cogent reasons for this division, there is a growing understanding that heritage sites throughout the Pacific are a fragile, limited and significant cultural resource that need urgent protection. Combining the archaeological 'science' from Pacific archaeological sites with the living connection and stewardship of the local community can make a strong and often compelling case for site protection and preservation at national and international levels. Division between foreign experts and local groups, often glossed as debate about 'who owns the past', has ignored the reality that important cultural sites are being degraded and destroyed at an unprecedented rate. If groups and individuals with a shared historical focus and respect for the past do not combine their resources, there will be far fewer heritage sites in the Pacific for future generations.

1

Identity and alternative versions of the past in New Zealand

Geoffrey Clark

Archaeology and Natural History, College of Asia and the Pacific, The Australian National University, Australia

Introduction

During the 1990s, New Zealand/Aotearoa experienced tumultuous debate over indigenous land rights, and the use of Maori culture and language, debate which was associated with the settlement of historical and contemporary grievances between the Crown and Maori. The study of New Zealand's human past during this period became politicised and problematic because different versions of that past could be mobilised to support various agendas and cultural groupings. The redistribution of state-owned resources to Maori through the Waitangi Tribunal process and settlement negotiations with the government gave added intensity to debates about ownership and culturally appropriate use of the past, as did the fact that, with several notable exceptions, most professionally trained historians and archaeologists were of European descent.

The refashioning of the cultural landscape at this time allowed concepts of identity to be destabilised, essentialised and reconstructed. For instance, some people of non-Maori descent, often glossed as 'Pakeha' (but see Goldsmith 2005), who historically belonged to the dominant colonial group, felt threatened by the prospect of a Maori cultural and economic renaissance supported by government redistribution of assets and the assertion that Maori had ancestral rights to New Zealand, as opposed to everyone else. Within Maoridom there were schisms between groups and subgroups involving membership and affiliation, and uncertainty over the rights of urban Maori to access resources through the Waitangi Tribunal. Most of all, if Maori were enshrined as the indigenous people of the land then the non-Maori majority might be considered 'non-indigenous', a term that carries the negative environmental connotations of being foreign, exotic and invasive to the land.

To evade the potentially marginal status implied by a 'non-indigenous' classification many Pakeha appear to have constructed a dual, and I would suggest hierarchical, view of indigeneity in which Maori are held to be the essential indigenous people because they were the first to colonise and inhabit New Zealand, while native-born Pakeha are also held to be indigenous to New Zealand, but less so than Maori because they arrived later. The 1840 Treaty of Waitangi between Maori (*tangata whenua*, people of the land) and non-Maori (*tangata tiriti*, people of the Treaty) is taken to be the charter that preserves the occupation rights of both groups, but especially colonial-derived Pakeha. When queried, individual Pakeha are in no doubt they are indigenous to New Zealand, but express uncertainty about whether Pakeha as a group can be considered indigenous. This suggests that defining oneself as 'Pakeha' involves, in addition to being 'native born', an element of choice both in rejecting other potential homelands and supporting New Zealand biculturalism by consciously, at some level, asserting Pakeha identity. In short, Maori, it is assumed, cannot be anything other than indigenous, while native-born non-Maori have a choice. The basic division outlined above needs to be tested in public survey, but if it has any validity then it implies a third 'non-indigenous' group composed of non-native migrants/settlers, and native-born people of non-Maori descent who, for whatever reason, reject Pakeha identity, to which the general term 'New Zealander' might apply. The shifting meaning of group identity labels is shown by the common use of the term 'New Zealander' by explorers such as James Cook to describe Maori in the 18th century.

Claims to being 'indigenous', then, stem from the group membership of an individual, either, as I have suggested above, as Maori, Pakeha or New Zealander, or in some other grouping. Whichever is used, to be truly indigenous is usually taken to mean having an ancestral link to the first inhabitants of the land. Alternative prehistories can be used to claim indigenous identity by asserting the arrival of people prior to the arrival of the people held to have been the first arrivals. These claims in New Zealand impinge on the status of Maori as *tangata whenua* and on orthodox views of the past developed by archaeologists, historians and anthropologists. In this paper, I review the alternative prehistory and activities of the Nation of Waitaha in the turbulent 1990s and the media response of archaeologists and others to allegations that New Zealand had a hidden pre-Maori past. The review illustrates how a manufactured past can be an effective tool in contemporary forums even though the aim in promulgating such views is probably the desire by some non-Maori to realise indigenous status.

The Nation of Waitaha

Reference is made in this paper to two Waitaha groups, which need to be clearly distinguished from each other. The Maori of New Zealand refer to their earliest actual named ancestors in the South Island as 'Waitaha'. The subsequent arrival of tribes from the North Island, most notably Ngati Mamoe and Ngai Tahu, led to the integration of the Waitaha peoples with these tribes. Thus, 'Waitaha' refers here to those Maori who stress the genuine Waitaha strand of their ancestry. The 'Nation of Waitaha' is the second group. Many individuals in this group cannot legitimately claim Maori or Polynesian descent (O'Regan 1992; Anderson 1998). This group is identified in the text as the 'Nation of Waitaha' or as the 'Nation'.

The genesis of the Nation of Waitaha in the late 1980s is credited by one commentator to two people, Barry Brailsford and Peter Ruka (Tau 1995). Brailsford was a history lecturer at the Christchurch College of Education and had written numerous books including two that dealt with South Island prehistory. Peter Ruka, a secondary school teacher of Maori studies, was involved in gathering data on traditional fishing practices for a Ngai Tahu claim to the Treaty of Waitangi. The Tribunal agreed with Ngai Tahu that Ruka's fishing evidence was taken from a text book on fishing rather than an unnamed *kaumatua* (Maori elder) informant as claimed (Tau 1995:6; *Ngai Tahu Sea Fisheries Report* 1992:3.4.9). In 1988, Brailsford and Ruka were engaged to write a book on the interaction between South Island Maori (Rapuwai, Waitaha, Ngati Mamoe and Ngai Tahu) and the environment, based largely on archaeological data. The decision for book funding was made after an approach to the Minister of Internal Affairs. However, by 1989 Maori support for the project was withdrawn by Ngai Tahu, the major

South Island tribe. Brailsford claimed the work was based on the teachings of Te Maiharoa and Puao Rakiraki, but tribal historians found his texts had no similarity to tribal manuscripts written by their descendants and students such as Wikitoria Paipeta, Wi Pokuku, Hoani Kaahu and Herewini Ira (Prendergast-Tarena 2008). Ruka's genealogical connection to Ngai Tahu and knowledge of tribal matters was also challenged by tribal elders (O'Regan 1992; Tau 1995).

Brailsford received an MBE for his contribution to education and Maori scholarship in 1990, but by then the book's direction had taken a radical turn. In media reports from 1990 to 1991 the Nation of Waitaha members identified themselves as distinct from Ngai Tahu, the tribe which had withdrawn project support, and were asserting that their culture and history had been secretly preserved by unnamed Waitaha Elders (*Dominion Sunday Times,* 9 December 1990; *The Press,* 5 November 1991). The Nation of Waitaha claimed to be the first people in New Zealand and culturally distinct from later Maori arrivals, especially Ngai Tahu, which was portrayed as a warrior culture more concerned with securing economic assets from the Crown than with matters spiritual or environmental (O'Regan 1992).

Song of Waitaha

The Nation of Waitaha published its prehistory, entitled *Song of Waitaha: The histories of a nation,* in 1994. A new edition was published in 2003 and a companion volume *Whispers of Waitaha* (2006) is advertised online as: 'Pre Maori Folklore, Traditions and Oral Histories of the Waitaha people'.

The version of New Zealand's past contained in the 311-page *Song of Waitaha* can be characterised as alternative in the sense that while it has a semblance to conventional history – for example, some place names and the names of some gods and ancestors conform to published sources – it adds completely new elements, and provides a quite different chronological framework for events which are also said to have unfolded in locations that are foreign to most oral traditions (e.g. Shortland 1851; Anderson 1998; Prendergast-Tarena 2008).

According to *Song of Waitaha,* the world in the deep past was regularly traversed by different races of people using canoes which moved on sea-highways called Long Tides. An important focus for these journeys was the island of Waitangi Ki Roto, which can, using maps and textural details, be equated with Easter Island/Rapa Nui (Brailsford 1994:158–159; Howe 2003:146). An early and important figure from Waitangi Ki Roto was the well-known Polynesian demigod Maui who visited the South Island and dragged the North Island from the sea. He also discovered the birth place of the gods Te Kohanga in the South Island and, on departing, left four tribes (Maoriori, Moriori, Pakau and Maruiwi).

Further visits to and from Waitangi Ki Roto and Aotea Roa (South Island)–Whai Repo (North Island) followed, with Tamatea Mai Tawhiti visiting 70 generations ago (ca. 1750–2100 years ago) and, Ngahue and then Ra Kai Hau Tu 67 generations ago. Some of the ancestral personalities, like Ra Kai Hau Tu, are well known in New Zealand and can be found in the traditional genealogies of Northland, the South Island and Polynesia, but new elements are introduced beneath the veneer of tradition. For example, Ra Kai Hau Tu in *Song of Waitaha* does not appear to be Polynesian and is described as having pale skin and blue eyes (Brailsford 1994:99).

Greenstone (nephrite) was supposedly carried to Waitangi Ki Roto (Brailsford 1994:157), while kumara (sweet potato) was moved to New Zealand and planted at Te Kohanga – an area outside the climatic tolerance of this crop. New people arrived and were subsumed under the names of Waitaha and Rapuwai. These included the skilled canoe navigators called Urukehu, who were pale-skinned, blue-eyed and short-statured, the gardening Maoriori, distinguished by their tallness and dark colouring, and the Tu Takapo/Kiritea, or Stone People, with dark hair, light-brown coloured skin and a double fold over their eyelids (Brailsford 1994:57, 135; Brailsford in Paterson 1994).

The utopian lifestyle of the Nation, complete with schools of learning, a gardening culture and distinctive set of ceremonial activities, came to an end with the arrival of warriors from the Pacific. This happened gradually, with the North Island falling first and then the arrival of Tu Ma Tauenga signalling the destruction of the peaceful Waitaha Nation and the concealing of its history (Brailsford 1994:294).

Of the many prehistoric events listed in *Song of Waitaha* there are few which can be examined using archaeological data and then only through negative evidence. There are claims, for example, that the Nation had the knowledge to construct clay items (Brailsford 1994:186) and had introduced different types of potato and sweet potato into New Zealand (Brailsford 1994:11, 140, 143), in addition to transporting greenstone to Easter Island and other places (Brailsford 1994:157). Evidence for these activities has not been found, nor is there any sign that pre-Maori settlements existed at the locations of the principal villages of the Nation.

The issue of chronology is perhaps the weakest part of the Nation's prehistory, as an extensive suite of radiocarbon determinations from cultural and environmental contexts strongly supports the conclusion that Maori arrived from East Polynesia about 700 years ago (e.g. Anderson 1991; Wilmshurst et al. 2010). There are references to large stone monuments at Te Kohanga and other places such as the sub-Antarctic Auckland Islands (Brailsford 1994:185–188), but only Nation of Waitaha adepts can distinguish these from natural formations. An entwined spiritual-conservation ethic was said to allow the Nation of Waitaha to live in harmony with the environment (Brailsford 1994:182, 235, 260, 289), presumably to such a degree that a conventional prehistoric landscape did not form. Deforestation and the extinction of bird species is attributed to cataclysmic natural phenomena (Brailsford 1994:52, 287–289), in contrast to results from archaeological and palaeoenvironmental research that suggest many large-scale environmental changes were wrought by prehistoric people (e.g. Anderson 1989; Worthy and Holdaway 2002; Wilmshurst et al. 2008).

All of this would be of little importance if *Song of Waitaha* was, like conventional prehistories, advanced as a competing view of the past which the community could either accept or reject. But, unlike most conventional prehistory, the prehistory of the Nation of Waitaha had the potential to threaten Maori rights: '... various ideologies arising from Brailsford's work – while appearing harmless on the surface – may in fact, by reconstructing Pakeha and other non-Maori as equally Indigenous to Aotearoa [New Zealand] have more far-reaching consequences – threatening ultimately to undermine the status of Maori as Tangata Whenua' (Liddell 1997:32). In addition, the Nation of Waitaha was active in promoting its view of the past and achieved considerable success in obtaining resources and a public identity.

Publication and media coverage

Despite the damaging withdrawal of Ngai Tahu support, considerable funds were given to support publication of *Song of Waitaha* from the Ministry of Education, the New Zealand 1990 Commission, and various corporations, including Toyota New Zealand, the National Bank and Air New Zealand, among groups providing financial and logistical support (Brailsford 1994; King 1995). Two sources estimate that at least $500,000 was spent on the project (O'Regan 1992; A. Anderson pers. com. 1998). *Song of Waitaha* was published in 1994, but it is unclear how many copies were initially printed. The pre-publication cost of the book was $60, with a recommended retail value of $89.95. A special edition run of 525 copies, priced at $750 each, was also advertised.

Apart from the financial benefits associated with publication, the Nation of Waitaha, some members of which had strong links to the education sector, planned to distribute a copy of the book to every New Zealand high school (Paterson 1994:35). Out of 12 high schools from the North and South Island contacted by the author in 1998 six had a copy of the book. The standard text on New Zealand's past is *The Prehistory of New Zealand*, written by Janet Davidson (1984), yet it seems likely, considering the amount of funding involved, that *Song of Waitaha* has an equally wide distribution within the education system. Thus, there is every reason to believe that in some schools Brailsford's book will have been used as a genuine teaching and research resource by teachers and students. Exactly how *Song of Waitaha* was used in the education sector is unclear. For example, six copies of the book held by the National Library of New Zealand Schools Collection have been heavily used in Auckland and Christchurch. However, one school librarian noted that students are intimidated by the book's size and tend not to use it for research purposes (T. Agnew pers. com. 1998).

Media reports about prehistory commonly focus on new discoveries, especially results which suggest a much greater age for human occupation than has previously been considered. The Nation was able to exploit the media's predisposition for these themes and in 1996 received sustained media coverage. In late April an article in the popular weekly magazine, *The Listener* (circulation ca. 100,000; Country Press 1997/1998), reported Brailsford's belief that a stone outcrop in the Kaimanawa Forest Park in the Central North Island was evidence of a pre-Maori megalith culture. The article, titled 'Megalith Mystery: Are giant stones in the Kaimanawa Forest Park evidence of an Ancient New Zealand culture?' gave the Nation an unprecedented amount of coverage in the electronic and print media (Table 1; Ritchie 1996). No other story dealing with the prehistory of New Zealand in the 10 years (1996–2006) for which records were examined by the author generated as much media coverage. Headlines on the Kaimanawa wall suggest two stages of reporting. The first is the 'mystery' versus the 'no-mystery' viewpoints, where archaeologists and geologists debated with the Nation of Waitaha (Table 1). Critical in keeping public interest alive was a media quote from a scientist that the wall was 'highly likely' to be of human construction. Towards the end of the media's interest, which lasted about two weeks, and following the identification of the wall as a natural formation, a strong Maori reaction, culminating in a ban on the site, halted research. As the story breaker, Brailsford's views were prominent in much of the media coverage, while those from prehistorians received limited treatment (Table 1). Archaeologists were hampered by having to comment on a geological formation with little time for detailed study.

Nonetheless, the limited public response from professional archaeologists to the Waitaha Nation's assertion that the Kaimanawa wall was evidence for pre-Maori population was somewhat perplexing, given that the story, regardless of how one views Brailsford's opinions, was about the prehistory of New Zealand and through the media had reached a large public audience. For example, the New Zealand Archaeological Association decided not to issue a press release as it was felt that the Kaimanawa wall was not an archaeological issue (M. White pers. com. 1996).

The Nation of Waitaha defused archaeological criticism by focusing on geological features, but it is also worth noting that relations between Maori and archaeologists were substantially reshaped by the activities of the Waitangi Tribunal during the 1990s, particularly the use of archaeological data to assist in identifying the antiquity and extent of tribal activities to formally establish *manawhenua* (authority over land). Archaeologists and historians critical of indigenous history, even that of alternative groups like the Nation of Waitaha, could be seen as colonial, repressive and acting against indigenous interests and negotiations, often fractious, between Maori and the Crown. The limited public response of New Zealand archaeologists to the Nation

Table 1. Media coverage of the claim that the Kaimanawa wall was of pre-Maori origin.

Newspaper	Date	Headline
1. New Zealand Herald	1 May	Great Wall of Kaimanawas theory rubbished by experts
2. New Zealand Herald	3 May	Mystery surrounds origins of the Kaimanawa wall
3. The Listener	29 April – 4 May	Megalith mystery
4. The Dominion	6 May	Experts none the wiser about wall
5. Daily News	7 May	American joins debate on mystery stone wall
6. New Zealand Herald	8 May	Excavations to uncover wall secrets
7. Evening Post	8 May	Theory of ancient wall rejected by historians
8. Evening Standard	9 May	It's a hoax, says historian
9. Daily Telegraph	9 May	Wall game may make Maoris the losers
10. Daily Telegraph	9 May	Wall a lava flow, says historian
11. Taupo Times	10 May	Rock wall not part of mill
12. New Zealand Herald	10 May	Theories on ancient settlers rise from forest's rock pile
13. New Zealand Herald	10 May	Excavations to uncover wall secrets
14. Taupo Times	11 May	Leave wall investigation to experts, DOC urges
15. Taupo Times	11 May	Site off limits to public, says Maori spokesperson
16. Daily Post	11 May	Wall raises racism claims
17. Otago Daily Times	13 May	Maoris debate fate of controversial wall
18 The Dominion	14 May	Kaimanawa wall off limits: Taupo Maori
19. New Zealand Herald	14 May	Kaimanawa wall a natural volcanic rock formation
20. Otago Daily Times	15 May	Ban placed on wall
21. The Press	15 May	Tribe puts ban on tampering with wall
22. Evening Post	25 May	In search of lost civilisations

Commentator	Number of stories (n=22)	Description by newspaper and story reference
Barry Brailsford	18	rebel historian (1), specialist in South Island Maori history (1), Christchurch geologist (2), maverick of archaeology in New Zealand (3), [former] archaeologist and history lecturer at Christchurch Teachers College (3), South Island geologist (12), Hamilton archaeologist (20)
David Hatcher Childress	15	American archaeologist (3), author of popular books (4), United States ancient history researcher (11), visiting American archaeological researcher (12), American historian (16)
Neville Ritchie	6	Doctor and senior Department of Conservation archaeologist (12), nationally acclaimed expert on walls (19), archaeologist (4)
Perry Fletcher	4	from the New Zealand Archaeological Association (11), Taupo historian (8), local historian (4), file keeper for the Bay of Plenty branch of the NZ Archaeology Association (8)
Peter Adds	4	Victoria University Maori Studies senior lecturer (17)
Kerry Howe	2	Professor of history from Massey University (8)
Peter Wood	2	Doctor and geothermal geologist (2), a Geological and Nuclear Sciences Institute specialist in ignimbrite (19)
Janet Davidson	1	author of *The prehistory of New Zealand* (22)
Harry Keys	1	Doctor and scientist for the Taupo-Turangi conservancy (2)
Geoff Irwin	1	Professor and specialist in Pacific archaeology (1)
Trevor Hosking	1	former New Zealand Historic Places archaeologist (14)
Rex Gilroy	1	Director of the Australia-Pacific Archaeological Research Centre (22)

of Waitaha's alternative prehistory can be compared with Australia where 25% of all print media reports on the controversial (and later rejected) claim made in 1996 that the Jinmium site in Australia was 176,000 years old were written by archaeologists.

Media and public interest in the Kaimanawa wall was further developed by Brailsford and the American alternative prehistorian David Hatcher Childress, who gave a joint seminar (11 May 1996) at the Auckland College of Education on the ancient megalithic cultures of the Pacific. The seminar was mentioned in the initial *Listener* article and later advertised in daily newspapers, and, at a cost of $35 per person, reportedly was well attended. The Nation of Waitaha in the 1990s continued to receive publicity using alternative prehistory to attract the media and the public to its view of the past. Earthworks found in Northland were identified in the New Zealand and Australian media as the remains of an ancient Waitaha village. The reports carried the headlines 'Pre-Maori tribe theory gains support' and 'Ancient earthworks casts doubt over Maoris' claim to be first settlers' (*NZ Herald,* 2 June 1998; *Sydney Morning Herald,* 13 June 1998).

Indigenous identity

Media and publishing activities helped the Nation of Waitaha to be seen as an authentic indigenous group. Ngai Tahu, which now has tribal authority over more than 80% of the South Island, had, since 1986, negotiated with the Crown for the return of land and sea assets taken from it after the signing of the Treaty of Waitangi in 1840. The success of Ngai Tahu in arguing its case led the Crown to offer a $170 million package through the Ngai Tahu Claims Settlement Bill which was passed by Parliament on 29 September 1998. Before the settlement, factions from within Ngai Tahu, most notably members who have actual Waitaha ancestry (as, in fact, do nearly all Ngai Tahu), and who had discovered a potential strength in alliance with the Nation of Waitaha, argued that their rights would be extinguished under the Bill (*The Press,* 22 May 1998). O'Regan (1992) has suggested that factions like the Nation of Waitaha form and agitate in order to capture resources and funds when the opportunity to do so arises.

A desire for an authentic indigenous identity also helps to explain the content of *Song of Waitaha* and the activities of the Nation of Waitaha, which had a potentially large and cosmopolitan membership. Brailsford is quoted in a New Age publication as saying: 'we are all *tangata whenua* ... the white ones with their freckles and blue eyes and blonde hair, the dark ones who go to the gardens, the snow people from the Asian lands. We are all part of this land' (in Paterson 1994:34). In a later book, Brailsford (1995) who is of European ancestry, claimed direct descent from the founding Waitaha ancestor Rakaihautu.

Ko Barry Brailsford	*My name is Barry Brailsford*
Ko Tuhua te maunga	*My mountain is Tuhua*
Ko Mawhera te awa	*My river is Mawhera*
Ko Te Aka Aka o Poutini te marae	*My marae* [meeting place] *is Te Aka Aka o Poutini*
Ko Rakaihautu te tupuna	*My tupuna* [ancestor] *is Rakaihautu*
Ko Waitaha te iwi	*My iwi* [tribe] *is Waitaha.*
(Brailsford 1995:9)	

One Waitaha group with links to Brailsford specified that members of Waitaha were those who could conventionally trace their ancestry (*whakapapa*) from and through Rakaihautu, in addition to honorary members who could be Maori and Pakeha who were not of Waitaha (Waitaha Taiwhenua O Waitaki Trust Board 1996). What is perhaps unique to Waitaha was this fusion of disgruntled but genuine groups within Maoridom with non-Maori in the Nation of

Waitaha. One example is that some Waitaha claimed an antiquity of 67 generations as in the *Song of Waitaha* when arguing for their status as a distinct and older indigenous group than Ngai Tahu (*Otago Daily Times,* 17 June 1998; *The Press,* 10 July 1998).

It is not possible now to estimate how many people claimed to be part of the Waitaha Nation or the Nation's ethnic composition, because of the confusion between the two Waitaha groups. One Waitaha leader said that about 270 people from the South Island and 1000 in the North Island had registered as Waitaha (*Otago Daily Times,* 17 June 1998), while a Nation of Waitaha elder noted a similar total figure, but had the majority resident in the South Island (*NZ Herald,* 2 June 1998).

Conclusion

The late Michael King (1994, 1995, 2003) saw the *Song of Waitaha* as yet another example of colonialism affecting indigenous cultures through European appropriation and transmutation of the Maori past into synthetic forms. One of the ironies about the views contained in *Song of Waitaha* for archaeologists and historians is their similarity to ideas found in earlier and long-discarded scholarship. Elsdon Best and Percy Smith, both eminent workers in the emerging field of Maori studies, advanced the idea of a pre-Maori population called the Maruiwi/Moriori in a series of papers published in the *Journal of the Polynesian Society* (Smith 1913–15; Best 1913–14, 1916, 1928). The peaceful Maruiwi/Moriori were said to have been killed, assimilated or driven to the Chatham Islands by Maori. There are similarities between *Song of Waitaha* and these earlier studies, both in substance and style, which suggests a degree of familiarity with long-abandoned works like the *Lore of the Whare-wananga, Tuhoe – Children of the Mist,* and Adkin's (1950, 1960) thesis of a pan-New Zealand Waitaha tribe 2100 years old. Hyper-diffusionist explanations of cultural dispersal in the late 19th and early 20th centuries provide a permanent reservoir (e.g. Haast 1872; Tregear 1904; Brown 1907, 1924) of outdated and discredited ideas that alternative prehistorians will refer to and use (e.g. Childress 1995). One publisher of alternative prehistory in New Zealand (Dé Danaan Publishers) wants to: '... restore full integrity to the reliable works of Historians of the 19th and 20th centuries and those first hand accounts of New Zealand's colonial history, which have been supplanted by modern works written by social historians with P.C. agendas'. It is noteworthy that hyper-diffusionist and pre-Maori explanations of New Zealand's past supported colonial occupation by viewing history as a series of population movements by progressively more advanced ethnic groups which, along with their plants and animals, naturally supplanted those of the indigenous ecosystem. As others have pointed out, it is astonishing how the idea of a pre-Maori population periodically returns in a new guise (O'Regan 1992; Anderson 1998:21), in spite of the idea and its sources suffering frequent criticism in scholarly circles (Williams 1937; Golson 1960; Simmons 1976).

One explanation for the popularity of alternative prehistories in New Zealand during the 1990s might lie in the changing cultural spaces created by the activities of the Waitangi Tribunal between different sectors of New Zealand society, particularly the new relationships forged between the Crown and Maoridom. The alienation of some non-Maori and Maori from the redistribution-reconciliation process fostered a range of prehistories that proposed the colonisation of New Zealand by, among others, Celts, Phoenicians, Vikings, Chinese and South Americans (e.g. Wiseman 1998, 2001; Bolton 1999; Doutré 1999; Tasker 1999). Several published and online alternative prehistories explicitly state that the 'fact' of pre-Maori occupation extinguishes Maori rights under the Treaty of Waitangi. In summary, the argument runs that if Maori were preceded by another people, and they killed the Maruiwi/Moriori and took their lands by force, then European settlement and the subsequent alienation of Maori land is simply another example of social-Darwinism – with the weak making way for the strong. Further, the redistribution of state-owned assets under the Treaty of Waitangi is not warranted because the original inhabitants have been extirpated.

The *Song of Waitaha* is relatively benign in comparison with several of the more malignant alternative prehistories, although the Nation of Waitaha in the 1990s had the potential to unsettle and complicate the Ngai Tahu settlement, and contributed a unorthodox view of New Zealand's past that achieved a much wider distribution than others in the genre through its New-Age message and strategic use of publishing and the media. As has been noted, the descendents of settler societies occupy an uncertain cultural space between the 'mother' and the 'other' (Lawson 1995:25), and in post-colonial settings, group identity is constantly refashioned from conventional and unorthodox sources. Archaeologists and others involved in historical research need to be aware of the content, influences and activities of individuals and groups promoting alternative versions of the past, and mindful of the desire for indigeneity that is frequently embedded in them (Goldsmith 2009).

Acknowledgements

I would like to thank Atholl Anderson for access to his Nation of Waitaha file and his pertinent comments on previous drafts of this paper. Others who provided valuable feedback and comments during the paper's long development include Sir Tipene O'Regan, Michael Goldsmith, Matthew Campbell, Janet Davidson, Jack Golson, Kirsten Lawson, Foss Leach, and Michael King. Ailisa Cornelius (School Library Network), Kingsley Field (*NZ Herald*), Don Lawson (Kaikorai Valley High School), Rachel Lawson (Victoria University Press) and Kathy Prickett (Auckland Institute and Museum), and Neville Ritchie (Department of Conservation) kindly supplied information and answered queries. The opinions and content expressed in this paper are, however, the responsibility of the author alone.

References

Adkin, G.L. 1950. Supplementary data relating to the ancient Waitaha in the Horowhenua – Te Whanga-nui-a-tara area, North Island, New Zealand. *Journal of the Polynesian Society* 59:1–34.

Adkin, G.L. 1960. An adequate culture nomenclature for the New Zealand area. *Journal of the Polynesian Society* 69:228–238.

Agnew, T. Hillmorton High School, Christchurch. Personal communication, 17 September 1998.

Anderson, A. 1989. *Prodigious birds. Moas and moa-hunting in prehistoric New Zealand.* Cambridge University Press, England.

Anderson, A. 1991. The chronology of colonization in New Zealand. *Antiquity* 65:267–295.

Anderson, A. 1998. *The welcome of strangers.* University of Otago Press, Dunedin.

Anderson, A. Research School of Pacific and Asian Studies, Australian National University. Personal communication, October 1998.

Best, E. 1913. Tuhoe – The children of the mist. *Journal of the Polynesian Society* 22:149–167.

Best, E. 1914. Tuhoe – The children of the mist. *Journal of the Polynesian Society* 23:38–54, 159–172.

Best, E. 1916. Maori and Muruiwi. *Transactions of the New Zealand Institute* 48:435–447.

Best, E. 1928. Maori and Muruiwi. *Journal of the Polynesian Society* 37:175–225.

Bolton, K.R. 1999. *Lords of the soil: The story of the Turehu, the White Tangata Whenu*a. Spectrum Press, Waikanae.

Brown, J.M. 1907. *Maori and Polynesian: Their origin, history and culture.* Hutchinson, London.

Brown, J.M. 1924. *The riddle of the Pacific.* Fisher Unwin, London.

Brailsford, B. 1994. *Song of Waitaha: The histories of a nation.* Ngatapuwae Trust, Christchurch.

Brailsford, B. 1995. *Song of the stone.* Stoneprint Press, Hamilton.

Childress, D.M. 1995. *Lost cities of ancient Lemuria and the Pacific.* Adventure Unlimited Press, Illinois.

Country Press. 1997/1998. *Press, radio and T.V. guide.* Media Monitors NSW, Sydney, Australia.

Davidson, J.M. 1984. *The prehistory of New Zealand.* Longman Paul, Auckland, New Zealand.

Doutré, M. 1999. *Ancient Celtic New Zealand.* Dé Danaan Publishers, Auckland.

Goldsmith, M. 2005. Translated identities: 'Pakeha' as subjects of the Treaty of Waitangi. *SITES: New Series* 2(2):64–82.

Goldsmith, M. 2009. Struggling to be indigenous. Paper given at the Association for Social Anthropology in Oceania session at Santa Cruz, California.

Golson, J. 1960. Archaeology, tradition, and myth in New Zealand prehistory. *Journal of the Polynesian Society* 69(4):380–402.

Haast, J. 1872. Moas and Moahunters. Address to the Philosophical Institute of Canterbury. *Transactions of the New Zealand Institute* 4:66–90.

Howe, K.R. 2003. *The quest for origins.* Penguin Books, New Zealand.

King, M. 1994. Repairing the damage. *Metro* 155 (May):141–142.

King, M. 1995. The secret history. *Metro* 164 (February):120.

King, M. 2003. *The Penguin history of New Zealand.* Penguin Books, New Zealand.

Lawson, A. 1995. Postcolonial theory and the 'Settler' subject. *Essays on Canadian Writing* 56(Fall):20–36.

Liddell, T. 1997. The travesty of Waitaha: The New Age piracy of early Maori history. In: Pihama, L. and Waerea-i-te-rangi Smith, C. (eds), *Cultural and intellectual property rights. Economics, politics & colonisation,* Volume 2, pp. 32–43. International Research Institute for Maori and Indigenous Education, University of Auckland, Tamaki Makaurau.

Ngai Tahu Sea Fisheries Report. 1992. Waitangi Tribunal, Department of Justice, Wellington.

O'Regan, T. 1992. Old myths and new politics. Some contemporary uses of traditional history. *The New Zealand Journal of History* 26:5–27.

Paterson, K. 1994. Waka of dreams. *New Spirit* (August) 21:34–35.

Prendergast-Tarena, E.R. 2008. He Atua, He Tipua, He Takata Ranei: The dynamics of change in South Island oral traditions. Unpublished MA thesis, University of Canterbury.

Ritchie, N.A. 1996. A new age myth: The Kaimanawa 'wall'. *Archaeology in New Zealand* 39(3):175–183.

Shortland, E. 1851 [1974]. *The Southern Districts of New Zealand.* Capper Press, Christchurch.

Simmons, D.R. 1976. *The great New Zealand myth.* A.H. Reed and A.W. Reed, Wellington, Auckland, Christchurch.

Smith, S.P. 1913. The Lore of the Whare-wananga. *Journal of the Polynesian Society* 22:3–24, 45–61, 107–133, 169–218.

Smith, S.P. 1914. The Lore of the Whare-wananga. *Journal of the Polynesian Society* 23:1–18, 61–83, 127–149, 181–218.

Smith, S.P. 1915. The Lore of the Whare-wananga. *Journal of the Polynesian Society* 24:1–23.

Tasker, J. 1999. *Chain of evidence – Who were the first humans to visit New Zealand?* Kanuka Press, New Zealand.

Tau, R. Te M. 1995. Song of Waitaha – a descendant's point of view. *Te Karaka* (Spring) 6–7:20.

Tregear, E. 1904. *The Maori Race.* A.D. Willis, Wanganui, New Zealand.

Waitaha Taiwhenua O Waitaki Trust Board (HN/826450) Certificate of Incorporation, 1996. Ministry of Commerce Te Manatu Tauhokohoko.

White, M. New Zealand Archaeological Association. Personal communication, October 1996.

Wilmshurst, J.M., Anderson, A.J., Higham, T.F.G. and Worthy, T.H. 2008. Dating the late prehistoric dispersal of Polynesians to New Zealand using the commensal Pacific rat. *Proceedings of the National Academy of Sciences, USA* 105(22):7676–7680.

Wilmshurst, J.M., Hunt, T.L., Lipo, C.P. and Anderson, A.J. 2010. High-precision radiocarbon dating shows recent and rapid initial colonization of East Polynesia. *Proceedings of the National Academy of Sciences, USA* doi/10.1073/pnas.1015876108.

Williams, H.W. 1937. The Maruiwi myth. *Journal of the Polynesian Society* 46:105–122.

Wiseman, R.M. 1998. *Pre-Tasman explorers.* Discovery Press, Auckland.

Wiseman, R.M. 2001. *New Zealand's hidden past.* Discovery Press, Auckland.

Worthy, T.H. and Holdaway, R.N. 2002. *The lost world of the Moa.* Indiana University Press, Bloomington.

Newspaper reports

The Dominion Sunday Times, 9 December 1990. New book will reveal secret history of the Maori.

The New Zealand Herald, 2 June 1998. Pre Maori tribe theory gains support.

The Otago Daily Times, 8 May 1997. Historian touring South Island promoting new editions of books.

The Otago Daily Times, 17 June 1998. Subsumption key to Waitaha debate.

The Press, 5 November 1991. Waitaha make their stand.

The Press, 22 May 1998. Separate SI tribes reject $170m treaty settlement.

The Press, 19 June 1998. Waitaha wins right to challenge settlement.

The Press, 10 July 1998. Will the real Waitaha stand up?

The Press, 10 August 1998. Letter to the Editor.

The Southland Times, 9 May 1997. Evidence of human life in Southland from 1178.

The Sydney Morning Herald, 13 June 1998. Ancient earthworks casts doubt over Maoris' claim to be first settlers.

2

The Latte Period in Marianas prehistory
Who is interpreting it, why and how?

Rosalind L. Hunter-Anderson
1513 Wellesley Dr. NE, Albuquerque, New Mexico, USA

Introduction

'We know all about the Latte Period now so there is no need to dig anymore.'

Guam government official, 2006

Although most archaeologists familiar with Marianas prehistory would disagree with this statement, it indicates a widespread phenomenon in cultural-heritage matters, namely that many people tend to think about past cultures as composed of just a few essential elements. For some, Latte Period archaeology has already yielded all that is required.

This paper is about the various interpretations of Latte Period archaeological findings that one can find in the public arena today, and why and how they vary – even though they all refer to the 'same' prehistoric past. The paper is also about how people think about culture, particularly ancestral Chamorro culture, which is correlated with archaeological remains from the Latte Period. Variety in archaeological interpretation is apparent and inevitable in our pluralistic society: there are professional archaeological reports and publications, as well as newspaper, television and radio reports, video documentaries, internet blogs and websites, formal histories and textbooks. Cultural performances, celebrations and activities incorporating aspects of Chamorro heritage derived, in part, from Latte Period archaeology are also common both locally and on the internet.

These productions all share an interest in Marianas prehistory but they differ in their concepts of culture – from the very comprehensive to the minimal, or essentialist. Those that differ most from archaeological reports and publications, which tend to be comprehensive and detailed, hold an essentialist philosophical position regarding ancestral Chamorro culture. That is, they seem to assume that past cultures were unchangeable entities, each recognisable by a set of easily grasped defining elements. This tendency towards 'cultural essentialism' contrasts with a non-essentialist philosophical position and understanding of culture that is evident in much of the archaeological literature. Most archaeologists (although not all) think of culture as behaved, whether in the past or present, as a changeable, dynamic phenomenon, as adaptive systems that existed over time and space, invented by people and changed by them as needed.

As a dynamic system, a given culture cannot be reduced to a set of rigid, defining elements, like a list of ingredients on a cereal box (although some archaeological discussions include lists of culture traits that help identify the system under study and distinguish it from others). Philosophical differences over what a culture is, or was, lead to differences in goals and methods of involvement with the subject. To explain this idea further and to explore some of its implications, I have organised the paper as follows.

First, I introduce the concept of 'cultural essentialism' as it applies to current reconstructions and renditions of ancestral Chamorro culture, especially those invoking Latte Period archaeological data, and contrast this approach with that of most archaeologists working in this area. Next, I review some examples of popular treatments of ancestral Chamorro culture that reveal a cultural essentialist orientation, followed by some of my personal experiences in conveying archaeological findings in public venues. I conclude with some thoughts about how our communications with non-archaeologists can benefit from an awareness of pervasive cultural essentialism among the general public.

Essentialism and cultural essentialism

In philosophy, essentialism holds that for any specific kind of entity there is a set of characteristics or properties, all of which any entity of that kind must possess. The set of defining elements of the entity is permanent and unalterable; these elements are inherent in the entity. Plato may have been the first to formalise this idea. He asserted that there are two realities to the universe, the essential and the perceived, or what we might call the ideal versus the real (the one we experience every day). In the essential universe, everything is perfect and unchanging; there is no diversity. In the perceived universe, which Plato proposed was just a facade and by which we should not be fooled, diversity is rampant.

As you might expect, the founder of evolutionary theory, Charles Darwin, was not an essentialist. For Darwin, diversity not only affected the survival and reproductive prospects of the individuals in a population, it could be passed on to their offspring. Thus, a population could change, and given enough change, this evolutionary process would result in a new species. Anthropology and archaeology have similar notions regarding culture.

In our own lives as cultural beings, we usually do not operate under an explicitly essentialist position because we can easily see that our culture is complicated and always in flux. Our culture cannot be listed like the ingredients in a recipe. However, with respect to past cultures (and often cultures different from our own), many people seem to view them from an essentialist perspective: that far distant, or different, culture and its people are thereby reduced to a few easily recognised elements. A past culture becomes an ideal culture – frozen in a kind of timeless limbo not subject to outside influences.

Constructing a past culture

No one would dispute that ancestral Chamorro culture is no longer present as an entity to be experienced directly. Therefore, to give this concept meaning, one must (re)construct it. A strict essentialist approach would seek the set of defining elements untainted by outside influences. That Latte Period archaeology is a rich source of such untainted cultural evidence has not gone unnoticed by some of those interested in ancestral Chamorro cultural construction. For example, there are *latte* features, stone mortars, pottery bowls and jars, human burials in pits, human bone spears, *Spondylus* beads, sling stones, stone and shell adzes, marine-shell fishing gear, and volcanic-stone pounders and abraders, and much more, thanks to modern analytical techniques. For example, Latte Period archaeology provides descriptive evidence about foods, from microscopic and chemical analysis of organic residues on the interior surfaces of cooking-pot fragments. Certain shellfish remains and bones discarded in domestic middens indicate which animal species were processed and consumed. Archaeology also has excluded certain elements from the picture, such as pig and dog. These domesticates do occur in prehistoric contexts in some other Pacific Islands, but not in the Marianas.

A less strict essentialist construction of ancestral Chamorro culture would admit alien elements, apparently if they have a long enough history of assimilation. The term 'antigo' applies here, as found in the 35th issue of the internet zine called *Minaghet* ('truth'). The author distinguishes between ancient, antigo and contemporary Chamorro culture (see http://decolonizguam.blogspot.com/search?q=antigo). In Minaghet's usage, antigo refers to the olden times, after Spanish colonisation in 1668, well before modern times. Thus, for example, a lenient construction of ancestral Chamorro culture could include thatch-roofed huts on short wood posts, *carabao*, Sambar deer, Spanish dress styles and dances, the *belembaotuyan* (a single-string musical instrument), *titiyas mai'es*, (corn tortillas), older forms of Roman Catholicism, and Spanish-introduced items of material culture, such as the *hotno* (above-ground oven), *fuziños* (metal hoe) and *metati* (footed grinding stone).

What is remarkable to me, given the available information, is that relatively few of the total range elements are consistently invoked in contemporary discussions and depictions of ancestral Chamorro culture. Perhaps this reflects the operation of the process of reduction and simplification that has been noted among North American indigenous groups where there has been severe language loss, accompanied by loss or modifications of other traditions (Dauenhauer and Dauenhauer 1995). In this process, the ancestral culture is objectified and embodied by a core of essential elements that become fixed over time and ultimately become untouchable. For example, consider the case of the Tlingit of coastal Alaska. An audio tape collection of Tlingit stories told by elders in their preferred traditional manner, with clan affiliations and other introductory frames, recited by the tellers and considered integral to their storytelling tradition, was produced collaboratively by native-language-speaking linguists and Tlingit elders. The goal was to preserve the Tlingit language and culture. The recorded collection formed the basis for preparing culture-appropriate learning materials for tribal schools.

Two generations later, the collection resided in an archive that was off-limits to everyone by order of a tribal governing board whose members could not understand the stories that had been told in the manner considered right and proper by their elders. The board members insisted that simplified English 'translations' of these old stories should be used in the schools and the originals should remain locked up (as with holy relics). As Dauenhauer and Dauenhauer (1995) noted, in the process of heritage simplification, the ancestral stories so carefully preserved in that archive were reduced to a childish level, a format that also rendered them more acceptable to the surrounding dominant culture of English speakers.

A similar process seems to have been occurring with respect to depictions and invocations of ancestral Chamorro culture, and this is related to the severe heritage loss over the past 400 years amid the modern identity politics in an American-style political milieu found on Guam today. It certainly appears to have affected the way that archaeological findings are viewed by the public, including, and perhaps especially by, government officials. The belief that 'we know all about the Latte Period' may simply reflect the fact that, for essentialist purposes of ancestral culture construction, the few necessary elements provided by archaeology are well known and therefore need no further investigation.

Archaeology and a non-essentialist approach

Professional archaeological approaches to culture actually vary along an essentialist-non-essentialist dimension, and some archaeologists do discuss past cultures in terms of trait lists. Yet many of us working in Micronesia tend to think about our findings in a non-essentialist framework. Instead of fixating on naming and classifying and arguing about definitions – arguments such as, should a given artefact assemblage be called 'Lapita', 'Lapitoid' or something else – we non-essentialists have other interests and preoccupations. For instance, we assume that culture is a dynamic, changeable phenomenon and expect it to vary over time and across space. To many archaeologists, 'culture' is shorthand for 'cultural adaptive system' whose interrelated parts enable the system to persist over time and/or space by adjusting to and modifying (within limits) its social and physical environments. When these limits are exceeded cultural systems fail or evolve radically, so in this approach, the system is a 'moving target' for study.

In practice, non-essentialists seek patterns in archaeological and environmental data to help us imagine what past adaptive systems were like, how they were organised, how they functioned, and how and why they changed, if it appears that change and not just synchronous or cyclical variation has occurred. We are interested in the causes of system stability and instability, success and failure, over long and short time ranges and across small and large geographic areas. For example, Figure 1 is a graph of archaeological site types during the Latte Period (AD 900–1600) from the Manenggon Hills project in southern Guam, an area that encompasses about 1% of the island's 549 sq km landmass (Hunter-Anderson 2008).

These data suggest that the ancestral Chamorro cultural system at this place was far from static. Through technical and social adjustments, people were responding to something, as indicated by the flux in site frequencies and especially the increase in the number and proportion of storage/camp sites. I propose that after AD 1300, ancestral Chamorros were experiencing highly variable harvests due to more frequent and longer droughts, and accordingly, they intensified planting and increased food storage. It appears that people responded to climatic

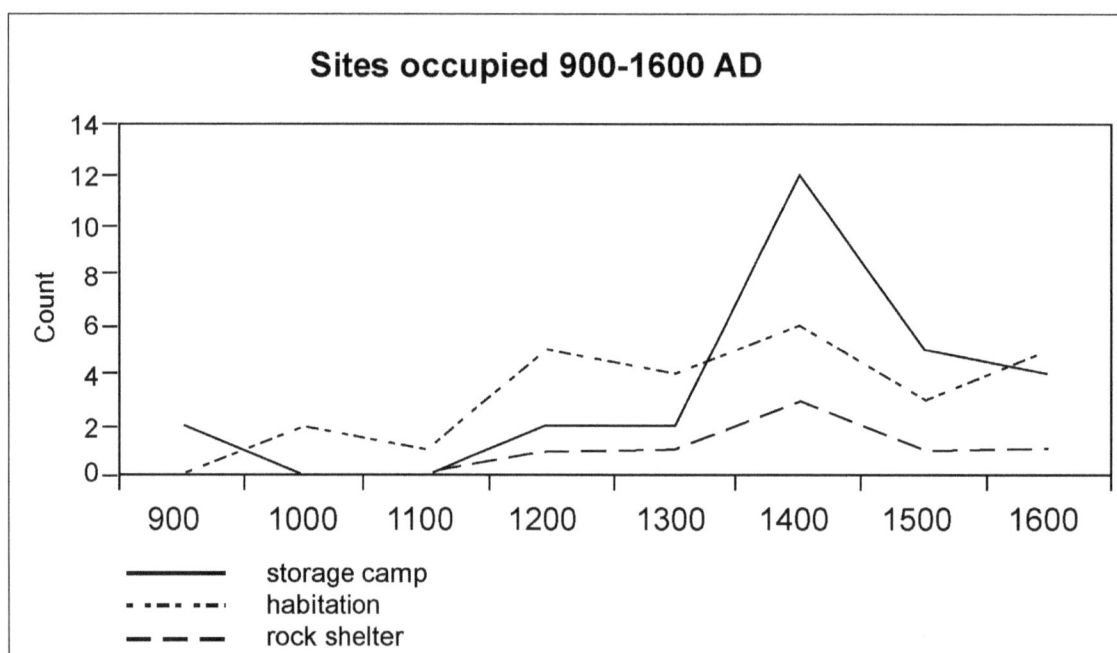

Figure 1. Frequencies of three types of site during the Latte Period at Manenggon Hills, Guam.
Data from Hunter-Anderson (2008).

change by doing more of what they already had been doing, namely, planting in the interior hills and using storage pits more intensively than they had previously. In ecology, this kind of behavioural response in a system experiencing environmental challenge has been called by van Valen (1973) the 'Red Queen Effect', after Alice's encounter with the Queen in Wonderland where increased effort in running was required to stay in the same place.

The non-essentialist archaeological approach is to explain the data, and the larger goal is to increase our knowledge of how cultural systems, including the dynamic ancestral Chamorro culture, acted under specific conditions. Data are generated by observation and are quantified to recognise significant patterns, for which a testable explanation is put forward.

Cultural essentialist goals and methods are different and less ambitious, at least as I have observed them. For example, the goals are limited to 1) preserving and protecting Chamorro culture, and 2) commanding respect for Chamorro culture. The methods used to further these goals include a) creating an attractive composite image of Chamorro culture by selecting elements known from archaeology and other sources, such as memory culture written down in the early 19th century and recorded in the early reports of foreign visitors, and b) transmitting this image in public venues. These efforts include museum and other static displays, paintings and drawings, wood and stone carvings, musical performances, recitation of poetry and chants, enactment of key events such as early encounters with foreigners and legends, and interpretations of archaeological features through websites, oral and written narratives and textbooks, and public protest demonstrations asserting proprietary control over archaeological materials and sites, especially human burials (see below), despite private property and historic preservation laws.

In 'multi-cultural' Guam, where ancient heritage loss is well documented and felt acutely by many, use of these methods by Chamorros whose ethnic identity is uncertain or ambiguous is strongly encouraged by those committed to the goals of preserving and protecting Chamorro culture and obtaining respect from outsiders. For example, a private K-12 school incorporating elements of Chamorro culture in the academic curriculum was formed in 1994 by 'Chamorro activists' (Twaddle et al. 2003:35). Chamorro culture and language classes in the public schools were mandated by the Guam legislature in 1992 and there are regularly occurring events that remind people of the island's Chamorro heritage. During Chamorro Week and Chamorro Month, annual events on Guam, a range of cultural elements are displayed in various venues, including arts and crafts, language recitals and musical performances in 'period' dress. The yearly Micronesian Island Fair, usually held in a large public park in the tourist district of Tumon Bay, also offers an opportunity for the display of some essentials of Chamorro heritage (Figure 2). These displays in preserving cultural heritage are the subject of a thoughtful essay by Michael Lujan Bevacqua, who avers that culture is not static after all (see http://minagahet.blogspot. com/2009/11/decolonization-and-loincloth.html).

As Dauenhauer and Dauenhauer (1995) noted for the Tlingit and other groups experiencing cultural heritage loss, traditional foods are served during cultural celebrations. Guam's monthly fiestas that mark each village's saint's day in the Catholic religious calendar are no exception, involving Chamorro dishes not normally part of day-to-day life, which serve as potent symbols of a unique ancestry. Historic Preservation Week, sponsored by the Federal government through Guam's local historic preservation office, is another occasion when selected elements of ancestral Chamorro culture are invoked, such as sling stones, large stone mortars, *latte* architectural features, and plainware pottery from the Latte Period, displayed on posters and in exhibits in hotels and other public venues.

Most essentialist treatments of ancestral Chamorro culture ignore, or have no use for, temporal changes in archaeological data, such as we found at Manenggon Hills. This kind of

Figure 2. Photo of Guam Chamorros asserting cultural identity through costuming and constructing traditional architecture; from http://minagahet.blogspot.com/2009/11/decolonization-and-loincloth.html

variability in cultural elements only confuses an essentialist picture of cultural continuity. Yet archaeologists immediately notice that certain elements are chosen for inclusion regardless of the time they were used or the systemic coherence that enabled these items and practices to exist. Consider, for instance, that the earliest archaeological evidence for human presence in the Marianas is consistently dated by radiocarbon assay no earlier than about 3500 years ago, give or take a couple of hundred years. This dating 'barrier' is not arbitrary and it is crucial for understanding the physical environment encountered by the first people to occupy the Marianas. Marine geological studies indicate that a high sea level before this time may have discouraged or even precluded successful landing and settlement (see Dickinson 2000, 2001). Figure 3 shows why mid-Holocene (pre-1500 BC) human occupation of the Marianas was unlikely. The high sea stand creates a high-energy sea-land interface, which, along with poor reef development, may have discouraged settlement.

While the existence of the Mariana archipelago may have been known to seafaring people of insular Southeast Asia, until environmental conditions improved, the Marianas remained uninhabited. After about 4000 years ago, sea level in the western Pacific began to decline from its mid-Holocene high stand. By around 3500 years ago, the sea had declined enough to allow the shores of the southern Mariana Islands to be approached by canoe and to serve as small camping platforms protected by reefs, which provided a rich source of marine foods.

These facts notwithstanding, and perhaps in the belief that earlier settlement is more admirable than the actual archaeological evidence for the timing of human advent in the Marianas, the human arrival date is often rounded up to 4000 years ago, or even more, on some popular websites and in text book discussions of ancestral Chamorro culture (e.g. Cunningham 1992:15; see also http://www.guam-online.com/history/history.htm; http://www.pacificworlds.com/cnmi/arrival/ancients.cfm; http://www.freewebs.com/allthingsguam/virtualhistorytextbook.htm).

Assertions of a great antiquity for human occupation of the Marianas ignore the significance of the sea-level barrier before ca. 1500 BC, while also missing the significant fact that the earliest people to leave archaeological evidence of their presence precede by at least 500 years human advent in the other remote Oceanic islands of the Pacific – as Craib (1999) noted more than a decade ago. We do not yet have an explanation for this anomaly, and few researchers have considered the issue (e.g. Hunter-Anderson 2005:30–31, 2008).

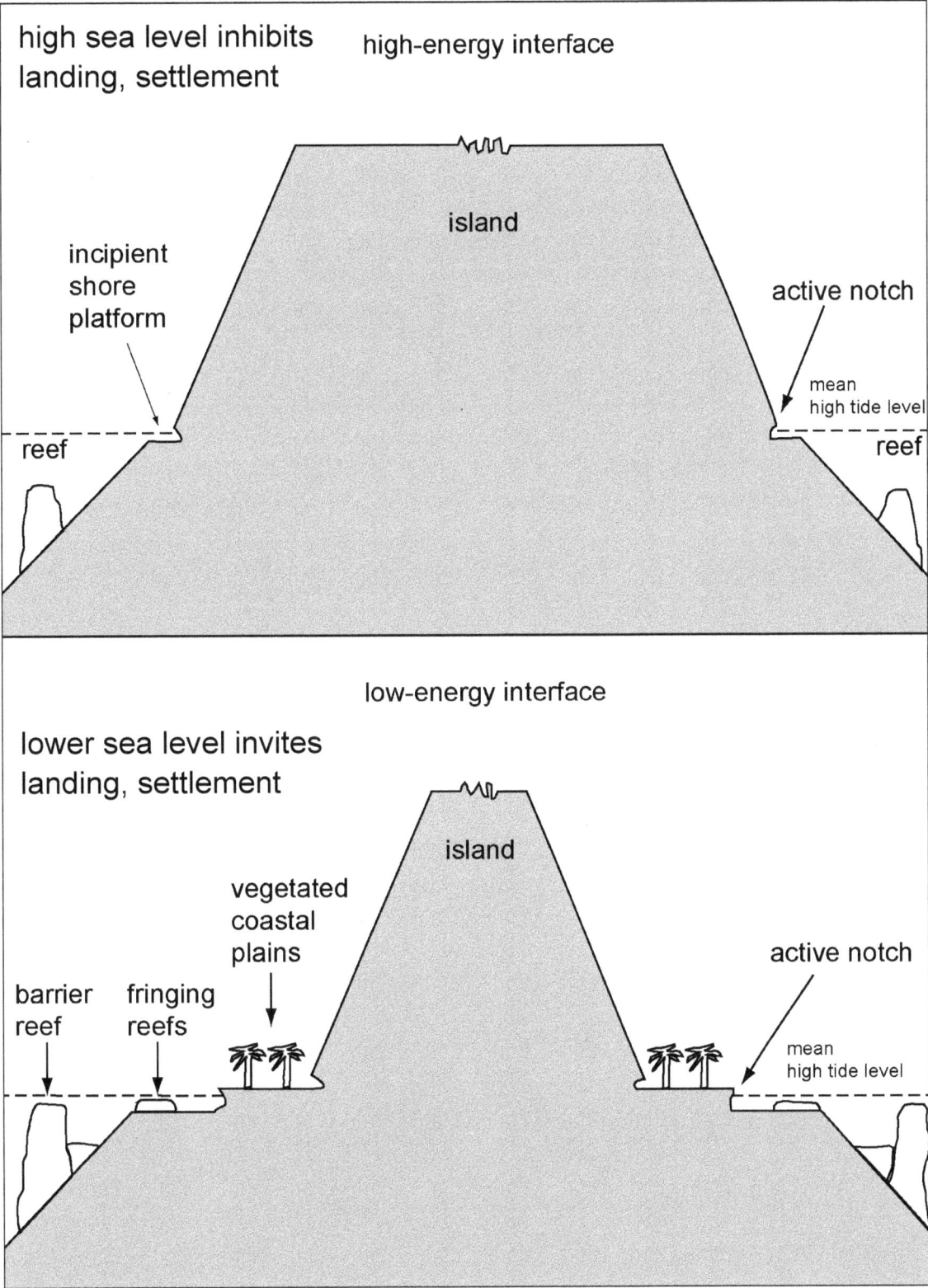

Figure 3. Mid-Holocene sea level and high-energy sea-land interface; late-Holocene sea level and low-energy sea-land interface. Modified from Nunn (1994).

Another questionable element in popular treatments of ancestral Chamorro culture is the assumption that the first people to arrive in the Marianas were fisher-farmers who pursued a way of life identical to that described in early historic accounts and from memory culture collected in the 19th century, despite the fact that the earliest Marianas cultural deposits, called Early Pre-Latte by archaeologists, contain no agricultural tools, nor any signs of a settled way of life, such as dense middens, substantial residential and other structures, or even human burials. While these anomalous absences are fascinating to archaeologists working in these islands, they tend to be ignored by cultural essentialists as they seek to connect the deep past of the Marianas with ancestral Chamorro culture.

Ancestral Chamorro culture in the local mass media

How do newspaper and television reports of Latte Period archaeology fit into an essentialist/non-essentialist distinction? Almost by definition, journalistic accounts are essentialist in that they must clearly inform us about essentials: what, where, who, when and how. The most common reason for local archaeological stories to appear in the local mass media is the accidental exposure of prehistoric human remains during construction projects, especially when historic preservation laws appear to have been violated. During reportage of 'what', the skeletal remains and any associated artefacts are automatically identified as ancestral Chamorros, usually on the advice of archaeologists. Photographs may be included in the piece, and they tend to be of recognisable objects such as stone and shell tools and human skulls. A skull and artefacts displayed on a local television station came from what archaeologists call Late or Transitional Pre-Latte cultural deposits and probably date between 2500 years ago and 2000 years ago (DeFant and Eakin 2009). If they are not re-interred, some day they could figure in public exhibitions and posters as elements of ancestral Chamorro culture, despite being made of stone exotic to the Marianas and having been found buried with individuals whose morphology is quite different from that of Latte Period burial populations.

Other journalism involving Latte Period archaeology includes reporting on protest demonstrations, such as events in which an activist group publicly objects to an archaeological mitigation project. In Guam, activists have characterised archaeological work on prehistoric materials as a desecration of ancestral Chamorro heritage (see entries at http://decolonizeguam.blogspot.com/2007/08/desecration-of-chamorro-remains-at.html). In such cases, the reporter focuses on the 'controversy' between local historic preservation laws and the activists' assertions of proprietary control of the remains, with the archaeologists caught in the middle and usually blamed for insensitivity or worse. Local laws mandate that the archaeological work be conducted on behalf of landowners or developers and paid for by them. Re-interment of human remains after minimal analysis is also required, and such ceremonies are reported in the local mass media, although there is usually only a small public attendance at these events.

A cultural essentialist position is generally adopted by activists and government officials in such cases. All human burials of early and late prehistoric age are considered essential elements of ancestral Chamorro heritage, and now have been accorded a near-sacred status similar to that of the Tlingit stories archive. Archaeologists familiar with the prehistoric record of human interments in the Marianas would know that secondary burials that often lack the skull and/or long bones testify to different funerary treatment accorded to many remains during the late prehistory of the Latte Period.

Journalistic alternatives to the quick report about the accidental finding of Latte Period remains include longer pieces in magazines, in video documentaries and on internet websites.

When based on adequate research, they serve as reliable references and ultimately reach a large audience composed of people more interested in the subject than the average newspaper reader or television viewer. Perhaps not surprisingly, however, a cultural essentialist view permeates many of these products. For example, the Guampedia (http://guampedia.com/) organises the Ancient Chamorro Era in an outline-list of separate cultural topics. From the topical presentation style, one might conclude that ancestral Chamorro culture consisted of separate, free-standing parts: a list of ingredients without the cooking instructions.

Formal histories offer longer and more reflective discussions. Russell's (1998) *Ancient Chamorro culture and history of the Northern Mariana Islands* and Rogers' (1995) *Destiny's landfall* elaborate on the various aspects of prehistoric occupation of the Marianas. In his archaeological summaries, Russell speculates on human motives for initial settlement and reviews several theories regarding variations and trends within the Latte Period; after all, the author is a historian. Rogers also recognises major archaeological changes in Marianas prehistory and proffers an explanation for the rise and persistence of Latte Period society, privileging population growth and resulting competition for limited resources. Both authors' interpretations reflect consultations with local archaeologists, and perhaps because of this come closest to a non-essentialist position regarding past cultures and their histories than do the views in popular literature.

From this brief overview, it seems archaeologists have their work cut out for them if they want to influence public thinking about past cultures. Cognitive scientists and linguists have found that new information is best assimilated in narrative form (Herman 2003). I suspect we need to work on our storytelling.

Experiences in conveying archaeological information to the public

Over the nearly 30 years that I have lived and worked in the Marianas and neighbouring islands, I have had the pleasure and challenge of trying various methods to convey archaeological findings to non-specialists. In addition to teaching university undergraduates and briefly hosting school children visiting archaeological sites where I was working, these efforts include producing a public radio series called *Island Archaeology: Reports from the field*, which later morphed into a live weekly broadcast called *Island Archaeology*; writing a chapter on Guam's prehistory for a textbook called *Guam history: Perspectives volume 2* (Carter et al. 2005); and most recently presenting a paper at a symposium called *The human dimensions of climate change* at the annual meeting of the Society for Human Ecology in Bellingham, Washington (Hunter-Anderson 2008). I will briefly describe these efforts and various reactions to them.

At the Society for Human Ecology symposium on climate change I was the only archaeologist presenting a paper and apparently the only one in the entire meeting. The climate-change session organiser was an environmental philosopher, Thom Heyd (University of Victoria, Canada), who had invited several of his colleagues as well as land management specialists and urban planners. Everybody in the presenting group and most of the audience was very concerned about the coming climate Armageddon due to global warming, but showed little or no awareness of long-term climate trends. For my presentation, I used some of the Manenggon Hills project data to remind people that such trends are known and to argue that a prehistoric cultural system had successfully coped with century-scale climate change towards more severe droughts in the western Pacific during the Little Ice Age. I proposed that the ancestral Chamorro coping mechanisms were both technical and social. After the session, people told me they had enjoyed my paper and some asked for copies, but I felt I had failed to accomplish my goal to quicken their interest in past climate oscillations and encourage them to consider the possibility that today we might be in just another one. Thus, my effort was evidently a diversion into another culture and era, but not a point of departure for thinking differently about human ecology as the study of human-environment relationships over long time scales.

Subsequently, I was asked by the session organiser to step down as a co-editor of the published papers. Here is part of his letter to me explaining why:

> … I appreciate your help with the special issue so far. Now, I did think about our completely opposite ways of thinking of our climate change situation, and I obviously made a mistaken assumption: that you would be of the same mind on anthropogenic climate change as I am. My mistake, obviously.
>
> Under these circumstances I do think that it would be better to have someone else as co-editor, since part of the task may be to think through how the urgency of the situation can be transmitted. In fact, I did ask a friend who has been working on that angle with me before and he says that he is very ready to take this on. I hope that you do not take this change personally.

I do not take it personally, but I do take it professionally. I have concluded from this polite exchange that the long interaction between people and the environment that archaeologists take for granted is quite alien to others and evidently holds few lessons for contemporary problems. We have some work to do to change that.

Another venue in which I have participated in conveying archaeological information is a local history textbook *Guam history: Perspectives volume 2* published by the Micronesian Area Research Center at the University of Guam. My 39-page chapter in this work was an informal, unfootnoted overview of Guam's prehistoric record. Naturally, my perspective is anthropological, and the discussion covers several aspects of the 3000-year-long span of prehistoric human presence in the island as a part of the Mariana archipelago and tropical western Pacific region. I believe it is the only textbook presentation on Marianas prehistory by an archaeologist designed expressly for secondary school students and the lay public. As for reactions to this piece, I am not aware of any. The first volume in the Guam perspectives series (Carter et al. 1997) can be purchased from Amazon.com and other internet bookstore sites, but volume 2 is nowhere to be found in the Guam public schools, cyberspace or local bookstores. Internet searches have revealed no reviews of the book, and according to Google Scholar, my chapter has not been cited in any article or book, and only one other contribution (Gracy 2005), about the late governor of Guam, Bill Daniels, has been noted on the internet (see http://www.ischool.utexas.edu/~gracy/research.html). I wonder whether all the effort expended by the editors, authors and production staff to produce a textbook was justified.

Another outreach project was the radio program called *Island archaeology: Reports from the field*, which I produced in the 1990s under a grant from National Public Radio (NPR) in collaboration with staff at Guam's new public radio station (KPRG). Making the series was fun, even though it required a lot of preparation and coordination of people and equipment. The sound man from KPRG and I visited archaeological projects as they were happening, as well as visiting the local archaeological laboratories of a contract firm where archaeological findings were being analysed. Some episodes were structured studio interviews that covered topics like prehistoric pottery and what can be learned from its detailed study; palaeoenvironmental investigations such as pollen analysis of ancient wetland sediments; and why people go into archaeology. We made 11 episodes, each about 10 minutes long, and the series got plenty of local play. Unfortunately, the recording quality was not up to NPR standards, and we had to abandon our plans to provide the series on Marianas archaeology for national airplay. Local listeners appeared to enjoy the program, and one even sent the station $100 to support the program.

A few years later, Richard Olmo and I co-hosted a similar program on KPRG. This one did not involve field recordings; rather, each episode was recorded in studio and ran about half an hour. The programs were conversations between the two of us about local archaeological projects and their implications. At first, we recorded each segment ahead of time, and later we did most of them live. The program came on during the lunch hour. Having been in graduate school in the 1970s, naturally our theme song was from the film *Raiders of the Lost Ark*. Occasionally, the station got telephone calls from listeners commenting that they enjoyed the program, but public interaction was quite limited. I believe these programs are still played occasionally.

One of the grant requirements for doing *Reports from the field* was to have the series evaluated by listeners. This was not practical to do over the radio, but fortunately, Professor Vince Diaz, then at the University of Guam, assisted with a student evaluation. For extra credit in his history of Guam class in 1996, students could listen to the tapes in their own time and answer questions about them. The listening environment was, of course, different: the 11 students who responded had to sit still and listen to the tapes one after another, rather than hearing the separate programs on the radio over a period of several weeks. The classroom setting is very different from how people usually listen to programs on the radio. However, in their overall evaluation of the program, most of the students said they enjoyed the series and learned new things. Many wished the episodes were longer, to include more information and clarification about specific points of interest. All remarked that making the series on video would have been better than simple audio recordings.

Below are a few quotes from the questionnaire. All the students were non-anthropology majors, and their ethnic backgrounds include Chamorro, Filipino and Chinese. Many were studying to become elementary or secondary-school teachers.

'I really enjoyed listening to the tapes. It was really interesting. I guess hearing things about our history or watching it on video has a better effect on people.'

'Dr. Diaz, I really didn't like this program. I found it to be very boring but of course educational. I'm not really interested in archaeology …'

'Overall I thought the program was interesting and I learned a lot about what archaeologists do and how they can tell of our past from pieces of artifacts they find.'

'Everyone has a right to learn about the past because everyone [is] a product of the past.'

'Whenever I hear the word "archaeology" I usually think of American scientists, but after hearing this episode, it really amazed me that there are Micronesian archaeologists out there.'

'The least interesting information to me was when some of the scientists talked too long on a certain subject that didn't need a lot of explanation, and also some of the information bored me. But overall the program was good and interesting. I learned a few things from the program.'

And my favourite:

'Make it a little more lively. The woman talking makes me want to fall asleep.'

Final thoughts

I have suggested that it is important archaeologists realise most people outside our field are 'cultural essentialists' and the latter realise that archaeologists do not share this view. This could explain why effective communication of our research seems so elusive. There will always be resistance to dissonant facts because they disrupt our previous conceptions; scientists have this problem, as does the general public. But I suspect we can broaden not a few minds if we produce compelling and accurate stories about our work and its meanings. Guam youth evidently prefers visual learning, but then many adults I know do as well.

Another communication issue is our credibility as professionals; this is surely important in this democratic age of self-proclaimed experts. More critical is that the information we try to convey stands on its own merits. In short, the messenger is not the message, the message is. Avoiding argument from authority and jargon that creates distance and distrust impels us to clarify what needs explaining and why: our stories must reflect the reasoning and data supporting our interpretations, and an honest airing of known problems with the data is also important. Some do this better than others, and judging from my own experiences, there is room for improvement among all of us.

References

Bak, P. 1996. *How nature works, The science of self-organized criticality.* Springer-Verlag, New York.

Carter, L.D., Wuerch W.L. and Carter R.R. (eds), 1997. *Guam history: Perspectives volume 1* MARC Educational Series No. 20. Richard F. Taitano Micronesian Area Research Center, University of Guam.

Carter, L.D., Wuerch, W.L. and Carter R.R. (eds), 2005. *Guam history: Perspectives volume 2.* MARC Educational Series No. 23. Richard F. Taitano Micronesian Area Research Center, University of Guam.

Craib, J. 1999. Colonisation of Mariana Islands: New evidence and implications for human movements in the Western Pacific. In: Galipaud, J.-C. and Lilley, I. (eds), *The Pacific from 5000 to 2000 BP, Colonisation and transformations*, pp. 477–485. IRD Editions, Paris.

Cunningham, L. 1992. *Ancient Chamorro society.* Bess Press, Honolulu.

Dauenhauer, R. and Dauenhauer, N.M. 1995. Oral literature embodied and disembodied. In: Quasthoff, U.M. (ed), *Aspects of oral communication*, pp. 91–111. Walter de Gruyter, New York.

DeFant, D. and Eakin, J. 2009. Preliminary findings from the Naton Beach site, Guam. Paper presented at the *Pacific Island archaeology in the 21st century* conference, Koror, Republic of Palau, July 1–3.

Dickinson, W.R. 2000. Hydro-isostatic and tectonic influences on emergent Holocene paleoshorelines in the Mariana Islands, western Pacific Ocean. *Journal of Coastal Research* 19:735–746.

Dickinson, W.R. 2001. Paleoshoreline record of relative Holocene sea levels on Pacific islands. *Earth-Science Reviews* 55:191–234.

Gracy, D.B. II. 2005. To build Rome in the morning: Bill Daniel's first days as governor of Guam, 1961. In: Carter, L.D., Wuerch, W.L. and Carter, R.R. (eds), *Guam history: Perspectives volume 2*, pp. 283–337. MARC Educational Series 27, University of Guam, Mangilao.

Herman, D. (ed), 2003. *Narrative theory and the cognitive sciences.* University of Chicago Press, Chicago.

Hunter-Anderson, R.L. 2005. An anthropological perspective on Marianas prehistory, including Guam. In: Carter, L.D., Wuerch, W.L. and Carter, R.R. (eds), *Guam history: Perspectives volume 2*, pp. 20–59. MARC Educational Series 27, University of Guam, Mangilao.

Hunter-Anderson, R.L. 2008. Cultural responses to late Holocene climatic oscillations in the tropical western Pacific: A new interpretation of the prehistoric Latte Period of Guam, Mariana Islands, Micronesia. Paper presented at the XVI International Conference of the Society for Human Ecology, Bellingham, Washington, September 10–13.

Nunn, P.D. 1994. *Oceanic Islands.* Blackwell Publishers, Oxford.

Rogers, R.F. 1995. *Destiny's landfall: A history of Guam.* University of Hawai'i Press, Honolulu.

Russell, S. 1998. *Ancient Chamorro culture and history of the Northern Mariana Islands.* Micronesian Archaeological Survey Report No. 32, Saipan.

Twaddle, I., Roberto, J.P. and Quitanilla, L.D. 2003. Chamorro perspectives on mental health issues in Guam: Cross-currents of indigenous and western cultural discourses. *South Pacific Journal of Psychology* 14:30–59.

van Valen, L. 1973. A new evolutionary law. *Evolutionary Theory* 1:1–30.

Websites

http://decolonizeguam.blogspot.com/search?q=antigo
http://www.gdoe.net/chamstud/
http://www.guam-online.com/history/history.htm
http://www.pacificworlds.com/cnmi/arrival/ancients.cfm
http://www.freewebs.com/allthingsguam/virtualhistorytextbook.htm
http://decolonizeguam.blogspot.com/2007/08/desecration-of-chamorro-remains-at.html
http://guampedia.com/
http://www.ischool.utexas.edu/~gracy/research.html
http://minagahet.blogspot.com/2009/11/decolonization-and-loincloth.html

3

Reinventing tradition
Archaeology in Samoa

Unasa L.F. Va'a
Centre for Samoan Studies, National University of Samoa, Samoa

Introduction

It can be argued that there are two sides to the study of archaeology. One is the scientific aspect, using modern methods of excavation, accurate recording, reliable carbon dating and competent analysis. The other is a discipline subjected to the demands of ideology, that is to say, a discipline that serves the purpose of an ideology. I am talking about tradition. The problem is that when the notion of tradition changes because of new influences, however these are generated, so does the perspective. An example is that a pagan country will highlight the validity of pagan principles and lifestyle, while a Christian country will do the opposite. That is to say, ideology will have an effect on how we describe and analyse the findings of a scientific discipline leading to different interpretations and solutions. In other words, we start from the same facts, but reach different conclusions.

In these situations, the facts must always be subordinate to ideology, an observation that is cogently argued in Marxist analyses of the relationship of structure and superstructure. It is also true of political analysis and, I contend, of archaeological analysis. The ideology can never be prised from the structure, nor the structure from the ideology, and that is because we are not just mechanical beings, we are also emotional ones. Our experiences are coloured by our feelings and this extends to all the sciences, however much we might preach about 'objectivity'. In traditional societies such as Samoa, feelings change when traditions change.

The beginnings of archaeology in Samoa

Understanding of the past in Samoa usually focuses on family genealogies, a body of knowledge which is usually memorised (Penisimani 1860; Krämer 1994). Little attention was paid by Samoans to the material remains of their ancient society. This is reflected also in the history of archaeology in Samoa. Thus, in the 19th century and early 20th century, relics of temples and sites of myths and legends throughout Samoa were places that people visited as modern-day tourists or as connoisseurs of exotic remains. The remains of an ancient temple at Magiagi, near Apia, was often visited by prominent citizens of the period, such as the Reverend John Stair, the first mission printer of the London Missionary Society (Lovett 1899), William T. Pritchard

(1985), one of the earliest traders in Apia, William Churchward (1971), the British Consul, and Chief Justice Schultz of the German Administration (1900–1914).

The real archaeological work, however, was started by Sir Peter Buck (1930), in his monumental study of Samoan material culture, followed by Derek Freeman in the early 1940s. Freeman (1944) introduced the methodologies of archaeology into his work, which involved excavations, collecting artefacts and measuring various prehistoric sites. These include the *Fale o le Fe'e* at Magiagi, the earth mounds of Vailele (near where the National University of Samoa now stands) and the historic cave at Seuao, Sa'anapu. He published his investigations in the *Journal of the Polynesian Society*. Freeman's work was continued by Jack Golson in the 1950s. He conducted the first systematic survey of archaeological remains on the big island of Savai'i, as well as Vailele on Upolu, and discovered the first ancient pottery from Samoa.

In the 1960s, Golson was followed by Roger Green and Janet Davidson (1974) from Auckland University. They and colleagues conducted extensive fieldwork at Vailele, Falefa and other sites in the 1960s, and edited the two volumes of *Archaeology in Western Samoa*, which are still the primary source of archaeological information for Samoa today. Noted American archaeologist Jesse Jennings and his student Richard Holmer (Jennings et al. 1982) also did extensive fieldwork in Samoa, principally at Faleasiu and Falelatai in the 1970s. At the same time, Jennings reviewed the progress of the work involved in the discovery of Lapita pottery at Mulifanua in 1973, which showed that Samoa had been colonised by the same cultural group that had spread from the Bismarck Archipelago to the Solomon Islands, Vanuatu, New Caledonia, Fiji and Tonga.

Interest in the archaeology in Samoa has been of a sporadic nature despite the stature of the scholars who pioneered investigations. But this approach has changed, and now archaeology, the study of the material and social culture of the past, has become a new and important field in Samoa. This is due to the following three actions:

1. Recent extensive archaeological work in American Samoa undertaken mainly by American archaeologists such as Patrick Kirch, David Addison and others during the past 20 years;

2. The adoption of archaeology by the National University of Samoa in 2007 as a compulsory subject in its new Bachelor of Samoan Studies degree; and

3. A renewed interest in environmental and heritage issues by the Samoan Government in the mid 1990s, resulting in the renaming of the former Ministry of Lands as the Ministry of Natural Resources and Environment.

On the whole, a renewed interest in environmental and heritage issues is good for the country, as reflected in the renewed interest of the government in heritage issues, which is in keeping with similar developments in other Pacific Island countries. As part of the new interest, archaeological research has received a considerable boost, which in the long term will result in significant change not only to government policies, but also to academic pursuits at the National University of Samoa. But the anticipated growth of archaeology as both an academic and an applied discipline will not be unproblematic for several reasons.

Firstly, one major problem that I foresee is the nature of tradition under culture change. Traditions keep changing as people change their values and beliefs. One of the most dramatic of these beliefs is change to religious affiliations. In the pre-Christian past, generally before the arrival of the first contingent of London Missionary Society ministers in 1836, Samoans followed a religion which is best described, according to Edward Tylor's 1871 classification in *Primitive Culture*, as animistic. In effect, Samoans believed in spirit-gods which appeared to them in the form of animals, birds, fish, reptiles, or as natural phenomena, such as the sun, stars, planets, the moon, lightning, earthquakes and so on.

In the 1830s and 1840s, evangelistic missionaries of the London Missionary Society from their base at Tahiti, Wesleyan missionaries from their base in Tonga, and Catholic missionaries from their base in Wallis and Futuna effected mass conversions of Samoans to Christianity (Williams 1837; Turner 1983; Moyle 1984). These conversions took place over a 30-year period and changed the religious belief and practice of the population in a basic and fundamental way. Everything that reflected Samoa's pagan religious beliefs and practices was condemned by European missionaries, and there was widespread destruction of ancient temples, shrines and sacred groves and visible incarnations of the ancient gods.

This act of destruction was so successful that very little of the old religious institutions remained, except in so far as they have been incorporated into the Christian religion, such as *lotu afiafi*, or evening prayer services (Va'a 1987). The *Fale o le Fe'e*, about 10 km inland of Apia, is the remnant of an old Samoan temple (Stair 1894, 1897) to the *Fe'e* (octopus), and though desecrated to a considerable degree, it managed to survive due to the fact that it was difficult to destroy the large stones that made up the posts of the temple.

The point about the re-invention of tradition, and in Samoa's case the change from paganism to Christianity, might have an important effect on future archaeological work, as religious fundamentalists try to discourage research which could remind Samoans of their pagan past. However, it is intriguing that in the British Isles and other parts of Europe there has been a revival in paganism by some sections of society.

The second major problem concerns the nature of internal politics in Samoa. One example happened recently in an archaeological project involving the National University of Samoa and Magiagi Village, 4.8 km southeast of Apia. The project concerned bush clearing and archaeological excavations at the *Fale o le Fe'e* temple, conducted in 2007–2008. In 2007, archaeology students from the National University of Samoa and archaeologists from Gotland University, Sweden, initiated a project which involved excavations at the *Fale o le Fe'e* temple, Magiagi (Martinsson-Wallin 2008). Before the research, we actively sought the support of both the Internal Division of the Ministry of Women and Social Development and the Electric Power Corporation (EPC). Meetings with the Internal Division were sought because it is the government arm which coordinates activities involving village councils, while the EPC controlled land though which our researchers had to pass to reach the temple site.

Of course, we also had to obtain the approval of the village council of Magiagi, mainly through the *Pulenu'u*, or government representative, in the village. As far as possible, we followed all of the necessary protocols to obtain access to the site.

However, unbeknown to us, there had been a political upheaval in the village in 2008, which resulted in a change in the *Pulenu'u*. The new government representative was not favourably disposed towards the project and he made known his opposition. When Associate Professor Helene Martinsson-Wallin (Gotland University) and I (National University of Samoa) visited Magiagi village to hand over the report of our 2007 research, we were subjected to haranguing by the new *Pulenu'u*. He accused us of not respecting our commitment (his words) to consult with the village, of not turning up for a scheduled meeting with the village council, and of not paying for village labour.

His diatribe was in Samoan, which I translated for the benefit of our European visitor. I told him that we did consult the village through the former *Pulenu'u* and that it was another government group that had failed to meet with the village council as scheduled. It was a case of mistaken identity, I told him. I also informed the *Pulenu'u* that we did contribute money for the village, again through the former *Pulenu'u*, as a token of our appreciation. Moreover, we did not make any commitments that we did not honour, such as payment for several villagers who helped clear the land and who carried surveying equipment between the base and the temple site.

The bottom line, however, is that we got caught up in the internal politics of the village. From what I had overheard from several of the villagers, there is disagreement in the village council about the proposed reconstruction of the ancient temple for tourism purposes. The *Pulenu'u* we originally dealt with represented the faction that favoured the reconstruction of the temple as a historical site that tourists could visit and our archaeological team was dedicated to helping make this a reality. The new *Pulenu'u*, we are were informed, represented the other faction.

The lesson, perhaps, is to have any future agreements with villages put down in writing, yet perhaps this can complicate matters further because the roots of the problem lie deeper. The Magiagi episode shows how complex these local issues are. It is possible that a political faction in the village did not want the old district war god of the Vaimauga, *Le Fe'e*, to re-emerge, and/or that supporting work on pre-Christian sites was seen as a culturally dangerous activity because it had the potential to challenge the contemporary belief system.

Thirdly, another problem for the future is the traditional concern for the physical remains of the ancestors, a common enough objection to archaeological investigations. This concern emerged in research at the Pulemelei Mound in Palauli, again involving archaeologists and students from Gotland University and the Australian National University. Some of the people of Palauli district voiced their opposition to archaeological excavations at the Pulemelei Mound because they said the work showed disrespect towards the physical remains of their ancestors who they claimed were buried there. Other issues were involved, of course, such as ownership of the mound. There was a court case disputing current ownership. The district lost. The Supreme Court held that the provisions of the Berlin Treaty (1899), under which the sales of certain traditional lands were legitimised, were Samoan law at the time, and therefore the sale of the Pulemelei lands was valid. The owner, O.F. Nelson and Co. Ltd, had its rights re-affirmed, but the village appealed the decision, with further court action likely in the future. By the time village politics intervened, much of the archaeological investigations had already been completed, with, it must be said, local labour from the village, but any further excavations have been effectively stopped, at least until a final decision is reached about land ownership. The O.F. Nelson and Co. Ltd performed a ritual to remove the various *tapu* involved in the project (Tamasese 2008), but this did not stop the village's opposition to the archaeology because the dispute also involved the question of authority over the land.

Already, archaeologists at the National University of Samoa are beginning to look elsewhere for fresh excavations – for instance, to Manono and Fagaloa. For example, Tautala Asaua (2005), the lecturer in archaeology at the Centre of Samoan Studies, is planning extensive work at the Manono site as part of her PhD field research. Archaeologists from Gotland University, Sweden, such as Helene Martinsson-Wallin and Gustav Svedmo, are also looking at new sites in both Upolu and Savai'i islands for institutional research and training postgraduate students. These researches, including student and staff exchanges between the National University of Samoa and Gotland University, are funded under the Palme Grant of the Swedish Government, and the National University of Samoa has been a beneficiary of this grant for many years.

Conclusion

Despite the anticipated problems outlined above, I am confident that solutions can be found in better and more formal negotiations about archaeological projects, which will help to identify and resolve internal village disputes before they escalate. Performing the necessary rituals and making appropriate payments will also ensure that locals support the investigations. In negotiating with the villages, the government protocol should be followed. That is to say, consultants, archaeologists and students should negotiate with interested parties through the agency of the Internal Division, the *Pulenu'u*, the village council and any other government department or corporation involved. The parameters of the project should be clearly spelled out and the extent and remuneration of village labour should be clearly identified, to avoid any misunderstanding. In the Samoan context, this may also involve making a formal gift to the village council (money or food, or both).

Internal politics in the village council are a reality in the Samoan context and it is not always possible to satisfy all factions. Failing an all-round agreement on the issues involved in the project, we can at least deal with the dominant part, then execute the project as quickly as possible in case the political climate changes. Proper respect should always be shown for the sacred sites of the Samoans, such as burial places, and above all for any physical remains excavated. American Samoan-based archaeologists have much experience in this area, and perhaps we can follow their example. For instance, remains can be collected and properly buried in a suitable location. There are no doubt many other obstacles to archaeological research in Samoa, but if we are to succeed in promoting the education, welfare and history of our people we must find ways of coping successfully with the challenges.

References

Asaua, T. 2005. Samoan archaeology: Bridging the gap between the spoken and the scientific. Unpublished MA thesis, Anthropology Department, University of Auckland.

Buck, P. 1930. *Samoan material culture.* Bernice P. Bishop Museum, Bulletin 75.

Churchward, W.B. 1971. *My consulate in Samoa.* Dawsons of Pall Mall, London.

Davidson, J. 1974. Samoan structural remains and settlement patterns. In: Green, R.C. and Davidson, J.M. (eds), *Archaeology in Western Samoa.* Volume II,. Auckland Institute and Museum Bulletin 7:225–244.

Freeman, J.D. 1944. *O le fale o le fe'e.* Journal of the Polynesian Society 53(4):121–144.

Jennings, J.D., R.N. Holmer and G. Jackmond 1982. Samoan village patterns: Four examples. *Journal of the Polynesian Society* 91:81–102.

Krämer, A. 1994. *The Samoa Islands. An outline of a monograph with particular consideration of German Samoa.* Volume I. Polynesian Press, Auckland.

Lovett, R. 1899. *The history of the London Missionary Society 1795–1895.* Henry Frowde, Oxford University Press, London.

Martinsson-Wallin, H. 2008. *Preliminary report of investigations at Fale o le Fe'e, June 21–25, 2007.* Gotland University, Visby, Sweden.

Moyle, R.M. (ed), 1984. *The Samoan journals of John Williams 1830 and 1832.* Australian National University Press, Canberra.

Penisimani. 1860. Penisimani Manuscripts. In the George Brown Papers, Mitchell Library, Sydney.

Pritchard, W.T. 1985. *Polynesian reminiscences or Life in the South Sea Islands.* Southern Reprints, Papakura, New Zealand.

Stair, J.B. 1894. O le fale o le fe'e: Or ruins of an old Samoan temple. *Journal of Polynesian Society* 3(4):239–244.

Stair, J.B. 1897. *Old Samoa or flotsam and jetsam from the Pacific Ocean.* The Religious Tract Society, London.

Ta'isi, Tui Atua Tupua Tamasese. 2008. *Su'esu'e Manogi. In search of fragrance.* The Centre for Samoan Studies, National University of Samoa, Papaigalagala, Apia.

Turner, G. 1983 [1884]. *Samoa a 100 years ago and long before. A study of a Polynesian society before the advent of European influence.* R. McMillan, Papakura, New Zealand.

Va'a, L.F. 1987. The parables of a Samoan divine. An analysis of Samoan texts of the 1860s. Unpublished MA thesis, Faculty of Arts, Australian National University, Canberra.

Williams, J. 1837. *A narrative of missionary enterprises in the South Sea Islands with remarks upon the natural history of the islands origin, languages, traditions, and usages of the inhabitants.* D. Appleton and Co., New York.

4

On cultural factors and
Marine Managed Areas in Fiji

Joeli Veitayaki, Akosita D.R. Nakoro, Tareguci Sigarua and Nanise Bulai
International Ocean Institute, School of Islands and Oceans, University of the South Pacific, Fiji

Introduction

Marine Managed Areas (MMAs) are spreading rapidly in Fiji and other countries in the Asia-Pacific region as local communities act to protect their marine resources that are in danger of depletion and overexploitation. Customary practices are the basis of these community-based resource management activities. This creates the need to better understand both the influence of cultural roles on the effectiveness of MMAs and how traditional practices can address the challenges faced today and in the years to come.

In Fiji, many local communities have demonstrated their commitment to manage their marine resources by using their customary rights to declare nearly all of the existing MMAs. In this case, the customary owners of the resources have shown more commitment to manage their resources than the Fiji Government, which pledged at the 2005 Mauritius Meeting of Small Island Developing States to manage 30% of its national waters by 2020. It is obvious that local communities have been more adept at making the hard decisions to restrict, reduce and manage their coastal resources for contemporary and future generations. The challenge is to support these community initiatives to effectively conserve their resources for the benefit of the communities and the resource users, as well as the environment.

The intimate relationship between the people in the Pacific Islands and their natural resources demonstrates the care that Pacific Islanders have for each other, future generations and the environment (Govan 2009:22). In these islands, community-based resource management is a dynamic system of social interventions, shaped by local practices and influenced by a combination of internal and external events. Aware that their resources recover quickly if their use is reduced, islanders have developed practices to restrict collecting, gleaning and fishing when it is justified. This is where people's knowledge, education, belief, community dynamics and perceptions influence their resource-management activities. Hence, for more effective contemporary community-based marine-resources management, the people's motives, ethics, interests and cultural conceptions need to be assessed and evaluated.

A customary marine tenure system based on local autonomy and self-reliance controls the use of marine space and resources in Fiji and many Pacific Island countries. While this tenure system is recognised in national constitutions and legislation in Papua New Guinea, the Solomon Islands, Samoa and Vanuatu, it is only an informal right in Fiji, which has 410 registered customary fishing rights areas (*qoliqoli*) that support the subsistence fishers as well as some commercial interests. In the heavily exploited *qoliqoli*, resource management is critical because local fishing pressure is no longer sustainable (Muehlig-Hofmann 2008).

The declaration of MMAs is determined by the social structure and circumstances of each community. In communities where there is strong, wise and respected leadership (Muehlig-Hofmann 2008), the customary system is offering an alternative to contemporary government-instigated resource management. This is important because these traditional communities have committed to manage their resources instead of waiting for government directive, guidance and leadership. However, respect for traditional chiefs, which is now dependent on their strength of character, knowledge and authority (Vunisea 2002), is important for the success of MMAs.

This paper is based on a Conservation International (CI) study that examines how cultural roles affect the effectiveness of MMAs and the factors that need to be taken into consideration by the communities involved. These community-based initiatives are supported by their non-government-organisation partners and are part of the Fiji Locally Marine Managed Areas (FLMMA) network, which demonstrates the popularity and effects of community-based resource management practices. However, FLMMA is still striving for efficient and effective MMAs and to make marine resources management more satisfying and meaningful to those involved. In the meantime, FLMMA partners have channelled increased resources into local communities and contributed to resource management as well as poverty reduction in rural communities that depend on marine resources (Aalbersberg et al. 2005:151).

Although most conservation review efforts to date have focused on MMAs' bio-physical and economic features, it is also critical to understand the cultural roles involved because of their influence on resource management decisions and compliance. After all, resource management is about managing the activities of people. As Jacques Weber contends (Henocque and Denis 2001:8), 'Environmental management is not a question of humans' relationship to nature; instead, it is a question of human relations on the subject of nature.'

Cooke and Moce (1995), Muehlig-Hofmann (2008) and Sano (2008) show that management strategies and the level of government participation vary greatly throughout Fiji and depend on the individual fisheries officers, chiefs and communities involved. In some places, people alter their resource-management activities when their social and economic conditions change. In other cases, problems and conflicts arise when community resource managers feel they are treated poorly or with disrespect. The lack of funds and capacity within Government has forced the reliance on the local governance and self-regulation of the coastal communities. However, the CI study shows that with their present structure, skills and resources, local communities alone cannot establish and carry out the management measures needed to mitigate the increasing pressure on their resources. Therefore, effective management of marine resources by community groups needs government support.

Marine resource management in its various forms is undertaken in Fiji's communities. Most of these communities collaborate with partners from non-government organisations (NGOs) and institutions (Veitayaki et al. 2005a, 2005b; Veitayaki 2006; Muehlig-Hofmann 2008; Sano 2008) to establish their MMAs, while others work independently or through local chiefs, officials and academics, or they learn from neighbouring communities and relatives. In many cases, resource management activities are dependent on the ambitions of the communities and individuals involved (Muehlig-Hofmann 2008) and the approach adopted by the group.

Some cultural features

The basis of Fijian organisation are the villages that people live in. Villages were originally small, and the main regulators to their size are the minimum viable defence force or workforce or the maximum number that the food supplies will support (Frazer 1973:78–79). Despite continually increasing in size over the years, village composition has remained the same, with each consisting of one or more closely related clans. Clans consist of *mataqali*, commonly the land-owning units, which include a number of extended families, or *tokatoka*, that are made up of individual households. From the different *mataqali* or *tokatoka* come the chiefs (*turaga ni vanua*), heralds (*mata ni vanua*), warriors and planters (*bati*), fishers (*gonedau*), priests (*bete*) and carpenters (*mataisau*).

The village operates because the different groups (*mataqali* or *tokatoka*) within it have specific tasks they are responsible for performing (Seruvakula 2000:21–29). People know who they are and what is expected of them. The *sauturaga*, for instance, are responsible for maintaining respect and order for the chief and the village. They ensure that all their responsibilities are fulfilled and that the protocol is observed (Capell 1991).

The chiefs and their clansmen are the traditional owners and guardians of the land, waters, resources and people. Previously, Fijians did not attribute monetary value to land or have the concept that land could be bought and sold for personal gain (Farrell 1972:38). This has changed, as land as a commodity is now a major cause of conflict among close family relations. Fortunately, laws and institutions have been put in place to address land issues and other aspects of Fijian affairs.

Customary marine tenure (CMT) is the formal and informal ownership of sea space by a Fijian group ranging from *tokatoka* to *tikina* (district) (Calamia 2003). The CMT system is built on local autonomy and self-reliance that controls the use of local marine space and resources. The use and management of customary fishing areas is determined by the group that owns the area. The use of customary fishing grounds by outsiders is permitted, provided access conditions are met. This system is seen by some as a hindrance to economic progress because the indigenous owners of the resources may not support important developments, as they are not convinced the proposed development projects will bring benefits to them.

Indigenous Fijians have exclusive customary fishing rights in their *qoliqoli*, extending from the coast to the barrier reefs and some offshore reefs. The location and size of the tenured fishing grounds is not based on ecologically optimal management units but on historical developments and societal, traditional and geographic factors. Thus, the size of the fishing ground and the quantity of its resources reflects the owner's historical status and prominence and is not related to the size of the population that depends on it or the boundaries of the ecological region (Muehlig-Hofmann et al. 2005).

Village life has evolved since European contact in 1643. In 1864, the first Melanesian farm labourers were shipped to Fiji because it was believed the local population's custom and kin ties would prevent them from working hard. In subsequent years, some 20,000 Ni Vanuatus, I Kiribati, Tuvaluans, Tokelauans and Solomon Islanders were brought to Fiji (Narayan 1984:23).

In 1874, Fijian chiefs ceded their country to Britain and became subjects of Queen Victoria to formalise the transition to contemporary Fiji. Shifting cultivation, which provided food for consumption and social obligations, was replaced by permanent plantations. The communication lines, health services, education and European goods that became a part of village life in the 1960s (Frazer 1973:78–79) continue to transform villages to mirror modernising societies elsewhere. Cash crops, wages and commercial activities are now established in villages throughout the country.

Decision-making was transferred from the hereditary chiefs and community councils to the government officials and judiciary (Frazer 1973). In addition, individuals and groups became more independent. Fijian villages were no longer limited in size and were influenced by their proximity to urban areas. Furthermore, villagers were attracted to urban life, with its opportunities for higher income and status.

The development expected after attaining political independence in 1970 has not materialised and the country is divided between the urban centres and peripheral rural areas. Political upheaval has hindered the country's social and economic development. After four coups in 20 years, the people are now working with the National Charter for Building a Better Fiji (Daurewa 2008) to redirect development towards sustained peace and prosperity.

Currently, traditional marine resource management promotes improving existing conditions, with the general population regulated to the role of spectator and the state responsible for resource management activities. Intensive and habitual fishing of Fiji's reefs by the ever increasing population using effective and destructive fishing methods is causing extensive damage that is threatening the fishing areas. In Macuata's Qoliqoli Cokovata, the high number of school dropouts adds more pressure to the area's already diminishing marine and terrestrial resources (Bolabola et al. 2006). In these areas, commercial and subsistence fishing are driving people further into deeper and distant offshore areas, increasing their costs and threatening their sources of livelihood and food.

Poaching is common even in MMAs, while destructive fishing practices such as fish drives are still used in Vanua Balavu, Bua and Gau. These harmful fishing methods are blamed for the extensively damaged reefs and the algae and seaweed now dominating some of the coastlines. The pollution and sedimentation associated with poor development practices is also a major threat to customary fishing grounds (Veitayaki 2006). Fiji's hillsides are commonly burned, threatening farmlands, while biodiversity and pesticide use is increasingly affecting the environment. In Vanua Balavu in the Lau Group, the villagers are asking why destructive chemicals are being introduced so freely into the villages when they are so damaging to the environment.

Customary roles and duties are less clear and effective in Fiji today. The traditional tenure system and resource management strategies, for example, experienced gradual erosion due to the impact of 20th century colonisation (Govan 2009:25). While traditional roles and resource-use systems within the communities are still well defined, leadership structures, protocol, respect, practices and beliefs are changing and are increasingly questioned by the people (Vunisea 2002). Moreover, intermarriages and the use of modern equipment have allowed people to fish in areas far away from their home base.

Muehlig-Hofmann (2008) argues that qoliqoli and other traditional systems are unable to independently cope with the rapid exogenous change and hence fail to perform their role in fisheries management; a role others believe they are capable of fulfilling (Anderson and Mees 1999). While there is strong support for the MMA, there are differences about the length of MMA closure, which some say could be alleviated by periodically relaxing activities in MMA (Van Beukering et al. 2007).

Contrary to the customary marine tenure system, the sea and sea floor stretching from the high-water mark belongs to the state (South and Veitayaki 1998). This mixed arrangement has been a source of confusion for more than 130 years (Ruddle 1994; Cooke and Moce 1995) and needs to be the basis of co-management. Since political independence, attempts have been made to return full ownership of the *qoliqoli* areas to the indigenous owners. In August 2006, in an attempt to resolve the situation, a Qoliqoli Bill was put before the Fiji Parliament that proposed returning all proprietary rights to *qoliqoli* areas to the identified traditional owners. The Qoliqoli

Bill caused controversy among the diverse stakeholders, some of whom harboured the idea that it privileged the indigenous Fijian population. According to this group, the legislation undermined responsible community-based resource management as ownership rights are in the hands of the land-owning groups (*mataqali*) (Muehlig-Hofmann 2008). In addition, issues such as community leadership and responsibility for community resource management efforts need to be appropriately addressed.

Fiji's MMAs are driven by the idea that sustainable healthy living standards and income can only be achieved with properly managed marine environment and fisheries resources. The varying degree of success seen in the more sustainable approach to exploitation pursued over the past decade is indicative of the people's inability to get organised and committed to resource management (Veitayaki 1998; Zann and Vuki 1998). Contrary to the MMAs, many communities are trying to modernise their fishing methods to increase their output. In fact, commercial fishing in rural Fiji has continued to expand and intensify, challenging MMA initiatives undertaken by local communities.

Given the current harvesting capacity, a fisheries resource can easily be exploited beyond sustainable levels. Thus, the precautionary approach to fisheries needs to be implemented at the village level. According to Muehlig-Hofmann (2008), who worked on Gau Island, community challenges can only be met by a strong bond between official agents and communities that is based on continuity, community consensus and trust. This can be achieved if every community has experienced officials working with it to formulate and implement conservation measures, surveillance, compliance, communication, networking, data collection and analysis.

The influence of cultural roles on MMAs in Fiji

Cultural roles are crucial to the declaration and support of local MMAs. However, they are not effective outside the local community context, where government regulations, policies and legislation are of greater consequence. Maintaining community MMAs is also challenging as the people need to be unanimously convinced that resource management improves their lives. Unfortunately, most of the villagers are unable to sustain their MMAs to realise the benefits because of outside pressure by traders and poachers, whose activities compromise the effectiveness of MMAs. As a result, Fiji's rural MMAs are vulnerable and targeted by poachers who consider these spots premium fishing grounds.

The establishment of MMAs in local communities was supported by traditional institutions and customs that are now eroding. Traditional protocols, for instance, are not strongly followed, while the enforcement of noncompliance within a community has changed. At times, traditions are abused for the benefit of a limited few. Traditional relations and ties are at times used to access the resources of rural communities. For example, some commercial operators present a *sevusevu* (the traditional offering of kava to announce arrival and welcome visitors) worth US$15 and earn between US$150 and $1500 from the fisheries products caught in their host's *qoliqoli*. In other instances, unscrupulous operators establish markets in rural areas to entice people to relax their management activities. This is the reason why effective communication is critical.

MMAs have greatly benefited coastal communities. People have realised the critical importance of maintaining the health and productivity of their fishing grounds and how these are related to and affected by all the ecosystems around them. Through training, the villagers are realising their responsibilities as stakeholders who depend on these resources for their livelihoods and who need to sustain their resources for current and future sustenance. They see the need to make the right choices for their children. In Verata, the permanent MMA is now surrounded by an area that is allowed to be fished whenever the villagers want. Under this arrangement, a portion of the MMA is always permanently closed, providing seeds for the recovery of the fished areas.

Communities now understand the need for an integrated resource management approach and have adopted the ecosystem-based method for managing their resources. This method is the basis of resource management activities in Verata, Muaivusu, Kubulau and Gau. People involved with MMAs now enjoy better lives; they are spending less time to get more resources and are earning more money than before. Fishing is now conducted in areas previously avoided and the abundance of fisheries resources and the reappearance of resources that have not been seen in recent times have been noticed. In general, communities are realising the recovery of their fisheries resources and the marine environment. This success in marine resource management is being extended to other areas of people's lives and responsibilities. The people are looking for alternative sources of income and are searching for better ways of using their natural resources. People's living conditions are being improved with the assistance of conservation partners through sustainable tourist activities, fisheries development, land use and forestry activities and the sale of traditional art and crafts.

The community-engagement approach in MMAs improved the management of marine resources and boosted rural-development activities. Villagers have enhanced their income-generating activities and established new sources of income such as mat making and ecotourism. Some conservation efforts have been rewarded with assistance such as village halls, outboard punts and engines that were given to communities in Ono and Navakavu, and trust funds that have been set up for communities such as Verata and Kubulau.

Socially, the villages, *tikina* and islands are working together with a better sense of purpose and cohesion. Social units have been strengthened, and district meetings (*bose*) and church services (*lotu ni vanua*) are now operating. The social institutions are revitalised and strengthened through development assistance that has allowed regular consultation and meetings. The social units are now more relevant because they are supporting the people's development aspirations. Community leaders are supported by being involved in consultative meetings and training, and visit other communities to widen their experiences and expand on their ideas.

Some of the community groups are earning steady incomes from their resource management activities. In Kubulau, there is a scholarship program for the villagers' children attending secondary and tertiary institutions, while the villagers now host divers from Lautoka hotels in their MMAs. In addition, the development partners are collecting money to support the protection of the marine environment. In many of the operating MMAs, assistance from the development partners is offered to the villages, village schools, kindergartens and health centres.

Studies in Fiji supported the increased income earned from resource management activities. Since 2006, the women of Vanuaso Tikina in Gau have earned about US$500 per month from the sale of their mats in Suva. In Vanuaso village, the youth opened a store that had not operated for more than 20 years, and in the villages of Malawai and Lekanai, the youth groups now own cattle farms that provide for the communities' ceremonial obligations. These initiatives demonstrate the link between economic development and care of the environment. The people are learning that they need to take care of their environmental resources because their lives depend on it.

Challenges

Unfortunately, many improvements are needed to ensure the effective operation of MMAs in Fiji. Many of these improvements involve the incorporation of traditional practices and cultural roles into contemporary resource management plans. In many cases, for instance, not everyone in the village is aware of what is going on, with resource management decisions made by a small group including the chief. In such cases, the involvement of the larger group depends on how well the message and decision is disseminated through the community. In other instances, there is an incorrect assumption that the entire community is involved. This study highlighted that this is sometimes not the case and that wrong assumptions compromise community support.

The importance of effective communication is also crucial to a community's resource management efforts. The strength of the traditional system is based on everyone observing the group's decision. This is only effective in cases in which the entire community is continually reminded of its resource management activities. Successful communication requires regular visits and follow-up activities so the stakeholders are consulted and kept informed on issues such as the ownership of MMAs and what is being and still needs to be done.

The 2009 indictment of the high chief of Macuata Province for authorising his honorary fish wardens to confiscate fish catches from fishers allegedly illegally fishing in his domain illustrates the need for government support to sustain customary resource management practices. The Fiji Government needs to put in place legislation to protect community-based resource management initiatives. Moreover, the Government needs to promote resource development and resource management. At present, the Government's emphasis on fisheries development is exemplified by the requirement that its support is subject to an applicant's possession of a fishing licence, which communities observing MMAs do not have.

Poaching is prevalent in rural communities because the Government has not assisted those who are least able to defend their resource management decisions. Without the local resources required for enforcement of environmental regulations, poaching will continue to occur. In many cases, the people's resolve to maintain their MMAs is badly undermined by the extent of poaching. This forces the community to relax its management activities so it may receive some benefit from its own MMA. These communities feel it is pointless to refrain from using their MMAs if outsiders are the primary beneficiaries. Poaching is stealing and should be treated seriously by the Government, which also needs to acknowledge that commercial fishers and businesses are supporting people that are stealing from rural communities. Many of these are the same communities the Government should be assisting to improve their living conditions while sustainably utilising their resources.

Poaching also tempers the effectiveness of MMAs, providing an inaccurate reflection of the recovery of the resources. An accurate resource-recovery picture is necessary to convince people that the MMAs work. In some cases, communities give up their MMAs because others are benefiting from their sacrifices. In these cases, the people ignored the effort put into the establishment of the MMAs and the benefits they have been witnessing.

Communities practising resource management are under continuous pressure to relax their management plans because their MMAs are a potential source of instant income. In many villages, there are limited opportunities to earn an income to pay for necessities and responsibilities, so the MMAs are seen as the community's last resort.

Sadly, people in rural areas are seldom given ample time to prepare for their financial obligations. Rural people therefore regularly turn to their MMAs to secure much-needed income. Hurriedly organised village income-earning activities such as collections and contributions are often conveniently supported by the arrival of commercial operators who easily convince the people to relax their MMA activities and earn the needed money from the sale of their products.

People in rural areas today need money to pay for food, electricity and transport to harvest their natural resources, as well as for their community obligations, church contributions and education. They periodically open their MMAs to pay for some of these obligations. In order for people to treat their MMAs seriously, the villagers need to have alternative avenues for generating income. People also must note that once an MMA is relaxed, it is difficult to re-close the site or commit to another MMA. In many instances, local fishing businesses, backed by middlemen in the cities, have sprung up in villages with MMAs to buy fish from the villagers. These commercial ventures are often non-sustainable.

Many communities, perceiving the MMAs as belonging to their partners, are weakly supportive of their resource management activities. This perception is related to the role played by the partners in the initial empowerment of communities and their declarations of MMAs. Unfortunately, people in these areas expect compensation for their contributions to MMAs, wait for directives from the partners and at times threaten the MMAs if their demands are not met. Obviously, these communities have not been convinced about their ownership of their MMAs, and so it is easier for them to trade their MMAs for much-needed goods or income.

Shifting demands from local communities of their partners are common. In some cases, the local people expect their partners to provide for their evolving needs even though they themselves are not committed to the MMAs and the partners have met all of their promised support. There is a need for local people to see their partners as generous and dedicated people who want to assist them and not as sources of unlimited riches to be used. The work in Vanuaso Tikina in Gau Island (Veitayaki et al. 2005a, 2005b) proves that local communities can take ownership of their MMAs if they are allowed ample time to make the determinations. Thus, long-term engagement of local communities is crucial to the process of establishing and maintaining effective MMAs.

Village meetings are regularly conducted but they are not all well organised and not well attended. The meetings are held mostly for the men who, it is assumed, will inform their women. Even if the women were expected to or wanted to attend, meetings are often held at times when the women are busy preparing breakfast and attending to the children. Minutes of the meetings are not well kept so reiteration of the discussions that took place and decisions made is commonly inconsistent and disorganised and often contradictory. Moreover, follow-up activities are not regularly communicated to the villagers, who are then left in the dark about what the village or district is undertaking and their expected contribution.

The community system of representation is ineffective due to poor communication and organisation. Without full knowledge of the undertaking, community members will not be fully engaged in their MMAs. The lessons from the training workshops, for instance, are not well relayed to the communities, while the information from the communities is not accurately reported to the partners. Local representatives do not consult the villagers before attending the various meetings where they speak for the community, while the local representatives, who are expected to articulate the meeting's decision in the community, do not share the information. Written reports are often in English or appear in formats that the villagers have problems understanding or using. Hence, people generally have only limited knowledge of the events impacting their community, while the lack of organised communication hinders the collective effort needed for operating effective MMAs.

Traditional leaders need to regularly seek advice on issues in which they are not well versed. Community leaders should guide and lead their people into the modern world, as well as look after the interests of their future generations. It is here that well-organised community-based committees can play an important advisory role to the traditional leaders. In fact, many local communities have formed committees to look after both resource management and development issues. These committees should be encouraged because of the complexities of contemporary community issues. Some of the issues that today's communities have to address and be trained for are good leadership and governance, development planning and implementation, sustainable use of resources and improvement of livelihood.

The changing of the guard is an unstable period in many local communities. Some people take advantage of this time to seek the relaxation of their community's resource management activities. In some cases, the MMAs are relaxed when a chief dies or shortly after when the community is asked to host a gathering for which the people are not adequately prepared. In other cases, the new chief's vision on the MMAs is different from the last chief's, so the community has to re-adjust its resource management activities accordingly.

It is important to note that local commitment is critical to the success of MMAs. This is due to the reliance people have on the resources and the impacts these resources have on people's livelihoods. Nevertheless, the long-term commitment to sustainable development is difficult to achieve under current conditions. People often only seek the fast money and instant gratification that they will get for exploiting their resources. In comparison, long-term conservation is not as attractive because people need to pay for essentials and assistance now. The few options available for earning an income make people look to their MMAs as a first and last resort to earn money.

The last challenge is the conflict and differences that arise in local communities. Some villagers do not fully comply with their community's resource management activities because of long-standing community conflicts and rivalries. These differences are deep rooted and difficult to solve as they are based on traditional and historical reasons often associated with customary roles. Such conflicts can hinder MMA operation unless there is effective leadership and measures to amicably resolve such differences.

The way forward

MMAs are one of the traditional resource management practices that have the potential to benefit local communities. However, the MMAs' effectiveness can only be realised if the issues that hinder their establishment and maintenance are addressed. This requires the assessment and strengthening of the cultural roles that are an integral part of these MMAs.

Good and visionary leadership is required in local communities where the bulk of the population has never left the village and is unfamiliar with the contemporary challenges it must address. This leadership is needed to ensure that the interests of all of the people, including future generations, are protected, and that they are allowed the opportunity to thrive in a contemporary setting. Leaders need to convince their people that protecting their food sources and their natural resources are the bulwark against starvation and poverty and the best safeguard for the wellbeing of future generations.

Governance and leadership issues need to be addressed to improve community living standards in general and enhance marine resource management in particular. The Fijian administration at all levels needs to ensure that Fijians look after their interests and responsibilities. In terms of organisation, the church is already showing the way forward. The challenge is to extend this success into all facets of life in the local communities.

People need to better organise village meetings where the minutes and records must be properly kept and tasks followed through to completion. The population must be regularly reminded of resource management decisions. For example, during village meetings the Turaga ni Koro (village headmen) must broadcast all of the village activities. This follow-up action is crucial for ensuring that the resource management decisions are endorsed and supported by all community members.

Villagers should improve the maintenance and management of their records. Community discussions, decisions and activities should be accurately recorded both for reference and for monitoring the changes. These community reports should be regularly lodged with the community's development partners and the Government so that the villagers' positions on issues are clearly known and their activities documented.

Villagers need to focus on long-term planning. Many of these initiatives, such as those addressing income-generating activities, sustainable development, climate change and altered habitats, require strategic planning and prudent implementation. Development activities need to be identified and undertaken to bring about better results and life for all.

Capacity building is critical, as new solutions are required to deal with the contemporary challenges that are unusual in traditional systems and therefore must be learned and mastered quickly. In many cases, the chiefs can better use their appropriately trained people who, if in positions of responsibility, need to diligently perform their duties in a transparent and trustworthy manner.

Communities need to make resource management decisions because their resources are unlikely to support their ever increasing demands within a continually degrading environment. Although decision making is the privilege of a few, such as chiefs and elders, their decisions are critical and will influence the quality of life of their people now and into the future. These decisions must be made carefully as they must be adhered to by all. For example, critical resource management decisions have to be endorsed and supported by all stakeholders and should be regularly reviewed and effectively communicated to ensure that the village's resource management commitments are known and honoured by everyone.

At the same time, community partners need to fulfill their long-term obligations. The partners should understand that their community counterparts alone cannot pay the expenses required for looking after the MMAs. Some communities are complaining about the irregularity of their partner's visits and are feeling abandoned. In some areas, community partners are perceived as uninterested in the individual sites because they now only work through the FLMMA network. As it was put to us, FLMMA is now the self-serving focus of Fiji's MMAs that is benefiting from using the individual sites that are otherwise left on their own after their initial empowerment.

Communication within the village and all levels of Fijian administration needs to be improved. Village decisions must be adequately recorded and then shared with everyone involved. Traditional communication protocol is not effectively informing all the stakeholders, who use this breakdown in communication as an excuse not to adhere to the group's decisions.

The Fijian Government, particularly the Fisheries Division, must lead resource management at the local, national and international levels. If MMAs are to succeed, the Government needs to recognise their importance and render its support through appropriate policies, legislation, plans and strategies. By enforcing existing laws, legislation can empower local communities to protect their resources. For example, fishing licence numbers should be easily identified by being clearly marked on the side of fishing vessels. Local community members can curb lawlessness by submitting the licence numbers of the boats fishing in their waters to the Government for identification. Those found violating the Fisheries Act must be penalised harshly so that others are discouraged from acting illegally.

Poaching can be better controlled if licence current conditions are enforced. Anyone selling fish must have a licence, which cannot be transferred. Department of Fisheries officials accompanied by the police must man all of Fiji's main docks to inspect fishing licences. People need to fish in their own designated areas and be encouraged to report suspicious events that may be in violation of the law to the authorities. Those found in violation of their licences should be dealt with harshly.

MMAs need to be relevant to local communities, which must incorporate them into their community initiatives. To allow for this, external partners must genuinely involve local people in project activities that are meaningful to the community. This requires that villagers be engaged in activities that are significant enough to convince them of the importance of resource management to the improvement of their lives.

Given the societal changes taking place, long-term commitment to sustainable development is required in rural communities and across the land. Sustainable development is related to the tradition of relying on the resources available in an area and the need to look after the welfare of the current as well as future generations.

The CI study has highlighted many useful lessons that must now be taken into consideration in the maintenance of effective MMAs. Of course, many of the cultural roles and influences have to be properly addressed. These issues must be amicably addressed because the children of current and future generations in Fiji and other Pacific Islands expect their parents and elders to be good role models who carefully balance their development activities with their maintenance of the integrity and health of their environmental systems. This is a big responsibility because life in years to come will depend on the decisions made by the current generation. Fortunately, customary and traditional practices already provide the basis for sustainable development and effective MMAs. What is needed is to ensure that communities are prepared for the realities they will face in the future and a commitment to address the associated challenges.

References

Aalbersberg, B., Tawake, A. and Parras, T. 2005. Village by village: Recovering Fiji's coastal fisheries. In: UNDP, UNEP, WRI, *World Resources 2005 – The wealth of the poor: Managing ecosystems to fight poverty*, pp. 144–152. World Resources Institute, Washington, DC.

Anderson, J.A. and Mees, C. 1999. The performance of customary marine tenure in the management of community fishery resources in Melanesia. *Final Technical Report* to the UK Department for International Development, MRAG Ltd, London.

Bolabola, A.,Veitayaki, J., Tabunakawai, K. and Navuku, S. 2006. Socio economic baseline survey of Qoliqoli Cokovata area – District of Mali, Dreketi, Sasa and Macuata, Vanua Levu. Ecosystem-based management project. Unpublished WWF report, Suva.

Calamia, M. 2003. *Expressions of customary marine tenure and environmental entitlements: A case study involving common property regimes in a Fijian outer island group*. Unpublished PhD thesis, University of Colorado.

Capell, A. 1991. *Fijian dictionary*. Obtainable from the Fiji Government Printer.

Cooke, A. and Moce, K. 1995. Current trends in the management of *qoliqoli* in Fiji. *SPC Traditional Marine Resources Management Knowledge Information Bulletin* 5:2–7.

Daurewa, A.W. 2008. There is no such thing as a poor Fijian. *Fiji Times* Online Wednesday 29 October.

Farrell, B.H. 1972. The alien and the land of Oceania. In: Ward, R.G. (ed), *Man in the Pacific Islands*, pp. 34–73. Oxford University Press, London.

Frazer, R. 1973. The Fijian village and the independent farmer. In: Brookfield, H.C. (ed), *The Pacific in transition: Geographical perspectives on adaptation and change*, pp. 75–96. Martin's Press, New York.

Govan, H. 2009. Status and potential of locally-managed marine areas in the South Pacific: Meeting nature conservation and sustainable livelihood targets through wide-spread implementation of LMMAs. SPREP/WWF/WorldFish-Reefbase/CRISP. Online at http://www.crisponline.net/Portals/1/PDF/0904_C3A_Govan_MMAs.pdf

Henocque, Y. and Denis, J. (eds), 2001. A methodological guide: Steps and tools towards integrated coastal management. *IOC Manuals and Guides* No. 42. UNESCO.

Muehlig-Hofmann, A., Veitayaki, J., Polunin, N.V.C., Stead, S. and Graham, N.A.J. 2005. Community-based marine resource management in Fiji – from yesterday to tomorrow. Proceedings of the 10th International Coral Reef Symposium 2004 In: *10th International Coral Reef Symposium 2004, 28 June – 2 July 2004*, Okinawa, Japan.

Muehlig-Hofmann, A. 2008. Ownership of Fijian inshore fishing grounds: Community-based management efforts, issues of traditional authority and proposed changes in legislation. *Ocean Yearbook* 22:291–321.

Narayan, J. 1984. *The political economy of Fiji*. South Pacific Review Press, Suva.

Ruddle, K., 1994. Traditional marine tenure in the 90s. In: South, G.R., Goulet, D., Tuqiri. S., and Church, M. (eds), *Traditional marine tenure and sustainable management of marine resources in Asia and the Pacific*, pp. 6–45. International Ocean Institute – South Pacific, Suva.

Sano, Y. 2008. The role of social capital in a common pool resource system in coastal areas: A case study of community-based coastal resource management in Fiji. Unpublished PhD thesis, The Australian National University.

South, G.R. and Veitayaki, J. 1998. The constitution and indigenous fisheries management in Fiji. *Ocean Yearbook* 13:452–466.

Seruvakula, S.B. 2000. *Bula Vakavanua*. Institute of Pacific Studies, Suva.

Van Beukering, P.J.H., Scherl, L.M., Sultanian, E., Leisher, C. and Fong, P.S. 2007. Case study 1: Yavusa Navakavu locally managed marine area (Fiji). The role of marine protected areas in contributing to poverty reduction. http://www.prem online.org/archive/19/doc/Country%20Report%20Navakavu%20_Fiji_.pdf

Veitayaki, J. 1998. Traditional and community-based marine resources management system in Fiji: An evolving integrated process. *Coastal Management* 26(1):47–60.

Veitayaki, J. 2006. Caring for the environment and the mitigation of natural extreme events in Vanuaso Tikina, Gau Island, Fiji: A self-help community initiative. *Island Studies Journal* 1(2):239–306.

Veitayaki, J., Tawake, A., Bogiva, A., Radikedike, P., Meo, S., Ravula, N., Vave, R. and Fong, S.P. 2005a. Partnerships and the quest for effective community based resource management: Mositi Vanuaso Project, Gau Island, Fiji. *Journal of Pacific Studies* 28(2):328–349.

Veitayaki, J., Tawake, A., Bogiva, A., Radikedike, P., Meo, S., Ravula, N., Vave, R. and Fong, S.P. 2005b. Addressing human factors in fisheries development and regulatory processes in Fiji – The Mositi Vanuaso experience. *Ocean Yearbook* 21:289–306.

Vunisea, A. 2002. Community-based marine resource management in Fiji: The challenges. *SPC Women in Fisheries Information Bulletin* 11:6–9.

Zann, L.P. and Vuki, V.C. 1998. Subsistence fisheries in the South Pacific. In: Fisheries and marine resources, pp. 103–114. Papers presented at Symposium 8, 8th Pacific Science Inter-Congress. The University of the South Pacific, Fiji. 13th–19th July, 1997. *Marine Studies Technical Report* No. 98/3. The University of the South Pacific, Suva.

5

The Guampedia experience
Creating a community online historical and cultural resource

Shannon Murphy

Guampedia Foundation, Inc., Guam

Introduction

Guampedia (http://guampedia.com) is an online encyclopedia that developed as a community project. Guampedia is dedicated to creating an easily accessible, comprehensive and informational internet resource about Guam's history, culture and contemporary issues. It debuted in April 2008 as the island's first online encyclopedia which synthesises scholarly and indigenous considerations in a user-friendly framework (Figure 1). It is intended to spur critical thinking about the island's complex history.

The primary objectives of the Guampedia project revolve around preservation, access and education. Information about important events and people conveyed in accurate and well-written encyclopedia entries ensures the preservation of Guam's history and culture. An internet platform provides everyone with easy access to text, photographs, audio and video that might otherwise be difficult to locate. Locally produced material focused on the island's heritage educates schoolchildren and a worldwide audience, which strengthens local and global knowledge of Guam's traditional and contemporary society and culture. Dr Nicolas Goetzfridt (2006:340) defines Guampedia's goal as:

> ... holistically describing its [Guam's] past and present, both locally and globally, in an electronic format that makes its heritage available to the world (and particularly to the American public whose influence in Guam remains an element of its own heritage) and to the local environment where it promises to make significant contributions to the island's educational, cultural and economic environments.

The Guam Humanities Council initiated the Guampedia project in 2002 and launched it online in 2008 with some 350 entries and approximately 900 photographs. In 2008, Guampedia became its own organisation, the Guampedia Foundation, with offices at the University of Guam in a professional affiliation with the Micronesian Area Research Center. Currently, the international community has access to an interactive, engaging and scholarly encyclopedic

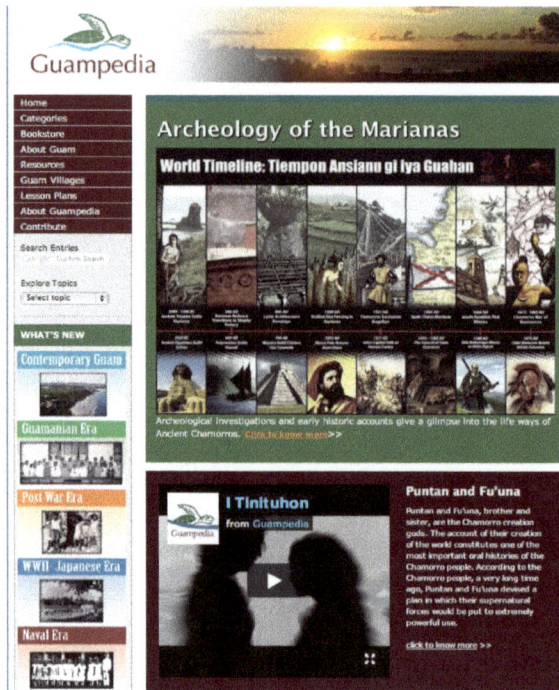

Figure 1. Homepage of Guampedia, Guam's online encyclopedia (August 2011).

online resource offering more than 680 entries, 2000 photos, about 15 videos, and 20 audio files describing Guam's culture and history.

Guampedia is intended to be a comprehensive reference work for students, advanced scholars and the public, including the federal government, investors and the press. The goal has been for Guampedia to be media rich, filled with historic and contemporary photos, video and audio. Information about those significant people, places, events and institutions that have shaped Guam is updated regularly, with each entry signed by its author(s). Guampedia will continue to be an evolving, dynamic project that will be updated and added to regularly as events unfold and technology allows.

The lessons learned during the evolution of Guampedia are presented here in the hopes that other island nations will consider the value of an online encyclopedia showcasing their cultures and societies. By sharing our experiences, Pacific Island communities will have the tools needed to create their own internet sites in the manner best suited to preserve and teach their natural and cultural heritage.

The need for a community heritage resource

An online encyclopedia such as Guampedia accomplishes a crucial mission. While the people of Guam embrace the global community that has emerged from the rise of technology, many vocalise their belief that it is increasingly important to preserve the culture of Guam's indigenous Chamorros. The island's unique history and information about local events, people and organisations should and can be available to everyone – from schoolchildren to adults, from local residents to newcomers, to people living around the world. Without efforts like this, these historical and cultural treasures might be lost to future generations, a tragedy for our ancestors, Micronesia and the Pacific. Guampedia helps Guam's culture survive by keeping the island's people informed and educated and bringing what is special about Guam to the world's attention.

Online accessible projects can be a needed bridge between traditional, customary and scholarly experts and the public. Oftentimes, those with expert knowledge do not have the time or the ability to share their information with the community by writing articles and books that are readily available to a public audience. Much of the scientific information produced by academics and environmental and cultural-resource managers is only published in specialised technical journals or in the grey literature housed in government offices. The valuable information held by traditional sources is often taught and passed down from generation to generation orally. An online encyclopedia is a venue that provides people with information that may never have been expressed in written form or may only have been presented in a technical manner.

Anyone with a computer and access to the internet can learn about a Pacific Island nation's history and culture through an online encyclopedia. Guampedia's target audience is students and teachers, visitors, Chamorros (those indigenous to the Mariana Islands) and Guamanians (peoples of Guam; see Eclavea 2010), both on and off-island. With an increasing number of islanders living abroad and the availability of computers in island school systems, online access to information is an extremely important educational tool. In addition, online encyclopedias are a valuable resource for the media, potential businesses and investors, and the federal government, in that they provide accurate information and save precious time in data collection. Guampedia offers a variety of ways for the community, both on and off-island, to learn about its homeland.

Through Guampedia, fact-checked, peer-reviewed and up-to-date information about Chamorro communities and ancient and contemporary data about Guam and the Mariana Islands is easily available and free. Encyclopedia entries typically serve as general, straightforward introductions to the topics, with readers guided to where they can find more in-depth information through either a reading list or links to further entries. Interpretive essays written by scholars are available for those wanting a deeper understanding about pertinent issues affecting Guam. Many topics include photos, drawings, illustrations, video and audio files. The multiple-media formats that can be produced on the internet allow for dynamic styles of expression, some of which better capture the data's significance, the receiver's imagination, or the traditional way of expressing that knowledge.

Accurate information has been a primary concern for the Guampedia Foundation. The Guampedia Project Author Manual (Guam Humanities Council 2004) offered this guideline for its contributors:

> Accuracy, accuracy, and again accuracy! Do not reproduce errors that appear in older secondary sources. Check every fact. Each person working with Guampedia has an obligation to generations yet unborn to dispel misinformation and to write without distortion.

The Guampedia manual further advised authors to: 'Be as specific as possible. Give precise information when you can ... If you know that an event took place in a particular village, include the community's name.' Another guiding principle has been to emphasise Guam: 'Every entry in Guampedia is being included because of its importance to Guam, and this fact should be reflected in the writing' (Guam Humanities Council 2004). Too often, historical and other sources have given the primacy of focus to others (such as colonising forces) or have only minimally included Guam and its peoples. This creates a variety of challenging issues for the island community. Guampedia aims to re-align such a non-localised focus to make the people and history of Guam the main focal point. This emphasis better meets the public desire for community-specific information and serves as an educational tool for island teachers and youth.

Guampedia is a growing repository of historical and cultural information. A motivating issue is the limited printing of island-centred materials; another is that much of what has been printed is at an academic level that is not readily digestible by the general public, specifically school-aged island children. Additionally, academic material is often issue- and time-specific, requiring a great amount of effort to fully understand the topic. Guampedia strives to balance maintaining the integrity of up-to-date expert knowledge and providing an accessible reading level, keeping in mind that a main goal is to have the online encyclopedia serve upcoming generations of the island's youth.

The public can offer critiques and corrections of Guampedia's online articles. At the bottom of each entry, readers are asked whether the information is useful and whether they have comments or questions. In the two years since the site was launched, Guampedia has had nearly 2000 responses. As a testament to Guampedia's role in filling a gap within the community, about 80% of the responses are from people saying thank you, that the online encyclopedia is a wonderful and amazing site, and similar submissions. Most of the other comments are from those looking for more information about the topics or additional entries. Three percent of the submissions are from people who offer corrections or dispute the information. The Guampedia staff responds to each of these comments.

How to make an online encyclopedia

The creation and up-keep of an online encyclopedia requires a dedicated community effort. As a first step, the Guampedia team created a mission statement to help keep the focus on the goals. The Guampedia Mission Statement is:

> We believe that the future of our island is dependent upon an informed, educated citizenry. Scarce resources result in limited opportunities to learn and understand about Guam's unique history, culture, environment and present-day society. Guampedia exists to provide a comprehensive, accessible resource about Guam that will educate the global community and increase opportunities for the enlightenment of our people, allowing us to chart our destiny.

The mechanics involved in constructing such a large and public project can be complex. Presented here is a discussion of the four key points that need to be considered during the planning process. The points are:

1. Site content

2. Community participation

3. Internet technology

4. Cost and funding sources

Site content

The Guampedia team had to decide what the site would contain and how this would be organised for ease of use. To determine content, we first came up with a list of topical categories which could be broken down into smaller sections. Amended over the years, Guampedia now has categories covering: Art, Architecture, Body Adornment, Music and Food; Chamorro Culture; Economics and Commercial Development; Education; European Exploration, Trade and Scientific Studies; Health and Medicine; Historic Eras; Justice; Language; Natural Resources; Non-Chamorro Ethnicity; People; Politics and Government; Religion; Sports and Recreation; Transportation, Technology and Communications; Trends; Villages, Historic Places and Island Life; and Wars and Factors of Peace.

We then invited scholars and local experts from a variety of fields to help develop outlines of what to include in each of these broad categories to provide comprehensive coverage of the topic. For example, we asked Father Eric Forbes, a Capuchin scholar and historian, to help develop the Religion section. We asked Professor Rosa Palomo, the head of the Micronesian Language Institute and former Chair of the Chamorro Language Commission, to assist with outlining the Chamorro Language section. Several professors from the University of Guam's Micronesian Area Research Center (MARC) were invited to work on categories such as local art, politics, European exploration and trade, the history of wars that have affected Guam, and so on.

Next, we developed a timeline of Guam history to create a content grid. Based on archaeological and historical findings, the Guampedia Foundation developed this timeline:

- Ancient Guam (3800 years ago–1668)

- Spanish Era (1668–1898)

- US Naval Era (1898–1941)

- WWII/Japanese Era (1941–1944)

- Post-War Guam (1944–1950)

- Guamanian Era (1950–1970)

- Contemporary Guam (1970–present)

Once the grid was established, we decided on organisational principles to guide the length, style and content of the five types of entries, ranging from short basic entries to longer interpretive essays. We then developed standards, contracts and a writer's fee and invited people to submit text and photos for each topic.

The result is the set of 19 categories, most of which are broken down into subcategories, many further subdivided, and linked back to one another. Not all categories use the timeline, as some topics range over several time periods or are not applicable to such an organisational structure. The Religion category (see below) contains 10 subcategories, divided into 58 topical entries. For example, the Contemporary Guam section has six topics and the WWII/Japanese Era section presents three topics.

Religion (58)
    Ancient Guam: Religion (5)
    Catholic (39)
    Christian (7)
    Contemporary Guam: Religion (6)
        Ancestral Worship Today
        Dominican Sisters
        Guam Buddhism Society
        Muslim Association of Guam
        Redemptoris Mater Seminary
        Sisters of the Good Shepherd
    Guamanian Era: Religion (10)
    Other Religion (4)
    Post WWII: Religion (6)
    Spanish Era: Religion (14)
    US Naval Era: Religion (15)
    WWII/Japanese Era: Religion (3)
        Father Jesus Baza Duenas
        Monsignor Oscar Calvo
        Religious Life during the Japanese Occupation

The homepage also links directly to overall information about Guam, educational lesson plans and interpretive essays. There is direct access to a bookstore and MARC publications, audio and photo galleries, information on Guampedia staff and contributors, and information on resources used by Guampedia. The audio gallery can include oral histories provided by the elders to preserve these older and experienced voices and musical performances. Visual documentation is provided in photos and the videos that present entire dances, re-enactments of legends, virtual tours of a location, and historical war footage.

Community involvement: Organisers, contributors, advisors

From its inception, the Guampedia team wanted Guampedia to be a community resource, created by and for the community. The team met with numerous agencies, institutions and organisations, including leaders of the public schools, the libraries, the museums, the legislature, the Governor, Guam's congressional office and the Catholic Church. We described our goals and asked for their input and support, and use of their resources. These groups were assured that this was a community effort with everyone working together to create something that we could all be proud of so that people on Guam and around the world could learn more about the island and its people.

Our next step was to list and contact the experts connected to each topic. Some of these experts were academics and researchers, others were community members with experiences to share, while others were keepers of traditional and cultural knowledge. We also identified in what publications or through which institutions we could find particular information. As the entries arrived, community members were chosen to fact-check, peer-review, advise and edit the documentation before it was placed online.

Today there is a permanent staff of three people: a managing editor, a content editor and a media editor. Guampedia relies on its volunteers, who form an Advisory Board, as its editorial team. Volunteer community members are educators, politicians, environmentalists, housewives, fishermen, economists, anthropologists, artists and others from every walk of life. To date, well over 100 Guamanians and Chamorros have participated in the Guampedia project by conducting research, writing entries, peer reviewing, fact checking or copy editing the entries and media. Authors are paid fees generated from grants for their research and writing.

Technology

Once the content was mapped out, the Guampedia team began talking to internet technology (IT) companies about the options available for a website that was user-friendly for both the site's visitors and its creators. Many online encyclopedias and comparable websites were examined and assessed for their strengths and weaknesses in serving their communities. An inspirational website was a New Zealand site called Te ara, a Maori term for pathway (www.teara.govt.nz). These evaluations allowed for a broader perspective of what best suited the Guam community and the available technology.

An important consideration in Pacific communities is the strength and capability of the local internet service provider. Many islanders pay by the minute for internet services and have only slow dial-up internet access. Complex entries containing numerous photos, maps, or even links can take several minutes to download and thus not be worth the time and cost required to wait for each page. Online encyclopedias in these island nations need to have simple entries that can be easily updated in the future when there is access to faster internet services.

An IT company thought to be the most capable of meeting Guampedia's specific needs was selected. Although not the lowest bidder, the company was chosen because the staff and community felt the most comfortable working with it. Trust is a very important consideration at this point of the development process. Additionally, it was decided that a top priority for this particular type of project was hiring a company that was proven to be able to provide a high-quality result. Of course, Guampedia had its limitations and the final price was negotiated.

In 2002, when Guampedia was just starting, computer programmers had to be hired to design codes used in tailoring the website to look and work according to our desires and specifications. For example, if a navigation sidebar was desired, then it had to be programmed as a feature. If links to submit feedback or make contact with Guampedia were deemed necessary then these features required specific programming.

Despite the passage of only nine years, today's (2011) online environment is much different. During this period, computer programmers banded together to create universal internet programs that are more easily replicated. Now there is free, open-source software available on the web that has all the options an entity might envision for itself and its audience. An IT company is still needed to set up a website, but the process will not be as lengthy or as expensive as Guampedia experienced in its embryonic years. Guampedia is now using WordPress, free software available to all. For a minimal cost, Guampedia currently subscribes to services such as Flickr (www.flickr.com/) to store photos, Vimeo (http://vimeo.com/) to store video and Issuu (http://issuu.com/) to share large documents and books.

There are numerous other web options available to those creating an interactive website. These days, a site can be developed for very little money and then maintained for less than US$1000 a year. Website developers may tell you otherwise, but the knowledge Guampedia has learned over the years is testimony to the fact that even quite large websites can be maintained with a annual small budget. Our staff of three, none 'techies', has learned to post entries, photographs, video and audio, and update our front page. This serves as an example that other Pacific Island communities can also accomplish these tasks without a great deal of technical knowledge or funding.

Guampedia is following the established technical and information standards of the National Initiative for a Networked Cultural Heritage's Guide to Good Practice in the Digital Representation and Management of Cultural Heritage Materials (www.nyu.edu/its/humanities/ninchguide).[1] By following these freely accessible standards, it is ensured that digital resources are compatible with each other now and in the future as technology evolves.

Funding

Finding the funding to initiate a project of the magnitude of Guampedia can be a strenuous experience, with many learning curves and challenges. First, a comprehensive work plan and feasible budget must be developed. Then, entities seeking funding have to accurately map out why their project is important and how capable their team is to people who have no knowledge about their culture, island area or project visions. Additionally, funding sources for the particular type of project that the particular type of organisation is qualified to apply for must be identified. Soon, one learns that some grants are only available to government agencies, for example, while others will only be awarded to non-profit organisations with federally recognised tax-exempt status. Guampedia, which developed from the ground up, advises building your organisation first, next creating a focused project work plan, and then looking for grants that match that particular phase of your project.

After submitting numerous grant applications to local and federal governments and to private organisations, Guampedia was successful in obtaining several federal grants from the US National Endowment for the Humanities (NEH) and the US Department of the Interior (DOI). As a US territory, NEH grants were available to Guam through the island's local humanities council. There are other NEH grants that US-based non-profit organisations can receive. As a United States commonwealth, the northern Mariana Islands can apply for assistance from NEH. However, the Federated States of Micronesia (FSM) and the Republic of Palau do not directly qualify for US NEH funding.

Locally, Guampedia was funded largely by the Guam Preservation Trust (GPT, a semi-autonomous entity) and the Bank of Guam. The Guam Preservation Trust's mission is to preserve Guam history and Chamorro culture. Funded by building permit fees, GPT acquires a sizable budget that enables it to fund projects like Guampedia. As Guam's local bank, the Bank of Guam has demonstrated leadership in funding projects promoting Chamorro culture. Bank of Guam president Lou Leon Guerrero also sits on both the Guam Humanities Council and Guampedia Foundation's board of directors. To help establish the organisation, Guampedia received an appropriation (and is expecting another) from the government of Guam.

As island visitors are among Guampedia's target audiences, it received a smaller grant from the Guam Visitors Bureau. Guam visitor surveys document a strong desire by tourists for more historical and cultural information about the island. An online encyclopedia, freely accessible via the internet, enhances the visitor experience by providing a deeper and broader understanding about the destination.

Development tales

Once the first funding arrived, Guampedia immediately set about developing online encyclopedia content. Computers were purchased and two more editors – one to handle text and another to control media issues – were hired. At the same time, Guampedia contracted software designers who estimated it would take nine months to a year to develop the 'back-end' software that was needed at the time. In the year the software was being developed, Guampedia prepared its first 350 entries.

At first, Guampedia used what I call a 'scattershot' approach. This entailed asking dozens of people to write entries on a wide variety of topics, sending them contracts, setting deadlines and determining fees for their work. In hindsight, it would have been better to have taken a step-by-step approach, deciding, for example, to work on a single time period, or two or three topics at a time, so that the development process would be more focused. The Guampedia staff found that even strong project supporters and dedicated professionals need to be regularly reminded that promised entries were due – otherwise, many of them would or did not submit the entries they had agreed to write. The Guampedia Foundation understands that islanders are busy and have many other obligations besides contributing to Guampedia. Additionally, some contributors were unable to recognise Guampedia's importance before it went online. The Guampedia staff spent a lot of time following up on entries and learned the fine art of petitioning and pleading.

The Guampedia media editor set about identifying historic photograph collections and gaining permission to use them for illustrating the Guampedia entries. This was no easy task, as many community members did not want to share their photos and artwork. Eventually, once it was understood that their display was strictly for educational purposes, most allowed Guampedia to use the photos and illustrations.

Finally, when our carefully set deadlines had come and gone, when the software was completed and it was nearly time to go online, dozens of entries scheduled to be submitted months before were submitted at the last minute, written in a wide variety of styles. Launching the site was delayed for six months in order to spend needed time editing, fact-checking and peer-reviewing the late entries before including them. Once Guampedia felt comfortable with the accuracy of the content, the foundation went full speed ahead to publish the site online.

Testimonials

A Chamorro man wrote to us from the eastern United States asking for help with his daughter's marriage preparations. He knew that part of the Chamorro Catholic wedding ceremony had to do with coins, but he could not remember exactly what it was. We contacted a priest who described the ceremony and what the priest, bride and groom were to say and sent it to the man, who was enormously grateful for the information.

Among many other issues, others have asked our staff for translations from Chamorro, for information on where to find a particular historic book, or to verify some bit of information. One woman asked to find the prayers for a novena her mother used to say so that she could continue the tradition. A student needed help finding information about Chamorro children's games for his presentation. We try to answer each one of the queries as best we can.

Recently, a cable television show producer contacted Guampedia for ghost stories to be used in an upcoming series on the supernatural. His crew loved it when we informed him about our *taotaomo'na* (ancestral spirits, see Bevacqua 2010). They spent a week on the island interviewing people and filming sites.

The community has embraced Guampedia. Guam's governor and senators have shared with the Guampedia Foundation that the online encyclopedia has helped them because whenever people ask for information about Guam, from the history of the Guam hymn or flag, to the schedule of village fiestas, they tell them to access Guampedia. Guampedia is being used by middle and high-school students for their homework projects, by college students for papers and presentations, and by teachers when preparing lessons relevant to Guam's history, art, culture and economics.

Many military personnel have written to let us know that Guampedia helped them learn about their new home. Likewise, business people and new contract hires have told us that it helped them to understand Guam better before taking a job on island. Guampedia has also helped the artists, musicians, dancers and community organisations featured in the online encyclopedia, as the public can easily find out about their work and contact them.

The next steps

Beginning in 2009, Guampedia worked with the Micronesian Area Research Center (MARC) and local archaeologists to build up Guampedia's Ancient Guam section, an effort supported by funding from the Guam Preservation Trust. Many of MARC's research and publications describe Guam history after European contact and settlement of the Mariana Islands that began with the Spanish in about AD 1668. In contrast, there has been little knowledge collected, organised and presented in a readable format from the hundreds of archaeological reports (the grey literature) describing and discussing Chamorro settlement of the Mariana Islands nearly 4000 years ago. Guampedia set about to rectify this discrepancy.

Chamorro society passed information along orally rather than in written text during more than three millennia of pre-contact settlement history. Hence, the most comprehensive information concerning these early times is found in the archaeological record. Archeologists can inform the public about ancient Chamorro diets, fishing practices, pottery making, diseases and health, settlement patterns and burials, based on findings from ancient villages, agricultural fields, activity areas and other archaeological sites. Chamorro scholars privy to traditional narratives that have been passed down through the generations will be consulted to gain their understanding of these times and practices. Guampedia scheduled a year for the writing and editing of this new section. The final entries will provide Guam's communities with much important information about its ancestral population and environment from the time the island was first colonised until Padre Luis San Vitores arrived and Spain began inhabiting the archipelago in AD 1668.

Using maps and an interactive timeline, Guampedia also proposes to show which villages and settlements are known to have been inhabited 3000, 2000, 1000 and 500 years ago. For each of these timeframes, Guampedia users will be shown a map of Guam that pinpoints where archaeological sites have been identified. Users will be able to click on some of the sites to learn what life was like in that location at that time. Photographs, drawings and maps will illustrate some of these entries.

New ideas for categories, sub-sections and topics are constantly being suggested by community members. Guampedia will continue to evolve, as it must, to survive and keep up with new technology and ways of engaging a variety of audiences. For instance, Guampedia now has a presence on Facebook and Twitter, where followers can easily be led to new additions and relevant timely topics. Encyclopedia entries treating subjects that can become dated have a feature that notifies editors within a specified timeframe that the information needs to be reviewed.

The work of Guampedia is a monumental mission. There are times when it seems that there are too many tasks to accomplish or too many difficulties in securing funding. And the Guampedia vision keeps growing. With the help of local community members, Guampedia will continue to meet its goal of better informing the island population and the world about Guam and the Chamorro people.

Note

1.   Founded in 1996, the National Initiative for a Networked Cultural Heritage (NINCH) is a US-based coalition of some 100 organisations and institutions from across the cultural sector. NINCH's objective is to build a framework within which these different elements can effectively collaborate to build a networked cultural heritage.

References

Bevacqua, M.L. 2010. Taotaomo'na, © 2009 Guampedia™. Referenced January 20, 2011. http://guampedia.com/taotaomona-taotaomona/.

Eclavea, G.E. 2010. Adoption of "Guamanian". © 2009 Guampedia™. Referenced January 20, 2011. http://guampedia.com/adoption-of-guamanian/.

Goetzfridt, N. 2006. GUAMPEDIA: A work of legitimacy. *Micronesica* 5(1/2):340–344.

The Guam Humanities Council. 2004. *Guampedia author project manual*. Hågatña, Guam.

6

Plants, people and culture in the villages of Oikull and Ibobang, Republic of Palau

Ann Hillmann Kitalong[1,3], Michael J. Balick[2], Faustina Rehuher[1], Meked Besebes[1], Sholeh Hanser[1,3], Kiblas Soaladaob[1], Gemma Ngirchobong[1,3], Flora Wasisang[1], Wayne Law[2], Roberta Lee[4], Van Ray Tadeo,[1] Clarence Kitalong[3] and Christopher Kitalong[1,3]

1. Belau National Museum, Republic of Palau
2. The New York Botanical Garden, Institute of Economic Botany, USA
3. The Environment, Inc., Republic of Palau
4. Beth Israel Medical Center, New York City, USA

Introduction

Ethnobotany is the investigation of the interaction between plants, people and culture (Jones 1941; Arvigo and Balick 1998; Balick and Cox 2005). The body of knowledge and practices developed and maintained by people interacting with their natural environment over time is known as traditional knowledge. This can include information on plants used for food, shelter, medicine, tools, arts and crafts, aesthetic beauty and spiritual purposes. Due to its dynamic nature, traditional knowledge is difficult to quantify (Lee et al. 2001). The loss of traditional practices is a threat to biodiversity globally (Balick and Cox 2005) and to Palau's communities (Palau National Biodiversity Strategy and Action Plan 2004). Lee and colleagues (2001) found that in Pohnpei traditional knowledge had significantly eroded within three generations for such daily tasks as planting taro, fermenting breadfruit, using plants for fish poison, making canoes and catching turtles. To counteract this threat in Micronesia, the Biodiversity and Human Health Project was initiated in Pohnpei in 1997 (Balick 2009), and as of 2007, has been ongoing in Palau and Kosrae. The goal of this project is to establish a link between ecosystems and human health.

Traditional medicines have been used for thousands of years worldwide. It is probable some of the canoe plants that arrived with Palau's early settlers 3000–4000 years ago were transported due to their medicinal properties. Healers still refer to the ca. 1700-year-old Chinese text *Materia Medica*, attributed to Shen Nong, that describes the medicinal properties of 252 plant species. India has made use of more than 7500 plants (Kapoor 1990; Mukherjee and Wahile 2006). The World Health Organisation estimates that 80% of the world's inhabitants continue to rely significantly on traditional medicine systems for their primary health care. The remaining 20% of the population depends on pharmaceutical medicines – and one in four of these contain plant extracts or active chemicals derived from 90 different plant species (Farnsworth et al. 1985). Although Western health care is available to varying degrees in many parts of the world, including the Pacific, traditional medicine is still widely practised in Oceania (Whistler 1992, 1996; Balick 2009). These traditional medical systems employ native tropical island plants, some of which are found nowhere else in the world. Health care based on traditional practices that are consistent with international standards of quality control is now being advocated in the worldwide medical community, including Micronesia (Lee 2009).

Ethnobotanical studies in the Palauan archipelago in western Micronesia have focused on the medicinal uses of plants (Okabe 1941; Black 1968; Salsedo 1970; Salsedo and Smith 1987; Defilipps et al. 1988; Friend and Tabak 1995; Palau Society of Historians 2000, 2001; Machiko 2002; Del Rosario and Esquerra 2003) and construction of the *bai*, the traditional men's meeting house (Telmetang 1993). The medicinal studies in Palau have documented more than 80 plant species with more than 235 medical uses, with the most recent study showing activity against the Hepatitis C virus for several native Palauan plant species (Kitalong 2007). Palau's early ethnohistorical sources (Krämer 1917, 1919, 1929) address plant use in Palauans' daily lives. These early studies lack records crediting the informants and do not detail the step-by-step processes for the use of many species. There may be several reasons for this, including the lack of translators, a society that was more protective of its knowledge, and a lack of understanding the value and significance of this information for future studies.

Previous studies of Palau's flora include Kanehira (1933) and Fosberg and his colleagues' extensive 45 years of floristic surveys and systematics (Fosberg 1946, 1947, 1957, 1960; Fosberg and Sachet 1975a, 1975b, 1977, 1979, 1980a, 1980b, 1981, 1984, 1987, 1991; Fosberg et al. 1979, 1982, 1987, 1993; Fosberg et al. 1980; Fosberg and Raulerson 1990). Palau's other vegetation studies consist of descriptions of wetland communities including mangrove forests (Stemmermann 1981), a comprehensive vegetation survey (Cole et al. 1987), a rapid ecological study of the Ngeremeduu Bay Drainage (Canfield et al. 1992) and a botanical reconnaissance of Babeldaob (Raulerson et al. 1997). Palau's forests have been systematically inventoried (Donnegan et al. 2007) and important forest areas, long-term vegetation trends and species diversity were studied (Hillmann Kitalong and Holm 2004; Costion and Kitalong 2006; Hillmann Kitalong 2008; Hillmann Kitalong et al. 2009).

Palaeoenvironmental studies using charcoal and palaeobotanical remains are reconstructing Palau's ancient landscape (Athens and Ward 2001, 2002, 2005). Palau's lowland forests cover 87% of the land, of which 75% is native forest. Prehistoric earthworks cover a minimum of 20% of Babeldaob and impact an area double that size due to the intensive erosion resulting from their construction (Liston 2009). This erosion may explain the alluvial soils of the lowlands (Athens and Ward 2005; Liston and Tuggle 2006; Masse et al. 2006). Integration of ethnobotanical and archaeological studies provides a better understanding of long-term changes in plant communities and their impact on human culture over time.

This ethnobotanical study was initiated at the Belau National Museum (BNM) in partnership with the New York Botanical Garden and the National Tropical Botanical Garden. The goal of the program is to document the traditional knowledge and practices regarding the use of plants through life's passage from birth to death. Presented here is a preliminary ethnobotanical study of the villages of Oikull and Ibobang on Babeldaob.

Materials and methods

The Republic of Palau, located within latitudes 08°12' to 2°48' and longitudes 131°07' to 134°44', is the westernmost archipelago of the Caroline Islands in Micronesia (Figure 1). The study sites are located on Babeldaob, Palau's largest island, in the village of Oikull in Airai state, and in the village of Ibobang in Ngatpang state. Oikull, in southeast Babeldaob, has volcanic, limestone and mangrove forests and freshwater wetlands and grasslands. Due to Oikull's unique transitional location on both volcanic and limestone soils, it contains a diverse assemblage of plants. Although with a similar habitat, Ibobang, on the shores of Ngaremeduu Bay in southwest Babeldaob, is on volcanic soils so does not have the limestone forest habitat of Oikull.

Oikull and Ibobang were chosen as study sites by the Belau National Museum Board based on a number of considerations, including local interest, accessibility, the level of cultural knowledge and the presence of plant diversity. These two villages are considered 'proof of principle' sites, where development of methodologies and training for studies elsewhere in Palau will be undertaken.

Earthworks complexes, pottery scatters and abandoned stonework villages connected by a network of stone paths attest to the fact that Oikull is an ancient village area that was once densely populated. Many people can trace their roots to Oikull as it plays a significant role in Palau's migration stories. The original settlers came from Metuker Rikull, a small rock island near Oikull where fishermen were famous for their shark-hunting skills.[1] Today few residents live in the village due to lack of adequate roads providing access to schools. The villagers have moved to locations that are more convenient and closer to schools although they would like

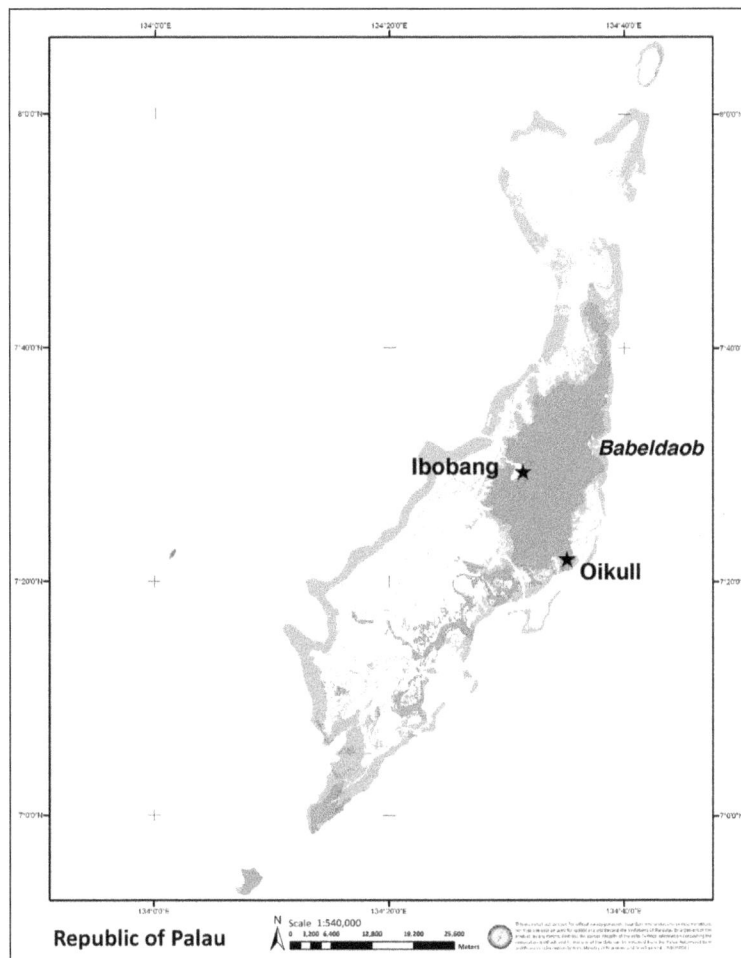

Figure 1. Study sites on Babeldaob, Republic of Palau (Source: PALARIS).

to move back to Oikull. Oikull was chosen for study due to the large number of community members who originated from this village with potential knowledge of traditional skills.

Ibobang, a village established in the recent historic era, is the centre of the Modekngei religion whose followers believe in the ancient gods and follow customary rituals and healing practices (Machiko 2002). Ibobang was donated by the Inglii clan to the founder of the Modekngei religion, Tamadad, who came from Choll, a village on Babeldaob's northeast coast. Ibobang was chosen for the study due to the large number of community members who are active practitioners of traditional skills.

A preliminary meeting was held with village elders at the Belau National Museum to explain the project's purpose and obtain informed consent. After community meetings in the two states, informal interviews were set up with those villagers recommended by the elders as knowledgeable about the use of plants. Interviews began by obtaining background information about the individuals, including age, place of birth, time in villages, migrations between villages and the activities they participated in or observed during childhood and adulthood. Specific questions focused on recreation, food preparation, medicine for primary care, building and special customary practices. Several interview approaches were used, although the preferred method was to walk in the informant's neighbourhood forest as the informant indicated specific plants for a given purpose. Replicate voucher specimens could then be collected on site.

Some elders preferred that plants be brought to them for verification, while others came to the BNM herbarium for interviews and voucher species were presented for authentication. The interviewer would ask whether a given species had a use, but did not state a use or ask for confirmation of a use for a given plant. Most interviews were carried out in one session, although time constraints required some informants to have several interviews. Both individual and group interviews were conducted. In the latter interviews, it is difficult to attribute information to a single person, so information was accredited to the group. Attributing information to specific people documents ownership of their intellectual property, their rights for its use and any benefits derived from this knowledge under the principles of the Convention of Biological Diversity. It also establishes the concept of prior art and prior knowledge to identify the source of the information.

During field interviews, voucher specimens were collected in a field press and the site was georeferenced using a Garmin GPS unit. Specimens were processed in the BNM herbarium within 24 hours of collection and results were entered into the herbarium database. GPS points were downloaded, analysed and mapped using Arcview© software. Transcribed field notes provided data for voucher specimen labels that list the name(s) of the informant(s), the identification of taxa, the description of the plant, the plant habitat and associated plants, and the documented uses provided by the informant(s). The voucher specimens were distributed to regional and international herbaria for specialists to confirm their identification. The informants reviewed and modified interview summaries. Below, the names of individuals who contributed information appear in parenthesis following specific use data. The information collected in the project was shared with the village communities in a series of PowerPoint presentations.

Plant uses

A total of 43 interviews were conducted: 27 in Oikull (17 women, 10 men) and 16 in Ibobang (nine women, seven men). In Oikull, interviewees provided 448 uses for 170 plants, while in Ibobang, informants provided 271 uses for 127 plants. Medicine, food and construction were the top three categories of recorded plant usage. Other categories included in the study were menstruation and childbirth, recreation, ropes and ties, firewood, cleaning, fishing and hunting.

A list of 28 categories of uses was derived from the information given by the interviewees during this study (Appendix 1). The frequency of reported plant uses divided into major use categories is listed in Table 1. These plants are commonly found throughout Palau's urban landscape.

Table 1. Frequency of reported plant uses by major categories.

Major categories	Total	Oikull (n=27)	Ibobang (n=16)
Medicine	248	123	125
Food	198	132	66
Construction	104	54	50
Toys	43	27	16
Tools	28	20	8
Cleaning	26	15	11
Rope	22	14	8
Fishing	21	14	20
Canoe Building	18	8	11
Total	**708**	**407**	**315**

The main categories of usage and the number of plant species used according to the male (Table 2) and female informants (Table 3) indicated that men are more knowledgeable about plants used for construction, firewood, fishing, and fashioning tools, canoes and rope. Women provided more information about plants used for food preparation and medicinal plants used in childbirth. Both men and women are knowledgeable about plants used for food, toys and general-purpose, primary-care medicines.

First menstruation

In one clan, a ritualistic cleansing using *Pandanus tectorius* (*ongor*), *Areca catechu* (betel nut, *buuch*) and *Citrus maxima* (pomelo, *malchianged*) is performed after the first menstruation (F. Wasisang). Another clan in Ibobang uses *Cymbopogon citratus* (lemongrass, *keskus*), *Citrus* sp. (*cheluchau*), *Decaspermum fruticosum* (*kertaku*), *Eurya japonica* (*cheskiik*) and roasted *Cocos nucifera* (coconut, *lius*) for the cleansing (G. Emesiochel).

Childbirth

After giving birth to their first child, women undergo a complex bathing process (*omengat*) that lasts from four to 10 days. The ritual's purpose is to heal the new mother and celebrate her first child. At least two months of preparation are needed for this event. Activities include constructing the bathing and steam hut, gathering firewood, gathering herbs, preparing ginger and coconut oil for the bath, preparing food, and making the traditional skirt and accessories for the mother for the last day of celebration. This ceremony culminates in a final bath and display of the young mother in her traditional dress for the father's family. The mother's family prepares a banquet of food, the father's family provides money, and a life-long bond is then established.

A variety of herbs is used in the ritual to energise and heal the new mother. There is no single prescribed set of plants used in the first bath ceremony and many clans have their own particular formula. Twenty plant species were listed as being used during the hot-bath process by the female interviewees from Oikull (16 species) and Ibobang (13 species) (Table 4). The most commonly listed plant (n=11) is *Curcuma longa* (turmeric, *kesol*), with the remaining plants described by at the most only two informants each.

Table 2. Main plant uses and number of plant species given by the men interviewed.

Use category	Number of species	Oikull (n=10)	Ibobang (n=7)
Food	25	17	8
Medicine	67	41	26
Construction	81	38	43
Toys	23	17	6
Fishing	19	9	10
Canoe building	10	4	6
Rope or tie	16	12	4
Total	**241**	**138**	**103**

Table 3. Main plant uses and number of plant species given by the women interviewed.

Use category	Number of species	Oikull (n=17)	Ibobang (n=9)
Food	26	17	9
Medicine	95	45	50
Construction	6	1	5
Toys	12	6	6
Fishing	6	4	2
Food wrap	12	5	7
Total	**157**	**78**	**79**

Recreation

Men and women, mostly elders, described different types of recreational activities in which they participated from an early age. Some of these activities employing plant products are practised by children today. A total of 22 plant species were used for childhood games and recreation according to the interviewees. Seven plant species were frequently described by the interviewees to make blowguns, spin wheels, balls, jump rope, bean bags and puzzles (Table 5). The three most frequently described plant species are *Heterospathe elata* var. *palauensis* (*demailei*) used to fashion blowgun bullets, *Schizostachyum lima* (*lild*) used to make the blowgun spears, and *Merremia peltata* (*kebeas*) used for jump ropes. Both *Flagellaria indica* (*bangernguis*) and *Leucaena leucocephala* (*telentund*) were made into bean bags. Balls and spin wheels were created from *Cocos nucifera* and puzzles were assembled from *Xylocarpus granatum* (*meduulokebong*).

Traditional food and food preparation

Thirty-two plant species were recorded as sources of food and useful in food preparation with 27 species being classed as important foods. As this list focused on the elders' favoured traditional food types, the actual number of food plants is under-represented. Documentation of plants used as traditional foodstuff will be expanded on in future interviews.

The most frequently mentioned plant species described as a source of traditional food are two types of taro, *Colocasia escuelenta* (wet taro, *dait) and *Cyrtosperma chamissonis* (giant swamp taro, *prak*), *Manihot esculenta* (tapioca, *diokang*), *Cocos nucifera* and *Inocarpus fagifer* (Tahitian chestnut, *keam*). Tapioca is believed to have been introduced by the Germans in the early 20th century (Mayo 1954).

Table 4. Plants used in the first-birth bath and ceremony.

Species (Palauan name)	Oikull (n=17)	Ibobang (n=9)
Curcuma longa L. (kesol)	8	3
Cocos nucifera L. (lius)	1	2
Cassytha filiformis L. (techellela chull)	1	1
Melastoma malabathricum L. var. *mariannum* (Naudin) Fosb. and Sach. (matakui)	1	0
Phaleria nisidai Kaneh. (ongael)	1	1
Dianella carolinensis (kobesos)	1	0
Limnophila chinensis (Osb.) Merr. subsp. *aromatica* (Lam.) (iaml)	1	1
Phyllanthus palauensis Hosok. (dudurs, udoud)	1	0
Melicope denhamii (Seem.) T.G. Hartley (kertub)	1	1
Pandanus tectorius Parkinson ex Du Roi (ongor)	1	1
Cymbopogon citratus (DC. ex Nees) Stapf (keskus)	1	1
Cinnamomum carolinense (ochod)	1	0
Citrus maxima (Burm. ex Rumph.) Merr. (malchianged)	0	2
Cananga odorata (Lam.) Hook. F. and Thomson (irang irang)	1	0
Syzygium samarangense (Blume) Merr. and Perry (rebotel)	2	0
Millettia pinnata (L.) Panigrahi (kisaks)	1	1
Eurya japonica Thunb. var. *nitida* (kertaku)	2	0
Eugenia reinwardtiana (Blume) DC. (kesiil)	0	1
Pouteria obovata (R. Brown) Baehni (chelangel)	0	2
Derris trifoliata Lour. (kemokem)	0	1
Total	**25**	**18**

Table 5. The most frequently named plants with recreational uses.

Species (Palauan name)	Use	Total interviewed (n=43)	Oikull (n=27)	Ibobang (n=16)
Heterospathe elata Scheff. var. *palauensis* (Becc.) (demailei)	Blowgun bullet	7	3	4
Schizostachyum lima Merr. (lild)	Blowgun	5	1	4
Cocos nucifera L. (lius)	Spin wheel, balls	2	2	2
Merremia peltata (L.) Merr. (kebeas)	Jump rope	5	1	4
Flagellaria indica L. (bangernguis)	Bean bags	2	1	1
Leucaena leucocephala (Lam.) de Wit (telentund)	Bean bags	2	2	0
Xylocarpus granatum Koenig (meduulokebong)	Puzzle	2	1	1
Total		**25**	**11**	**16**

The main starch of customary significance is *Colocasia escuelenta*. The plant is referred to as *dait* and the cooked corm is referred to as *kukau*. Traditionally, taro is the most important and most revered (prestige) food and crop in Palau. It is included in all rituals and customs and features prominently in Palau's legends, stories, songs, chants and proverbs. Taro is the most important starch used in Palau's customary exchanges. The cultivation of taro is the main role of women and a source of pride for women and their families. The inheritance of taro gardens is through the women (Figure 2).

Both the foliage and the root of the taro plant are used as a food source. *Colocasia* and *Cyrtosperma* can be prepared in different ways: the corm can be simply boiled (*meliokl*), boiled and cooked with coconut milk (*cheluit*), boiled and ground (*belsiich*), or ground and mixed with sugar and baked as a dessert. The leaves can be mixed with coconut milk and other ingredients to make a favourite Palauan soup (*demok*) and the stems can be cooked with sugar for a dessert *(chelang)*.

Traditionally, Palauan food is often boiled, steamed or baked inside a leaf casing. This not only imparts the flavour of the leaf to the food, but also holds the food together during cooking and protects it from exposure to adjacent contaminants such as charcoal or sand. Once cooked, the leaf package is easily portable and can be stored as is. The plants used to wrap food were given as *Cordyline fruticosa* (*sis*), *Cocos nucifera* and *Areca catechu*.

Taro patch

The majority of *Colocasia* grows in prepared wetland plots (*mesei*). Production systems relied on less frequently include damp gardens (*dechel*) and dryland gardens (*sers*). *Mesei* are paddy-like systems with channels and dikes used for water control, to divide the gardens into functional sections indicating the ultimate use of the taro grown, and to isolate plots from diseases. The *mesei* serve as an agroforest, with various useful trees and shrubs grown on the dikes and perimeter, mainly for food, green manure, medicine and ceremonies.

Figure 2. Ellen Adelbai preparing her wetland taro garden (*mesei*).

Leaves from many species of trees can be used as green manure for the taro patches, including *Osmoxylon oliveri* (*kesiamel*), *Musa* spp. (banana, *tuu*), *Cocos nucifera*, *Areca catechu* and the large leaves of the giant taro, *Cyrtosperma merkusii (prak)*. In Ngatpang, the women also use *Elaeocarpus joga* (*dekemerir*) and *Cerbera manghas* (*chemeridech*) as fertiliser (G. Emesiochel). Fertiliser, most commonly green manure, is both placed in the planting hole and spread on the top of the prepared beds as mulch to promote soil fertility.

Taboo food

Dietary taboos in Palau are most often associated with fish and other sea creatures. Papaya or *Carica papaya* is considered a taboo food during menstruation (F. Wasisang). Women who are either pregnant or breast feeding should avoid pineapple (*Ananas comosus, ongor ra Ngebard*) because it irritates the baby and gives a bad odour (E. Singeo).

Construction

A total of 41 species of plants were described as construction materials (Table 2). Metal tools have replaced the traditional shell or stone adzes once used to fell and shape the tree. Tool handles continue to be fashioned from Palauan wood species, including *Calophyllum inophyllum* (*btaches*) (C. Kitalong, R. Emesiochel, V.R. Tadeo), *Cocos nucifera*, *Hibiscus tiliaceus* (*chermall*), *Macaranga carolinensis* (*bedel*), *Rhizophora mucronata* (*tebechel*), *Terminalia catappa* (*miich*) and *Syzygium samarangense* (*rebotel*) (C. Kitalong).

Structures

Those plant species most frequently named by the informants as used to build structures are listed in Table 6. *Intsia bijuga* (*dort*) is a very heavy and strong hardwood used to build houses (C. Kitalong), house frames (T. Tesei) and flooring (T. Belchal). *Stemonorus ammui* (*ngmui*) is used for beams and posts (R. Emesiochel), crossbeams (H. Nabeyama) and flooring (S. Ubedei). *Gmelina palawensis* (*blacheos*) is used for posts (S. Ubedei), flooring and walls. Flooring is also constructed from *Bruguiera gymnorrhiza* (*kodenges*) (H. Nabeyama), *Bambusa vulgaris* (*bambuu*) and *Serianthes kanehirae* (*ukall*). Trees used to build the main frame of the house include *Lumnitzera littoralis* (*mekekad*) and *Calophyllum pelewensis* (*chesemolech*) (S. Ubedei). *Lumnitzera littoralis* is also used for a structure's posts and the upper house, as is *Campnosperma breviopetiolata* (*kelelacharm*) (R. Emesiochel) and *Sonneratia alba* (*urur*) (H. Nabeyama). Trees used to construct the frame of a dock and for posts include *Rhizophora mucronata* and *Sonneratia alba* (R. Emesiochel, T. Belchal). *Ceriops tagal* (*buit*) is also used for construction (C. Kitalong, T. Tesei, R. Alii), to build canoe houses (*diangel*) (W. Metes), for posts (T. Belchal) and for house frames (H. Nabeyama).

Canoe building

The men interviewed provided information about 10 trees that produce wood suitable for crafting canoes (Table 2). The most common species reported (Table 7) is *Serianthes kanehirae* (T. Belchal, R. Bausouch, S. Yano, C. Kitalong, R. Emesiochel, H. Nabeyama, S. Ubedei). Other wood taxa for canoe construction are *Artocarpus atilis* (*meduu*) (C. Kitalong, S. Ubedei), *Artocarpus mariannensis* (*chebiei*) (C. Kitalong, R. Emesiochel), *Calophyllum inophyllum* (C. Kitalong, H. Nabeyama, J. Emesiochel), *Calophyllum inophyllum* var. *wakamatsui* (*btachesked*) (T. Belchal), *Terminalia catappa* (C. Kitalong) and *Campnosperma brevipetiolata* (C. Kitalong).

Five species of trees are specifically used for making the hulls of canoes. *Gmelina palawensis* is used to make canoe sides or covers (Ucheldekes Rebluud). *Lumnitzera littoralis* wood is good for the canoe outriggers, with its curved branches straightened by heating (S. Ubedei). The sides, body and covering of canoes can be made from *Gmelina palawensis* (E. Rebluud).

Table 6. Tree species most frequently mentioned by males for use in construction of structures.

Species (Palauan name)	Use	Males interviewed (n=17)	Oikull (n=10)	Ibobang (n=7)
Gmelina palawensis H.L. Lam var. *palawensis* (blacheos)	Posts, flooring, walls	8	4	4
Bambusa vulgaris Schrad. ex Wendl. (bambuu)	Flooring	7	4	3
Lumnitzera littoralis (Jack) Voigt (mekekad)	Main frame, posts, upper and lower house	7	2	5
Rhizophora mucronata Lam. (tebechel)	Frame of dock, beam	6	2	4
Ceriops tagal (Perr.) C. B. Robinson (biut)	Frame	5	2	3
Serianthes kanehirae Fosb. var. *kanehirae* (ukall)	Flooring	4	4	0
Sonneratia alba J.E. Sm. (urur)	Frame of dock, posts	4	2	2
Stemonorus ammui (Kaneh.) Sleumer (ngmui)	Posts, crossbeams,	4	1	3
Intsia bijuga (Colebr.) O. Kuntze (dort)	Frame, flooring	2	2	0
Calophyllum pelewensis P.F. Stevens (chesemolech)	Main frame	2	0	2
Total		**49**	**23**	**26**

Table 7. Tree species most frequently mentioned by males to construct a canoe.

Species (Palauan name)	Males interviewed (n=17)	Oikull (n=10)	Ibobang (n=7)
Serianthes kanehirae Fosb. var. *kanehirae* (ukall)	6	4	2
Calophyllum inophyllum L. (btaches)	3	1	2
Calophyllum inophyllum L.var. *wakamatsui* (Kaneh.) Fosb. and Sach. (btachesked)	3	1	2
Artocarpus atilis (Parkinson) Fosb. (meduu)	2	1	1
Terminalia catappa L. (miich)	2	1	1
Artocarpus mariannensis Trécul (chebiei)	2	1	1
Campnosperma brevipetiolata Volk. (kelelacharm)	1	1	0
Total	**19**	**10**	**9**

Trees used to make canoe paddles include *Terminalia catappa, Campnosperma brevipetiolata, Syzygium samarangense, Hibiscus tiliaceus, Dolichandrone spathacea* (*rriu*), *Inocarpus fagifer, Swietenia mahogany* (*mahogani*) and *Cerbera manghas.* Canoe sails (*yars*) are fashioned from woven *Pandanus* leaves.

Cordage

Rope is used in construction, to carry loads, to tie food packets and for numerous other everyday tasks. Rope is made from fibres (C. Kitalong) of the bark of *Wikstroemia elliptica* (*tebudel*), *Hibiscus tiliaceus, Commersonia bartramia* (*chermalluang*), *Ambroma augustata* (*lab*), *Trichospermum ledermannii* (*chelsau*) and the *Cocos nucifera* husk (E. Singeo). Fibres from the stems of *Cyrtosperma merkusii* and *Musa textiles* (*blantalos*) are used to wrap light loads (C. Kitalong, E. Ridep, M. Rehurer). The leaves of *Draceana multiflora* (*orredakl*) are used for general tying (K. Tesei), while the vine of *Derris trifoliata* (*kemokem*) is used to tie bamboo together for rafts (S. Ubedei) and to tie packages of food items (C. Kitalong). *Canavalia cathartica* (*kldelleland*) and *Merremia peltata* (*kebeas*) are used to tie light items (C. Kitalong), as is *Nepenthes mirabilis* (*meliik*) (D. Otobed).

Firewood

The best firewood is *Maranthes corymbosa* (*bkau*), although *Rhizophora mucronata* and *R. apiculata* (*bngaol*) are also good because they burn slowly (T. Belchal). Other trees used as firewood include *Casuarina equisetifolia* (*ngas*), *Cocos nucifera*, *Rhus taitensis* (*eues*), *Pouteria obovata* (*chelangel*), *Alphitonia carolinensis* (*chelebiob*) and *Macaranga carolinensis*. *Excoecaria agallocha* (*ias*) is used for firewood, but is also known to be poisonous to the eyes (V.R. Tadeo).

Cleaning

Many plants are used in personal hygiene, for cleaning the body, teeth, hair and clothes, and to produce a nice smell. *Barringtonia racemosa* (*koranges*) is used as soap (W. Metes, C. Kitalong). *Ceratopteris thalictroides* (*tiela uek*) produces suds and is used as shampoo (I. Ngiraibai). The *Colubrina asiatica* (*derikel*) stem is pounded until suds appear and is used both to wash clothes and as bathing soap (I. Ngiraibai). *Limnophila aromatica* (*iaml*) is used to wash after working in the taro patch (N. Kitalong, B.S. Chiokai). The tendril of *Nepenthes mirabilis* is used to clean teeth (M. Ngirametuker, C. Kitalong, E. Rebluud). *Averrhoa bilimbi* (*imekurs*) fruit is used to clean teeth, as well as boats, as it acts as a bleaching agent (C. Kitalong). The leaves of *Cananga odorata* (*irang irang*), *Cymbopogon citratus* and *Melicope denhamii* (*kertub*) produce a fragrant odour and are used to wipe the body (E. Rebluud). *Macaranga carolinensis* and fibres from *Cocos nucifera* are used as a natural tissue paper (C. Kitalong, T. Belchal, R. Bausouch, S. Yano).

Fishing

Fishing is a key activity for Palauan males, who practise such traditional fishing techniques as line fishing, netting, poisoning and spearing (Masse 1989; Johannes 1992). Fish are also caught in basket traps and fish weirs and propagated in fish ponds. Fishing techniques vary with the fish taxa being sought and the habitat being exploited.

Bamboo and wood basket traps (*bub*) are commonly used in Palau. Basket traps vary depending on the type of fish to be caught. Smaller basket traps like the *kosekl* and *bub el dech* are used in shallow water to catch small goatfish, sea bass, surgeonfish and wrasse. Larger traps such as the *techioll* and *bub el komud* are lowered into deeper water to catch bumphead parrotfish, humphead wrasse, large sea chup, sea bass, sharks and turtles. Fish traps (*semael*) are made with *Bambusa vulgaris* and lashed together with the *Derris trifoliata* vine, which is also used to tie bamboo rafts (S. Ubedei). *Loeseneriella macrantha* var. *palauica* (*kerrangel*) is also used to tie fish and crab traps (S. Ubedei, T. Belchal).

Traditionally, a large variety of fishing nets was used in Palau. As with baskets, the net and the mesh size varies according to the prey sought. Palauans created nets that could be operated by an individual, nets for a small fishing party, or extremely large nets (*direkorek*) necessitating a group. Some of the smaller, single-person nets include the *derau a mekebu*, *derek*, 'aikurs', *kual a chemang*, 'garn' (*charm*?), *kual a ngoaol*, *mangidab* and *methilab*. The *bilokl*, *ruul* and *sab* are some of the nets that can be operated by a single individual or a small group. Typically, net types are used for specific prey; for example, 'aikurs' nets are reported to catch sea bass, emperor and rabbitfish, while *direkorek* was used primarily for humphead wrasse, bumphead parrotfish, surgeonfish and rays.

Smaller nets were generally made from *Cocos nucifera* husk fibre (S. Ubedei). Larger fish nets (*ruul*) are made with *Heterospathe elata* var. *palauensis* leaves (H. Nabeyama), which are preferred over coconut leaves because they are stronger (S. Ubedei). The leaves are tied using either *Derris trifoliata* or *Hibiscus tiliaceus* (S. Ubedei). The frame for a small hand net (*derau*) is fashioned from *Allophylus timoriensis* (*chebeludes*) (R. Bausouch, S. Ubedei) and *B. vulgaris* (T. Belchal). *Macaranga carolinensis* is used to make light wooden floats for the net (S. Ubedei). The prop roots (*raod*) of the mangrove trees *Rhizophora mucronata* and *R. apiculata* are used to lure fish out of the rocks (H. Nabeyama) before they are caught by a net, spear or natural poison.

Spearing is a common Palauan fishing technique. Ethnographically, there were two main spear types, the *klebiskang*, with a single hardwood point, and the *taod*, with a cluster of barbed points. The *klebiskang* is used to catch taxa such as large species of parrotfish, triggerfish and wrasse, as well as rays and sharks. The *taod* is used on such fish as cornetfish, jacks and needlefish. Spears are made with *Areca catechu* (E. Singeo) and *Schizostachyum lima* (C. Kitalong, T. Belchal). *Lumnitzera littoralis* is used to make spear handles (S. Ubedei). *Intsia bijuga* is used for spear guns (C. Kitalong, V.R. Takeo).

Plants are not only employed to make fishing nets, traps and spears, but provide cues to signal the appropriate time to catch particular species. When *Melastoma malabathricum* var. *mariannum* (*matakui*) is in full bloom, sea urchins and clams are ripe and ready to be harvested (M. Ngirametuker). When *Serianthes kanehirae* are in full bloom, there will be many fish, especially during the high tide (R. Alii).

Hunting

Few terrestrial animals contributed significantly to the traditional diet. In the ethnohistorical records, terrestrial protein sources are limited to crabs, bats and birds, such as the duck and pigeon and the eggs of the Micronesian megapode (*Megapodius laperouse senex*) and the white tern (*Gygis alba pacifica*) (Kubary 1892). Archaeological evidence exists for the consumption of pigs as a status food (*Sus scrofa*), although they were apparently extirpated by the first substantial Western contact with the islands in 1783 (Masse et al. 2006). Today, men hunt for birds, bats and wild pigs and set traps for wild chickens and crabs.

Land traps (*bedikl*) are made with the flexible stem of *Ixora casei* (*kerdeu*) (S. Ubedei, T. Belchal, C. Kitalong, V.R. Takeo) and *Cocos nucifera* fibre (S. Ubedei). Once the chicken takes the bait, it trips the trap and is caught in the fibre snare as the stem springs backwards (C. Kitalong). *Symplocos racemosa* var. *palawensis* (*chebtui*) is used to make the slingshots used in bird and bat hunting (T. Belchal).

Medicine

The medicinal plants category contains the greatest number of species for a given task. Informants provided a medicinal use for 95 plant species. Oikull interviewees described 80 medicinal plant uses, with 41 provided by the men and 39 by the women. In Ibobang, 52 medicinal plant uses were described, with men and women each giving 26 uses. Frequently mentioned uses were pain relief from toothaches, earaches and headaches; cures for diarrhoea, bleeding and boils; and overall cleansing and healing (Table 8). *Premna serratifolia* (*chosm*) and *Phaleria nisidai* (*ongael*) were the two species most commonly referred to as providing a medicinal value.

Premna serratifolia is used to stop cuts from bleeding (C. Kitalong, M. Rehuher) – one young chewed leaf is applied to small cuts and the inner slimy bark to deeper cuts (F. Wasisang, J. Emesiochel, S. Obedei, V.R. Tadeo, M. Besebes, G. Emesiochel). The bark is peeled and drops of the clear inner sap are placed on stings or wounds caused by sea urchins or fish spines, to ease the pain. Another preparation method for *P. serratifolia* as a pain medication is to place the extracted sap into a spoon with hot coconut oil and put the infected area into the resultant steam or smoke (T. Belchal, R. Bausouch, S. Yano). *Premna serratifolia* also stops bleeding from

Table 8. Most frequently mentioned medicinal plants.

Species (Palauan name)	Use	Total interviewed (n=43)	Oikull (n=27)	Ibobang (n=16)
Premna serratifolia L. (chosm)	Cuts, weight loss, asthma, mosquito repellant, pain reliever	16	10	6
Phaleria nisidai Kaneh. (ongael)	Cleansing, flushing, build immunity, aches and pain, heart ailment, diarrheoa and abortion	15	6	9
Morinda citrifolia L. (ngel)	Cuts, weight loss and boils	9	6	3
Curcuma longa L. (kesol)	Medicinal ointment for skin and stretch marks	9	6	3
Cocos nucifera L. (lius)	Cleansing, earache, external ointment strengthening immune system, boils, diarrhea	8	3	5
Syzygium samarangense (Blume) Merr. and Perry (rebotel)	Cuts, sore throats, colds stretch marks, herbal bath, external rash or itch	7	5	2
Millettia pinnata Panigrahi (kisaks)	Use in herbal bath after first born	6	2	4
Calophyllum inophyllum L. (btaches)	Asthma, strength	5	3	2
Epipremnum carolinense Volk. (toilalech)	Menstruation, abortion	5	5	0
Barringtonia racemosa (L.) Spreng. (koranges)	Heartburn, stop bleeding, abortion	4	4	0
Casuarina equisetifolia L. (ngas)	Toothaches, abortion	4	3	1
Total		**88**	**53**	**35**

head injuries (R. Alii, C. Kitalong) and is used in combination with other plants for weight loss (O. Belaio). The leaves are mashed and placed on the body to act as a mosquito repellant (H. Yuri). Four leaves of *P. serratifolia* and four leaves of *Codiaeum variegatum* (*kesuk ianged*) are boiled for one minute and drunk as tea to treat asthma (E. Rebluud).

Phaleria nisidai heals many illnesses and is used in combination with other plants for bodily cleansing and flushing (C. Kitalong, M. Ngirametuker, T. Watanabe, N. Kitalong). Its leaves are boiled into a tea drunk in specific amounts to build immunity and relieve aches in the stomach (M. Ngirametuker) and body (H. Nabeyama, G. Emesiochel). *Phaleria nisidai* is used for headaches, menstruation pain and to strengthen the body (M. Rehurer, F. Wasisang, M. Besebes). The plant acts as an energiser (B.S. Choikai) and is used for heart ailments (I. Spesungel). Combined with *Psidium guajava* (*kuabang*) leaves, *P. nisidai* is a remedy for diarrheoa (M. Besebes). It is also one of the plants used during the first birth ritual and ceremony (F. Wasisang).

As part of the Modekngei religious ritual, its members gather on special dates to worship and share a herbal drink that cleanses the body. Some of the plant species in this drink are *Dianella carolinensis* (*kebesos*), *Phaleria nisidai*, *Melastoma malabathricum* L. var. *mariannum*, *Nepenthes mirabilis*, *Lycopodiella cernua* (*olechuila beab*) *Dicranopteris linearis* var. *ferruginea* (*itouch*), *Cassytha filiformis* (*tellelachull*), *Trema cannabina* Lour. (*chelodechoel*) and *Hedyotis korrorensis* (*chemudalech*) (M. Ngirametuker).

Two keystone plants

The elders provided 39 separate uses for *Cocos nucifera*, making it the study's most useful plant species (Table 9). Due to its importance, as reflected in the number of different uses, *C. nucifera* is a 'cultural keystone species' (Garabaldi and Turner 2004) in many Pacific Island nations

Table 9. Most frequently mentioned trees with a specific use.

Species (Palauan name)	Total interviewed (n=43)	Oikull (n=27)	Ibobang (n=16)
Cocos nucifera L. (lius)	67	39	26
Areca catechu L. (buuch)	19	15	9
Premna serratifolia L. (chosm)	13	5	8
Syzygium samarangense (Blume) Merr. and Perry (rebotel)	11	11	0
Macaranga carolinensis Volk. (bedel)	11	7	4
Rhizophora spp. (tebechel and bngaol)	9	6	7
Spondias pinnata (titimel)	9	7	3
Calophyllum inophyllum L. (btaches)	8	6	5
Averrhoa bilimbi L. (imekurs)	8	8	1
Melastoma malabathricum L. var. *mariannum* (Naudin) Fosb. and Sach. (matakui)	8	6	3
Terminalia catappa L. (miich)	7	3	4
Ixora casei Hance (kerdeu)	7	2	6
Total	**177**	**112**	**76**

(e.g. Samoa, Whistler 1996) and in Central and South America (e.g. Belize, Arvigo and Balick 1998). Ridep Emesiochel calls the coconut tree the 'mother of Belau' because of its many uses. The recorded uses of coconut are similar in Oikull and Ibobang, with multiple interviewees providing similar uses. With 19 documented uses, *Areca catechu* is the second most identified plant in the study and is another cultural keystone species.

Clarence Kitalong listed 24 uses for the nut (n=7), trunk (n=8) and leaves (n=9) of the coconut palm. The coconut meat (endocarp) is a food and the fluid a drink. The hard outer nut (exocarp) is used for cups, bowls and utensils. Coconut oil is used singly or as one of several ingredients in food and medicine, to protect the skin after bathing from bites, infection or skin diseases, as a hair conditioner and as a mosquito repellent. The exocarp fibres start fires and keep them burning hot, and are fashioned into sieves and rope. The trunk of the coconut palm is used as firewood and to make trap doors, stirring utensils, taro-pounding implements, tool handles, walking canes, spears, benches and wall and flooring material. Coconut leaves are woven into baskets (Figure 3), folded as wraps for fish and ground tapioca, used as torches to provide light and made into ropes and toys such as balls, canoes and windmills. The midrib of the frond is used to make brooms and catch shrimp.

Fourteen uses for the coconut leaves (n=4), nut (n=9) and trunk (n=1) were provided by T. Watanabe, including its use as an ingredient in herbal hot baths, as food, and to make ropes, handbags, hats, brooms, water dippers, buttons, bras, belts, hair picks, baskets, hair oil and sieves. Dirratkelkang M. Ngirametuker provided 13 uses for the coconut leaves (baskets, brooms, firewood and toys), the branches (toys), the trunk (implements, canes and construction material), and the nut and its fibres (sieve, rope, oil, food and syrup).

Dirratesei E. Singeo described other uses of coconut, including the exocarp being used as a lime holder for the preparation of betel nut, and the nut's oil being rubbed on the stomach to ease stomach aches. Because the healthy coconut juice cleanses the intestines, babies, young children and elders drink it to strengthen their immune systems. The young soft meat is sweet and good for desserts or snacking. After the nut is mature and the meat is hard, it is tasty when eaten with *Cyrtosperma merkusii*. Grated coconut meat is placed in a white cloth and wrung to

Figure 3. Dirrngerchemuul (Hinako Ngirmekur) weaving a *terkill* (a basket used to carry food for travelling) from *Cocos nucifera (lius).*

extract the milk used in food preparation and to revitalise hair by making it shiny, silky and strong. The grated meat can also be placed in a coconut sheath and heated and the warm oil used to heal a wound cleaned with *Morinda citrifolia* (*ngel*) (C. Kitalong). Coconut fronds are cut off the main midrib and stripped to leave the rachis, which is gathered and tied to make a broom. Individual pieces of the rachis are used to catch shrimp and small lizards. The young fronds can be woven to make small balls and animals to entertain children. Benches and flooring are constructed from the trunk.

After childbirth, the male or female placenta is wrapped in coconut fronds to symbolise manhood or womanhood and prosperity (W. Metes, C. Kitalong). The young frond is a symbol used during the passing of a chiefly title (E. Singeo, H. Takeo, N. Luii, M. Kim, A. Bintorio). Dirrngerchemuul H. Takeo demonstrated how the young coconut leaf is prepared with the wild taro leaf to symbolise the transfer of clan titles. While the ritual to transfer traditional titles is practised or performed by men, it is the women who are the recipients of the title symbolised by the coconut and wild taro leaf.

The process of making rope from coconut husk fibres was described by Dirratesei E. Singeo. After the husks are buried under the sand in the ocean for about a month, they are pounded to remove excess fluid and stray fragments, rinsed with water and left to dry. Once dried, the fibres are placed in one's lap to be rolled in a circular motion and elongated by connecting one end to another. It takes many coconut husks to make a single rope. One basket full of fibres from the coconut husk can make about 7 m of thick rope used for constructing a house or 12 m of thin rope to make tools (C. Kitalong). This rope can be used in tying together parts for traditional canoes, tools and structures such as a men's meeting house.

The coconut endocarp is used as food and drink, the fibres from the husk are used to make rope and to embellish fish hooks, the husk is firewood, the meat is ground for milk and oil that is used to remove skin boils and water from the ear, and the leaves are used to wrap food. Coconut fibre is used to make small hand nets (*derau*) and land traps for crabs and chickens (S. Ubedei) and to wrap food and cleanse the body (I. Ngiraibai). The leaves are woven into toys (*btul* or *eberdord*), the nut's oil is used for ear aches and the husk is used to make smoke (F. Wasisang). The leaves can be made into brooms, baskets and food wrapping; the nut is a source of food and drink; the trunk is used for firewood and to make small bridges and benches; the meat from young coconuts (*kleu*) is mixed with salt and eaten to prevent dehydration, the young sprout (*meolt*) is used to wrap tapioca and make grass skirts (G. Emesiochel, S. Chiokai). The husk (*ulengchidel*) is used to clean pots and make rope or cords, and the trunk is used for compost and flooring (S. Chiokai).

Nineteen uses for *Areca catechu* were given by women from Oikull (E. Singeo, M. Kim, N. Luii, H. Takeo). The nut is chewed with lime and *Piper betle (kebui)* leaf as a stimulant. The *Areca catechu* nut and *Piper betle* leaves are an integral part of customary exchanges between clans during important rituals such as first-birth, marriage and funerals. The *Areca catechu* palm has numerous medicinal purposes. The root is used with *Leea guineensis (sngall)* to ease menstrual cramps, and in Ibobang, is one of the plants in the ritual cleansing after the first menstruation (F. Wasisang). Juice from the pounded roots relieves toothaches. Five to seven days after the umbilical cord has fallen off, betel-nut juice is applied to a newborn's navel as a natural antiseptic. Heating the ripe nut softens it so that juices can be extracted and applied mornings and evenings after the newborn's bath. To prevent bed wetting, the nut is cut in half and given to babies to chew and suck on.

The betel-nut trunk is cut into flooring and benches (G. Emesiochel). The lower portion of the trunk is used to make spears, dancing paddles and sticks. *Areca catechu* leaves are used for fertiliser. Its smooth inner sheath is good for long-term food storage (up to a week, depending on the type of food), to wrap a baby and as a raincoat. Sheaths are fashioned into dancing skirts and, when sewn together with *Hibiscus tiliaceous* fibre, used to make coats and handbags. The outer sheath is stripped and pounded to make a loincloth. Infants bite down on the young fronds when teething. Children play by sitting inside the fronds and sliding down hills (F. Wasisang).

Conclusion

During 2006 to 2010, an ethnobotanical study was conducted in Oikull, Airai State, and Ibobang, Ngatpang State, on Babeldaob, Palau's largest island. The objective of this pilot study was to document in as much detail as possible the use of plants in all aspects of Palauan culture, using the theme 'the cycle of life', or from birth to death. During interviews, we recorded uses for 200 plant species; 171 species in Oikull and 127 in Ibobang. Plants were mainly used for medicine (70 species), construction (41 species), food (27 species) and toys (22 species). Knowledge differed depending on traditional gender roles and practices. Men described plants used for construction, tool making, firewood, fishing and canoe making. Women described plants used for medicinal uses for the first-birth ceremony (Figure 4). Men and women described how

Figure 4. Uodelchad ra Esel (Terue Daniel) and her daughter Uwai Skebong sorting the inner bark fibres of *Hibiscus tiliceaus* (*chermall*) in preparation for making a grass skirt for a first-birth ceremony.

plants were used for food, recreation, art and medicine for primary care. Two palm species, *Cocos nucifera* and *Areca catechu*, had the most uses and were considered cultural keystone species.

This preliminary study shows that Ibobang and Oikull use many plant species for similar purposes. The communities continue to maintain strong ties between their plants and culture. We found that there are certain families or individuals who are renowned for their knowledge and have very specific skills that are part of their own family knowledge and a source of prestige and wealth. There is much more knowledge that needs to be documented in Palau. This is only the beginning. We were heartened by a summer youth program in Ibobang where we observed and documented the elders teaching their youth how to build crab traps, weave baskets, fish and fix Palauan food. Oikull's traditional leaders have also begun youth programs.

Conservation of plant diversity, integration of traditional knowledge and practices in educational programs, and promotion of culture thorough local, regional and international fairs will ensure that the Palauan culture and its plant diversity survives through the next millennium.

Acknowledgements

This paper results from a multidisciplinary field project studying the relationship between plants and people in Palau, and in the larger context, throughout Micronesia. This effort is focusing on botany, ethnomedicine, traditional land management and resource systems, conservation and education. We are grateful to the The V. Kann Rasmussen Foundation, Edward P. Bass and the Philecology Trust, the Marisla Foundation, the MetLife Foundation, the Germeshausen Foundation and the National Geographic Society Committee for Research and Exploration. We thank the people of Oikull and Ibobang and the Board of Trustees of the Belau National Museum for their support, guidance and participation in this project.

Note

1. Sharks were hunted from sail boats with special hooks. Mlamitoi from Peleliu who grew up in Oikull's Ngesileong clan was known for trapping a shark by himself. He could both manoeuvre the sail of his canoe and catch the shark by throwing a coconut to it to bite on (A. Rufino). There is a legend in Oikull of how an Airai god, Medechii, claimed Ngerduais Island. Medechii challenged the other gods that whomever could throw the betel nut fiber (*ulemachel*) the furthest would own Ngerduais Island. While the gods were fixing their betel nut, chewing it and preparing to throw, Medechii put the red honeyeater bird (*chesisebangiau*) into his mouth pretending it was his betel nut as it was red like a chewed betel nut. The gods threw their betel nut and Medechii grabbed the bird out of his mouth quickly without being detected. The bird flew all the way to Ngerduais and Medechii claimed the island as his own.

References

Arvigo, R. and Balick, M. 1998. *Rainforest Remedies*. Lotus Press, Twin Lakes, Wisconsin.

Athens, J.S. and Ward, J.V. 2001. Paleoenvironmental evidence for early human settlement in Palau: The Ngerchau core. In: Stevenson, C.M. and Morin, F.J. (eds), *Proceedings on the fifth international conference on Easter Island and the Pacific*, pp. 165–178. Easter Island Foundation, Los Osos.

Athens, J.S. and Ward, J.V. 2002. *Holocene paleoenvironmental investigations on Ngerekebesang, Koror, South Babeldaob, and Peleliu Islands, Palau*. Report prepared for Palau National Communications Corporation, Republic of Palau. International Archaeological Research Institute, Inc., Honolulu.

Athens, J.S. and Ward, J.V. 2005. *Palau Compact Road archaeological investigations, Babeldaob Island, Republic of Palau; Volume IV: Holocene paleoenvironment and landscape change*. Report prepared for the Department of the Army, U.S. Army Engineer District, Honolulu. International Archaeological Research Institute, Inc., Honolulu.

Balick, M.J. (ed), 2009. *Ethnobotany of Pohnpei: Plants, people, and island culture*. University of Hawai'i Press/The New York Botanical Garden, Honolulu.

Balick, M.J. and Cox, P.A. 2005. *Plants, people, and culture. The science of ethnobotany*. Scientific American Press, New York.

Black, P.W. 1968. Notes on medicinal plants of Tobi. Unpublished manuscript on file at the Palau Bureau of Arts and Culture, Koror, Palau.

Canfield, J., Herbst, D. and Stemmerman, L. 1992. *Rapid ecological assessment of areas in Palau considered for conservation: Ngeremeduu Bay drainage area (Draft)*. Report prepared for U.S. Fish and Wildlife Service, Pacific Islands Office.

Cole, T.G., Falanruw, M.C., MacLean, C.D., Whitesell, C. and Ambacher, A.M. 1987. *Vegetation survey of the Republic of Palau*. Resource Bulletin PSW-22. Pacific Southwest Costion, C. and Kitalong, A. 2006. *Babeldaob forest survey*. Belau National Museum and The Nature Conservancy, Palau Field Office, Koror, Republic of Palau.

Forest and Range Experiment Station, U.S. Forest Service, U.S. Department of Agriculture, University of California Press, Berkeley.

Defilipps, R.A., Marina, S.L. and Pray, L.A. 1988. The Palauan and Yap medicinal plants – Studies of Masyoshi Okabe, 1941–1943. *Atoll Research Bulletin* No. 317. National Museum of Natural History, Smithsonian Institution, Washington D.C.

Del Rosario, A.G. and Esquerra, N.M. 2003. *Medicinal plants in Palau, Volume 1*. PCC-CRE Publication 28/03 (3.0C).

Donnegan, J.A., Butler, S.L., Kuegler, O., Stroud, B.J., Hiserote, B.A. and Rengulbai, K. 2007. *Palau's forest resources, 2003*. Resource Bulletin PNW-RB-252. U.S. Department of Agriculture, Forest Service, Pacific Northwest Research Station, Portland, Oregon.

Farnsworth, N., Akerele, A.O., Bingel, A.S., Soerjarto, D.D. and Guo, Z. 1985. Medicinal plants in therapy. *Bulletin of the World Health Organization* 63:965–981.

Fosberg, F.R. 1946. Botanical report on Micronesia. *U.S. Commercial Company Economic Survey of Micronesia* 13(1).

Fosberg, F.R. 1947. Micronesian mangroves. *Journal of the New York Botanical Garden* 48: 128–148.

Fosberg, F.R. 1957. Vegetation of the oceanic province of the Pacific. In: *Proceedings of the VIII Pacific Science Congress* (Quezon City 1953) 4:48–55.

Fosberg, F.R. 1960. The vegetation of Micronesia. I. General descriptions, the vegetation of the Marianas Islands, and a detailed consideration of the vegetation of Guam. *Bulletin of the American Museum of Natural History* 119:1–75

Fosberg, F.R. and Sachet, M.H. 1975a. Flora of Micronesia, 1: Gymnospermae. *Smithsonian Contributions to Botany* 20:1–15.

Fosberg, F.R. and Sachet, M.H. 1975b. Flora of Micronesia, 2: Casuarinaceae, Piperaceae, and Myricaceae. *Smithsonian Contributions to Botany* 24:1–28.

Fosberg, F.R. and Sachet, M.H. 1977. Flora of Micronesia, 3: Convolvulaceae. *Smithsonian Contributions to Botany* 36:1–33.

Fosberg, F.R. and Sachet, M.H. 1979. *Maesa* (Myrsinaceae) in Micronesia. *Phytologia* 44 (1):363–369.

Fosberg, F.R. and Sachet, M.H. 1980a. Flora of Micronesia, 4: Caprifoliaceae-Compositae. *Smithsonian Contributions to Botany* 46:1–71.

Fosberg, F.R. and Sachet, M.H. 1980b. Systematic studies of Micronesian plants. *Smithsonian Contributions to Botany* 45:1–44.

Fosberg, F.R. and Sachet, M.H. 1981. Nomenclatural notes on Micronesian ferns. *American Fern Journal* 71(3):82–84.

Fosberg, F.R. and Sachet, M.H. 1984. *Micronesian Poaceae: Critical and distributional notes.* Botany Department, Smithsonian Institution, Washington, D.C.

Fosberg, F.R. and Sachet, M.H. 1987. The Genus *Timonius* (Rubiaceae) in the Palau Islands. *Micronesica* 20(1–2):157–164.

Fosberg, F.R. and Sachet, M.H. 1991. Studies in Indo-Pacific Rubiaceae. *Allertonia* 6(3):191–278.

Fosberg, F.R. and Raulerson, L. 1990. New and noteworthy Micronesian plants. *Micronesica* 23(2):150.

Fosberg, F.R., Sachet, M.H. and Oliver, R.L. 1979. A geographical checklist of the Micronesian Dicotyledonae. Botany Department, Smithsonian Institution, Washington, D.C. *Micronesica* 15(1–2):41–298.

Fosberg, F.R., Sachet, M.H. and Oliver, R.L. 1982. A geographical checklist of the Micronesian pteridophytes and gymnosperms. Botany Department, Smithsonian Institution, Washington, D.C. *Micronesica* 18(1):23–82.

Fosberg, F.R., Sachet, M.H. and Oliver, R.L. 1987. A geographical checklist of the Micronesian Monocotyledoneae. Botany Department, Smithsonian Institution, Washington, D.C. *Micronesica* 20(1–2):19–129.

Fosberg, F.R., Sachet, M.H. and Oliver, R.L. 1993. Flora of Micronesia, 5: Bignoniaceae-Rubiaceae. *Smithsonian Contributions to Botany* 81:1–135.

Fosberg, F.R., Otobed, D., Sachet, M.H., Oliver, R.L., Powell, D.A. and Canfield, J.E. 1980. *Vascular plants of Palau with vernacular names.* Department of Botany, Smithsonian Institution, Washington, D.C.

Friend, N. and Tabak, N. 1995. *Medicinal plants of Ngaraard.* Center for Island Management Studies, School for Field Studies, Ngaraard State, Republic of Palau.

Garabaldi, A. and Turner, N. 2004. Cultural keystone species: Implications for ecological conservation and restoration. Ecology and Society 9(3): 1. URL: http://www.ecologyandsociety.org/vol9/iss3/art1

Hillmann Kitalong, A. and Holm, T. 2004. *Forest habitat assessment project.* Report prepared for the Palau Conservation Society, Koror, Palau.

Hillmann Kitalong, A. 2008. Forests of Palau: A long term perspective. *Micronesica* 40(1/2):9–31.

Hillmann Kitalong, A., DeMeo, R.A. and Holm, T. 2009. *Native trees of Palau.* The Environment, Inc, Koror, Palau.

Johannes, R.E. 1981. *Words of the lagoon: Fishing and marine lore in the Palau district of Micronesia.* University of California Press, Berkeley.

Jones, V. 1941. The nature and scope of ethnobotany. *Chronica Botany* 6(10):219–221.

Kanehira, R. 1933. *Flora of Micronesica, Book I: General sketch of the flora of Micronesia.* South Seas Bureau under Japanese Mandate. Translated by the Office of the Engineer, U.S. Army Pacific, Tokyo, Japan 1958.

Kapoor, L.D. 1990. *CRC handbook on ayurvedic medicinal plants.* CRV Press, Boca Raton.

Kitalong, C. 2007. Hepatoprotective and HCV-protease inhibitory activity of Palauan medicinal plants. Unpublished MA thesis, Toyama University.

Krämer, A. 1917, 1919 and 1929. Palau. In: *Ergebnisse der Südsee-Expedition:1908–1910.* Teilbands 1–4. Hamburg: L. Friederichsen and Co.

Kubary, J.S. 1892. Ethnographical material for the knowledge of the Caroline Archipelago. In: *Volume*

II: Industry of Palau, pp. 117–219. Verlag Von P.W.M. Trap, Leiden.

Lee, R., Balick, M., Ling, D., Sohl, F., Brosi, B. and Raynor, W. 2001. Cultural dynamism and change – An example from the Federated States of Micronesia. *Economic Botany* 55(1):9–13.

Lee, R. 2009. Traditional medicine, Pohnpei and its integration. In: Balick, M. (ed), *Ethnobotany of Pohnpei: Plants, people, and island culture*, pp. 204–216. University of Hawai'i Press, Honolulu.

Liston, J. 2009. Cultural chronology of earthworks in Palau, western Micronesia. *Archaeology in Oceania* 44:56–73.

Liston, J. and Tuggle, H.D. 2006. Prehistoric warfare in Palau. In: Arkush, E. and Allen, M.W. (eds), pp. 148–193. *The archaeology of warfare: Prehistories of raiding and conquest.* University Press of Florida, Gainesville.

Machiko A. 2002. *Modekngei: A new religion in Belau, Micronesia.* Shinsensha Press, Tokyo Japan.

Masse, W.B. 1989. *The archaeology and ecology of fishing in the Belau Islands, Micronesia.* Unpublished PhD thesis, Southern Illinois University.

Masse, W.B., Liston, J., Carucci, J. and Athens, J.S. 2006. Evaluating the effects of climate change on environment, resource depletion, and culture in the Palau Islands between AD 1200 and 1600. *Quaternary International* 151(1):106–132.

Mayo, H.M. 1954. *Report on the plant relocation survey and agricultural history of the Palau Islands.* Office of the Forestry Conservation. Trust Territory of the Pacific Islands, Saipan.

Mukherjee, P.K. and Wahile, A. 2006. Integrated approaches towards drug development from Ayurveda and other Indian systems of medicines. *Journal of Ethnopharmacology* 103:25–35.

Okabe, M. 1941. Folk medicine of the Palau islander. *Journal of the Anthropological Society of Nippon* 56:413–426. Translated by H. Takeda for the Military Geology Branch, U.S. Geological Survey for Intelligence Division, Office of the Engineer Headquarters, Far East Commander, Tokyo, Japan.

Palau Society of Historians 2000. *Medicine and therapy. Traditional and customary practices.* English Series 6. Division of Cultural Affairs, Republic of Palau.

Palau Society of Historians 2001. *Traditional items and properties of a household, clan, and village.* English Series 7. Division of Cultural Affairs, Republic of Palau.

Palau National Environmental Protection Council 2004. *Republic of Palau national biodiversity strategy and action plan.* Report prepared for the Office of Environmental Response and Coordination, Republic of Palau.

Raulerson, L., Rinehart, A.F., Falanruw, M.S., Singeo, Y., Slappy, S. and Victor, S. 1997. *A botanical reconnaissance of the proposed Compact Road alignment on Babeldaob Island, Republic of Palau.* Report prepared for Wil Chee Planning, Honolulu. University of Guam Herbarium (GUAM) Contribution No 32.

Salsedo, C.A. 1970. The search for medicinal plants of Micronesia. *Micronesian Reporter.* Third Quarter. pp. 10–17.

Salsedo, C.A. and Smith, D.G. 1987. Medicinal plants of Palau. *Phytologia* 64(1):63–77.

Stemmermann, L. 1981. *A guide to Pacific wetland plants.* Report prepared for the Department of the Army, U.S. Army Engineer District, Honolulu.

Telmetang, M. 1993. *Bai.* Imuul Series No. 1, Belau National Museum, Inc., Republic of Palau.

Whistler, A. 1992. *Tongan herbal medicine.* Isle Botanica Press, Honolulu.

Whistler, A. 1996. *Samoan herbal medicine.* Isle Botanica Press, Honolulu.

Appendix 1. Use categories with the total number of plant species for each village.

Use	Oikull	Ibobang
Medicine	48	39
Food	23	7
Construction	14	43
Toys	12	10
Fishing	7	9
Cleaning	6	2
Rope	6	3
Canoe	4	10
Farming	4	5
Accessories	3	0
Baskets	2	1
Canoe paddle	2	0
Clothing	2	0
Custom	2	1
Firewood	2	10
Tools	2	7
Chicken trap	1	3
Decoration	1	3
Dye	1	3
Fibre	1	0
Food wrap	1	1
Magic	1	0
Pillow	1	1
Storyboard	1	1
Bridge	0	1
Chewing	0	3
Sail	0	2
Taboo food	0	1
Total	**147**	**166**

7

Selecting cultural sites for the UNESCO World Heritage List

Recent work in the Rock Islands–Southern Lagoon area, Republic of Palau

Christian Reepmeyer[1], Geoffrey Clark[1], Dwight Alexander[2], Ilebrang U. Olkeriil[3], Jolie Liston[1] and Ann Hillmann Kitalong[4]

1. Archaeology and Natural History, College of Asia and the Pacific, The Australian National University, Australia
2. The Palau Bureau of Arts and Culture, Ministry of Community and Cultural Affairs, Palau
3. Department of Conservation and Law Enforcement, Koror State Government, Palau
4. The Environment, Inc., Koror, Palau

Introduction

In this paper, we discuss approaches and issues raised by the nomination of cultural properties in the Pacific Islands to the World Heritage List. The World Heritage Committee in 2003 acknowledged the under-representation of the Pacific region on the World Heritage List. In response, the action plan *World Heritage Pacific 2009* (UNESCO World Heritage Centre 2004) was launched to build capacity in the region and encourage nomination of sites to the Tentative List through identification of properties of potential outstanding universal value (OUV), including transboundary and serial site nominations. Since 1992, Pacific cultural-heritage research has taken an active role in reshaping notions of cultural significance and OUV criteria traditionally employed to achieve World Heritage status. Archaeological expertise in partnership with traditional knowledge and local community involvement is increasingly relied on to provide the material necessary for World Heritage site nomination and heritage management in the Pacific. Emerging issues include tensions between traditional/community structures and government/federal organisations over World Heritage cultural and mixed properties, and the means by which Pacific nations can accumulate the resources and expertise necessary for a World Heritage nomination.

World Heritage: The Pacific context

The World Heritage (WH) List is an exceptional success story since the World Heritage Convention was adopted in 1972. The WH List in 2010 has 911 properties (704 cultural, 180 natural, 27 mixed) and 187 state parties have ratified the World Heritage Convention (UNESCO World Heritage Centre 2010a). Balancing the geographic representation of the WH List is a recurring problem which has yet to be fully resolved, as stated in the 2005 analysis by ICOMOS, *Filling the gaps – an action plan for the future* (2005:14):

> The idea of 'balance' in relation to the World Heritage List should not be seen to refer to a balance between countries or types of properties, but rather to how well a particular type of heritage of outstanding universal value is represented on the List.

An early focus in the WH List on monumental and religious structures has resulted in several site types now being identified as over-represented, including historic towns and religious buildings (particularly of Christian contexts), 'elitist' architecture and an overall disproportionate number of properties in Europe (Titchen 1996).

The uneven distribution of WH sites globally is exemplified by the presence of only 15 sites in the wider Pacific area (including sites in New Zealand, Chile and Ecuador), and only five sites nominated by developing Pacific Island nations (Kiribati, the Marshall Islands, Papua New Guinea, the Solomon Islands and Vanuatu). It is perceived that the under-representation of WH sites in the Pacific is caused by the grouping of Pacific Island nations with the more economically developed, resource-rich and densely populated nations of Asia (Smith and Jones 2007). An Asia-Pacific grouping is significant as the submission of Tentative Lists by State Parties should be initiated by local communities, with external experts involved in the process only as facilitators (Aim 1 in ICOMOS 2005:102). In comparison with some Asian countries, many Pacific Island nations are still developing their heritage capacity and have fewer human resources to devote to the site nomination process. Assembling information networks of local communities, external and local archaeologists, anthropologists and other heritage experts is likely to be a key strategy for Pacific Island nations wishing to produce WH cultural-site nominations.

To address low representation in the WH List, the action plan *World Heritage Pacific 2009* (UNESCO World Heritage Centre 2004) was launched. Its aim is to build capacity in the region and to encourage nomination of sites to the Tentative List through identification of individual properties of potential Outstanding Universal Value, along with possible transboundary or serial site nominations. Since its launch in 2003, eight of the 14 independent Pacific Island nations (including New Zealand and Papua New Guinea) have submitted properties to the World Heritage Commission, and in total 38 sites have been registered on the Tentative List.

Six sites have been inscribed from the Pacific region to the WH List since 2003. These include one site, *Lagoons of New Caledonia: Reef Diversity and Associated Ecosystem* (2008), in an overseas French territory and the *Papahānaumokuākea* (2010) property in the US state of Hawai'i. Whereas the lack of human resources seriously limits the capability of Pacific Islands nations of submitting nomination dossiers for sites now listed on the Tentative List, it is interesting to note that, except for the June 2010 nomination of *Les Iles Marquises* in French Polynesia, none of the Western developed nations with overseas territories in the Pacific have nominated new properties for the Tentative List, although potential cultural sites have been suggested in an ICOMOS thematic study (Smith and Jones 2007).

Since 1992, Pacific cultural-heritage research has taken an active role in the progress of reshaping notions of cultural significance and of OUV criteria traditionally employed to nominate sites for WH status. The incorporation of associative cultural landscapes into the criteria and the inscription of the *Tongariro National Park*, New Zealand, in 1993 and the *Uluru-Kata Tjuta National Park*, Australia, in 1994 set the foundation for the more than 66 properties (UNESCO World Heritage Centre 2010b) specifically inscribed as cultural landscapes on the WH List. The inclusion of cultural landscapes in the OUV criteria acknowledged the dominance of monumental sites and the under-representation of cultures whose heritage was non-monumental on the WH List (Fowler 2003, 2004). With a large number of properties (26 out of 52 sites on the WH and Tentative Lists) having a cultural-landscape component, this step is particularly important for Pacific Island nations. Associative cultural landscapes were defined as a priority for Pacific Island nominations (Smith and Jones 2007:9).

In this paper, we review the nomination process of a mixed cultural/natural site in the Palau Islands of western Micronesia to the WH List, concentrating on the selection of prehistoric sites in the cultural section of the dossier. The Rock Islands–Southern Lagoon (RISL), the second site submitted by the Republic of Palau, is nominated due to international recognition of its outstanding natural and cultural attributes (Figure 1). In the case of the RISL nomination, archaeological expertise in tandem with traditional knowledge and local community involvement is providing the material necessary for cultural-site nomination and future management plans. The Rock Islands' cultural properties include non-monumental stone structures and ancient cultural deposits dominated by subsistence remains, both of which are attributes of archaeological sites on many Pacific Islands. The selection of OUV criteria and use of scientific data and traditional information in Palau's RISL dossier may be instructive, therefore, for future WH nominations in other parts of the Pacific.

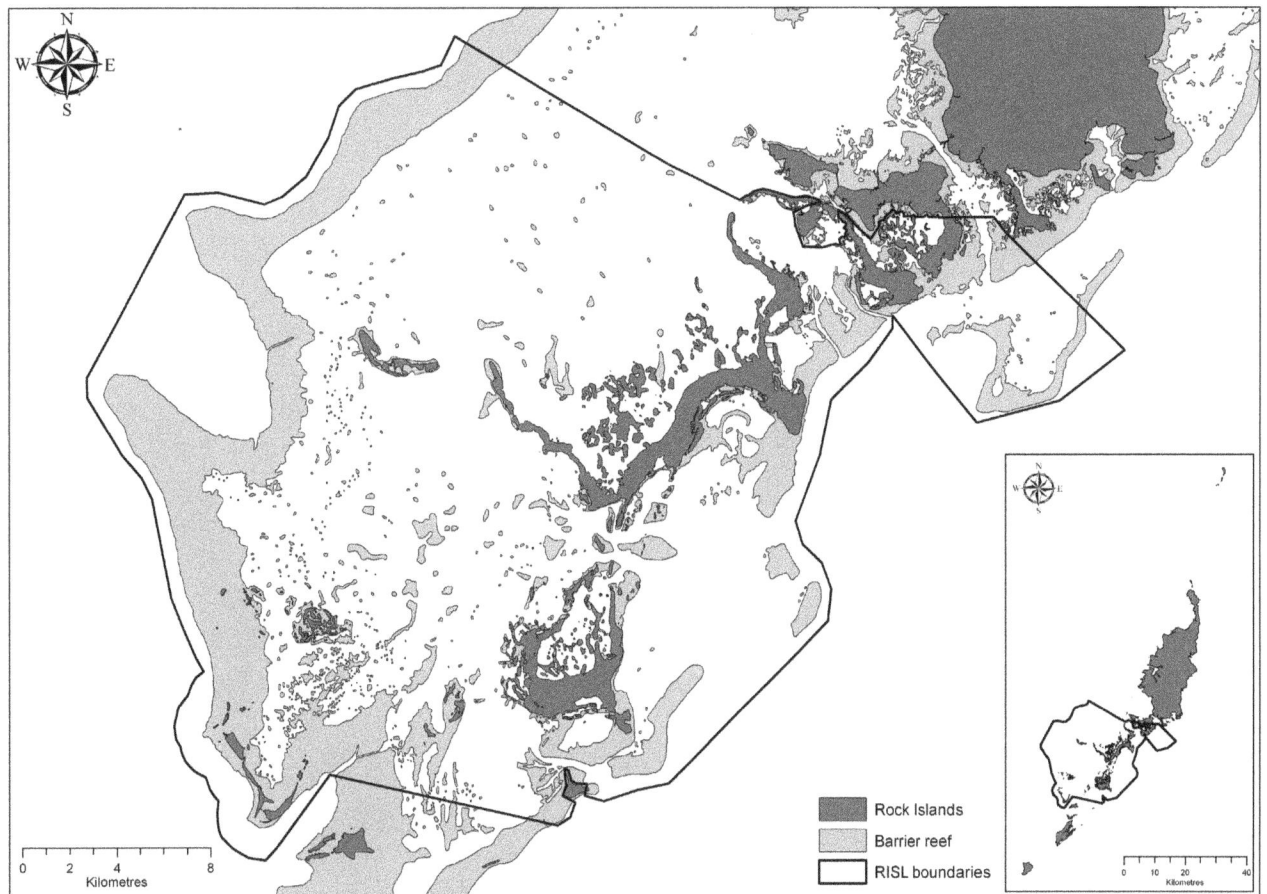

Figure 1. Location of the Rock Island Southern Lagoon area in the Republic of Palau being nominated as a mixed cultural-natural World Heritage site.

Site description

The Rock Island/Southern Lagoon area is located in the Pacific Island archipelago of Palau, 850 km north of West Papua in Indonesia and 900 km east of the island of Mindanao in the southern Philippines. Palau forms the southwestern island group of the Caroline Islands of Micronesia. The RISL site is located in Koror State, one of Palau's 16 states. The RISL site comprises 847 sq km of lagoon in which numerous small raised limestone islands are enclosed by nearly 200 km of barrier reef (Colin 2009).

The first Europeans to visit Palau noted that all of the limestone Rock Islands south of Malakal and north of Peleliu were uninhabited (Keate 1789). Palauans reported, however, that a population numbering in the thousands had once lived in the Southern Lagoon, with traces of their abandoned village sites found on many islands. Oral traditions frequently place the origin of social groups and the invention of customary practices in the limestone islands south of volcanic Babeldaob. The origin stories trace the migration of individuals, families and entire villages from the Rock Islands to contemporary villages on the large islands of Babeldaob, Oreor and Ngerekebesang, many of which have village names, chiefly titles and community deities retained from the original village site.

Archaeological investigation of Rock Island cultural sites began in the Japanese era with the collection of ceramics and artefacts from limestone caves (Suzuki 1938). Recording of Rock Island rock art, ceramics, artefacts and burial caves was included in the first systematic survey and excavation of prehistoric sites in Palau made by Douglas Osborne in 1953–1954 and 1968–1969 (Osborne 1966, 1979). Osborne identified several ancient village sites comprising stonework features such as walls, platforms, wells and trails associated with extensive deposits of marine food remains. The broad overview of prehistoric remains made by Osborne directed subsequent research by Takayama (1979), and extensive research by staff and PhD students from the Southern Illinois University (SIU) on several village sites in the Rock Islands (Masse 1989; Snyder 1989; Carucci 1992).

At the conclusion of the SIU investigations, the antiquity of human occupation in Palau was thought to extend to 2000 years ago, but subsequent projects on human burials and cultural deposits on Chelechol ra Orrak Island and Ulong Island have lengthened Palauan history to 3000 or more years (Fitzpatrick 2003a; Clark 2005; Liston 2005), similar in time to the expansion of early ceramic cultures into Island Southeast Asia and the western Pacific. The rugged terrain and large number of Rock Islands have prohibited complete archaeological survey, and many additional prehistoric sites, including stonework villages, Yapese stone money quarries, burial caves, rock art and early cultural deposits remain to be documented in the Southern Lagoon.

Based on current archaeological and historical investigations, it is possible to tentatively divide the Rock Island culture sequence into five phases, each associated with distinct artefactual remains, human behaviours and sets of environmental interactions (Clark 2005; Liston 2005, 2009; Phear et al. 2003; Masse et al. 2006; for a detailed characterisation of the cultural sequence, see Clark and Reepmeyer 2010). The culture sequence, although based on radiocarbon dates, is tentative, and is used to characterise prehistoric human occupation in the Rock Islands to understand the selection of specific OUV criteria.

Phase I: Colonisation and mobile encampment (3100–2700 years ago)
The first evidence for human activity in the Rock Islands dates to 3100 years ago on Ulong Island. At this time, sea level was declining, after being 1.5–1.8 m higher than it is today. Subsidence of the Palau archipelago (estimated at 0.6 mm/year by Dickinson and Athens 2007) ensured there were relatively few beaches and landing spots suitable for people to access the Rock Islands.

Excavated ceramic vessels consist of medium-sized red-slipped jars made with a mineral temper that was collected from volcanic or volcanic-limestone islands. Marine-resource use focused on the collection of large locally available clams (Tridacnidae) and inshore fish species. Island use was short-term and consistent with the presence of mobile camps that skimmed pristine stocks of marine foods from accessible Rock Island locations.

Phase II: Human burials and rock art (2700–1000 years ago)

Caves and shelters in the Rock Islands were consistently used for human burial for almost 2000 years (Osborne 1966; Fitzpatrick 2003a; Berger et al. 2008). Many of the larger caves contain multiple human remains while smaller caves appear to have been used for individual interments. Burials occasionally contain grave goods such as shallow bowls/dishes (grog tempered) marked with a red slip or paint, personal ornaments and knives/scrapers made of pearl shell, stone adzes and painted stones. Territorial rights might be represented in the placement of highly visible rock art in exposed locations, although some art was, like human burials, hidden from view in limestone caves. The most spectacular remaining art site is on Ulong Island where there is a large gallery of red painted art.

Continued use of the marine resources of the Rock Islands is indicated during this phase, but there is no evidence for permanent settlement until about 1300–1000 years ago when large *Strombus* shell middens were deposited. This suggests that the technological and cultural adaptations necessary for occupying harsh limestone landscapes had not yet developed before 1300 years ago and/or that an increasing population and possibly deteriorating social conditions made the Rock Islands appealing settlement locations about this time.

Phase III: Village settlement and intensified use of marine resources (1000–350 years ago)

Permanent villages may have first been established in the Rock Islands about 1000 years ago on indented sand plains, with trails connecting stone terraces, platforms and walls in the rugged limestone landscape. Location was strongly defensive, with high stone walls, some with an additional interior foot ledge, built across beaches that provided canoe access (Clark 2005:353). Defensive walls were also placed across trails connecting the coastal and interior parts of the village. Large or elaborate platforms and stonework consistent with social stratification and activity specialisation were built on high limestone points and ridges. Domestic space was generally focused on coastal sand plains, where house platforms and substantial midden remains were deposited. Burials were also made in sand plains and often in areas with stone structures, although cave burial might also have been practised. Swampy ground at the interface between the limestone bedrock and the coastal sand plain was used to grow swamp taro (*Cyrtosperma chamissonis*), as were damp sink holes, while tree crops such as coconut were grown on sand plains.

The overwhelming components of the prehistoric village deposit are fragments of marine shells and ceramic containers. The ceramic sherds are from large flanged-rim bowls made with crushed pottery temper. Marine shellfish and finfish were taken for food and shell was used to make domestic artefacts. Food shell mostly derives from small taxa, particularly *Strombus*, while large clams were collected from outer reefs and the shell was used to make adzes, pounders, knives and other utensils. The diversity and abundance of fish taxa increases in this phase, with pelagic species such as tuna (Scombridae) and mackerel sharks (Lamnidae) captured.

As the total Rock Island population size is estimated to have been 4000–6000 during the stonework village phase (Masse et al. 2006), the environmental impact of human occupation on the terrestrial and marine environments of the Southern Lagoon must have been substantial.

Phase IV: Village abandonment and Yapese stone money quarrying (350–100 years ago)

The Rock Islands were depopulated over several centuries, with relocation of groups to the large volcanic island of Babeldaob to the north and to the large platform-like reef islands of Peleliu and Angaur in the south. The tenuous economic conditions of limestone-island occupation are indicated by the inhabitants' dependence on pottery and food staples imported from the nearby volcanic islands. Abandonment of the Rock Islands had significant consequences for the remainder of the Palauan archipelago as village groups were incorporated into already established large and powerful socio-political structures, particularly in Koror.

After the migration of population to the volcanic islands, Yapese voyagers were drawn to the Rock Islands to quarry the limestone islands' calcite deposits to make stone disk money. Yapese stone money was valued according to its shape, weight and colour, and the effort involved in quarrying and transport. The money was displayed in Yap along the front of stone residential platforms to signal the status, power and prestige of the individual and clan (Fitzpatrick 2003b).

During Phase IV, the marine and terrestrial environments in the Southern Lagoon would probably have experienced some rejuvenation with the expansion of indigenous forest on now largely uninhabited limestone islands and less intensive collection of coral reef marine taxa.

Phase V: Colonial era and WWII effects on the Rock Islands (230–65 years ago)

In 1783, the East India packet, the *Antelope*, wrecked on Palau's western barrier reef. On the crew's return to England, the account of the newly 'discovered' Palauan people became, after James Cook's volumes, the most popular voyaging book of the late 18th century (Keate 1789). During its stay on Ulong Island, the *Antelope's* crew assisted the High Chief (*Ibedul*) of Koror to overcome his enemies on Babeldaob and Peleliu. In subsequent years, these favourable relations between the *Ibedul* and the foreigners assisted Koror in becoming Palau's central place, albeit under successive colonial administrations (Spain 1885–1889, Germany 1889–1914, Japan 1914–1945, United States 1945–1981).

As a result of US and Japanese forces garrisoning troops, concealing caches of military supplies, establishing defensive positions and mooring naval and supply ships, World War II had severe impacts on the Rock Island landscapes. Historical remains from the conflict range from small fragments of shrapnel, equipment and unexploded munitions to gun emplacements, troop shelters, sunken ships and planes (Bailey 1991). Many stonework defences constructed by Japanese military affected prehistoric Palauan stonework, and numerous caves and rock shelters were cleared of prehistoric remains by military forces.

Selection criteria for Outstanding Universal Value

The RISL area is nominated by the State Party under the criteria 'iii', 'v', 'vii', 'ix' and 'x', outlined in the operational guidelines for the implementation of the World Heritage Convention (UNESCO World Heritage Centre 2008:20–21). The selected natural criteria ('vii', 'ix' and 'x') focus on the exceptional natural beauty and biological/ecological diversity of the marine ecosystem. The Rock Island's marine lakes have specific ecosystems and endemic species which are emphasised along with the diversity of marine, terrestrial and coastal habitats.

Cultural OUV criteria are defined in the WHC operational guidelines as having 'cultural and/or natural significance which is so exceptional as to transcend national boundaries and to be of common importance for present and future generations of all humanity' (UNESCO World Heritage Centre 2008:14). For the RISL property, this is best represented in criteria 'iii' and 'v'. Although the RISL site was not mentioned in ICOMOS's thematic study on the Pacific (Smith and Jones 2007), it was decided by the State Party that the natural/cultural attributes of the

RISL site and its conservation needs merited nomination to the WH List.

The RISL area is nominated under OUV criterion 'iii' as a cultural landscape. The distinct environmental conditions of the raised-reef Rock Islands sustain a range of prehistoric sites (e.g. rock-art sites) and evidence for past cultural behaviour not preserved elsewhere in Palau. They incorporate aspects of an organic evolved relict landscape, as defined in Annex 3 of the operational guidelines (UNESCO World Heritage Centre 2008:86), in that intensive permanent settlement ended in the 17th–18th centuries. Within an archipelago continuously inhabited for at least three millennia, many of the Rock Island's archaeological sites and culturally significant places are recorded in oral history, myths, dances, proverbs and the traditional place names of its landscapes and seascapes. A connection with the seascape, seen in the archaeological record of human use, adaptation to, and reliance on the marine ecosystem, continues today.

Second, the RISL site is described as an associative cultural landscape in that the significant aesthetic and cultural values of the landscape are integral to the identity of the nation. The cultural landscape is central to national identity as articulated in traditional history, island place names and the origin-migration stories of Palauan people. In these traditional narratives, Palauans originated from ancestral settlements in the Rock Islands. It is from here that their ancestors subsequently moved to the larger volcanic and volcanic-limestone islands, such as Oreor and Babeldaob. Place names of the abandoned Rock Island village sites were retained by the transference of old names to new village sites during the migration. Examples include the association of stonework structures on Uchularois Island with the high chief Uchermelis ('high chief of the Ngemelis Group'), the transfer of place names from Ngermiich village on Ngeruktabel Island to Ngerekebesang Island after village relocation, and the perpetuation of place names at the abandoned village of Metukeruikull (e.g. Bai era Iechell and Iillebai) on Ngeruktabel Island.

Under cultural criteria 'v', the RISL site is nominated for its traditional human use of land and sea as representative of human interaction with the environment, especially when it has become vulnerable under the impact of irreversible change. Three human-environment responses are identified to support the nomination under criterion 'v': 1) evidence of climate change in the transition of the 'Medieval Warm Period' (MWP) to the 'Little Ice Age' (LIA), 2) human impact on the marine ecosystem, and 3) adaptation to a precarious environment. All of the responses are supported by scientific data, particularly the existing archaeological and palaeoclimate records.

Climate change

The abandonment of the Rock Islands in the second millennium AD is probably associated with population growth and climate change affecting a human society living in a marginal environment. The Rock Islands consist of small raised karst landmasses with sparse pockets of sand plains and suitable gardening soil. This terrestrial environment is highly susceptible to climatic fluctuations. Recurrent droughts limit the production of starchy crops in sink holes and on sand plains, while access to potable water is dependent on a high and consistent level of precipitation into the freshwater aquifer (the Ghyben-Herzberg lens). Recent studies on marine lake sediments in the Rock Islands indicate that the transition from the MWP to the LIA was associated with an increase in the frequency of ENSO events (Sachs et al. 2009), with its resulting decrease in precipitation. In addition to changes in precipitation regimes, El Niño/La Niña events disrupted marine organisms – especially subsistence taxa commonly collected by people – due to increased variability in tidal range, sea temperatures and nutrient concentration.

The vulnerability of prehistoric societies to periods of dramatic climate change such as the climatic optimum in the Medieval Warm Period (MWP) to the Little Ice Age (LIA) is included within the WH criterion 'v' concept of: 'landscape abandonment because of irreversible environmental change' (UNESCO World Heritage Centre 2008:20, Article 77). This is comparable to the relict landscape of the Mapungubwe Cultural Landscape in South Africa (R.S.A. Department of Environmental Affairs and Tourism 2002), where increasing droughts during the LIA in the 14th century limited the agricultural capacity of the land to sustain a large population. The direct consequence of climate change in Mapungubwe was the large-scale migration of people into neighbouring regions, which supported the rise of substantial political entities, particularly that of the World Heritage site of Great Zimbabwe (Zimbabwe). Similarly, in Palau, climate change restricted the subsistence capacity of the Rock Island population to a point where social fragmentation and migration resulted in a relict island landscape and the rise of more powerful political entities in other parts of Palau.

Human impact on the marine ecosystem

Human occupation and population growth has had negative effects on the biota of many islands in the Pacific and elsewhere (e.g. the Hawaiian Islands, Fiji, New Zealand, Mauritius, the Caribbean Islands) (Erlandson and Rick 2010). When combined with climatic factors, such ecosystem changes can have consequences that are catastrophic for human societies (e.g. suggested at Rapa Nui National Park [Chile] WH site) (ICOMOS 1994).

Scientific research on the prehistoric use of Palau's coral reefs has focused on the Rock Islands due to the generally benign preservation conditions of the limestone/calcareous sediments. Two archaeological sites have finfish and shellfish remains that record human use of marine resources for more than 3000 years. Assemblages from several sites date to the past 1000 years when stonework villages briefly flourished in the Rock Islands before the extinction of the stonework village system in the smaller islands. Over-harvesting of local marine resources is witnessed in the progressively smaller size of marine shellfish and inshore finfish remains through time (Masse et al. 2006; Ono and Clark 2010). The archaeological record correlates well with traditional Palauan explanations referring to resource deprivation and warfare as the primary causes of settlement extinction in the Rock Islands (Nero 1987; Masse 1989).

Adaptation to a precarious environment

The Rock Islands' cultural sequence is a three millennia long record of human adaptation to an environmentally depauperate landscape. In this, cultural sites in the Rock Islands can be compared with several other WH sites, such as the 2000-year human sequence of the St Kilda Archipelago in northern Scotland where the small population inhabiting a marginal environment was similarly reliant on a combination of wild foods (fish and sea birds) and small-scale agricultural production for its survival (ICOMOS 1985).

Adaptation to a precarious environment is evidenced by differentiation in the subsistence approach, village architecture and spatial organisation in contemporaneous Rock Island and volcanic island villages. The production of starchy root crops was very limited in the Rock Islands compared with the abundance of the Southern Lagoon's marine food resources. The stonework remains in the Rock Islands are less formal, smaller in scale and less diverse than volcanic-island village remains. Whereas in the volcanic-island villages, house platforms and terraces were largely organised according to a culturally prescribed plan, those in the limestone islands appear to be positioned according to the constraints of the unpredictable and rugged topography. The Rock Island villages were protected from attack by defensive walls guarding beach flats, trails and paths, while thick bands of mangrove forest protected villages on the volcanic islands. In summary, the differences indicate that the subsistence economy of the Rock Islands was highly specialised on marine foods, while the architectural remains indicate that village social structure was less hierarchical than village systems on volcanic islands.

Boundaries and buffers

The boundaries of the RISL site are defined by the extension of the barrier reef and the adjacent open ocean, or, as in the case of the southern and northern boundaries, through the Koror State's jurisdictional borders, excluding the urban area of Koror, which is Palau's economic and population centre. The RISL is legally owned by Koror State. As defined in Article 1 of the Palau Constitution, land sales and property development inside the RISL area are prohibited. The RISL has historically belonged to the clans of Koror and has been held in stewardship and guarded for the good of all by the Chiefs of Koror State (see below).

The use of buffer zones has been part of the nomination process of WH sites since the first version of the operational guidelines was published in 1977 (Martin and Piatti 2009:25). They were implemented to add an additional layer of protection for core zones of WH properties. Buffer zones are usually areas adjacent to the WH core zone which have defined legal and/ or customary restrictions (Martin and Piatti 2009:60–61). In the operational guidelines, buffer zones are still exclusively linked with this function (UNESCO World Heritage Centre 2008:26, Articles 103–105). However, according to an ICOMOS position paper on buffer zones (ICOMOS 2009:23), these zones have evolved from their original context to interaction zones around WH sites which provide a linkage between the OUV of the core area and socio-economic development outside of the WH zone.

Since the recognition of the first WH site involving communal land on East Rennell in the Solomon Islands in 1998, conflict over land rights has been a perpetual issue, particularly in buffer zones. Buffer zones are defined in the operational guidelines as not being part of the WH site, however modifications to this zone are subject to the approval of the World Heritage Committee (UNESCO World Heritage Centre 2008:27, Article 107). Wilson et al. (2007; also Waters 2009) have discussed problems over the sale and related economic development of land surrounding the Chief Roi Mata's Domain WH site in Vanuatu.

In the nomination file of September 2010, no buffer zones were proposed for the RISL as the current boundaries are perceived to be adequate for the protection of the property. The eastern and western boundaries are surrounded by open ocean and the southern boundary borders a conservation zone administered by Peleliu State. The northern boundary, particularly that bordering the highly urbanised area of Koror, is managed through the RISL Area Management Plan 2004–2008, which places restrictions on property development, waste management and pollution, access and infrastructure (cf. Table 1). Key indicators for monitoring conservation and general impacts on the WH sites are defined in Table 2. In general, key indicators are evaluated annually. Exceptions are made for certain indicators, which are evaluated on a five-year frequency.

Stakeholders

An emerging issue for Pacific Island nations is tension between traditional/community structures and government/federal organisations over WH property site/land. The nomination of the RISL area is an example of the necessity of properly informing decision makers about the WH concept and the consequences of implementing UNESCO cultural-heritage values. The RISL area is perceived in Palau as a premier site incorporating both natural and cultural attributes of

Table 1. Management restrictions applicable to all zones.

Prohibition of any new mining and dredging activities
No entry to foreign commercial fishing vessels and other large vessels such as large luxury boats, commercial cruise liners, cargo and military ships (excluding registered live aboard boats), except in designated channels/routes
No entry by foreign yachts and boats, except in designated channels/routes, without a cruising permit from Koror State
Harvesting restrictions (seasons, size limits and methods) designated in national and state laws
No removal of cultural and historical artefacts (protected by national monument legislation)
No damage allowed to any portion of the coral reef ecosystem (e.g. via anchoring, resource harvesting or ship grounding)
No harvest of timber, except for cultural purposes with permit from Koror State
Dumping of trash is prohibited; all litter must be removed from land and marine areas
Use of personal water craft (jet skis) is restricted to designated watersport zones
Tourists require a valid Rock Island Permit to undertake recreational activities in any zone
Only approved structures/facilities in support of flood and erosion prevention, conservation activities, and visitor use as defined in the Koror State 'CD' conservation zone can be built on the Rock Islands
No domestic animals (cats, dogs, monkeys) may be brought to the Rock Islands at any time

Outstanding Universal Value. However, the site nomination was delayed because of uncertainty about the legislative impact of the WH status on public access to the area (an issue addressed at the 2007 Study Tour for Leaders from Micronesia, http://whc.unesco.org/en/events/346/) and the relatively recent recognition in OUV of associative cultural landscapes of non-monumental character.

The inscription of the RISL site as a mixed property was initiated and led by Adalbert Eledui of Koror State's Division of Coastal Management, with support of the House of Traditional Leaders, those chiefs traditionally associated with the RISL. The Bureau of Arts and Culture within Palau's Ministry of Community and Cultural Affairs and the Palau National Commission for UNESCO assisted in the process. Participation of traditional landowners in the process of WH nomination, management and conservation is actively encouraged by the World Heritage Convention (UNESCO 1972, Article 14). Acknowledging that many Palauans migrated from the RISL, criterion 'iii' of the operational guidelines featured prominently in the nomination file. A historical connection with ancestral sites in the Rock Islands is preserved in the retention of chiefly titles brought from the Rock Islands to other parts of Palau, especially Koror. The people of Ngerchemai village in Koror, for example, used to live in Rock Island villages, and after assisting Koror to defeat its enemies in the RISL, they were allowed to settle and garden on the fertile volcanic island. The Ngerchemai chiefs kept their former titles, and along with Koror State, have been key stakeholders involved in managing and preserving the Rock Islands.

Uncertainty about the impact of a WH nomination to access and stewardship of the RISL resulted in a series of meetings between Palau's Bureau of Arts and Culture, Koror State and the House of Traditional Leaders, and the chiefs have been seeking legal clarification about the ownership of the RISL. Pacific Islanders have strong ancestral, economic and cultural ties to the environment and are particularly sensitive to potential changes in access and ownership of the land and sea, like those involved in the nomination of a property to the WH List in the Pacific. It is important to note that the traditional chiefs promoted the cultural values of the RISL during its nomination to the WH List as a mixed natural-cultural property. Nomination of Pacific cultural sites to the WH List is likely to coincide with ongoing negotiation, and at times tension, between groups traditionally associated with a nominated area, and the government/

Table 2. Key Indicators for measuring state of conservation.

Indicator	Periodicity	Location of records
Biophysical status		
Coastal habitat coverage (km²)	Ground truthing/spot annual checks	PALARIS, PICRC
Forest cover (km²)	Ground truthing/spot checks annual	PALARIS
Marine lake species (list species)	Annual	CRRF
Marine lake species (no. jellyfish/area)	Annual	CRRF
Extent invasive species in marine lakes (no. species / area)	Annual	CRRF
Reef substrate/Benthic community structure (% cover)	Annual	PICRC
Coral recruitment (no./area)	Annual	PICRC
Fish species (no. species/area)	Annual	PICRC
Fish abundance (no./area)	Annual	PICRC
Sea turtles (no./area)	Annual	PICRC
Sea turtle nesting sites	Every five years	Ministry of Natural Resources
Environment and tourism		
Crocodiles (no.)	Every five years	Koror State
Dugong (no.)	Every five years	Koror State
Fruit Bats (no./station)	Annual	Belau National Museum
Birds (no./station)	Annual	Belau National Museum
Plants (no. *Ponapea*)	Annual	Ministry of Natural Resources
Water quality (turbidity, nutrients)	Annual	EQPB
Cultural site integrity		
No./% sites documented/inventoried	Annual	Koror State/Cultural Affairs
Presence/absence of documented removable artefacts	Annual	Koror State/Cultural Affairs
% sites restored	Annual	Koror State/Cultural Affairs
% sites with documented visitor damage	Annual	Koror State/Cultural Affairs
% sensitive sites with restricted access	Annual	Koror State/Cultural Affairs
Socioeconomic status		
Perception of resource (% categorisation)	Every five years	Koror State
Resource use patterns	Every five years	Koror State
% buy-in	Every five years	Koror State
Household income distribution by source	Annual	Office of Statistics
No. visitors	Monthly	Koror State
Threats		
Invasive species (presence/absence, no.)	Annual	Koror State
Visitor impacts	Annual	Koror State
Management effectiveness		
Level of funding	Annual	Koror State
No. staff/no. empty staff positions	Annual	Koror State
No. citations	Annual	Koror State
Presence/absence authorised management plan	Annual	Koror State

state entities responsible for managing a proposed WH property.

As a relict landscape, the cultural sites in the RISL have high integrity, with several ancient settlements in pristine condition. This is an additional argument for OUV status in the nomination dossier. The rugged terrain of the islands restricts access to many sites, and there is limited knowledge of the location of cultural sites by the general public. Hence, most of these sites receive few visitors and are therefore relatively well preserved. Land use for recreation is largely restricted to selected coastal sites monitored and managed regularly by Koror State; however, in some of these areas there has also been substantial prehistoric human impact.

A concern in promoting the OUV of cultural sites in the RISL area is the possible impact that WH status might have on the preservation of these same sites. It is assumed that limited public knowledge of archaeological sites restricts vandalism and potential illegal antiquity sales. At publicly known sites, both activities occur very occasionally, such as the recent graffiti at the Ulong rock-art site and the illegal removal of Yapese stone money. The nomination dossier proposed three objectives for cultural-heritage management which focus on sustaining the RISL landscape. The first objective involves a detailed survey of prehistoric sites in the RISL, managing access to key sites and providing educational material and general information for RISL cultural sites. The second objective is to strengthen and enhance the cultural aspect of the RISL visitor experience. Actions involved in developing a more sustainable visitor flow include: a) cultural site training for Koror State Rangers, and possibly extending this training to tourist operators, b) upgrading current visitor infrastructure at 'arrival points' with explanatory signage located at cultural sites, and c) construction of guided pathways from 'arrival points' to the periphery of prehistoric sites to avoid visitor impact on the cultural resources. The third objective is to protect sensitive and fragile cultural sites such as rock-art panels and burial caves by prohibiting visitation.

Tourism is a major source of income for Palau's economy. An issue for the future management of the RISL area will be the conflicting economic interests of different stakeholders. The relatively unspoiled nature of the environmental and cultural aspects of the RISL are under threat from an increasing number of tourists, especially package tours from East Asian countries (Marino et al. 2008:516, Table 16.3).

The initiation of the WH bid derived, in part, from recognition of the negative effect that mass tourism is having on the integrity of the RISL area. It is hoped that the branding of the RISL as a WH site, accompanied by a potential increase in entrance fees, might diversify future increases in the package-tour component to other states in the archipelago, subsequently minimising degradation of premier sites in the RISL. This approach might also include marketing of the RISL area as an environmentally sustainable and upmarket tourist experience.

Conclusion

In this paper, we have outlined the recent Rock Islands–Southern Lagoon submission to the World Heritage List. The WH List and criteria of Outstanding Universal Value is a relatively new field for natural and cultural scientists, conservationists and decision makers to comprehend in the developing island nations of the Pacific. Although Pacific heritage research has been directly involved in reshaping notions of OUV, the implications of adding associative cultural landscapes of non-monumental character to the WH List are not yet fully understood, and are seen in the delay of the RISL site submission to the Tentative List.

The main cause for the under-representation of Pacific cultural sites on the WH List lies in the limited human resources available to develop and support site nomination. The past decade of detailed research into the Pacific's prehistory is delivering new evidence about potential WH properties in the region that might realistically fulfil the OUV criteria, as well as providing significant information about the integrity and authenticity of cultural properties, needed for long-term site management. This mounting knowledge has helped boost the number of sites nominated to the Tentative List by Pacific nations to 38, including the RISL site.

It has been emphasised that archaeological data is required to establish the significance of non-monumental sites, particularly cultural landscapes in the Pacific. The RISL area, with its 3000-year-long history of human occupation, is a prime example of a relict island landscape. The exceptional preservation conditions of the RISL derive from the limestone environment, but also from the abandonment of the islands in the 17th–18th centuries AD, with no later permanent habitation. As a result there was surviving archaeological evidence for the intensification of prehistoric human settlement combined with an increasing reliance on marine resources at the same time that climate data indicated that Rock Island occupation would have been increasingly difficult to sustain. OUV criteria 'iii' and 'v' were applicable because they focused on the non-monumental character of cultural sites. The importance of migration traditions following the abandonment of the Rock Islands is emphasised as they are fundamental to the national identity of many Palauans.

Our experience suggests that the number of WH sites in the Pacific will grow primarily through the establishment of information networks comprising foreign and local researchers, community groups and government agencies. Such groups can assemble the required WH documentation and develop realistic and sustainable management plans for potential properties. Support of WH nominations in the Pacific might also be encouraged by the greater involvement of developed nations which have long and continuing relationships with the islands and peoples of Oceania, as well as nations such as China and India which are increasingly involved in the region.

References

Berger, L.R., Churchill, S.E., De Klerk, B. and Quinn, R.L. 2008. Small-Bodied Humans from Palau, Micronesia. *PLoS One* 3(3):e1780. doi:10.1371/journal.pone.0001780.

Bailey, D.E. 1991. *WW II wrecks in Palau.* North Valley Diver Publications, Redding, California.

Carucci, J. 1992. Cultural and natural patterning in prehistoric marine foodshell from Palau, Micronesia. Unpublished PhD thesis. Southern Illinois University, Carbondale.

Clark, G.R. 2005. A 3000-year culture sequence from Palau, western Micronesia, *Asian Perspectives* 44:349–380.

Clark, G.R. and Reepmeyer, C. 2010. World Heritage Rock Island Dossier: Cultural sites. Report to The Palau National Commission for UNESCO for the nomination of the Rock Islands–Southern Lagoon area to the World Heritage List. The Australian National University, Canberra.

Colin, P.L. 2009. *Marine environments of Palau.* Indo-Pacific Press, San Diego, California.

Dickinson, W. and Athens, J. 2007. Holocene paleoshoreline and paleoenvironmental history of Palau: Implications for human settlement. *The Journal of Island and Coastal Archaeology* 2(2):175–196.

Erlandson, J.M. and Rick, T.C. 2010. Archaeology meets marine ecology: The antiquity of maritime cultures and human impacts on marine fisheries and ecosystems. *Annual Review of Marine Science* 2:231–251.

Fitzpatrick, S.M. 2003a. Early human burials in the western Pacific: Evidence for a ca. 3000 year old occupation on Palau. *Antiquity* 77:719–731.

Fitzpatrick, S.M. 2003b. Stones of the butterfly: Archaeological investigation of Yapese stone money quarries in Palau, western Caroline Islands, Micronesia. Unpublished PhD thesis. University of Oregon, Eugene.

Fowler, P.J. 2003. *World Heritage cultural landscapes 1992–2002.* World Heritage papers (6). UNESCO World Heritage Centre, Paris.

Fowler, P.J. 2004. Landscape and world heritage. In: Fowler, P.J. (ed), *Landscapes for the world: Conserving a global heritage*, pp. 1–14. Windgather Press, Bollington.

ICOMOS. 1985. St Kilda, Advisory Body Evaluation, 31 December 1985. http://whc.unesco.org/ archive/advisory_body_evaluation/387bis.pdf (accessed: 20/05/2010).

ICOMOS. 1994. Rapa Nui National Park, Advisory Body Evaluation, 13 June 1994. http://whc. unesco.org/archive/advisory_body_evaluation/387bis.pdf (accessed: 18/08/2010).

ICOMOS. 2005. *The World Heritage list: Filling the gaps – an action plan for the future, monuments and sites (XII).* International Secretariat of ICOMOS, Paris.

ICOMOS. 2009. ICOMOS Position Paper. In: Martin, O. and Piatti, G. (eds), *World heritage and buffer zones: International expert meeting on world heritage and buffer zones in Davos, Switzerland 11 – 14 March 2008* with contributions of Rössler, M., Fuchs C. and Delsol, C. World Heritage papers (25), pp. 23–57. UNESCO World Heritage Centre, Paris.

Keate, G. 1789. *An account of the Pelew Islands, situated in the western part of the Pacific Ocean. Composed from the journals and communications of Captain Henry Wilson and some of his officers, who, in August 1783, were there shipwrecked, in the Antelope, a packet belonging to the Honourable East India company*, 3rd edition, London.

Liston, J. 2005. An assessment of radiocarbon dates from Palau, western Micronesia. *Radiocarbon* 47:295–354.

Liston, J. 2009. Cultural chronology of earthworks in Palau, Western Micronesia. *Archaeology in Oceania* 44:56–73.

Marino, S., Bauman, A., Miles, J., Kitalong, A.H., Bukurou, A., Mersai, C., Verheij, E., Olkeriil, I., Basilius, K., Colin, P.L., Patris, S., Victor, S., Andrew, W. and Golbuu, Y. 2008. The state of coral reef ecosystems of the Republic of Palau. In: Waddel, J.E. and Clarke, A.M. (eds), The state of coral reef ecosystems of the United States and Pacific Freely Associated States: 2008, *NOAA Technical Memorandum NOS NCCOS* 73:511–540. NOAA/NCCOS Center for Coastal Monitoring and Assessment's Biogeography Team, Silver Spring, Maryland.

Martin, O. and Piatti, G. (eds), 2009. *World heritage and buffer zones: International expert meeting on world heritage and buffer zones in Davos, Switzerland 11 – 14 March 2008* with contributions of Rössler, M., Fuchs, C. and Delsol, C. World Heritage papers (25). UNESCO World Heritage Centre, Paris.

Masse, W.B. 1989. *The archaeology and ecology of fishing in the Belau Islands, Micronesia.* Unpublished PhD thesis. Southern Illinois University, Carbondale.

Masse, W.B., Liston, J., Carrucci, J. and Athens, J.S. 2006. Evaluating the effects of climate change on environment, resource depletion, and culture in the Palau Islands between AD 1200 and 1600. *Quaternary International* 151:106–132.

Nero, K.L. 1987. *A cherechar a lokelii: Beads of history of Koror, Palau, 1783–1983.* Unpublished PhD thesis. University of California, Berkeley.

Ono, R. and Clark, C. 2010. A 2500-year record of marine resource use on Ulong Island, Republic of Palau. *International Journal of Osteoarchaeology* DOI: 10.1002/oa.1226.

Osborne, D. 1966. The archaeology of the Palau Islands. *Bernice P. Bishop Museum Bulletin* 230. Bishop Museum Press, Honolulu.

Osborne, D. 1979. Archaeological test excavations Palau Islands 1968–1969. *Micronesia Supplement* (1), University of Guam, Guam.

Phear, S., Clark, G.R. and Anderson, A. 2003. A ^{14}C Chronology for Palau. In: Sand, C. (ed), *Pacific Archaeology: assessments and prospects. Proceedings of the International Conference for the 50th anniversary of the first Lapita Excavation, Koné–Nouméa 2002, Les Cahiers de L'Archéologie en Nouvelle-Calédonie,* pp. 255–263, Museum of New Caledonia, Noumea.

R.S.A. Department of Environmental Affairs and Tourism. 2002. *Mapungubwe cultural landscape – World Heritage nomination dossier,* January 2002. http://whc.unesco.org/uploads/nominations/1099.pdf (accessed: 19/07/2010).

Sachs, J.P., Sachse, D., Smittenberg, R.H., Zhang, Z., Battisti, D.S. and Golubic, S. 2009. Southward movement of the Pacific intertropical convergence zone AD 1400–1850. *Nature Geoscience* 2:519–525.

Smith, A. and Jones, K. 2007. *Cultural landscapes of the Pacific Islands: ICOMOS thematic study.* International Secretariat of ICOMOS, Paris.

Snyder, D. 1989. Towards chronometric models for Palauan prehistory: Ceramic attributes. Unpublished PhD thesis, Southern Illinois University, Carbondale.

Suzuki, M. 1938. One example indicating the situation of recovery of the artifacts in Palau. *Nanpou* 5:53–61 (in Japanese).

Takayama, J. 1979. Archaeological investigation of PAAT-2 in the Palaus: An interim report. In: Kusakabe, H. (ed), *Report, cultural anthropological research on the folk culture in the Western Caroline islands of Micronesia in 1977,* pp. 81–103. The Committee for Micronesian Research, Tokyo University of Foreign Studies, Tokyo.

Titchen, S. 1996. On the construction of 'outstanding universal value': Some comments on the implementation of the 1972 UNESCO World Heritage Convention. *Conservation and Management of Archaeological Sites* 1:235–242.

UNESCO. 1972. *The World Heritage Convention*, Paris.

UNESCO World Heritage Centre. 2004. Action plan: World Heritage – Pacific 2009 Programme. http://whc.unesco.org/uploads/activities/documents/activity-6-1.pdf (accessed: 04/11, 2010).

UNESCO World Heritage Centre. 2008. Operational Guidelines for the Implementation of the World Heritage Convention (WHC. 08/01). UNESCO World Heritage Centre, Paris.

UNESCO World Heritage Centre. 2010a. World Heritage List. http://whc.unesco.org/en/list (accessed: 04/11, 2010).

UNESCO World Heritage Centre. 2010b. Cultural Landscape. http://whc.unesco.org/en/culturallandscape (accessed: 04/11, 2010).

Waters, J. 2009. Heritage council demands Vanuatu explain bulldozing. ABC News, 10/05, http://www.abc.net.au/news/stories/2009/05/10/2565765.htm.

Wilson, M., Ballard, C. and Kalotti, D. 2007. Chief Roi Mata's domain: Challenges facing a World Heritage-nominated property in Vanuatu. Paper presented at the session: Cultural Heritage Management in the Pacific, 21 July 2007. ICOMOS 2007 conference.

8

The complexity of an archaeological site in Samoa
The past in the present

Helene Martinsson-Wallin
Gotland University, Visby, Sweden

Introduction

This paper discusses post-colonial perspectives on archaeology and studies of materiality in the Pacific. It uses the Pulemelei investigations at Letolo plantation on Savai'i Island in Samoa as a case study, including events and activities that have taken place after the completion of archaeological research (Martinsson-Wallin 2007). These investigations shed light on the entanglement of values and actions in the performance of past and present power relations.

Archaeology is a relatively young science in the Pacific, developed mainly in the 20th century. Extensive archaeological excavations were not initiated until the 1940s–1950s (Gifford 1951; Gifford and Shutler 1956; Emory et al. 1959; Heyerdahl and Ferdon 1961; Emory and Sinoto 1965), but initial ethnological, anthropological and linguistic studies were made in the 18th and 19th centuries. Before these approaches, traditional history and mythology provided the primary explanation for the origin, migration and structure of contemporary societies in Oceania. The traditional history of Pacific Islanders does not separate the past from the present, as does much archaeological research, and the 'past' is seen as living within contemporary culture. There is therefore a divide between a classical evolutionary and a contextual way of looking at culture and the 'past'.

The post-processual archaeological perspective of the 1980s opined that the 'past' does not exist in its own right, but is excavated, related and interpreted in relation to the present, including to many subjective elements of contemporary culture (Hodder 1986; Shanks and Tilley 1987). This approach appears to partly bridge the traditional and scientific views of history, but it has also generated a style of archaeology that deprecates analytical methods and interprets the prehistoric material-culture record by comparison with behaviours seen in contemporary societies that may be quite different to those found in prehistory. The end result is an individualistic and deterministic form of history. Instead, I argue here that the 'past' of Oceania was collective, family based and multivocal, and archaeological methods and the study of material culture add greatly to the understanding of past events and cultural processes.

Post-colonial archaeology

The Polynesian islands are among the most recently populated places in the world. Since the colonisation of these islands by humans in prehistory, many events have shaped and reshaped island societies. These events include exchange, interaction and colonialism, which can creolise societies, but contacts can also produce multiculturalism, separatism, cohabitation and apartheid (Vergès 1999:166). Gosden (2004) stresses the importance of material-culture studies to better understand how colonialism changes societies. He suggests that consumption is a vital factor to determine when relations are built within and between cultures. Earlier approaches such as world-system and core-periphery theory have been used to determine the archaeological impact of colonial movements but have been criticised, since they use modern economic behaviour to interpret consumption (Gosden 2004:7).

In recent years, there has been a focus on post-colonial archaeology, which aims to create an alternative history from that of the colonisers by focusing on the indigenous people. The colonisers and the colonised are in one way connected, but they are also historically and culturally separated from each other. This creates ambiguity in the post-colonial discourse so that questions about the location of culture arise between individuals and groups (Gosden 2004). The aim of post-colonial discourse is the writing of an alternative history that is conscious of the colonial situation. It does not entail a dualistic standpoint, but acknowledges the hybrid nature of social action and material expression (Van Dommelen 2006).

The post-colonial approach was forcefully presented by Said (1978) in his book *Orientalism*, and has been applied by Spivak (2002) and Bhabha (2004). Their discourse has been of a textual nature and material expressions have not been a focus. Gosden (2004:4) makes the point that: 'colonialism is crucially a relationship with material culture, which is spatially extensive ... and destabilising of older values so changing all concerned – incomers and natives. It is less to do with production and exchange, unlike in old models, and more centred on consumption.' Gosden (2004) suggests a comparative model which examines the materialisation of symbolic power in various regions rather than in the colonies alone. Archaeology can contribute to the understanding of various colonial formations over long periods, since colonialism itself has a great antiquity. Archaeology also has a major role to play in investigating materiality at broad and local scales. Local agency, for instance, can be examined from the exchange of material goods between the coloniser and the colonised through the different meanings and values each place on categories and types of materiality.

Symbolic power is significant as religions/belief systems changed during the colonial contact phase. Creolisation or hybridisation at the cognitive level and the material expressions attached to this are especially interesting as they create meaning which is both a part of the local production/consumption system but also reaches beyond this to the systems of the coloniser/ colonised. With culture contact came culture change, especially the introduction of Christianity to Samoa, and there is today a hierarchy among the congregations of Samoa, with the LMS (London Missionary Society), which was the first to arrive and convert the 'natives', ranked as the 'original' and most prestigious congregation.

Samoan history

In Samoa, there has been interest in finding the 'original' or 'oldest' version of Samoan oral tradition taken down by European explorers and missionaries (Meleisea 1980; Krämer 1994). There is also a focus on 'traditional' Samoan culture, rather than the modern one that is heavily influenced by European lifestyles and values. Meleisea (1980:27) has suggested that this can cause Samoans to think of their culture as ancient instead of something lived today. The essential elements of the 'ancient' Samoan culture then have to be protected so that Samoan values are not lost. Meleisea further suggests (1980:28) there is confusion between history and culture in Samoa that has to be sorted out. Culture is something that is relative and lived (i.e. *fa'asamoa*) and therefore cannot be lost, although it constantly changes and evolves, in contrast to history, which consists of specific events and traditions/behaviours from the 'past' that if not protected can be lost. Unlike New Caledonia, which is a multicultural society with past inputs from several Pacific Islander and European groups (Sand et al. 2005), one would think it should be straightforward to present an overarching Samoan past, but as history is very much family based and tied to land and titles, with identity tied to *fa'asamoa*, there is a dense set of social and exchange relations among and between families that makes the telling and presentation of a 'Samoan history' highly complicated.

Cultural heritage

In society today, the most obvious functions of cultural heritage are to establish and support cultural identity. The use of cultural heritage to legitimise and promote group identity and political activities is clear (Aplin 2002) and needs to be recorded (Lilly 2005). In the Pacific area, there can be divisions between 'colonial' heritage and 'indigenous' heritage that are problematic. Smith (2005) has discussed the town of Levuka, Fiji's first colonial capital, situated on Ovalau Island. Even if Ovalau is considered to be national heritage and recognised as a tourist attraction, it has been difficult to determine a management plan and allocate funding, since the property is associated with processes of European colonisation. Should the protection and preservation of such sites be a government priority in post-colonial Fiji?

Karlström (2005:4–5) notes that in relation to the UNESCO World Heritage convention: 'The question is – how a global organisation, which operates according to general guidelines, can recognize and appreciate the complexity and diversity of the cultural expression that it seeks to protect.' post-colonial agendas have been used both to confront and to reconcile, but to move forward it is also necessary to raise the level of education and awareness of the past within the frameworks of traditional and scientific culture heritage. In many parts of the world these issues are complicated by migration, interaction and colonisation, which have created partly creolised societies. Even in Pacific Islands, complexity is apparent concerning archaeology, archaeological sites and issues about heritage management, and I use my scientific investigations at the large Pulemelei mound and extensive prehistoric settlement at Letolo plantation on Savai'i as a case study to illustrate the different approaches to the past in Samoa.

The relationship between European colonisation and post-colonial discourse is more subtle in Samoa than in Fiji, New Caledonia, French Polynesia, Rapa Nui and several Micronesian states as there is no overt tension between the indigenous people and later migrants/colonists. Samoa is populated and governed by Samoans, but the society is affected by past colonial oppression, the introduction of Christianity and social and economic influences of modernity and globalisation. Archaeology programs were introduced just after independence in 1962, which potentially could have supported nation building and the creation of a Samoan identity. However, the social structure marked by a kinship-based title system that is tied to customary land tenure and a semi-autonomous village structure has so far had little engagement with archaeology. The cultural heritage is comprised mainly of the oral traditions and customs denoted as *fa'asamoa*. Studies of the material remains of Samoa's past are not widely viewed as historically significant.

The Pulemelei mound excavations and aftermaths

The archaeology of Samoa (excluding American Samoa) is confined to the archaeological program initiated by Roger Green and Janet Davidson in the 1960s and excavations by Jennings and colleagues in the 1970s. (Green and Davidson 1969, 1974; Jennings et al. 1976; Jennings and Holmer 1980; Jennings et al. 1982). A re-evaluation of the archaeology of Samoa by Green (2002) provides a general understanding of Samoan prehistoric society, with reviews of archaeology by Martinsson-Wallin (2007) and investigations of the mound tradition (Martinsson-Wallin et al. 2007). Most research to date has focused on the island of 'Upolu, including the first and so far only site featuring Lapita pottery (Jennings 1974; Leach and Green 1989; Petchey 2001).

In 2002, I initiated an archaeological project with colleagues at the large Pulemelei mound on the extensive Letolo prehistoric settlement in the southwest part of Savai'i (Figure 1). The Letolo plantation is one of the few large 'freehold' properties in Samoa and is owned by O.F. Nelson and Co. Ltd. This was the first major archaeological excavation on the island, but an extensive survey of the Letolo plantation had been made by US Peace Corps volunteer Gregory Jackmond in 1977–1978. The survey data and other surveys of prehistoric settlement in Savai'i and 'Upolu had been used to compare the prehistoric settlement pattern with the post-European settlement pattern (Jennings et al. 1982). During the European contact period, the large inland settlements at Letolo, Sapapali'i, Mount Olo and Falefa'a valley were depopulated, indicating a shift from extensive use of inland zones to an extensive use of near-costal locations (Davidson 1979).

The purpose of the project at the Pulemelei mound was to investigate the origin and development of monumental architecture in West Polynesia. The rise of Polynesian chiefdoms and

Figure 1. East view of Pulemelei mound during excavations 2004.

the relationship between the monument-building traditions of West Polynesia and East Polynesia was also investigated (Wallin 1993; Martinsson-Wallin 1994, 2007; Clark and Martinsson-Wallin 2007). Activities at the Pulemelei site involved clearing vegetation from the mound so that it could be properly mapped, geophysical survey and archaeological excavations. Training for local students in field techniques and the heritage management of a prehistoric monument impacted by tourism were also involved (Figure 2).

Since the Letolo copra plantation had not been active for the past 25 years, there was heavy vegetation growth over the multitude of prehistoric mounds, walls, walkways and raised rim earth ovens that had been surveyed by Jackmond in the 1970s. The plantation includes the large Pulemelei mound, which measures some 65 m x 60 m x 12 m, and is located about 2 km from the coast. The Pulemelei stone mound and surrounding area was initially surveyed and mapped during the 1960s (Scott 1969), but only a small trench some distance from the main mound was excavated. The Pulemelei mound when cleared of vegetation was exposed, allowing a deeper understanding of its monumentality and strategic location on the landscape. The excavations indicated that the Pulemelei mound and surrounding area comprise a complex prehistoric site. At least 2000 years of human occupation were uncovered in the archaeological research. The mound itself is likely to have been built around 700–900 years ago and was used, added to and re-used in various phases, until being abandoned in the past 200–300 years (Martinsson-Wallin et al. 2003, 2005, 2007).

The exposure of the Pulemelei mound and archaeological finds recovered from the site triggered renewed interest in the prehistoric past from different quarters. Before excavations in 2003, the landowners suggested a ceremony should be carried out at the Pulemelei mound.

Figure 2. Ms Siumaga Setisefano and Helene Martinsson-Wallin taking soil samples during excavations at Pulemelei mound in 2004.

The *asi* (sandalwood) ceremony was a purification and holy oil ritual that took place at sunset and at sunrise. The proposed reason was to lift the *tapu* of the mound in case human remains were found during excavation (Tamasese 2003). In performing the ceremony, the mound was transformed into a contemporary monument. There were numerous aspects to the ritual, including indigenous religious revival and the bridging of new and old religions (Tamasese 2003, 2007). Other interests could be interpreted in terms of land ownership related to local and national politics, while the view that the Pulemelei mound was an ancient diaspora site from which West Polynesians left to settle East Polynesia might be seen as supporting pan-Polynesian connections. The purpose of the ritual was transmitted through the involvement of local and national chiefs and the national and international media.

The land in Samoa is for the most part customary land, owned by villages (Ward and Ashcroft 1998). During the European contact phase with Germany, and especially when Samoa was governed by Germany, large parts of the land were sold to foreigners. By the end of the 19th century, freehold land was regulated by the Berlin Act of 1889 (Ward and Ashcroft 1998). According to the Berlin Act, only 7–8% of Samoa's land was considered freehold. The Letolo plantation has long been freehold land, but ownership of it has been disputed. It belongs formally to O.F. Nelson and Co. Ltd. and probably came to the Swedish merchant August Nelson when he married a chief's daughter, Sina Masoe, from Safune, about 100 years ago. The *matai* (chiefs) of the nearby village of Vailoa of the Palauli district claim the Letolo plantation is traditional land belonging to their village, a view which has caused major conflict. This view has been prevalent particularly since the copra plantation ceased to operate on a large scale and many locals employed on the plantation lost their income. Disputes and even violence occurred between the current landowners and Vailoa village before the archaeological excavations and after the *asi* ceremony. A new archaeological project at the Pulemelei site in 2004 initiated opposing action from the *matai* of Vailoa and put a stop to the excavations, and in a separate incident, the burning down of the plantation manager's house in April 2005 and the taking of cattle from plantation lands. These actions can be seen as a struggle between the landowners, who themselves have different ideas about what to do with the property, and the *matai* of Vailoa for the land, as well as a struggle more generally between the *matai* and the government of Samoa. Since 2005, there have been several court cases and a struggle over the land and assets at Letolo plantation. The village sued the landowners and demanded economic compensation of SAT$80 million. In 2010, the landowners won all of the court cases and the people of Vailoa village are now legally banned from the site.

According to current traditional history, the large Pulemelei mound at Letolo is a *tia seu lupe* (pigeon-snaring mound), but it is also said to be the residence of chief Lilomaiava Nailevaiiliili, who according to Samoan genealogies dates to around AD 1650 (Scott 1969; Krämer 1994). According to Asaua (2005), this chief is associated with the Palauli district, which is one of the six districts on Savai'i. The village of Vailoa is the closest village to the Letolo settlement and Pulemelei mound. The Vailoa *matai* claim that Letolo is their ancient burial ground and belongs to them and insist Pulemelei should not experience excavation. In 2004, their actions stopped the archaeological excavations. This was both an action against the landowners in a struggle for authority and funds, but also a way to try to be in control of 'outsiders' moving around and disturbing 'spirits'. Meleisea's (1980:21) statement on culture and change in Samoa in the proverb 'We want the forest, yet we fear the spirits' may be appropriate.

The activities that stopped archaeological investigations were subsequently explained by the village *Pulenu'u* (mayor) as an act against the landowners and not against archaeological research as such. In 2006, we were able to carry out further investigations, under a new plantation manager, and the *matai* of the district and village of Satupaitea on the west side of Letolo plantation were involved (Martinsson-Wallin 2006). In the conflict over land, a whole set of social relations tied to the Pulemelei mound site surfaced. Since the Letolo plantation is freehold land which was alienated from the local village by the 19th century colonisers, it is part of the colonial inheritance. There are the old colonial aspects to consider, but O.F. Nelson and Co. Ltd is not just a group of outsiders, but a group that might be considered as a creolised group of individuals with Samoan and European decent who have owned the plantation for at least 100 years. On the other hand, the archaeologists might be seen as a new colonial group aligned with the former colonisers, while the archaeological investigations have reinforced the value of the site as a symbolic place and as a tourist attraction. From this, the primary value of the land has moved from being a plantation to grow and produce food. The *matai* of Vailoa village hold the view that even if O.F. Nelson and Co. Ltd comprises Samoans (and one of them is the current head of state), the village's traditional rights to the land should be respected.

In 2006, the Pulemelei mound was also nominated by the World Monument Funds as one of the world's 100 most endangered sites (Martinsson-Wallin 2007). A suggestion to nominate the site to the tentative World Heritage list was also presented by the author to the cultural heritage committee at the Ministry of Natural Resources and Environment (MNRE) in Samoa and to members of ICOMOS and UNESCO, who were included in the Pacific 2009 World Heritage program working on the nomination of cultural sites in the Pacific region. Members of the nomination group visited the Pulemelei site, but jointly with the cultural committee at MNRE, they considered that the political difficulties and land dispute were too problematic to support nomination. It is important to note here that World Heritage sites are those identified officially as meeting the criteria of Outstanding Universal Value, rather than sites that are realistic to nominate based on current political conditions, and that the 2009 selection of sites was aimed at identifying potential World Heritage properties rather than producing nomination dossiers for sites to be inscribed on the UNESCO WH List.

Samoa signed the World Heritage convention in 2001 and started working out cultural heritage policies. Two policies on cultural heritage have been published by the Ministry of Education, Sports and Culture: the Heritage Policy (2002–2005) and the Cultural Policy (2008). A draft of a Cultural and Natural Heritage Conservation Policy for the Cabinet Development Committee was developed in 2010. The Ministry of Natural Resources and Environment and the Ministry of Education, Sports and Culture have organised a Heritage Coordinating Committee to work on cultural management, as part of the 2002 Heritage Policy, which states that the Pulemelei mound is a national heritage site. In 2008, a display of the Pulemelei excavation, including two *toi ma'e* (stone adzes) and soil from the Pulemelei mound excavations, was given as a coronation gift to the new Tongan king from the head of state of Samoa.

Archaeology, CHM in Samoa: Education and legislation

In the wake of the Pulemelei excavations, the Centre for Samoan Studies at the National University of Samoa suggested a development course in archaeology, and in 2005 it invited the author to assist. To conceptualise archaeology in Samoan terms a new word was invented: *tala eli* (history from the soil). The venture was made possible by an educational exchange from the Swedish International Development Agency (SIDA). This exchange also included both Swedish and Samoan students who have had the opportunity to undertake an exchange semester. Swedish students have also been involved in minor fieldwork studies in Samoa (SIDA sponsored) and have written BA theses about issues in archaeology, cultural and natural-heritage management in Samoa (Brødholt and Vuijsters 2004; Listfeldt 2005; Nord 2006; Wehlin 2006;

Bornfalk-Back 2008; Johansson 2008; Enström 2009; Jonsson 2009; Fosselius 2010; Rosén 2010) (Figure 3). The projects have included studies of the legislation, policies and education relating to the tangible heritage of Samoa, as well as interviews about heritage. A synthesis of the student projects indicates that the tangible archaeological heritage and its management do not have a high priority in Samoa. On the positive side, since 2006 NUS has provided courses in archaeology and CHM, and since 2007 a permanent lecturer in archaeology has been employed. From 2010, NUS students can choose archaeology as a minor subject. The fact that there are higher-education courses evidences both a will and an interest to engage in archaeology and CHM (Figure 4). This interest is partly about using archaeology and CHM in cultural tourism, but is also suggested as an addition to *fa'asamoa* and the preservation of Samoa's cultural heritage (Jonsson 2009).

The concept of archaeology and CHM of tangible heritage is almost nonexistent in the school curriculum at elementary, secondary and senior level in Samoa. So far, it is not until the 11th grade Social Studies curriculum that the prehistory of Samoa is touched on. The students are given three different versions of the origin of the Samoans. One version states the common scientific view that Samoans originated ultimately from island Southeast Asia through the Austronesian expansion of maritime-oriented groups carrying so-called Lapita pottery. Another view is the one put forward by Thor Heyerdahl, suggesting a South American origin for the Polynesians, and the third states that the god *Tagaloa* placed humans in Samoa.

The two cultural-heritage policies have led to an increasing interest in protecting Samoa's cultural heritage, both the tangible and the intangible (Heritage Policy 2002–2005, Cultural Policy 2008). However, the lack of funding and human resources has delayed implementation of measures to do this. The 2008 cultural policy states that the past should be treasured and covers the following sites and activities:

- heritage sites, including legends and myths, mountains including volcanic mountains, stone mounds and monuments

- museums and archives

- visual arts, crafts and literatures

- traditional sports

- fusion of animate and inanimate or tangible and intangible qualities

In Samoa, the word 'culture' can be defined in three words: *fa'asamoa, aganu'u* and *faia*. The *fa'asamoa* is often used as a synonym for 'traditional Samoan culture', and does not commonly include contemporary behaviours, nor the culture of other groups living in Samoa. It does include how people treat their environment, not only the land and the sea, but also the social environment. *Aganu'u* stand for social rules, often associated with the power of the village council (*fono*) in terms of governing social cohesion. Culture can also be referred to as *faia*; the relationship of people, families and villages to each other, to their titles and to their lands.

The cultural policy has used Dr Melenaite Taumoefolau's definition of culture (Cultural Policy 2008):

> We can define culture for now as the typical kind of behaviour of a particular people and the characteristic pattern of behaviour which renders them different from other groups of people – their particular life ways which set them apart, including the ways in which they cook, the things they characteristically eat, the customs they regularly keep, the ways in which they dress, their religion, their dances, their music, their technologies, their medicines and the kind of language that they speak – [one thing about culture is that it changes, but just because it changes this doesn't mean it is not there].

Figure 3. The Swedish MFS student Ms Moa Nord and Ms Katrin Litsfeldt interviewing the Honorable Tui Atua Tupua Tamasese Taisi Tupuola Tufuga Efi (current head of state in Samoa) on Samoan history and cultural heritage in 2005.

Figure 4. The two Samoan archaeology students Mr Silau Vagai and Mr Akuso Kafe excavating at the monument *Fale o le Fe'e* (the house of the Octopus) in 2007 during the first field school given at the National University of Samoa.

To tie back to the post-colonial discourse on the location of culture, Bhabha (2004:163) notes that culture is something that is acted and is the outcome of actions and power relations between individuals and groups.

In 2007, a summary of existing laws, policies and conventions referring to cultural issues in Samoa was published on UNESCO's website in its Cultural Heritage Laws Database (www. unesco.org/culture/natlaws 2009-05-26). The protection of the tangible archaeological heritage in Samoa under the Planning and Urban Management Agency from 2004 provides:

> A planning framework for the management and protection of land in Samoa, integrated with environmental, social, economic, conservation, and resource management policies, at national, regional, district, village and site specific levels. This includes the development of national, local and site specific management plans, which plan and regulate a development of an area e.g. can restrict or prohibit construction work on an archaeological site.

Other laws that can reinforce the protection of the tangible historical cultural heritage are the *Samoa Antiquities Ordinance* from 1954 (revised 1972). This regulates what can be done with an object/site considered to be a 'Samoa Antiquity', with the head of state having the final decision about an antiquity and the ability to acquire it on behalf of the government. In the Lands, Survey and Environment Act of 1989, Part VIII Conservation and Environment states that management plans should include '… objects and sites of biological, archaeological, geological and geographical interests'.

The National Parks and Reserves Act 1974 furthermore states that:

> Historical reserves, where in the opinion of Cabinet, any public land that is not set aside for any other public purpose is of national, historical, legendary or archaeological significance, the head of state, acting on the advice of the cabinet, may by order declare the land to be an historic preserve, for the benefit and enjoyment for the people of Western Samoa.

The Forest Act from 1967 states that if an archaeological place is found in the forest, the Minister may demand that the owner should leave it undamaged. A new bill on the Land Titles Registration Act passed in 2008 includes changes to land ownership, but the implications of this act are yet to be seen. In 2006, Government-owned land in Samoa constituted 10.7% of the total, and freehold land comprised only 2.8% of the total, with the majority customary land (Jonsson 2009:18).

As outlined above, there is education and legislation regarding the protection and preservation of the tangible historical heritage in Samoa. However, there is currently no mechanism to maintain and reinforce legislation. A Cultural and Natural Heritage Conservation Policy has been developed by the Division of Land, Survey and Environment at the Ministry of Natural Resources and Environment. Education in archaeology and heritage management is also in its infancy and increased human-resource capacity in heritage management is needed to move from legislation to practice and reinforcement of the laws. Further education and awareness programs involving archaeology and CHM are a priority, but how these programs should be run and who should run them must be discussed by Samoans. A key contributor, given its interest and expertise in archaeology, will be the Centre for Samoan Studies at the National University of Samoa.

Some last words

The archaeological excavations at the large Pulemelei mound site raised issues about post-colonial discourse and the role of archaeology and cultural-heritage management in Samoa and the Pacific region. Problems and possibilities have been experienced in the introduction of archaeology and cultural-heritage management to Samoan society as in any post-colonial setting. The customary land tenure in Samoa, which is tied to the chiefly *matai* system is a vital part of the *fa'asamoa* (the Samoan way of life). Since land is limited and titles have been split and have proliferated over time, there has been an increasing amount of conflict among chiefs, people and villages over land. Oral traditions and history are important in the Samoan society, but these are tied in the main to the extended family history, and are important assets in land and title disputes. Oral traditions also evolve in a society like that of Samoa which has a rapidly changing culture. Even if policies are worked out and legislation exists, the above facts, along with lack of funding and education, make the protection and preservation of the archaeological remains and historical sites difficult to undertake. On the other hand, archaeological remains and historical sites are also seen as potential assets to be used in the tourist industry, which is a major income source in Samoa. A possible way to move forward and protect and preserve these sites could be to incorporate them into *fa'asamoa*, and at the same time to strengthen legislation and work out practical means of preserving cultural heritage. To make this happen, there is an urgent need to develop human expertise in archaeology and heritage. Most important of all, in my view, is that there is a will and initiative from the authorities and the academic community in Samoa to pursue these issues because: 'Facing the future, we treasure the past. For without history, we have no roots, and without roots, there is no future.' (Cultural Policy 2008).

Acknowledgements

'You started this thing, so you have the responsibility.' This is what my good friend and colleague Rapanui archaeologist Sonia Haoa-Cardinale has said to me many times. In stating this, she is not referring just to me, but to me as one of many archaeologists who have worked on Rapanui. In recognising my responsibility to the past, present and future of archaeology and heritage management in the Pacific, I would like to thank my Samoan and Swedish students and colleagues who have made me recognise the problems as well as the promise that our work holds. In pursuing these positive possibilities, I am forever grateful to two of my Pacific Island colleagues, Tautala Asaua and Sonia Haoa-Cardinale. Fa'afetai lava and Maururu Nui.

References

Aplin, G. 2002. *Heritage: Identification conservation and management*. Oxford University Press, Oxford.

Asaua, T. 2005. Samoan Archaeooratory. Bridging the gap between the spoken and the scientific. Unpublished MA thesis, University of Auckland.

Bhabha, H. 2004. *The location of culture*. Routledge, London and New York.

Bornfalk-Back, A. 2008. New approaches to old remains. Awareness and handling of the tangible cultural heritage in the Samoan educational system. Unpublished BA thesis, Gotland University.

Brødholt, E. and Vuijsters, I. 2004. Archaeology, heritage and cultural tourism development at the Letolo plantation Savai'i, Samoa. Minor fieldwork report, Gotland University.

Clark, G. and Martinsson-Wallin H. 2007. Monumental architecture in West Polynesia: Origins, chiefs and archaeological approaches. In: Martinsson-Wallin, H. (ed), Archaeology in Samoa. The Pulemelei Investigations, *Archaeology in Oceania* Supplement (42):28–39.

Davidson, J. 1979. Samoa and Tonga. In: Jennings, J.D. (ed), *The prehistory of Polynesia*, pp. 82–109. Harvard University Press, Harvard.

Emory, K. and Sinoto, Y. 1965. *Preliminary report on the archaeological investigations in Polynesia. Field work in the Society and Tuamotu Islands, French Polynesia, and American Samoa in 1962, 1963, 1964*. Bernice P. Bishop Museum Polynesian archaeological program, Honolulu.

Emory, K., Bonk, W.J. and Sinoto, Y.H. 1959. *Fishhooks*. Bernice P. Bishop Museum Special Publications 47, Bishop Museum Press, Honolulu.

Enström, I. 2009. Subsistence use and management of mangrove ecosystems. A study of community-based conservation in Samoa. Unpublished BA thesis, Gotland University.

Fosselius, S. 2010. The Samoan kava in a long time perspective – an attempt to touch intangible heritage. Unpublished BA thesis, Gotland University.

Gifford, E.W. 1951. Archaeological excavations in Fiji. *Anthropological Records* 13:189–288. University of California Press, California.

Gifford, E.W. and Shutler, R. Jr. 1956. Archaeological excavations in New Caledonia. *Anthropological Records* 18(1):1–148. University of California Press, California.

Goffman, E. 1967. *Interaction ritual – essays on face-to-face behavior*. Anchor Books Press, New York.

Gosden, C. 2004. *Archaeology and colonialism: Cultural contact from 5000 B.C. to the Present*. Cambridge University Press, Cambridge.

Green, R.C. 2002. A retrospective view of settlement pattern studies in Samoa. In: Ladefoged, T.N. and Graves, M.W. (eds), *Pacific landscapes. Archaeological approaches*, pp. 125–152. Bearsville press, Easter Island Foundation.

Green, R.C. and Davidson, J.M. (eds), 1969. *Archaeology in Western Samoa*. Volume I. Auckland Institute and Museum Bulletin 6, Auckland.

Green, R.C. and Davidson, J.M. 1974. *Archaeology in Western Samoa*. Volume II. Auckland Institute and Museum Bulletin 7, Auckland.

Heyerdahl, T. and Ferdon, E.N. Jr. (eds), 1961. Reports of the Norwegian archaeological expedition to Easter Island and the East Pacific. *Archaeology of Easter Island*, Volume 1. Monograph of the School of American Research and the Kon-Tiki Museum No. 24, Stockholm.

Hodder, I. 1986. *Reading the past. Current approaches to interpretation in archaeology*. Cambridge University Press, Cambridge.

Jennings, J.D. 1974. The Ferry berth site, Mulifanua district, Upolu. In: Green, R.C. and Davidson, J.M. (eds), *Archaeology in Western Samoa* Volume II, pp. 176–178. Auckland Institute and Museum, Auckland.

Jennings, J.D. and Holmer, R.N. 1980. *Archaeological investigations in Western Samoa*. Pacific Anthropological Records 32. Bernice P. Bishop Museum, Honolulu.

Jennings, J.D., Holmer, R.N. and Jackmond, G. 1982. Samoan village patterns: Four examples. *Journal of the Polynesian Society* 91:81–102.

Jennings, J.D., Holmer, R.N., Janetski, J.C. and Smith, H.L. 1976. *Excavations on Upolu, Western Samoa*. Pacific Anthropological Records 25. Bernice P. Bishop Museum, Honolulu.

Johansson, T. 2008. LAPITA – thriving culture or gone forever? Unpublished BA thesis, Gotland University.

Jonsson, M. 2009. Once it's gone it's lost – perceptions of Samoa's archaeological heritage. Unpublished BA thesis, Gotland University.

Karlström, A. 2005. Spiritual materiality: Heritage preservation in a Buddhist world? *Journal of Social Archaeology* 2005(5):338–355.

Krämer, A. 1994. *The Samoan Islands: An outline of the monography with particular consideration of German Samoa*. Polynesian Press, New Zealand.

Litsfeldt, K. 2005. Kulturarv i skilda världar, en komparativ studie mellan Sverige och Samoa – om kulturarvets betydelse. Unpublished BA thesis, Gotland University.

Leach, H. and Green, R.C. 1989. New information for the Ferry Berth Site, Mulifanua, Western Samoa. *Journal of the Polynesian Society* 98:312–329.

Lilly, I. (ed), 2005. *Archaeology of Oceania. Australia and the Pacific Islands*. Blackwell Studies in Global Archaeology, Malden, MA.

Martinsson-Wallin, H. 1994. *Ahu – the ceremonial stone structures of Easter Island. Analysis of variation and interpretation of meanings*. Aun 19. Societas Archaologica Upsaliensis, Uppsala, Sweden.

Martinsson-Wallin, H. 2006. Report of archaeological excavation at Letolo plantation, Savaii, Samoa. Unpublished report, Gotland University.

Martinsson-Wallin, H. (ed), 2007. *Archaeology in Samoa. The Pulemelei investigations. Archaeology in Oceania* Supplement 42.

Martinsson-Wallin, H., Clark, G. and Wallin, P. 2003. Archaeological investigations at the Pulemelei Mound, Savai'i, Samoa. *Rapa Nui Journal* 17(2):81–84.

Martinsson-Wallin, H., Clark, G. and Wallin, P. 2005. The Pulemelei project, Samoa, Savai'i. In: Stevenson, C.M, Ramirez, J.M., Morin, F.J. and Barbacci, N. (eds), *The Reñaca papers. VI International Conferences on Rapa Nui and the Pacific*, pp. 225–232. Easter Island Foundation, Los Osos.

Martinsson-Wallin, H., Clark, G. and Wallin, P. 2007. Monuments and people: The longevity of monuments. *Journal of Samoan Studies* 2:57-63.

Martinsson–Wallin, H., Wallin, P. and Clark, G. 2007. The excavation of Pulemelei site 2002–2004. In: Martinsson-Wallin, H. (ed), Archaeology in Samoa. The Pulemelei investigations *Archaeology in Oceania* Supplement 42:41–59.

Meleisea, M. 1980. We want the forest, yet fear the spirits: Culture and change in Western Samoa. *Pacific Perspectives* 9(1):21–29.

Nord, M. 2006. Linking local and universal values. Managing and protecting cultural heritage in Samoa. Unpublished BA thesis, Gotland University.

Petchey, F. 2001. Radiocarbon determinations from Mulifanua Lapita Site, Upolu, Western Samoa. *Radiocarbon* 43:63–68.

Rosén, A. 2010. Without roots, there is no future. Discussing the future for cultural heritage management in Samoa. Unpublished BA thesis, Gotland University

Said, E. 1978. *Orientalism*. Pantheon Books, London.

Sand, C., Bole, J. and Quetcho, A. 2005. What is the archaeology for the Pacific? History and politics in New Caledonia. In: Lilley, I. (ed), *Archaeology in Oceania*, pp. 321–345. Blackwell publishing, Malden, MA.

Scott, S.D. 1969. Reconnaissance and some detailed site plans of major monuments of Savai'i. In: Green, R.C. and Davidson, J.M. (eds), *Archaeology in Western Samoa*. Volume I, pp. 69–90. Auckland Institute and Museum Bulletin 6, Auckland.

Shanks, M. and Tilley, C. 1987. *Social theory and archaeology*. Polity Press, Great Britain.

Smith, A. 2005. Levuka, Fiji Island – a case study in Pacific island Heritage management. In: I. Lilley (ed), *Archaeology in Oceania*, pp. 346–362. Blackwell publishing, Malden, MA.

Spivak, G. 2002. Kan den subaltern tala? In: Lundahl, M. (ed), Postkoloniala studier. *Karios* 7:73–146.

Tamasese, T. 2003. Pulemelei mound, purification rituals and breaking tapu. *Green Bananas* 17:2–3. Centre for Pacific Studies, Univeristy of Auckland.

Tamasese T. 2007. In search of Tagaloa: Pulemelei Samoan mythology and science. In: Martinsson-Wallin, H. (ed), Archaeology in Samoa. The Pulemelei investigations. *Archaeology in Oceania* Supplement 42:5–10.

Van Dommelen, P. 2006. Colonial matter. Material culture and postcolonial theory in colonial situations. In: Tilley, C., Keane, W., Kuechler-Fogden, S., Rowlands, S. and Spyer, P. (eds), *Handbook of material culture*, pp. 104–124. Sage Books, London.

Vergés, F. 1999. *Monsters and revolutionaries. Colonial family romance and métissage.* Duke University Press, Durham, NC.

Wallin, P. 1993. *Ceremonial stone structures. The archaeology and ethnohistory of the marae complex in the Society Islands*, French Polynesia. Aun. 18. Societas Archaologica Upsaliensis, Uppsala, Sweden.

Wehlin, J. 2006. Let the remains ask the questions. In search for prehistoric relations on a Samoan settlement pattern through a correspondence analysis. Unpublished MA paper, Gotland University.

Ward, R.G. and Ashcroft, P. 1998. *Samoa: Mapping the diversity.* Institute of Pacific Studies. University of the South Pacific and National University of Samoa, Suva and Apia.

Internet source

http://www.unesco.org/culture/natlaws 2009-05-26

Samoan Government policies

Heritage Policy 2005. The Samoan Ministry of Natural Resources and Environment.

Cultural Policy 2008. The Samoan Ministry of Education, Sport and Culture.

9

Is a village a village if no one lives there?
Negotiated histories on Mabuyag in the Western Torres Strait

Duncan Wright[1] and the Goemulgaw *Kod*
1. School of Geography and Environmental Science, Monash University, Australia

Introduction

Partnership (or community) archaeology has become increasingly prominent in the Australia/ Pacific region (see Marshall 2002 and McNiven and Russell 2005). A community-led approach acknowledges the importance of indigenous control of the cultural-heritage process. This is designed to enable indigenous communities to 'maintain or establish community pride, cohesion and identity', as well as creating a 'more nuanced and textured view of the past' (Smith 1999; Nicholas 2000; McNiven and Russell 2005:244; Smith and Wobst 2005).

Divergent 'symbolic and metaphoric strategies' in oral history and archaeology are likely to result in the creation of different histories (McNiven and Russell 2005:248). This may be further influenced by methodological constraints (e.g. the validity, accuracy and representativeness of oral/archaeological histories) or the reluctance of communities to divulge secrets about their sites and practices (Sand 2000:68; McNiven and Russell 2005:48). When archaeological and ethnographic results do not correspond it is important to avoid both selective criticism of oral histories and censoring of instances where archaeology conflicts with oral accounts (Allen 1983:8; Echo-Hawk 1997; McNiven and Russell 2005:256). Partnership archaeology recognises that the cultural-heritage process requires ongoing negotiation between indigenous and archaeological communities, and in some cases the alteration of existing indigenous and/or non-indigenous cosmologies and methodologies (Nicholas 2000; McNiven and Russell 2005:248; Smith and Wobst 2005).

In 2001, a community project was initiated in the western Torres Strait to track 'archaeological signatures of ethnographically documented cultural practices back from a recent to a more distant past' (David and McNiven 2004:203). As well as providing significant information on key points of cultural change, it has also provided a case study about community-based archaeology and the methods used to explore prehistoric sites and cultural material (e.g. McNiven and Feldman 2003; David et al. 2004; McNiven et al. 2009). This paper stems from doctoral

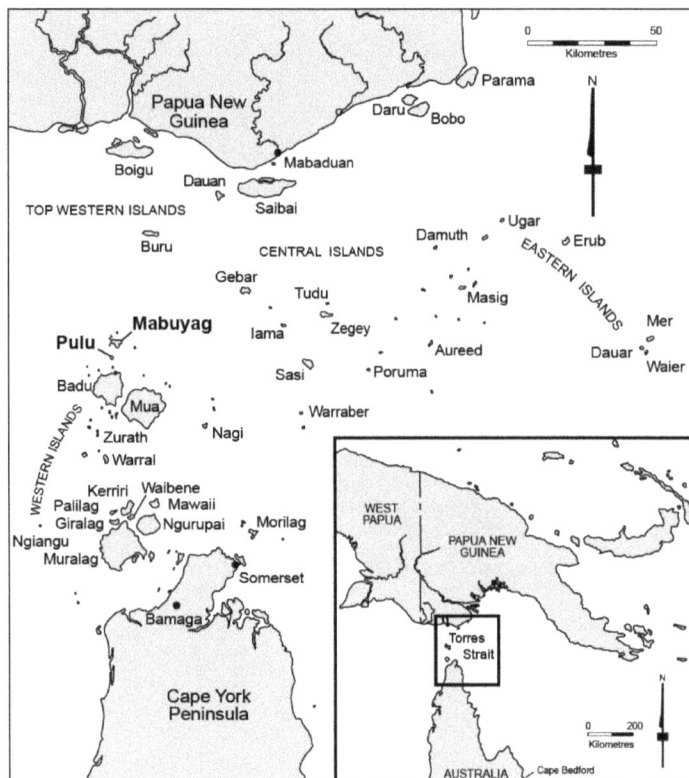

Figure 1. Map of Torres Strait Islands showing regional groupings.

research conducted during the Western Torres Strait cultural history project. It negotiates the competing histories for two ethnographically prominent 'villages', Wagadagam and Maidh, on Mabuyag in the central western Torres Strait (Figure 1).

Archaeology of villages in the Torres Strait

Two methods have been proposed to interrogate the notion of 'village' in the Torres Strait. The first conceives these sites to be 'semi-permanent to permanent places of residence containing groups of houses' (David and Ash 2008:428; see also McNiven et al. 2004:88). Using extracts from diaries, books and letters written by early European voyagers, 71 such 'villages' have been identified across 20 Torres Strait islands in the Torres Strait (McNiven et al. 2004:77, 88). In the western islands these locations were frequently abandoned during the dry season or due to sickness/death (Haddon 1890:353; Moore 1984:26), and similar practices are noted on a number of islands in the southwestern and central Torres Strait (Jukes 1847:155, 294; Thompson cited in Moore 1984:33). The term 'village' is flexible and can include occupied garden or feasting areas (McNiven et al. 2004:88; David and Ash 2008:429).

A second method of classification considers villages to be 'meaningful places connected to how people structure and understand their social spaces' (David and Ash 2008:428). This follows community histories which identify socio-political-ceremonial centres of activity relating to individual clans (cf. Haddon 1904; McNiven et al. 2004; Shnukal 2004). Such links to place continue to be firmly held by contemporary communities despite frequent relocation from traditional villages (Edmund Bani pers. com. Mabuyag 11/09/2006).

Despite the apparent disparity between these conceptions, they are not considered mutually exclusive but represent two sides (physical and metaphysical) of the village (Ghaleb 1990; McNiven et al. 2009).

The archaeological implications of both conceptions have been broken down into a set of archaeological expectations and related methodologies. Based on the first conception, it is expected that a certain amount of spatial and temporal homogeneity will exist in the archaeological record, with villages revealing 'archaeological traces of occupation in the form of structural features (houses, fences) and occupational debris such as food remains (shell middens) and artefacts of stone, shell and bone' (McNiven et al. 2004:88; see also Harris et al. 1985; Ghaleb 1990:219–222; Barham 2000; David and Weisler 2006; McNiven 2006:9; David and Ash 2008:428; McNiven et al. 2009). The semi-permanent conception of 'village' implies that archaeologists look for evidence of residential structures or activities (e.g. post holes, house platforms, paths, hearths and earth ovens) (Fitzpatrick et al. 1998; David and Ash 2008:446–447). For example, midden materials and clear activity areas (cooking, refuse) at Kurturniawak on Badu were used as evidence for village occupation despite the lack of confirming oral histories (David and Weisler 2006:21).

The second conception is harder to examine archaeologically, with villages assumed to contain both tangible (e.g. structured space, middens, paths) and intangible (e.g. story sites, trees, stones, rivers) markers (Haddon 1904:197; Shnukal 2004:323). Such sites are identified through experience and social interaction, and do not necessarily involve human modification of the landscape. In large measure, archaeologists identifying the social components of the 'village' are guided by oral and written histories (Ghaleb 1990; 1998; Ash and David 2008; McNiven and Wright 2008; McNiven et al. 2009).

The ethnography of Goemulgaw villages

Four traditional 'villages' are prominent in Goemulgaw cosmology: Wagadagam and Dabangai on the north coast of Mabuyag, and Maidh and Goemu on the east coast (Haddon 1904:266, 1935:56; Figure 2). Further smaller villages on the island include Mui and Udai (east coast), Dogai (southeast coast), Sao, Awbayth and Kodakal (north coast), Ii and Sopolai (west coast) and Dadakul and Maitan (interior) (Haddon 1904; Vanderwal 1973:178). These villages have independent totemic affiliations: the major moiety (*Koey awgadhaw kazi* or *Koey Buway*) with Wagadagam, while the minor moiety (*Moegi awgadhaw kazi* or *Moegi Buway*) is associated with most villages on the east and south side of the island (Haddon 1904:55; Eseli et al. 1998:87; Shnukal 2004:323; Adhi Cygnet Repu pers. com. Mabuyag, 12/08/2006). Villages are further divided by primary and subsidiary clan affiliation (Haddon 1904:266, 1935:56; Table 1). A further village (as well as the 'national kwod' (ceremonial men's meeting house) of the Goemulgal) is recorded for the adjacent island of Pulu (Haddon 1904:207; Lawrie 1970:85–87).

Table 1. Totemic affiliation (from sketch map drawn by Ned Waria in 1898, cited in Haddon (1904:163).

Village	Primary totem 1	Subsidiary totem 1	Primary totem 2	Subsidiary totem 2	Primary totem 3	Subsidiary totem 3
Wagadagam	Crocodile	Sucker fish	Snake	Dugong	Turtle	Frigate bird, fruit bat
Goemu	Turtle	Crocodile, dog				
Maidh	Snake	Turtle, sucker fish				
Dabangai	Dugong	Crocodile				
Pulu	Dugong	Sucker-fish	Cassowary	Dugong, snake	Dog	Turtle

Figure 2. Map of ancestral Goemulgaw villages on Mabuyag (topographic map courtesy of Schlenker mapping; GIS by Matthew Coller). Aligned grid north.

Totemic affiliation influences the behavior and spiritual and ceremonial roles practised by the people of each village. For example, Dabangai is reputed to be the place of great dugong hunters and the location of ceremonies relating to the dugong (Haddon 1904:162, 182, 1932:76, 1935:182–183; Eseli et al. 1998:74). The people of Goemu were largely concerned with turtle fishing, and were responsible for success in turtle hunting by conducting a number of key ceremonies (Haddon 1904:164, 183, 214, 330–331, 334–345, 1935:59). The families and clans associated with each location identify the individuality of villages through tangible and intangible features (Haddon 1904:4; McNiven et al. 2009).

Archaeological research at two Goemulgaw villages

To date, archaeological research on Mabuyag has concentrated on Goemu (Barham and Harris 1987; Ghaleb 1990, 1998; McNiven and Wright 2008) and Dabangai (McNiven and Bedingfield 2008; Wright 2009). Both ethnographically prominent sites contained rich surface and sub-surface deposits, leaving little doubt of a correlation between oral history and archaeology. This research comes at the expense of two equally important Goemulgaw villages, Wagadagam and Maidh, neither of which contain substantive archaeological evidence for cultural activity (Ghaleb 1990:158). Following the partnership approach, both villages were chosen for archaeological research in 2006 and are examined in detail below. It is recognised that significant problems surround the reconstruction of Aboriginal boundaries and land ownership, with the publication by Sutton (1995) singled out for criticism. While this paper does not support the validity of bound social groups, it accepts that much of the material collected by Davis and Prescott (1992) parallels ethnographic material collected by Alfred Haddon (1890, 1904, 1935), Margaret Lawrie (1972) and myself.

Wagadagam

The Wagadagam region encompasses the northwest side of the island, from the forested hills inland (an area known as 'Bari') to the coastal grasslands of Wagadagam proper (Davis and Prescott 1992:118, 124). A number of adjacent islets (e.g. Woeydhul and Aipus) also appear to have been affiliated with and used by the people of Wagadagam (Haddon 1904:58, 368; Davis and Prescott 1992:124). As the divisions between regions remain contested and obscure, they are roughly illustrated in Figures 2 and 3.

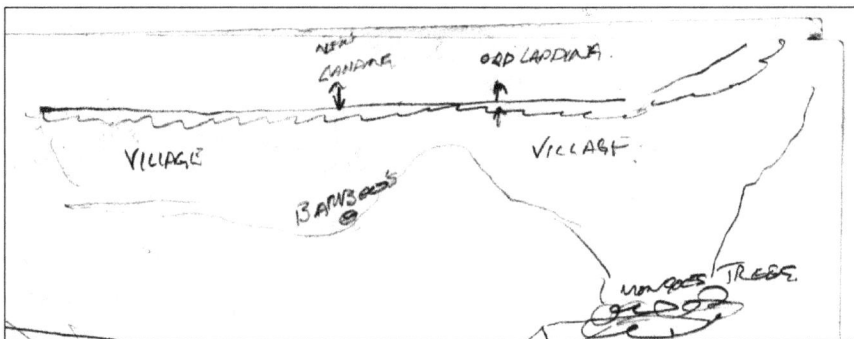

Figure 3. Sketch by Tim Gizu (of Mabuyag) of the Wagadagam village(s).

Ethnography

Lawrie (1970:105, 108) suggests there were two large villages, Wagadagam and Urabal Gagait. These two locations lie adjacent to one another, with the former at the end of the current road and near the new landing place, and the latter slightly further to the west (towards Ii). Both of these villages were large enough to contain sub-districts such as Kulapis (in east Wagadagam) and Buru in Urabal Gagait (Lawrie 1970:105). An alternative arrangement recorded by Ghaleb (1990:134) was that everything from Kula pis to bur was part of the single gigantic village of Wagadagam.

Wagadagam is recorded to have been an extremely important and influential place on Mabuyag, and the focus of activities relating to the *Koey awgadhaw kasi* moiety, which had the *koedal* (crocodile) as the main totem (Haddon 1904:164, 172; Adhi Gabriel Bani pers. com. Mabuyag, 21/9/2006). At Wagadagam, decisions relating to warfare and headhunting were made by people who were 'fierce and politically minded' (Haddon 1904:185; 1935:56; Adhi Gabriel Bani pers. com. Mabuyag, 21/9/2006). According to legend, Wagadagam was also the ancestral village of the Goemulgal, with all other villages founded by the chief of Wagadagam at the time, Bari (Haddon 1904:164, 236, 267; Tabeta cited in Mooke and Simpson 1972:1; Edmund Bani pers. com. Mabuyag, 12/11/2006).

Archaeological research

Until this study, no excavations had been conducted at Wagadagam. The only conclusive evidence of former occupation was several relict mound-and-ditch fields in the northeast quarter of the valley, and in the same area: 'a large grove of tall bamboo growing around a water hole' (Ghaleb 1990:158; Wright 2009).

Two excavations were conducted on the Wagadagam foreshore, adjacent to the new landing place (Figure 3). As Square A had been substantially disturbed by bulldozing, this excavation was discontinued and a second 70 cm² unit (Square B) was positioned 4 m away from the mangrove line on an elevated platform. With the exception of a few fragments of glass, no surface materials were observed in the locality of the excavation. Square B was excavated to a maximum depth of 63 cm (18 excavation units/XUs), with bedrock reached in some sections at 33 cm depth. There was little stratigraphic change, with sediment consistently dry and silty and mildly acidic throughout. A slight change in colouration occurs at the base of SU 1 (between 3 cm and 6 cm) from very dark grey to black (Figure 4). This transition is reflected by a shift from consolidated, organic rich sediment to increasingly friable and unconsolidated sediment. The transition between SU 2 and SU 3 (between 27 cm and 30 cm) was marked by substantial increases in rock, pumice and cultural materials (see Figure 4). Although the sediment is similar in texture to SU 2, it gradually reverts in colour to a very dark gray.

The main period of cultural activity at Wagadagam was dated to 800–1057 cal. BP by three AMS dates in correct stratigraphic sequence and overlapping at two standard deviations (Table 2). Ephemeral cultural deposits continue until 5–8 cm below the ground surface, before disappearing in the top four XU. This transition was dated to 464–535 cal. BP.

Marine vertebrate bone makes up the bulk of the Wagadagam cultural assemblage (total weight = 1.4 kg), with the majority of remains attributed to unidentified large vertebrates

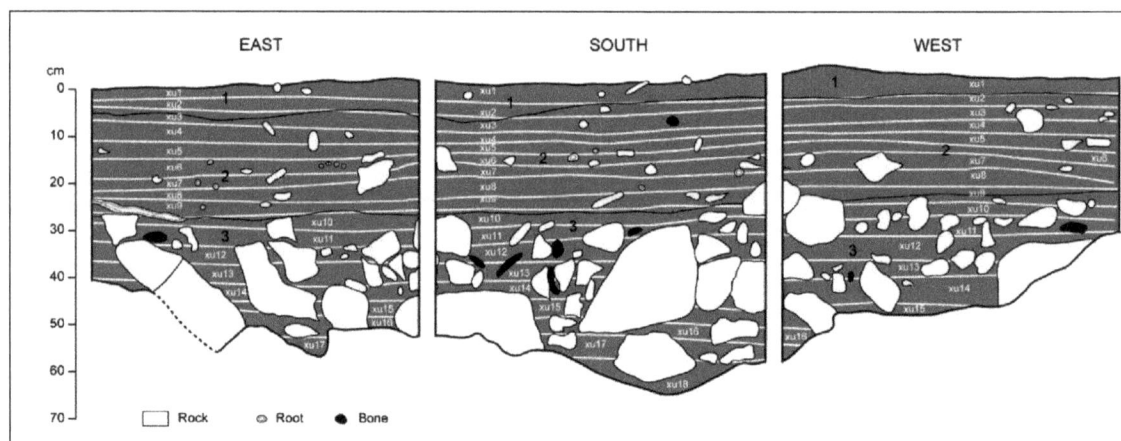

Figure 4. Section of Square B, Wag 1 showing stratigraphic units (SU 1–3).

Table 2. AMS radiocarbon dates, Square B, Wag 1. Dates in calendar years using Calib 5.0.2

Laboratory code	Square B: XU	Depth below surface (cm)	Sample type	Sample weight (g)	¹³C	¹⁴C age	Calibrated age (cal. BP)
WK-24932	B: 4	7–11	Charcoal	0.43	25.7 ± 0.2	486 ± 30	464–535
WK-24933	B: 10	30–32.5	Charcoal	0.38	24.4 ± 0.2	1050 ± 40	896–968* 800–890
WK-24934	B: 16	53–56	Charcoal	0.14	25.3 ± 0.2	1134 ± 30	932–1018* 1022–1056
WK-24935	B: 18	60–63	Charcoal	0.5	25.3 ± 0.2	1140 ± 30	951–1057* 934–948

Dates expressed as cal. BP = before AD 1950. * = highest probability calibrated age range.

(88.5%) and dugong (11%). The remaining turtle and fish bone makes up less than 0.5% of the total. Marine vertebrate bone was present in small quantities within SU 1 (total of 55.5 g per 10 l of deposit), increasing in SU 2 (total of 286.7 g per 10 l of deposit). The majority of bone comes from the top of SU 3 (XU 10–15), at which stage there is total of 472.7 g per 10 l of deposit. After this point, the quantity of marine vertebrate bone drops considerably (total of 26.3 g per 10 l of deposit). During excavation it was noted that the transition was matched by a significant drop in bone size, suggesting some bioturbation (Figure 5).

Considerable charcoal (40.3 g) was excavated from all XUs until XU 12, with 73% (17.0 g per 10 l of deposit) recorded between XU 7 and XU 11. There is a further minor charcoal peak in the basal two XUs, although this is considered to be the result of natural bioturbation of small fragments.

Square B contains a total of 3143 flaked stone artefacts and a further three ground stone/ ochre pieces. Quartz was the prominent material used to make flaked artefacts (n=3043), followed by igneous (n=93) and glass (n=7). The remaining non-flaked artefacts consisted of two fragments of ground ochre and a single stone implement with use impact. The bulk of artefacts (by number) comes from the upper 12 excavation units (SUs 1, 2 and the top of 3). This accounts for 96% of the quartz and 92% of the igneous flaked assemblage (Figure 6). Of the igneous flaked artefacts, the bulk come from between XU 6 and XU 12 (75%), while the ground stone and ochre is restricted to XU 3 and XU 4. Flaked glass is restricted to the upper three XUs, roughly corresponding with the SU 1 deposit.

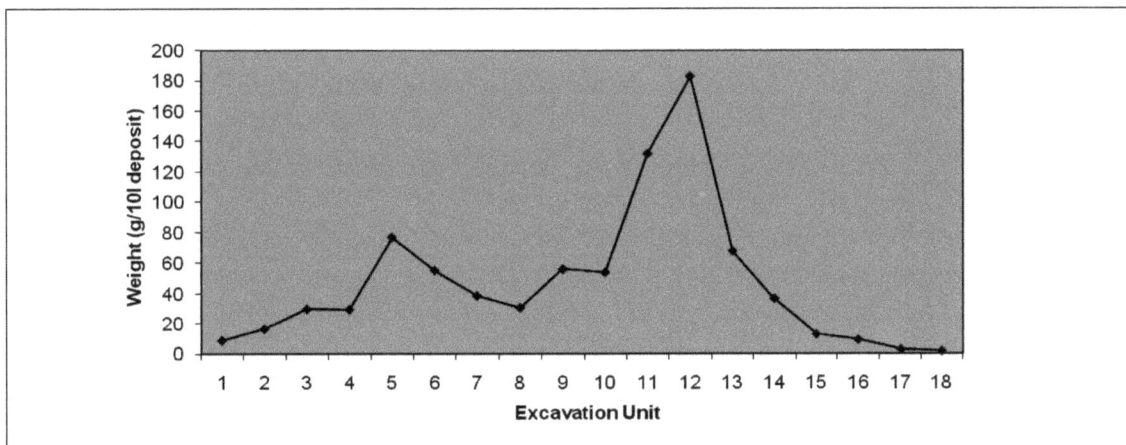

Figure 5. Vertical change in marine vertebrate bone density, Square B, Wag 1.

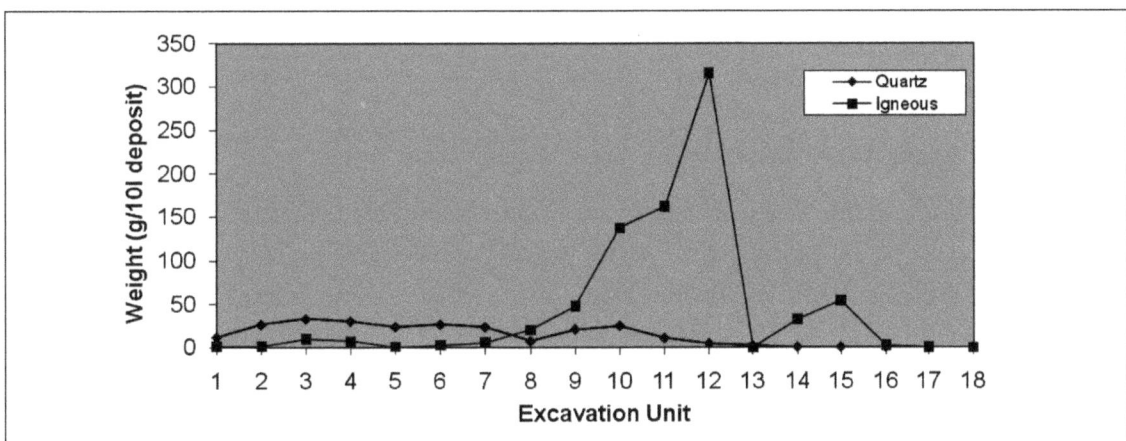

Figure 6. Vertical change in flaked stone artefact density, Square B, Wag 1.

Maidh

Davis and Prescott (1992:127) suggest that: 'the boundary between Wagedagam and Maidh follows a ridge line, a criterion which also accords with the northern boundary between Maidh and Panai' (see Figure 2). The southeast boundary of Maidh generally follows a line excluding the beach and foreshore area, which has become the focal residential area for the Mabuiag population. Other sources suggest that Maidh includes the villages of Bau, Maidh and Mui, with all of these areas falling within the jurisdiction of *thabu* (snake) and *koedal* (crocodile) clans (Haddon 1935:56; Rivers cited in Haddon 1935:55; Aaron Whap pers. com. Mabuyag, 1/12/2006).

The paucity of cultural material was explained by traditional owners as evidence for the different role of Maidh within the community. This was not considered a residential place but rather an important totemic and ceremonial site (Young Bani pers. com. Mabuyag, 1/12/2006; see Haddon 1904:97, 327). The 'village' (for that is what the Goemulgal call this site) was used by the *Maidhelaig* (or spiritual people) to conduct ceremonies at a large house (*merkai mud* or 'dead man's house'), with a high, steep roof and low walls (Haddon 1890:399). The area was restricted to certain members of the community: 'if an unauthorised man or any woman entered a *merkai mud* they would die' (Haddon 1890:399; Adhi Dimple Bani pers. com. Mabuyag, 1/9/2006). During the early 19th century, these restrictions appear to have been lifted, with the village increasingly used for gardening (Mooke and Simpson 1972:17; Done cited in Stevenson 1987; Eseli et al. 1998:27; Figure 7).

Archaeological research

Site surveys were made between July and October 1984 by archaeologists from University College London (Harris et al. 1985; Barham and Harris 1987). Investigations revealed few cultural surface materials or sites associated with cultural activity (Harris et al. 1985:48). The exceptions were relict fields and two stone arrangements in the shape of turtles observed on a hillside overlooking Maidh (Barham and Harris 1987:32). A survey in 2006 by the author revealed stone cairns in the Maitan valley region of Maidh. These were attributed by the Goemulgal to a recent period of land clearance for gardens (T. Gizu pers. com. Mabuyag, 8/11/2006).

Two 'test pits' were dug at an unspecified location at Maidh (Harris et al. 1985:48). The pits did not reveal any buried soil or former land surface that might have provided charcoal or other datable organic material (Harris et al. 1985:48). Due to site disturbance relating to the expansion of the modern village of Bau, further excavation of this site was not considered feasible (Wright 2009). An examination of bulldozed spoil heaps and house foundations in the eastern margins of Maidh also revealed little evidence for human settlement. The eroding creek bed which runs through the centre of Maidh did not contain any evidence of significant human activity.

Discussion and conclusion

Two villages that from the outset were expected to reveal little archaeological information about human settlement on Mabuyag were examined archaeologically. The lack of surface (and in the case of Maidh, sub-surface material) was initially conceived as evidence for contradictory histories between archaeology and ethnography. Following the partnership model, both sites were investigated to give insight into the broader cultural heritage of the indigenous communities.

The antiquity of 'villages' was expected to date to between 850 cal. BP and 550 cal. BP (cf. McNiven 2006). However, as evidenced by Mabuyag, archaeological research frequently considers the culturally rich areas (e.g. Goemu and Dabangai) as priority sites for research

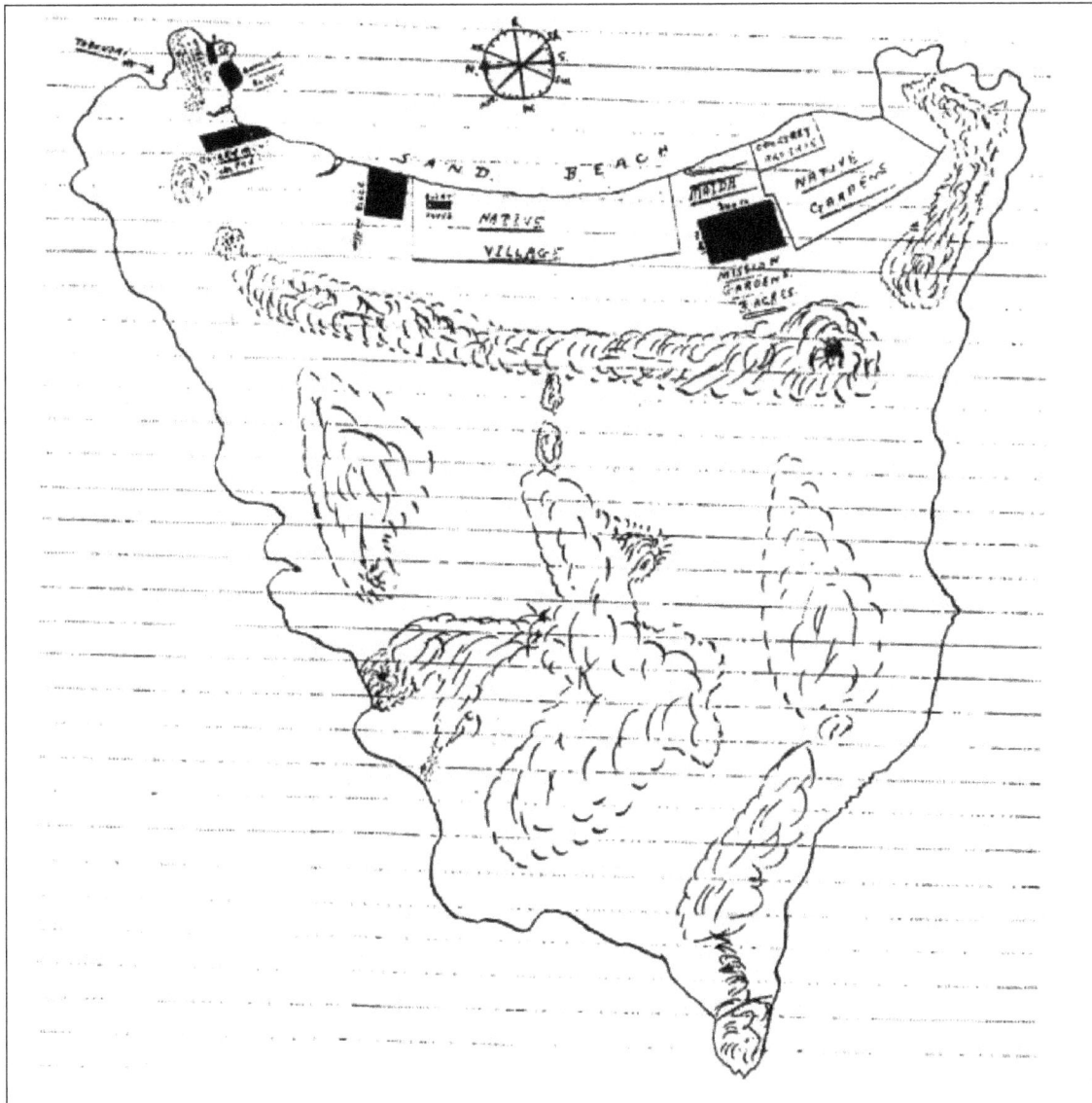

Figure 7. Sketch map of Mabuyag in 1914 (Queensland State Archives file A/58755: Islands, Torres Strait, sketcher unknown. From Eseli et al. 1998:27).

(Barham and Harris 1987:28; Ghaleb 1990, 1998; McNiven and Wright 2008). This is broadly representative of research elsewhere in the Torres Strait, which has a recognised bias towards highly visible, late-Holocene sites (e.g. Barham et al. 2004; David and McNiven 2004). As evidenced by excavations at Wagadagam, such an archaeological approach can ignore early phases of village occupation in the Torres Strait. Archaeological research at Wagadagam identified sub-surface deposits of bone from large vertebrates that date to 1100–550 cal. BP. A similar partnership project at the ethnographically known village of Totalai (on Mua) revealed an antiquity of 1300–1400 cal. BP for the initial phase of village settlement (Ash and David 2008). These excavations reveal the value of partnership archaeology and suggest that the methodology will improve our understanding of late-Holocene settlement in the Torres Strait.

While oral histories may or may not always converge with archaeological remains, this paper suggests that negotiation between indigenous and non-indigenous archaeologists is likely to enable the mutual development of both the prehistoric record and the oral history. Adhi Cygnet Repu (pers. com. Mabuyag, 20/04/2010) identifies the reciprocal role and importance of archaeology and ethnography within the cultural heritage process, saying: 'it [archaeology] is useful for us [Goemulgal]. It makes us ask questions about our important villages. There are some points we can ask why the archaeology is not the same as our stories.' Community histories provide archaeologists with an equally distinct (and in some cases) confronting set of questions.

It is recognised that cross-cultural distinctions exist in the classification of 'villages'. Such locations are regarded as both residential areas and the meaningful places connected with community identity (McNiven et al. 2004; David and Ash 2008). However, Maidh is ethnographically known to be a site deliberately restricted from the majority of the Goemulgaw. This was an important socio-political and ceremonial centre, but was not expected to be a residential centre. It is equally clear that Wagadagam (along with all other ethnographically known villages) continues to be conceived by the resident Mabuyag population as a village (in the present rather than past tense) despite the physical relocation of the Goemulgal away from this site at least 150 and possibly 550 years ago. These different ideas about what constitutes a village contribute to a broader understanding of what is 'significant' about these sites. An archaeological perspective is frequently (although not always) grounded in domesticity and utilitarian material culture, while the indigenous conception frequently identifies material culture as secondary to, and a result of, how people look at and organise a social space. Oral histories identify villages to be socio-politically and ceremonially distinct, with individuality often inscribed on to the landscape through totemic markers and monument architecture (Wright In prep). In effect, representing 'conflicting' views of what constitutes a 'village' requires a partnership approach whereby villages are recognised to be unique and the presence/absence of material culture can be viewed as the result of different types of social activity.

Following previous research, this paper highlights a partnership model for negotiating indigenous cultural heritage. While cultural materials and site visibility remain useful methods of site selection, it is important that cultural-heritage practitioners recognise the limitations of this approach. It is also essential that expectations of variation/disagreement between oral and archaeological histories should not result in the avoidance of such sites or situations (Echo-Hawk 1997; McNiven and Russell 2005:256). While such an approach is liable to highlight divisions between different belief systems, it is important that the value and limitations of each historical perspective are recognised in establishing a cross-cultural working relationship. When discrepancies do exist, these need not be viewed as problematic, but instead an exciting opportunity to develop a deeper mutual understanding of the past.

Acknowledgements

I thank the Goemulgaw community for its help and support. In particular, Tim Gizu and Edmund Bani, who shared their time and stories with me. Thanks also to AIATSIS for funding the project and the field crew – Beboy Whap, Thomas Whap, Ben Watson, Cameo Daley, Alice Bedingfield, Matt Coller and Sally May. Thanks also to Tim Denham, Jeremy Ash, Ian McNiven, John Bradley, Matt Coller, Pamela Ricardi and Sara Booth for reviewing drafts of this paper.

References

Allen, J. 1983. Aborigines and archaeologists in Tasmania. *Australian Archaeology* 16:7–10.

Ash, J. and David, B. 2008. Mua 22: Archaeology at the old village site of Totalai. In: David, B., Manas, L. and Quinnell, M. (eds), *Gelam's homeland: Cultural and natural history of the island of Mua, Torres Strait* Volume 4, pp. 451–472. Memoirs of the Queensland Museum Cultural Heritage Series, Brisbane.

Barham, A.J. 2000. Late Holocene maritime societies in the Torres Strait Islands, northern Australia – cultural arrival or cultural emergence? In: O'Connor, S. and Veth, P. (eds), *East of Wallace's Line: Studies of past and present maritime cultures of the Indo-Pacific Region. Modern Quaternary Research in Southeast Asia* 16:223–314.

Barham, A.J. and Harris, D.R. 1987. Final report to the research and exploration committee of the National Geographic Society on the Torres Strait Research Project. Part IIB: July–October 1985. Archaeological and Palaeoenvironmental Investigations in Western Torres Strait, Northern Australia.

Barham, A., Roland, M. and Hitchcock, G. 2004. Torres Strait Bepotaim: An overview of archaeological and ethnoarchaeological investigations and research. In: McNiven, I.J. and Quinnell, M. (eds), *Torres Strait archaeology and material culture* Volume 3, pp. 1–72. Memoirs of the Queensland Museum Culture Heritage Series, Brisbane.

David, B. and Ash, J. 2008. What do early European contact-period villages in Torres Strait look like? Archaeological implications. In: David, B., Manas, L. and Quinnell, M. (eds), *Gelam's homeland: Cultural and natural history of the island of Mua, Torres Strait* Volume 4. Memoirs of the Queensland Museum Cultural Heritage Series, Brisbane.

David, B. and McNiven, I.J. 2004. Western Torres Strait cultural history project: Research design and initial results. In: McNiven, I.J. and Quinnell, M. (eds), *Torres Strait archaeology and material culture* Volume 3, pp. 199–208. Memoirs of the Queensland Museum Culture Heritage Series, Brisbane.

David, B. and Weisler, M. 2006. Kurturniawak (Badu) and the archaeology of villages in Torres Strait. *Australian Archaeology* 63:21–34.

David, B., McNiven, I.J., Manas, L., Manas, J., Savage, S. and Crouch, J. 2004. Goba of Mua: Archaeology working with oral tradition. *Antiquity* 78:158–172.

Davis, S.L. and Prescott, J.R.V. 1992. *Torres Strait Aboriginal frontiers and barriers in Australia.* Melbourne University Press, Melbourne.

Echo-Hawk, R. 1997. Forging a new ancient history for Native America. In: Swindler, N., Dongoske, K.E., Anyon, R. and Downer, A.S. (eds), *Native Americans and archaeologists: Stepping stones to common ground.* AltaMira Press, Walnut Creek.

Eseli, P., Shnukal, A. and Mitchell, R. 1998. *Eseli's notebook. Aboriginal and Torres Strait Islander Studies Unit Research Report Series* Volume 3. University of Queensland Press, Brisbane.

Fitzpatrick, J., Cordell, J. and McNiven, I.J. 1998. Torres Strait culture site documentation project. Unpublished report to the Island Co-ordinating Council, Thursday Island, Torres Strait.

Ghaleb, B. 1990. *An ethnoarchaeological study of Mabuiag Island, Torres Strait, Northern Australia.* Unpublished PhD thesis, University College London, London.

Ghaleb, B. 1998. Fish and fishing on a Western Torres Strait island, Northern Australia: Ethnographic and archaeological perspectives. In: Jones, A.K.G. and Nicholson, R. (eds), *Fish remains and humankind.* Volume 2. Internet Archaeology 4.

Haddon, A.C. 1890. The ethnography of the Western Tribe of Torres Straits. *The Journal of the Anthropological Institute of Great Britain and Ireland* 19:297–440.

Haddon, A.C. 1904. *Reports of the Cambridge anthropological expedition to Torres Straits: Sociology, magic and religion of the Western Islanders* Volume 5. Cambridge University Press, Cambridge.

Haddon, A.C. 1932. *Head-Hunters black, white and brown* (2nd edition). Watts and Co, London.

Haddon, A.C. 1935. *Reports of the Cambridge anthropological expedition to Torres Straits: General ethnography* Volume 1. Cambridge University Press, Cambridge.

Harris, D.R., Barham, A.J. and Ghaleb, B. 1985. Archaeology and recent palaeoenvironmental history of Torres Strait, Northern Australia. Preliminary report to the Research and Exploration Committee of the National Geographic Society on Part IIa of the Torres Strait Research Project, July–October

1984. Institute of Archaeology, University of London and Department of Geography.

Jukes, J.B. 1847. *Narrative of the surveying voyage of the Fly, Commanded by Captain F.P. Blackwood, in Torres Strait, New Guinea and other islands of the Eastern Archipelago during the years 1842–1846* (Volume 1). T. and W. Boone, London.

Lawrie, M. 1970. *Myths and legends of the Torres Strait.* University of Queensland Press, Queensland.

Lawrie, M. 1972. *Tales from Torres Strait.* University Queensland Press, Queensland.

Marshall, Y. 2002. What is community archaeology? *World Archaeology* 34(1):211–219.

McNiven, I.J. 2006. Dauan 4 and the emergence of ethnographically-known social arrangements across Torres Strait during the last 600–800 years. *Australian Archaeology* 62(1):1–13.

McNiven, I.J. and Bedingfield, A. 2008. Past and present marine mammal hunting rates and abundances: Dugong (Dugong dugon) evidence from Dabangai bone mound, Torres Strait. *Journal of Archaeological Science* 35:505–515.

McNiven, I.J. and Feldman, R. 2003. Ritually orchestrated seascapes: Hunting magic and dugong bone mounds in Torres Strait, NE Australia. *Cambridge Archaeological Journal,* 13(2):169–194.

McNiven, I.J. and Russell, L. 2005. *Appropriated pasts: Indigenous peoples and the colonial culture of archaeology.* Altamira Press, Lanham, New York, Toronto, Oxford.

McNiven, I.J. and Wright, D. 2008. Ritualised marine midden formation in Western Zenadh Kes (Torres Strait). In: Clark, G., Leach, F. and O'Connor, S. (eds), *Islands of inquiry: Colonisation, searfaring and the archaeology of maritime landscapes,* pp. 133–148. Terra Australis 29, ANU EPress, Canberra.

McNiven, I.J., Fitzpatrick, J. and Cordell, J. 2004. An islander world: Managing the archaeological heritage of Torres Strait. In: I.J. McNiven and Quinnell, M. (eds), *Torres Strait Archaeology and Matrial Culture* Volume 3, pp. 74–91. Memoirs of the Queensland Museum Culture Heritage Series, Brisbane.

McNiven, I.J., David, B., Goemulgaw Kod and Fitzpatrick, J. 2009. The Great Kod of Pulu: Mutual historical emergence of ceremonial sites and social groups, Torres Strait, Northeast Australia. *Cambridge Archaeological Journal* 19(3):92–108.

Mooke, T. and Simpson, B. 1972. Mabuiag Lag. Unpublished collected stories. Mabuyag Island Council, Mabuyag.

Moore, D. 1984. *The Torres Strait collection of A.C. Haddon.* British Museum Publishing Ltd, Britain.

Nicholas, G.P. 2000. Indigenous land rights, education, and archaeology in Canada: Postmodern/postcolonial perspectives by a non-Canadian white guy. In: Lilley, I. (ed), *Native Title and the transformation of archaeology in the postcolonial world,* pp. 121–137. Oceania Monographs 50. Oceania Publications, Sydney.

Sand, C. 2000. Reconstructing 'traditional' Kanak society in New Caledonia: The role of archaeology in the study of European contact. In: Clarke, A. and Torrence, R. (eds), *The archaeology of difference: Negotiating cross-cultural engagements in Oceania,* pp. 32–50. Routledge, London.

Shnukal, A.R. 2004. The post-contact created environment in the Torres Strait Central Islands. In: McNiven, I.J. and Quinnell, M. (eds), *Torres Strait archaeology and material culture* Volume 3, pp. 317–346. Memoirs of the Queensland Museum Culture Heritage Series, Brisbane.

Smith, L. 1999. *Decolonizing methodologies: Research and Indigenous peoples.* Zed Books Ltd, London and New York.

Smith, C. and Wobst, H.M. 2005. *Indigenous archaeologies: Decolonizing theory and practice.* One World Archaeology 47, Routledge, Abingdon and New York.

Stevenson, B. 1987. *Wings across the sea.* Boolarong Publications, Brisbane.

Sutton, P. 1995. *Country: Aboriginal boundaries and land ownership in Australia.* Aboriginal History Monograph 3, Canberra, Australian National University.

Vanderwal, R. 1973. *The Torres Strait: Protohistory and beyond* Volume 2. University of Queensland Occasional Papers, Queensland.

Wright, D. 2009. The archaeology of community emergence and development on Mabuyag in the Western Torres Strait. Unpublished PhD thesis, Monash University, Melbourne.

Wright, D. In prep. Approaching community through archaeology on Mabuyag in the Central Western Torres Strait, Northeast Australia.

10

Paths to knowledge
Connecting experts in oral histories and archaeology

Karen L. Nero

Macmillan Brown Centre for Pacific Studies, University of Canterbury, New Zealand

A long time ago people from Yap came to Palau for stone money. They used bamboo rafts to carry the money. The first time they came they went to one rock island and went under a hole [cave], to hide in the place to make stone money. That place had one house close to them with small children who cried all the time. One day the old lady took the children outside, going far from the house early in the morning, and then saw smoke from under the rock. She took the children home and told her daughter that she saw smoke under the rock. In the cave there was one Yapese who knew magic. That day he knew they had to kill the fire because he knew people might come and find us. And we were frightened. But the village chief was told, who told all his people to go look for smoke. He said if they found people, to call them to come so that we could know where they came from. And those Yapese killed the fire, but the chief came on top of the hole and called them and asked them to come outside and talk: 'I didn't come to fight. I want you to come outside.' When the Yapese came, they had brought plenty of food, so they took all their food, and gave it to the chief of the place. The chief asked where they came from – and they said they came from Yap. The chief asked why, and they responded 'we came here looking for stone money'. The chief said to come with his men and later to go look for stone money. And the place would be named for Yapese people.

Account by elder Yapese woman in Belau, 1991.

Introduction

The name of the village of Ngermid on the island of Koror in the Palau Islands is derived from *Remith* (Ngermid in Palauan), the Yapese word meaning 'place of hiding'. In the early 1990s, a Yapese female elder recounted this history to me, and it was then independently depicted for me in a contemporary wood carving (Figure 1) by a young member of a high-ranking Koror lineage. These oral historical and artistic performances demonstrate two of the media through which experts perform and thereby retain and transmit important histories over the centuries. The physical sites of these important encounters are still retained; bringing the appropriate elders to the sites will often elicit even deeper and more detailed accounts of the events that took place there, as they have been recounted over the centuries.

Figure 1. Storyboard showing the Yapese stone-money quarry, Ngermid.

Austronesian speakers separately settled the island groups of Yap and Palau in the Western Carolines. Roughly 450 km apart, the islands are situated just on the western edge of the Philippine continental plate, east of the Philippines and southwest of Guam in the Mariana Islands. Despite the designation of Palauan as a Western Austronesian language, and Yapese as an Oceanic Austronesian language, cognate terms for key cultural components in the two languages attest to long historical cultural exchange relationships connecting the two island groups, with especially strong ties between Koror in Palau and Yap. These historical relationships are maintained today through ongoing kin and marital linkages and close political and economical links connecting the Republic of Palau and Yap State of the Federated States of Micronesia.

Current archaeological research has confirmed settlement of Palau by at least 3100 cal. BP (Clark et al. 2006:215), and suggested that the original population was augmented but not replaced by later arrivals. Palauan oral historians refer to the ancient past as *Er a Ititiumd* or 'Mossy Past' (Nero 1987:38), evoking the image of stones covered by moss, by extension their knowledge not clearly visible. The flurry of recent archaeological work surrounding the construction of the Compact Road on Babeldaob (Wickler et al. 2005a, 2005b; Liston 2007, 2010) has provided a substantial body of data to support the development of more refined archaeological timelines (Masse et al. 2006; Liston 2009). Indeed, the term *Er a Ititiumd* might be an apt label for the era of early monumental earthwork that archaeologists call the Earthwork Era, with its moss-covered stones but few connected oral histories (see Liston and Miko, this volume).

The Rock Islands were permanently inhabited by about 1000 BP, with residents establishing sizeable stonework villages by about 700 BP, which eventually supported as many as 4000 to 6000 people (Masse et al. 2006:111–112). Most of the Rock Island villages were abandoned about 450 years ago. Occupation periods for the Rock Islands (including those off the shores of Ngermid, Koror and Babeldaob) may be helpful in establishing a timeline for Yapese quarrying, as oral histories in Palau and Yap agree that the Rock Islands were uninhabited when they were being quarried. Recent archaeological data from Omis Cave in Ngermid suggests that early Palauan settlers might have used it as a campsite. Fifteen charcoal and marine-shell samples from three Rock Island quarry sites, dated to ca. 300 BP, relate to intensive stone-money quarrying (Fitzpatrick 2002:239), supporting Descantes' (2005:94) analysis that quarrying intensified when European traders entered the region. There is still no conclusive data identifying the earliest dates that the Yapese might have first visited the Rock Islands for quarrying.

In this chapter, I consider the ways in which oral histories and archaeological data have been used to understand the early histories of the Palau islands and their relationships with the neighbouring island of Yap. I frame this reflection in the growing field of the study of experts and expertise, as a foundation of my discussion of Palauan and Yapese oral historians as experts, and the ways Palau's oral histories and its access may be structured – in ways some outside experts perceive as 'ill-structured'. I review definitions of key terms as they are generally used and open the discussion on how we might refine the use of these terms and their associated methodologies in conjunction with local oral historians. Summaries are provided of the characteristics of Palauan oral histories, and the protocols used in the 1980s research on Koror's oral histories. While the type of information available through oral histories differs from that of archaeology, a fruitful area of consideration is that of identifying relative sequences of events. I discuss excerpts from a few of the Yapese and Palauan oral histories, demonstrating how historians indicate the relative order of key events, and identifying potential ambiguities in trying to relate these to chronological time. I conclude with discussions of recent studies of Yapese stone-money quarrying as examples of archaeological approaches to integrating knowledge from the oral histories, in order to help identify ways in which the two disciplines might better work together. I have grounded these analyses in the Palauan histories with which I am most familiar, while recognising parallels with work done elsewhere in the Pacific (i.e. Burley 1998; Sheppard et al. 2004). These reflections should not be taken as a general discussion of oral historical protocols and practices as there are variations within Palau.

Throughout the chapter, I use Palauan metaphors such as the *iek* (bead money necklace) and the term *rael* (path) to communicate some of my understandings of the characteristics and practices of Palauan oral histories. *Rael*, one of the key Palauan icons, refers to the trails that connect villages, and serves as a multivalent reference to the social relationships established between groups and political units by past events, or also a method, strategy or pattern (see Parmentier 1987:109). Both archaeological and oral historical approaches offer different types of information useful in understanding the early settlement periods. After the disastrous depopulation of Palau from an estimated 50,000 people before European contact and introduced diseases, to 3743 people by 1900, we are fortunate that contemporary oral historians still retain and transmit some of these early histories (Palau National Committee on Population and Children 1997:7). Archaeologically based timelines may indicate the potential temporal depth of the oral historical records, while oral historical accounts focus on key actors and their local and inter-island relationships over time, including the relative order of key events. Often these oral historical and archaeological accounts appear to complement rather than contradict each other, and suggest that coordinated studies could be effective. The training of indigenous ethnographers and archaeologists should deepen the types of questions that could be addressed.

In the early 1980s, at the request of the current *Ibedul* of Koror, I worked with the chiefly councils and staff to record the oral histories of Koror and its constituent villages. Koror (in Palauan *Oreor* or *Sureor*, or the poetic name *Erengul*) is the official English name of the island, a state of the Republic of Palau and one of two paramount chiefdoms. At that time, although secure in their oral histories that reached deep into the past, the historians could not be certain of Koror's calendrical time depth or whether some of the cultural sites might have been made by people other than their own ancestors. In the 1970s and 1980s, most archaeologists and historians were reluctant to seriously consider information from the oral histories, as indicated by their labelling of the period before written documentation, as prehistory and those histories not personally witnessed as oral traditions. In the early 1980s, Bruce Masse and David Snyder, of the Center for Archaeological Investigations of Southern Illinois University at Carbondale, undertook archaeological research on Koror, under the direction of George J. Gumerman (Gumerman et al. 1981), partially overlapping with our oral historical research. By the mid 1980s, their team provided us with preliminary archaeological assessments of the dates that the Rock Island villages had been abandoned (Masse 1984; Masse et al. 1984). These dates, up to 400 years ago, were compatible with preliminary dates suggested by the sequence of the Rock Island village wars recounted in the histories. This cross-verification supported an argument that some of the Koror oral histories had a depth of perhaps 400 years – a time depth then not generally acknowledged by academics.

This led me to seek other forms of independent verification of oral histories: the early Yapese quarrying in Palau provided an excellent case study. Colleagues from the Yap State Historic Preservation Office and Palau Resource Institute, with whom I was working on a separate project, supported my suggestion to seek oral histories both on Yap and Palau about the early stone-money quarrying, and we were able to interview elders of both island groups.

Today's oral historians are carefully considering the histories that were passed on to them and how they might be best interpreted. After several decades of collaborative work by Palauan and outside researchers through the Palau Bureau of Arts and Culture, the Belau National Museum and the Ministry of Cultural Affairs and the increasing cadre of Palauan researchers trained in both Palauan and Western methodologies of cultural anthropology and archaeology, there is renewed excitement in researching the histories of the islands. The expertise of archaeological studies is welcomed as it provides a second 'path' (*rael*) through which knowledge may be augmented. Both disciplines, with their very different theoretical and methodological approaches, may offer insights that will create a more complete vision of the past.

Our research on early Yap-Palau stone-money quarrying coincided with preparations to hold the 8th Pacific History Association (PHA) conference on Guam in 1990 (see Rubinstein 1992), when organisers and participants sought new ways to access and integrate indigenous scholars and their knowledge into the early histories of the Pacific nations. We hoped to open up academic practices to include appropriate consideration of the local histories of the region and avoid undue reliance on documents often written after brief chance encounters during the early contact period. The papers from the 1990 session Oral Traditions and Alternate Media, co-chaired by David Hanlon and myself, are especially relevant to this chapter. Pohnpeian archaeologist Rufino Mauricio, then a graduate student, demonstrated how oral histories recorded and published by early researchers might be best understood through identifying the framework of indigenous Pohnpeian types of historical knowledge (what we might call genres) and the expectations the historian or the audience might have of the different types of narratives. Mauricio's (1992:239) paper is a major contribution towards inter-disciplinary studies and the ongoing work to bring archaeologists and oral historians into closer understanding of each other's work and to begin to integrate these approaches.

Cultural-knowledge custodians, anthropologists, archaeologists and historians continue to seek inter-disciplinary approaches. The conference, *Pacific Island archaeology in the 21st century: Relevance and engagement Dikesel a Beluu*, supported by the World Archaeological Congress, was held in Palau in June 2009. Dr. Rufino Mauricio, Chairman, ICOMOS Pacifica; Director, FSM National Historic Preservation Office; and Secretary General, FSM National Commission on UNESCO, was a keynote speaker. The session, Archaeology, oral traditions and the history of the past in the Pacific Islands, convened by Dr Christophe Sand, helped identify current challenges and ways forward. Members of our *Dikesel a Beluu* academic and community audiences were enriched by the insights of the increasing numbers of indigenous anthropologists and archaeologists directing this research.

Experts and expert systems of knowledge

I begin with the premise that the Palauan and Yapese oral historians are experts. They, like archaeologists, are formally trained in the theoretical and methodological approaches of their disciplines, the protocols under which they are practised, and rigorous verification processes. Their approaches and the types of data that archaeologists and formally trained oral historians collect, analyse and interpret differ substantially. While at times these interpretations may differ or clash (as they do on other Pacific islands), on Palau they may provide a more complete foundation to understand past events.

By definition, an expert is a 'person having special skill or knowledge', and expertise as an 'expert opinion or skill or knowledge' (*Concise Oxford Dictionary* 1964:426). Cambridge University Press has recently published a handbook of the new field of scientific research on expertise and expert performance (Ericsson et al. 2006:3, 4) that states 'expertise then refers to the characteristics, skills, and knowledge that distinguish experts from novices and less experienced people'. The handbook 'includes a multitude of conceptions of expertise, including perspectives from education, sociology and computer science, along with the more numerous perspectives from psychology'. The definition is thus limited for our purposes, as it does not include non-Western or indigenous perspectives, and fails to draw on the disciplines of anthropology, history and indigenous studies. Nevertheless, I believe that positioning this chapter within the framework of the study of experts and expertise may provide new perspectives and widen the discussion between anthropologists and historians, and cultural anthropologists and archaeologists.

The chapter by psychologists James F. Voss and Jennifer Wiley, Expertise in History, is grounded in Western approaches and reliance on written sources. They believe 'an expert in history is assumed to have a general and specialized knowledge of history as well as facility in the skills of historical research and writing', although paintings and objects are included among the otherwise written resources that might be 'examined for their reliability, validity, authenticity and usefulness' (Voss and Wiley 2006:569). One might question the utility of their division of the domains in which expertise may be formed into two types. The first 'because of their conceptual evolution, permit the use of mathematics, formal logic, or well-controlled experimentation … are termed 'well-structured', frequently dealing with problems having a single answer, readily identifiable constraints, and agreed-upon solutions'. The second domain is 'termed 'ill-structured', having more than one possible answer, requiring identification of constraints, and having no agreed-upon solution'. Political science and history are used as examples of this latter type of domain that has 'conceptual structures that allow relatively little opportunity to use mathematics, which leads to relatively less certainly in subject-matter in knowledge and more heterogeneity in constraint usage' (Voss and Wiley 2006:569–570). However, the authors do conclude that the expert historians' 'subject-matter knowledge' – [is the area in which] 'virtually across all domains, our understanding of the development of such knowledge is inadequate, in history as well as other domains. Longitudinal studies of knowledge development are especially needed …' (Voss and Wiley 2006:581).

The study of the development, retention and transmission of oral historical knowledge by recognised specialists could make a substantial contribution to the study of experts and expertise. John Wilding and Elizabeth R. Valentine's (2006:539–552) chapter on Exceptional memory reviews some of the universal foundations of exceptional memory, including 'semantic' memory or a body of information embedded in an organised structure that is added to and organised over a long time; 'episodic' memory, or 'the ability to reproduce a prior input, event, or episode'; and '*loci*', a mnemonic device that relates to its Latin root *locus* for place or location. The Carolinian, and other, oral historians demonstrate exceptional memory skills, such as the ability to retain and reproduce verbatim an oral account or instruction. Interestingly, Wilding and Valentine noted that using functional MRIs to understand the neurological basis of superior memory provided: 'no differences in any aspect of the brain recordings to match the differences of the experts for the different materials' (Wilding and Valentine 2006:548).

Palau's expert historians

In 1979, at the time of my early research in Palau, Malsol Ngiraibuuch Ngiraklang was recognised as the pre-eminent historian of Palau. This was true structurally as he held the title Ngiraklang, one of the high-ranking titles of Imeiong in Ngeremlengui. Imeiong, as the eldest stone son of the goddess Milad of the current world, was responsible for holding the histories and sacredness of Palau (Parmentier 1987). Ngiraklang was an expert in all aspects of Palauan history and a master fisher and expert on the land and seascapes of Palau. He was legendary for his exceptional memory and ability to recall verbatim a new account he had heard. Nor was his reputation limited to Palau or Yap; he became an internationally recognised expert after Robert Johannes (1981) published his seminal *Words of the Lagoon* on Palauan marine resource management, based on his work with Ngiraklang and other Palauan master fishers. Ngiraklang was the primary mentor for at least five international doctoral theses in different social and physical science disciplines. While pre-eminent, he was only one of Palau's expert male and female historians. The senior male and female elders of Palauan lineages and villages serve as custodians of the histories. Today, each of the 16 states in the Republic of Palau selects a historian as a representative to the Palau Society of Historians. The systems of knowledge the historians preside over are quite structured, involving many different levels with restrictions that may be opened in turn depending on the person seeking and the knowledge levels already attained. Age, clan and village affiliation, and the context and reason such information is sought may also affect access. Such restrictions may serve to protect the integrity of the oral histories, and may help ensure their transmission. Yapese similarly identify respected male and female historians.

Terminology

The use of certain key terms differs for members of the public and within disciplines. Through the lens of a cultural anthropologist working at the interface with history, I summarise the way in which I understand and use the terms oral histories, oral traditions, ethnohistory and prehistory and their relationship to the larger field of history. The dictionary definitions of terms[1] reflect the common Western bias towards written documents, and a polarisation of Western and non-Western peoples which is questionable in academic levels of discourse. It will need the combined efforts of the broader discipline of anthropology to influence and update public perceptions and biases.

Jan Vansina (1985:3–32) distinguished between *oral histories* and *oral traditions* on the basis that *oral histories* are based on memories of events witnessed by the person narrating them, limiting their range to the age of the oldest living individual. A series of individuals might be interviewed to access multiple accounts that could be compared with each other and other accounts, and permit initial assessments. The *Oxford Dictionary of English* draws on his work in its definition of oral history as 'the collection and study of historical information using tape recordings of interviews with people having personal knowledge of past events', retaining the primary requirement of personal experience, but adding the requirement that the account be recorded. Vansina used the term *oral traditions* to refer to accounts of those that were no longer contemporary, in turn subdivided between memorised traditions, and a number of different types of narrative accounts.

Vansina's (1985) work has been highly influential in the study of oral histories. He carefully identified the requirement that all accounts must be submitted to evidential questions in order to assess the value of a particular oral history or tradition. For its time, Vansina's research was innovative – encouraging scholars to consider the historical and cultural relevance of oral traditions. However, the debates have shifted as anthropologists and historians attempt to take these issues into account and work across disciplines (see Dening 1980; Sahlins 1983, 1985, 2004; Ohnuki-Tierney 1990; Biersack 1991; Comaroff and Comaroff 1992; Merwick 1994). It is time to reconsider how we might try to understand the various types of historical accounts, how they are meant to be used and understood, and whether these types or genres have any comparative validity.

I use the term *oral histories* simply to refer to any account verbally transmitted to another individual or group of people. For those engaged in learning oral histories, this term is considerably expanded below. I suggest the critical aspect of this type of history is that it covers a body of knowledge that is orally transmitted by recognised experts and that has been retained and transmitted over time by these oral historians. Access to oral historical accounts (including different types of accounts or genres) is often restricted but not closed. The distinction of personal witness may still be marked. A Palauan historian will preface the account of an event he or she witnessed with the statement: 'I saw this with my own eyes.' This gives the account a certain credibility, although of course, different witness reports might vary. There are a number of different types of oral histories that might be performed: in Palau, these include a chant, dance performance, verbatim memorised account, narrative that may be interrupted, proverb, or reference to a material sign of the event in the form of a stone or bead money or low-relief carving on a beam of the community meeting house (*bai*). In all cases, it is the oral historian who provides the necessary connections and interpretations. In the case of the lineage, village or state histories, the Palauan historian is entrusted to retain and appropriately pass on the story on behalf of the collective *dui* (title) he or she holds. This identification with past titleholders is often marked by an oral historian's use of the plural pronoun and present tense to describe events in the past. They often specify the relative order of events in the narrative, and certain place names or titles may indicate relative antiquity. It is important to foreground the oral historian as the source of the knowledge and its interpretation, not the recorded or written narrative.

I use only the term *oral history* to refer to all histories that are transmitted orally because personal witness may not be the most important characteristic of these differing types of oral histories, and as a reminder that all oral (and written) histories are subject to potential distortion and culturally appropriate verification.

I prefer not to use the term *prehistory* ('the period of time before written records; myths that stretch back into prehistory' according to the *Oxford Dictionary of English*), as it is clearly rooted in the requirement that history begins only with the availability of written accounts and by association only when Europeans enter the Pacific. Common in early accounts, today's Pacific archaeologists rarely use the term. Early accounts of Pacific peoples and places were generally based on very recent, partial and often biased observations that visitors recorded during brief visits that were often characterised by limited opportunities for good communication with the people visited. Indeed, Palauan oral histories recognise that Portuguese (Ritzenthaler 1954:11) and Spanish visits preceded that of Captain Wilson and his crew, who provided the first written account of their three-month stay in 1783 (see Nero 2002). All accounts must be subjected to assessment, in particular of length, breadth and depth of observations and the opportunities for communication across languages. While a demarcation of major transformations as a result of interactions with significant and often powerful outsiders is important, it should not be used to suggest that historical knowledge was not retained by the local peoples before the arrival of these most recent outsiders.

The term *ethnohistory* has a long controversial history as used by cultural anthropologists, historians and archaeologists. The general *Oxford Dictionary of English* definition of *ethnohistory* as: 'the branch of anthropology concerned with the history of peoples and cultures, especially non-Western ones' goes back to Dening's (1966:23) early discussion and distinction that 'We write the history of whites and the ethnohistory of the rest', despite challenges to such a conceptualisation as a form of intellectual apartheid. Anthropologists and historians have worked since to bridge their theoretical and methodological differences, best captured by Dening's (1980:35–44) historical review of the term's use, followed by his eventual strict limitations on how the term might appropriately be used (Dening 1991:347–377). I am aware of the long debates, and the importance of this disciplinary designation combining ethnology and history to study America's First Nations peoples in particular. While I support all theoretical and methodological developments in formal training on how to do oral historical research and how to relate it to ethnology, history and archaeology, I still find the term counterproductive (see Chaves 2008 for a current review). Some sub-disciplines and academics still use the term to refer to early written traveller accounts; this appears to compound the error of preferring early written accounts by outsiders. Others use the term to refer to oral histories. I suggest we need to reconsider academic uses of the term ethnohistory as a sub-category of the disciplines of history or anthropology to refer to the study of peoples and cultures without *written* histories, generally not according to the understandings and practice of the mainly non-Western peoples being studied.

I have used the term oral history to draw attention to the live performance and transmission of knowledge to one or more individuals, We must refine our methodologies to consider the effects of the audience, event, place, and context or query to which the historian was responding in a particular presentation. Each of these factors may influence what the historian chooses to include, emphasise, or exclude. While a written account of an oral presentation may later be produced from notes or recordings, such an account is not the same as the original presentation. We must sharpen our methodologies to capture and deal with these differences. In many of the definitions discussed above, there appears to be an underlying assumption a) that the oral history has been recorded and/or transcribed into a written account, and b) that the oral and written account may be considered the same. Any public speaker differentiates between oratory, in which Pacific elders excel, and a polished written account. Expert anthropologist, writer and lecturer Gregory Bateson insisted on this important differentiation: he permitted members of the audience to record his lectures or seminars, but not to transcribe them. He reserved the right to control and change the language of oral presentations to language appropriate for general or academic publication (Bateson seminar, 1982).

Translation is a critical issue for those working with indigenous histories. Oral histories often require access to local specialised vocabularies and an understanding of the specialised language of politics (Peterson 1990), including the identification of and access to multiple layers of appropriate meaning. There are many reasons why a written transcription/translation of an oral history must not be taken as a stand-alone resource document.

As we strengthen relationships with indigenous scholars, some of the basic premises may be adjusted. It seems that a history seeking to understand a people and place remembered through oral histories, the landscape and material signs, and architecture and performances needs to begin with the premises that:

- there are expert knowledge systems retained by peoples and cultures who may use other media for the retention and transmission of historical knowledge, which may or may not have been partially transferred to written accounts in the past several centuries;

- indigenous oral historians are the experts and any written accounts of the oral histories (that are generally partial) should not be used independently without consultation with those who speak for the histories;

- the different theoretical bases, accepted methods and expertise of archaeologists and oral historians must be respected; and

- we must find ways to engage with different types of knowledge and verification.

Reflecting on oral histories

While the oral histories are primarily held and transmitted by the appropriate lineages and villages, at the regional level the Micronesian national and state historic preservation offices have the responsibilities of recording and preserving the histories and cultural knowledge. They often have the difficult task of mediating between oral historical and archaeological approaches. The following summaries are offered of some of the characteristics, structures, types and protocols that might be useful as an introduction to outsiders. This is necessarily incomplete as access to certain levels of knowledge or specific details is only given based on the oral historian's assessment of the knowledge and understandings of the protocols and the reasons why such information is sought. While this may limit cross-cultural understandings that could be relevant to theoretical work on the roles and responsibilities of experts and the structure and protocols of historical knowledge systems, I also recognise that these protocols are followed to protect and manage the integrity of the knowledge.

Characteristics of oral histories in Palau

Palau and Yap's multi-layered oral histories range from highly accessible short stories told to children, to the guarded lineage and village histories, some so strictly limited that they require a code for access. In my doctoral thesis, I used the image of the Palauan *iek* (a necklace of Palauan bead money, Figure 2) as a metaphor for oral histories. These valuables are considered male money, although only women wear the necklaces. While individuals earn bead monies through service, lineage elders control how they may be used and occasions when they might be worn, and by whom. The composition of the beads on a necklace is based on the ranked relationships of the individuals who brought the money into the house, the values of the various pieces, and a sense of balance and aesthetics. Experts know the stories of the named high-ranking individual monies, and the histories of their transfers. This bead-money necklace thus embodies the multi-valence of the oral histories, with their discrete units of different types, values and histories; the control of the pieces and the histories by the elders; the proper ordering of the pieces; the emphasis on social and spatial relationships; the limited occasions when necklaces are to be seen or their histories discussed; the physical grounding and representation of social relations

Figure 2. *lek*: A metaphor for oral history.

and histories; use of mnemonic devices; and the prestige and power based in the control of knowledge (Nero 1987:20–22).

Small oral versions of important histories are well known – for instance, the love story of Osilek (chief of Ulong) and Oreng. At its chiefly levels, this history expands to provide more details and refer to other Rock Island village histories, love relationships, wars and migrations. Histories are linked from the clans/lineages to the series of polities that range from the small villages comprising the districts to the wider village federations and two paramount chieftaincies. The male and female elders of the lineages and villages have the rights to and are responsible for appropriately transmitting the histories, and selecting the level of information suitable to the occasion and audience. That there may be different 'variants' of stories largely relates to the occasion, and the kin position and knowledge level of the person to whom the information is transmitted, similar to the highly structured protocols for the transmission of knowledge among Yolngu (Morphy 1991, 1995). Care is taken that the appropriate elder speaks. To ensure its proper transmission, however, different levels of the story are generally more widely known by clan members and elders, partly to ensure their continuation. All societies restrict access to some types of knowledge and information by law and practices. This appears to especially be the case in Pacific societies that rely strongly on oral histories and therefore maintain control over how such knowledge is transmitted and verified (see Kesolei 1977; Meleisea 1987; Hanlon 1988; Petersen 1990, 1994; Morphy 1991; Mauricio 1992; Schwarz 1997; Tellei et al. 2005).

Kesolei's paper (1977:4–11) identified attitudes and practices that might affect access to Palauan knowledge: information is restricted; there is an unwillingness to make their knowledge public; the proper person must be asked; opinions of Palauans are more important than those of foreigners, affecting how such information might be received until verified; and Palauans are protective of close relations and fellow villagers. These issues affect local as well as outsider researchers. Members of the Palau Resource Institute (PRI) worked successfully with archaeologists on part of the Compact Road project, and noted: 'sometimes access to traditional information does not come easily' (Tellei et al. 2005:12). The restrictive protocols to protect the proper transmission of verifiable histories raise barriers to access unless historians are carefully approached. The proper identification of the appropriate person with the knowledge and position to speak for the history is paramount. As noted by Kesolei (1977) and Tellei et al. (2005), this knowledge is generally grounded within a lineage/clan or village. It is common for either a knowledgeable elder or younger clan members to refer the researcher to the person who speaks for the history. Once the proper person has been identified by the local chief and other contacts and confirmed by the Palauan Society of Historians, the research path may be smoothed (Tellei et al. 2005).

Genres

It is useful to consider the types of oral histories and stories that may be recounted and their specific characteristics. In the Koror histories, we encountered several types of histories that followed different levels of protocols and access. I will leave the characterisation of Palauan oral historical genres to a Palauan scholar, but as an analogy, I summarise from Mauricio's study (1992:362–363) of Pohnpeian genres in which he attempted to understand the ways in which the people of Pohnpei might have understood Hambruch's (1932, 1936) 1910 requests for their oral traditions. Some of the histories he collected would have been 'stories of Pohnpei' (folk tales, legends, life histories), or 'details of Pohnpei' (applied or practical knowledge of social behaviour and specialised technological skills). The latter are necessarily susceptible to relatively short-term change and are more descriptive and less explanatory. In contrast, the 'content of Pohnpei' is comprised of subgroups of histories of the land and the people. Considered sacred, these are interpretive accounts that are much more subjective and generalising: 'Authoritative explanations are a prerogative of the senior oral historian' (Mauricio 1992:363). The final category is the 'sacredness of Pohnpei' (i.e. spells, magical or sorcery formulas, esoteric changes, medicinal knowledge). These are highly guarded, not normally disseminated, and characterised by archaic terminology suggesting (Mauricio 1992:363):

> ... that they have remained lexically intact over a long period of time. The majority of them are neither descriptive nor interpretive in nature. Rather, they are believed; they are thought of as possessing *manaman* (a form of detached authority, force or supernatural power).

To my understanding, a similar set of descriptive, interpretative and apparently unchanging types of oral histories exists in Palau. I believe that for Palau, what Mauricio discussed as the 'content of Pohnpei' histories might include histories of the land, villages and peoples of Palau and would include bodies of historical knowledge from which historians might draw in responding to specific questions or events (i.e. be more interpretive). This might also include Palau's memorised verbatim histories that may be of great antiquity and carefully controlled; these would not be altered during their performance. Yet they might not be part of what Mauricio included as the 'sacredness of Pohnpei', which would include some of the older chants in archaic language. I note that Parmentier (1987) specifically used the term 'sacredness of Palau' in his work on the oral histories and the role of the historians of Ngeremlengui in maintaining this. There are complex analyses to be made, and this discussion suggests caution for non-specialists in interpreting and categorising written accounts.

Protocols followed in oral historical research in Palau

As a researcher employed by Palauans and working under their direction, I was taught some of the protocols governing research in Palau, first by Palauan anthropologist Katharine Kesolei and the staff and board (1979–1982) of the Palau Community Action Agency.[2] I observed the care with which elders opened all meetings by acknowledging those present, explaining the purpose of the research to be undertaken and asking their permission and support. Care was taken to ensure a proper mix of researchers with kin or village linkages, both elders and more junior workers, and gender balance. Initial research results were reported back to the communities for clarification and comments, and at times spurred lively debates. Extreme care was taken to check data and interpretations.

In 1982 at the request of *Ibedul*, I was part of a Koror oral histories project under the auspices of the chiefly councils of central Koror (*ordomel*, the spear head): Ngarameketii (male), Kerngab (female), and *Rubekulkldeu* (the highest-ranking male chief of each of the constituent *renged* – or tied villages of Koror).[3] This research focused on the village/state histories of Koror (Erengul), one of Palau's two paramount chieftaincies, including its consolidation in the late 1600s and early 1700s.[4] I worked in a counterpart relationship with then *Kloteraol* Alexander Merep, who had just returned to Palau after completing his master's degree in political studies in the United States. As the holder of the title of *Kloteraol* he had the responsibility to speak for the *beluu* (village) within the Ngarameketii council; these oral histories were thus transmitted orally to an appropriate titleholder. Koror State staff members assisted in recording, transcribing, at times providing translations and seeking the meanings of special terminology.

To an outsider, it might appear that the Palauan history so collected would necessarily be of the elites. While the recording of village histories tends toward that (Sahlins 1985), in Micronesian societies chiefly council members generally represent clans of all ranks. In Palau, each of the chiefly councils is comprised of the selected titleholders of the 10 major *kebliil* (normally poorly glossed as 'clan' in English) of the village. Each of the titles holds specific responsibilities within the council. In turn, each of the *renged* (tied) villages are governed by their respective male and female councils, and the highest male titleholder of each of Koror's *renged* form the Rubekulkldeu council under the direction of the Ngarameketii.[5] Normally, the oral histories are held by the senior male and female titleholders of each of the lineages/clans and jealously guarded within these units; quality control is maintained through limiting who has the right to speak the history. Younger members learn the histories at levels appropriate to their position and aptitude. This is true both for the central villages and for the *Rubekulkldeu* villages that had existed before the consolidation and creation of the new polity of Koror. The villages recounted their long histories before the establishment of Koror, and their particular entitlements, rights and responsibilities were confirmed as they joined the new federation of Koror (Erengul).

The histories of the *ordomel* and *renged* villages and the histories of their past and present relationships were recorded. It was the responsibility of the senior male and/or female titleholders to speak the history of that village and clan; in each case, we were directed to those elders who could speak (and verify) the relevant histories. While we followed a template of interview topics, each historian chose what information (at what level) would be recorded. Some of the historians chose not to discuss details of the village gods. A male elder was often accompanied by his wife and/or by female clan members who would join the discussion. When we were interviewing female titleholders, the male transcriber generally did not accompany us, so that when *Kloteraol* did not join us the interviewee's daughter or other female relative often translated my questions into Palauan. With the exception of one bilingual titleholder who chose to speak in English, the interviews were conducted in Palauan. In the process of transcribing the interviews, our skilled transcriber at times encountered Palauan words that were not in general use. Where possible, these words were explained and translated into English by one of the respected Koror staff members, or a former educator, or, if necessary, referred to other language experts. All those interviewed could decide whether the interview or any of its parts should not be recorded.

Our interviews varied by the topic and genre of material presented. Some of the old histories were told as performances, often using archaic language and recited without interruption. Other topics elicited a lively interaction as a way of assessing the interviewer's knowledge, and at least one follow-up interview was generally required to clarify and extend discussions and check possible interpretations. We held interviews at relevant sites to spur memories of past events, such as the Ngarameketii or Ngerkldeu meeting houses, titleholders' houses, or village or Rock Island sites.

A factor not always considered when reading written documents of interviews or events relates to the dynamic between members of the audience and the oral historian. As noted by Kesolei (1977), a historian might not wish to share particular knowledge with those present. The social characteristics of the interviewers (clan/village affiliation, ties to the person interviewed, knowledge level and especially age) affected the dynamics and presentation of the story, especially in the more interpretive genres. The presence of a particular person could elicit or preclude certain stories. Knowledge may be provided only for information but not further dissemination.

Appropriate historians may be able to verify or query accounts, although the type of history may affect this. Some of the village histories were verified by the appropriate knowledge holders at the time in a joint interview with village titleholders. Certain types of questions are better pursued with a single or a few historians. Rarely, we were advised to seek an appropriate historian to *melediich* or 'shine the light' on a sensitive issue. Multiple sources – a physical sign, a chant, or a dance depicting an event – may also be used to verify accounts. Some chiefly *kelulau* or 'secret or sensitive political matters' were raised; in one case, the historian advised that we could hear and record but not write the *kelulau*.

Even if an interview is carefully conducted according to appropriate protocols, the histories so recorded may not fully reflect the knowledge of the historians. First, historians carefully responded to a question as it was presented, which might not have elicited all the knowledge they held on the topic. Second, the historian's knowledge of a history is often multi-levelled in both the ways it is transmitted and the ways it should be used. The historian will choose the level on which to respond, if at all. Even when in agreement with the stated purpose, the historian might not reveal the level of his/her knowledge on a specific topic.

As with all historical sources, oral histories must be used carefully. Today, interviews are often kept in tape or digitised form, and many are transcribed in the language of the historian. A very serious consideration is the language the interview was originally in and how and why it may be translated. In Palau, where both English and Palauan are official languages, English is increasingly used in documents, even though glosses only incompletely 'translate' the concepts of the original language. A written account of a Palauan history might only have been 'partial' when recorded, some of its meanings might be lost in translation, or the reader's understanding might differ depending on the version read. Translations and back-translations will not easily resolve the difficulties.

Koror's histories were transmitted orally, recorded and transcribed, as were major events of the polity and its governance during this period. Protocols for recording Koror's oral histories were carefully followed. Information and interpretations were verified both in the process of interviews when multiple experts were present, and through subsequent interviews. While to a large extent these protocols mirror those generally used by socio-cultural researchers, when seeking privileged histories in Palau close attention to the protocols is critical to the quality of the knowledge shared. It is through these protocols that trust may be gained so that, in conjunction with cultural expectations, the oral historian understands the purpose of the research and the ways the information will be used. The Koror state-level research was possible only because it was done for the State of Koror.[6]

Oral historical accounts of early Yap stone money quarrying: Yap and Palau

We are fortunate that the oral historians of both Yap and Palau retain histories of the early political/economic activity of stone-money quarrying. Accessed independently, the histories agree on key issues important to island histories, such as identification of named money pieces presented from Rul to Koror and from Gachepar to Melekeok to confirm quarrying rights and to illustrate the significance of place names in indicating relationships.

I believe that the careful consideration of a variety of historical sources can supply a framework by which the 'snapshots' provided by outsider-written descriptions may be interpreted. In using these various media, I suggest two controls to test the reliability of the data:

- Within each island or polity, using indigenous tests of the reliability of sources, as well as more locally based tests such as the conjuncture of chant, stone record, and/or money piece – the latter of which, in Palau, validates important histories (see Parmentier 1987:12).

- Between islands or polities, verification is provided by using independent sources that relate to the same subject.

Yapese and Palauan oral histories of early stone-money voyages

Yapese histories

When Yapese and Palauan elders are asked about the histories of their relationships with other peoples before the European ships came, they turn to the stories of the transactions of valuables between the leaders of the two islands' polities. According to a Yapese money expert, in the beginning Yapese and Palauans used similar forms of money, a single piece worn on a necklace by the wives and daughters of the chiefs, as Palauan women wear them today, or kept in purses. The beads were of many materials, some glass, others stone or clam shell, and in many different colours.[7]

The opening: Ngermid history

The brief oral history quoted at the beginning of the chapter describes a very early visit by Yapese for quarrying stones to craft into a form of money. I believe this account refers to what is called Omis Cave in the archaeological studies of Fitzpatrick (2001, 2003), discussed below, and other oral histories. The Yapese elder's daughter translated her account into English during my interview, a language common to Yapese, Palauans and myself, and from which a written account was made and excerpted. This history provides an important record of the origin and meaning of the name Ngermid and documents the gifts of food used to establish friendly relationships between the Yapese and the chief of the village in order to secure his permission to quarry the stone needed to make money. The elder uses the personal plural, demonstrating her incorporation of the ancestors for whom she is speaking into the story, an important characteristic of traditional accounts in many societies. She refers to the Yapese use of magic and the Yapese fear of discovery (not always communicated in accounts by males). The name 'Ngermid' provides a time marker, albeit ambiguous.

Ngermid is one of the ancient villages of Belau from the time of Chuab (Nero 1987:185; Liston and Miko, this volume). It has its own side village division and two chiefly councils, and elders still point out the cave site associated with this story. The identification of Ngermid as an early site for stone-money work and the account of the direct relationship between the chief of Ngermid and the Yapese are important in suggesting that these might have occurred very early in the cultural sequence. It would be useful to establish tentative dates for this important inter-island network. These exchange networks as early international relationships, and the production of monetary valuables are long recognised as key to political development, especially of chiefly hierarchies (Kirch 1984; Nero 1990; Earle 1991). Ngermid continues to be an important village, and today is one of the tied Ngerkldeu villages that comprise the Koror paramount chieftaincy under *Ibedul*.

A Yapese oral historian recounted (with key passages indicated in bold):

The Yapese were industrious and started to look elsewhere for a new form of currency. There were two men who went to Palau, where they found a beautiful white stone. **This very first expedition was led by Fatha'an and Angumang, and were trips for Rull and Tomil, for Fatha'an was from Ngolog [Rull] and Angumang from Tomil. During this expedition they found the limestone islands and a place called Ramith; that's where they started to make some kind of medium of exchange.** There they made the stone pieces into a number of different shapes, including the shape of a fish. Then finally it was full moon. They looked at the full moon, and then made something in that shape. But they had a problem carrying the stone, so they put a hole in the middle to make it easier to carry.

Fatha'an and Angumang were both navigators, and they were competing to bring money back to Yap. They worked in the quarries they found in the rock islands, working during the quarrying and shaping of the pieces of stone money. And Fatha'an finished first, so Angumang told him, 'why don't you take the ones over first?' **So Fatha'an set out from Ngeremdiu,** and started for Yap. Fatha'an being Yapese, and knowing Yapese ways, knew that it was more than likely that Angumang would use magic to make a typhoon to kill him while he was travelling on the ocean, so that he would not be able to make it to Yap. So instead, as he was travelling north, when he came to some islands he went into them and hid. **And the place where he hid is called Ramith, Yapese for 'the place of hiding'.** And several days later the typhoon came. And seven days later, after the typhoon, Angumang sailed for Yap, and there were heavy seas. But Fatha'an didn't move, as he knew that Angumang would sail, so Angumang came and passed Fatha'an. Then Fatha'an created a typhoon for Angumang, so that the gales and waves were high, and split the canoes into pieces, and some of the rafts carrying the stones sank, and other rafts were separated from the canoes. But Angumang was able to bring some pieces on his rafts trailing after his canoes to Yap.

Then a little later Fatha'an came behind, and he collected some of the stone money still attached to rafts floating on the water, left behind by Angumang. So he added some of Angumang's money to his own, and proceeded to Yap. And he came very slowly, for he was towing a lot of stone monies on the rafts.

When Angumang arrived on Yap, people asked what had happened to Fatha'an. And he said that he must have died on the way to Yap. And Fatha'an's parents and the people of Rull started mourning. And it was several months later that Fatha'an came, pulling a lot of stone money on rafts. **It was night time when he arrived, and he came into the harbour here, at Nelil, then went up the mangrove channel and hid among the trees. And that place also is called Mamith, or hiding place. There are two places called Mith, the one in Palau, and the one in Yap called Mamith.** So before dawn Fatha'an went to his parents' house and woke them up. The parents turned around, saying, stop making fun of us, our son died a couple of months ago. No, he said, this is Fatha'an. He then told them what had happened, so they all gathered together and cried. So he was instructed by his father to take all the stone money to Balabat [the high village of Rull] early in the morning. The father went to tell all the people that Fatha'an had returned, for the people believed he had been lost at sea. And that is how Ramith was named.

And when the Yapese first went on expeditions to quarry rocks in Palau to make their money, there were fights. So the Yapese found some caves, and went there to protect themselves from attack. The Palauans call these yii.

During a later trip, in order to make peace, the chief of Rull made a present to the chief of Palau; he gave one of the Yapese money beads to Ibedul of Koror to buy a quarry site. The bead money, of the type called Churwoo, was from Yap, [he didn't know where they got it]. As there were two chiefs of Palau, so two monies were given. These two monies, which were given, Tabremdiu [Point of Ngeremdiu] and Beluulechab [Yap], were the biggest of all Palauan monies, so they could purchase the gogyal [rock islands], of Tabremdiu and Ramith. The money was used to buy the rights to take rock from Tabremdiu [a site in the rock islands south of the island of Koror]. The second money was presented to Palau by the chiefs of Gagil, from Gachepar. There were two gifts: one from Balabat [Rull] to Koror, the other from Gagil to Melekeok. The Palau chiefs didn't mind selling the rights to quarry in some of the gogyal, as there was no one living there. And that's when the disputes between Yap and Palau were settled.

And there were a number of expeditions between Palau and Yap after the one made by Fatha'an and Angumang, and before the Europeans came. And during the exchanges the people would help each other. There was a particular family of some influence, and the women of this family, the highest clan, helped the Yapese people by providing food for their living. And in return the men helped the family by building houses, or stone platforms for houses.

... During the time of Angumang and Fatha'an, there were no men from the outer islands on the trips. Because these two were the navigators. But during the later expeditions some of the men from the outer islands were invited. Later when they made expeditions they asked the outer islanders to join, which is their sawei [their path].

... And ever since then, when the Westerners came, they began using the ship to transport stone money to Yap. But those that came by canoe earlier are of higher value.

The chiefs later closed the channels of collecting stone money in Palau, for two reasons. The first is that if they allowed people to go there and bring so many pieces of money on the island, their value would go down. And the other reason is that then there were ships that went to Palau carrying the stone monies back, and these pieces were bigger than before, but there was no danger in getting them. The largest piece of money brought to Yap, now on Rumung, was brought by ship, and the traditional leaders during that time said this is a bigger piece, but there is a smaller piece which was gotten by hardship taken by canoes, so the smaller one is more valuable than the bigger piece. There were so many pieces it was hard to keep value in the whole system, so they stopped the quarrying.

Discussion of the oral histories: Yap

I have shown in bold key texts to be considered in trying to unravel the time-depth issue for Yapese quarrying in Palau. While the identification of Ramith, or Ngermid, is an important time marker, its meaning could relate to Ngermid either as a Child of Chuab, or as a *renged* village of Koror. Unfortunately, the narrative's identified sequence of events, as currently recorded, does not solve the problem. The historian indicated that quarrying began at Ramith led by men of Fatha'an of Rull and Angumang of Tomil. The historian noted that there was a time lapse and period of fighting before later expeditions. To end the fighting and establish quarrying rights, the Chief of Rull presented *Ibedul* of Koror the money *Tabremdiu*, while the Chief of Gachepar presented the named money *Beluulechab* to the *Reklai*, the chief of Melekeok. The shift in participation from Tomil to Gachepar may also signal a time lapse. While the sequence is clear, there is no apparent indication of the antiquity of the earliest quarrying voyages.

Palauan histories

Ngermid

Interviews with the elders of Ngermid village confirmed the Yapese history that the village's name is Yapese in origin, and that its naming had to do with the Yapese who hid there while on a stone-money quarrying voyage.

> While the origin of the name is not generally known in Palau, it is not hidden or secret, and can be discussed. When the Yapese first came they were quarrying for stone money at the rock islands on the Airai side, but they were fought there. So they came over to the rock islands by Ngermid, where they hid in a cave, which is not far from the main road. And then Bilung heard that the Yapese were there, and told her people to bring them to her, and she cared for them. And then they brought a money from Yap to give to Ibedul, the one called Tabremdiu, which was given from Rull to Idid [the Koror clan of which Ibedul and Bilung are the highest male and female titles respectively], which is why they are related today. It was at least the second or third quarrying voyage when the payment was made to Ibedul.

This account from elders of Ngermid adds information that before quarrying in Ngermid, Yapese had been quarrying on islands in Airai, and there were at least two to three voyages before the Yapese from Rull presented a bead money named *Tabremdiu* to *Ibedul* of the Idid clan of Koror.

Palau Society of Historians

The Palau Society of Historians also began its discussion of early linkages to the outside world with the Yapese quarrying of stone money in Palau. It provided information about other islands as well.

> The link, from the time long ago, had to do with the quarrying of **balang** [stone money]. They came, but it was a bit difficult that taking balang from Koror, for they belonged to Koror. And there was also a link with Melekeok, for Reklai bought the island **Toi er a Bisch** [Channel of the Wild Taro] so they could take their stone money there. And that happened for perhaps twenty or twenty five years. There was a treaty, which gave them the path to come to Palau. And this was the story of Ibedul and Reklai. For it was Ibedul who controlled the **chelebacheb** [rock islands], which was well explained. So they [the Yapese] should have been the people of Ibedul. But the reason that Reklai bought a rock island is that he was leader of the other heaven, and it would be bad for him not to have his hand on the spear as well. So they tied the relationship between Yap and Palau, those two heads. That was before the time of the Westerners, before the time of the Spanish, long before that. And the Yapese came by canoe to take the balang back to Yap on their rafts [trailing behind the canoes].
>
> But that time was difficult, for it was still a time of warfare in Palau. And so the Yapese were afraid. And it was during that time that Reklai and Ibedul were bringing together their peoples. And so the Yapese catered to those two leaders. And they came to Palau to make those large stone monies. And that's why Yap and Palau had one heart. And at that time Yap was also divided, and one side came, that of Rull, which came to Koror. And the other came to the small villages that went to Melekeok. And that's why, a few months ago, we went from Melekeok to visit in Gachpar, in Yap, for several weeks. And it was the relationship of the stone money, which was the basis for this visit. For the second group that came didn't have a way of working with those that were already here from Yap, for they were split. That's

why they went to find Reklai, and why he bought that rock island in front of Airai, so that the second group of Yapese could take their money there. So today we and those from Yap are linked together by that money.

And that was the rule of Palau in the past, that of hospitality, of taking care of people. It was the law, that the chief should humbly receive them, taking them to heart, to make them his people. It was the chief who took in the outsiders. And there is a chant, which records this.

And there is also the story of another stone money voyage, that of a chief of Melekeok who came to take stone money. He came and quarried the money and was on his way to Yap when he was struck by a storm. And he was drifted ashore at Ngchesar, but then he was taken to Melekeok where he became the third chief there, holding the title of Ngirkungil. Yes, he was Yapese, but he was given a high chiefly title in Melekeok. And this was before the ships had first come …

Because those that came from the two heavens of Yap couldn't come and work together here, those people of Tomil and Rull. And that's why they went to Reklai and begged of him for help. And during that time Ibedul and Reklai could communicate privately through their messengers. And that Ngirkungil took some money and gave it to Ibedul, saying, these are my people, please let them come and take their stone money here. So he sold them that rock island in front of Airai, so they could quarry there. That was a long time ago, taking stone money a very long time ago.

Discussion of the oral histories: Palau

The first oral history from Ngermid speaks of the earliest quarrying voyages, first to Airai and then, after fighting, to the Rock Islands by Ngermid. It states that following at least two or three voyages, the Yapese from Rull presented *Ibedul* with a money named *Tabremdiu* in return for the rights to quarry stone money. This history may be compared with the short history at the beginning of the chapter. Other oral historians referring to this site gave the name and history of the name 'Omis'.

The second oral history was provided by members of the Palau Society of Historians, speaking for Palau. They referred to Yapese quarrying voyages at the time that the two paramount chieftaincies of Koror and Melekeok were each being consolidated, before the arrival of European ships. Once again they recounted Rull's presentation of *Tabremdiu* to *Ibedul* and Gachepar's presentation of a money to *Reklai* for rights to quarry the stone money. This account provided greater details of *Reklai's* purchase of a Rock Island so that both chieftaincies could be represented in the relationships with the two villages of Yap.

Differing practices concerning time

A challenging but potentially productive difference between the expert practices of oral historians and archaeologists is the way in which they address and relate to time. Archaeological research emphasises chronologies established by thorough examination of carefully sampled and controlled stratified data, with date ranges proposed in a calendar time sequence. Western time is linear and is generally expressed within standard BC or AD, or BP (before present) categories. In contrast, Palauan oral histories focus on mnemonic devices to anchor and help verify the history given by respected historians. These devices range from places, titleholders or individuals involved in important events, to physical signs (i.e. landscape markers, stones, money pieces, certain plants, bas-relief carvings depicting histories) or performative genre (i.e. chants, songs, dances) that refer to events. This material is also 'sedimented' in a multi-layered way that is metaphorically similar to archaeological excavation units.

While it is common for an account to include markers referring to the relative order of events, the focus is on social relationships and places, and not calendar time. Information on the relative sequence of events may be of use, but may be ambiguous if the attempt is to identify a specific time period. More important, while Micronesian oral historians may identify a narrative's relative sequence of events, it is just as common for them to omit events in the sequence. Because oral histories, and other types of knowledge, are important components of power, the historian will often not divulge the entire story at one sitting. Hence, the presentation of a full sequence of events in any one narrative should not be expected. With diligence and careful analysis of multiple accounts, the skilled oral history researcher may be able to identify missing parts and frame further questions in order to piece together a complete sequence (see Petersen 1994).

As would be expected of experts, respected oral historians in Palau will very carefully identify areas of which they do not have any knowledge. They also judiciously consider what information they do hold for its relevance. The oral historians may be able to search their deeper knowledge of the narratives, and perhaps some of the *kelulau* histories they retain, to provide further insights into the early period of Yapese quarrying. This would assist in an issue that is still unresolved using archaeological methods and approaches.

Bringing together oral historical and archaeological approaches

The Micronesian Historic Preservation Offices (HPO) were originally established through the extension of a number of federal programs to the US Trust Territory of the Pacific Islands. During the region's transition to freely associated status, reduction of a block grant threatened the continuation of the Historic Preservation Offices. The offices in the newly freely associated nations of the Federated States of Micronesia, Palau and the Marshall Islands lobbied strongly and successfully with the US Congress for continuation of federal funding. The Micronesian HPOs[8] are still closely linked to American archaeological practices, including the challenges and opportunities created by the 1990 passage of the Native American Graves Protection and Repatriation Act (NAGPRA). Issues of the historical veracity of oral traditions have recently been strongly debated within that context. Mason (2000) analysed the challenging (n=4) and supporting (n=7) arguments for the incorporation of oral traditions in archaeological theory or practices from Native American perspectives. His conclusions focus on the dilemma concerning the relationships between calendrical time and relative chronologies and tendencies of oral societies to achronicity. He also recognises the dangers of what he calls 'cherry picking in a minefield' (Mason 2000:260). Mason concludes that the two epistemologies are fundamentally disparate, with his careful review of the arguments providing a foundation for future discussions.

Rock Island studies

The period of my first research in Palau (1979–1984) partially coincided with archaeological studies by the Center for Archaeological Investigations (CAI) of Southern Illinois University at Carbondale. I was working through Koror State and the archaeologists were based at the Bureau of Arts and Culture (BAC). It was impossible to schedule joint site visits, partly due to our positions in different agencies, but also because of time constraints for the work undertaken. Both the CAI and Koror State teams collected oral histories from living historians. The Koror State team focused on those titleholders or specialists whose traditional rights and responsibilities for sections of the Rock Islands continued into the present. This mainly included the villages of Ngerchemai, Ngerbeched, Ngerkebesang and Ngermid, while working with all the titleholders of Ngarameketii and Rubekulkldeu as appropriate.

As Tellei et al. (2005:11) noted, clan, lineage or family histories affect access to traditional information. The familial links of the BAC staff in some cases differed from those of Koror State. It appears that CAI might have recorded oral histories from historians linked to Koror and perhaps from descendants of former Rock Island villages whose people migrated elsewhere. If so, such histories could provide important insights into the dynamics of the out-migrations, as the resettlements of clans and villages established new allegiances in other states. As these oral histories and identifications of the Rock Island villages were conducted nearly three decades ago, they should be re-verified.

Verification is often a long-term project. In 1983–1984, the elders wished to make a map available to the general public that accurately recorded place names in the Rock Islands. My 1987 doctoral dissertation included a draft of the Koror map, although the included Rock Island place names were not immediately verifiable. Years later, establishment of the Koror State Rangers under the direction of Adelbert Eledui, and now Ilebrang Olkeriil, allowed this important verification to be appropriately completed. This map is now available (at different levels of precision) through the Palau Visitors Authority and the Rock Islands Southern Lagoon Management Area (Figure 3).

Study of early Yapese stone-money quarrying in Palau

In the early 1990s, I sought a different type of cross-validation of oral histories and their potential time depth by approaching the Yap HPO with which I had been working since 1979. With its assistance and the provision of staff to translate and transcribe, we were able to interview recognised elders who spoke for Yap-Palau stone-money quarry stories and could appropriately transmit them. Following Yapese protocols and state law, the Council of Pilung ultimately approved a Palau-Yap Linkages paper for presentation and publication (through the Yap HPO). I also conducted additional interviews with elders in Palau and with the Palau Society of Historians. The resulting paper was provided to the Palau and Yap HPOs and the Belau National Museum for use by local researchers. The experts quoted above are in this manuscript.

At the time, we did not have archaeological dates to use in considering the relative time period/s in which these stories took place. It was solely an oral history project working with Yapese and Palauan elders and there was no attempt to establish a timeline. In 1992, I simply noted that the identification of Ngermid did not resolve the ambiguity of potential dating of the earliest Yapese quarrying activities.

Recent archaeological research on Palau-Yapese stone money

There have been two recent doctoral studies and subsequent publications concerning the Palau-Yap stone-money exchange, by University of Oregon archaeology graduates Descantes (2005) and Fitzpatrick (2003). The two archaeologists used the term ethnohistory somewhat differently and both valued oral histories. The two differing approaches to the use of oral histories (or ethnohistorical data) provide an excellent foundation for a discussion of current practices.

Descantes' thesis concerned the development of the exchange relationships between Yap and Ulithi. While focused on *sawei* relationships between the villages of Yap Island and the Outer Islands of Yap, he included several sections considering Yapese stone-money quarrying. Descantes (2005:16) used the term ethnohistory, which he defined, in contrast with archaeological history, as:

> an ethnological study based on historical documents and indigenous histories, lends non-material contextual information about island interactions of a short time span while archaeological evidence, on the other hand, provides a representation of exchange practices in much longer time duration.

Rather than prehistory, he used the term protohistory, which he defined as: 'the time segment between European discovery and the settlement of the island's societies' (Descantes

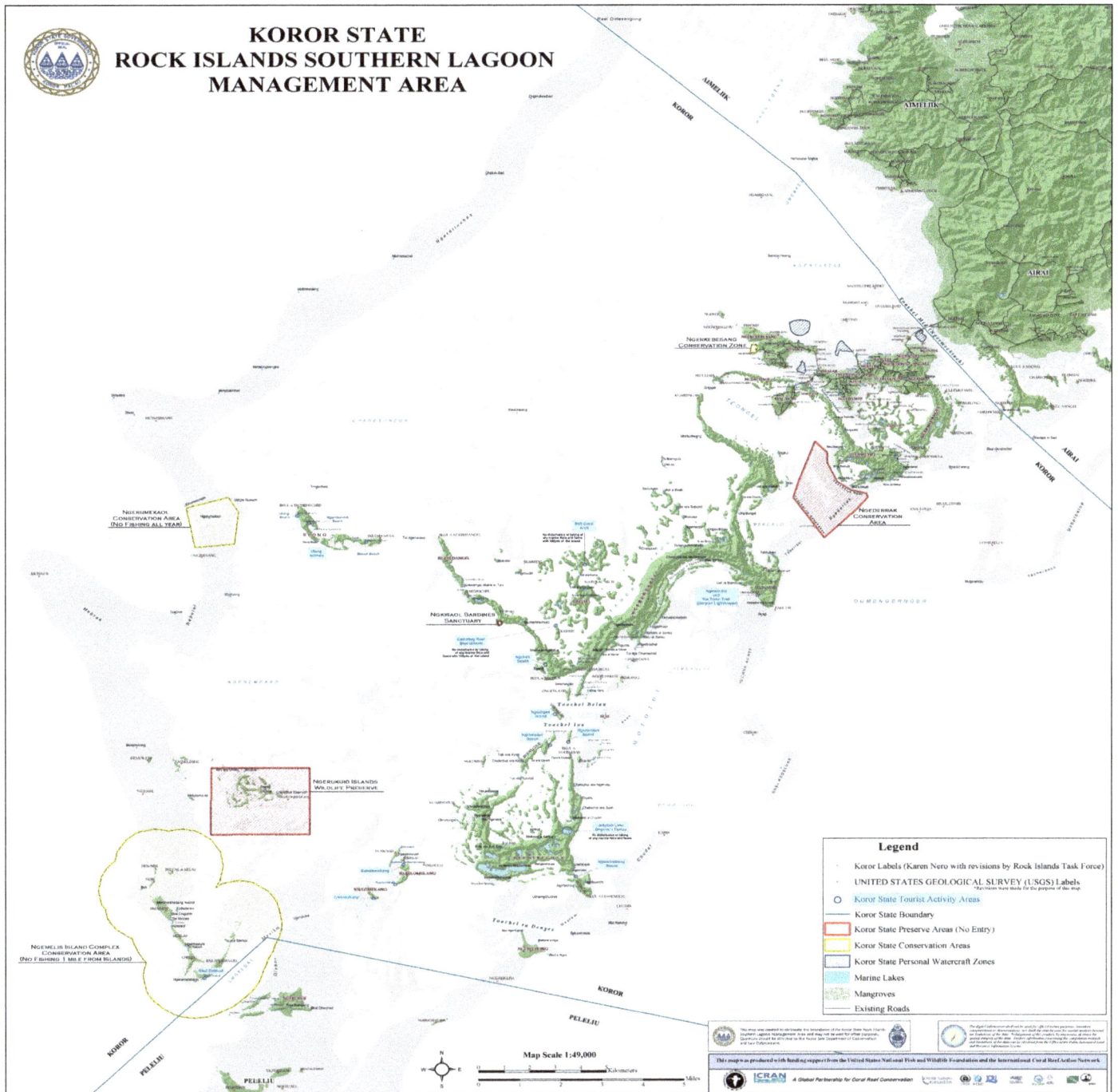

Figure 3. Map of the Koror State Rock Islands–Southern Lagoon management area.

2005:29). For Yap, he identified this as the period between AD 1525 and AD 1843. Descantes carefully analysed historical documents from the 16th century onwards, including the writings of early visitors, missionaries and traders, and the detailed 19th century scientific observations – the first 'ethnographic accounts' of the Polish naturalist Kubary (Descantes 2005:29–38).

In his discussion chapter, while considering the 'Epistemological Challenge … [of] the integration of archaeological and ethnohistoric records involved in his exchange model', Descantes noted (2005:95):

European contact is an important boundary point because not only major cultural transformations ensued, but also because this is when Western Carolinian cultures entered the European ethnohistorical records. The latter did not have a profound effect on the sedimentation of the archaeological record, but it did influence the ethnohistoric records and methodology for integrating both records. The last 400 years of the exchange model is a combination of both records. My construction of the pre-contact period relied, but for a few cases, on the archaeological records alone. I did this for the obvious reasons that the European-made ethnohistoric record was more accessible and understandable to me. While I relied little on indigenous oral histories for explaining the archaeological patterns, I did use it to frame the research ...

Protohistoric period interpretations, which depended upon archaeological and European-produced ethnohistoric data, were richer than either record alone. I used both records in a complementary fashion to focus on the problem of change.

Descantes (2005:95) chose to limit his use of indigenous oral histories to frame his research, provide leads for sites to be investigated or to add 'details of practice and the *mentalities* of the people'.

It appears that Descantes did not have access to, or recognised he did not have the specialised expertise to work with, contemporary oral historians. He also recognised that those oral histories of the *sawei* earlier recorded by anthropologists had been of historical, not modern practices. He used the term ethnohistory to refer to those indigenous histories recorded by anthropologists, perhaps marking their transformation in the process of writing such histories of the *sawei* system. Descantes (2005:29):

Anthropologists recorded ethnohistory from their informants who were taught by older relatives and friends about the formalized tribute system. Therefore, the ethnographic data represent how the system was meant to operate in the nineteenth and twentieth centuries.

Without access to oral histories that had been collected at the time of the *sawei* practices Descantes (2005:95) would consider contemporaneous, he followed Gosden (1996) in considering these as mythno-histories or ethnohistories, identifying specifically myths, histories and genealogies as:

... partial and distorted accounts of the past made to shore up particular interests and undermine others, in exactly the same way as other histories are, but they also contain information about past events and the cultural schemes through which events were appreciated.

Clearly, Descantes recognised the complexity and different epistemologies involved in working with oral historical as opposed to archaeological knowledge. He undertook the challenge of integrating several types of ethnohistorical accounts, although recognising that the oral histories could not have been recorded at the time of such developments. It appears that he did not work with contemporary oral historians from Yap or Ulithi, but relied on earlier anthropological records of oral histories. While he chose not to use recorded indigenous oral histories for the most part, he recognised their potential for other scholars to pursue. Descantes' (2005:96) thoughtful conclusion pointing to the value of closer work with 'ethnohistorians and native peoples' foregrounds my understandings, although his framing of indigenous oral histories as 'myth-history' and 'ideology' are worthy of debate:

The integration of mytho-history in my interpretations about the past is only as accurate as my understanding of the texts. Despite these challenges, I believe this rich data set of ideology is a potential source worthy of closer investigation by archaeologists *in collaboration with ethnohistorians and native peoples.* (emphasis added)

The second PhD dissertation, by Scott Fitzpatrick (2003), is an archaeological investigation of the Yapese stone-money quarrying in Palau. In his chapter on oral traditions, ethnohistory and ethnography, he attempted to broaden the ways in which oral traditions might be used to help understand the origins and transformation of stone-money production and exchange processes, and in his acknowledgements, he recognised the support of the chiefs and governors of Airai, the chiefs of Ngermid, the Palau Society of Historians, the Palau Cultural Advisory Board, and Kathy Kesolei. Like Descantes, Fitzpatrick began with ethnohistoric accounts generally drawn from early European explorers, travellers and traders. His second section, entitled 'Oral traditions'[9] and ethnographic observations, consists primarily of paraphrased or verbatim quotations of oral histories recorded (and excerpted) by Nero in the 1990s and one early account by Müller (1918, quoted by Gilliland 1975:188), from which Fitzpatrick took the title of his thesis. For the most part, the oral histories were simply quoted to provide a descriptive background of the early quarrying visits, supported by an ethnographic observation by Hunter-Anderson (1983:19) that the early relationship between Koror and Rull might explain the 1980s place of residence of Palauans in Yap. Fitzpatrick's use of the term ethnographic observations presumably also included those referred to in the following sections summarising accounts and photographs from early travellers, and traders[10] and scholars interested in how stone-money pieces were valued (strongly based on the work of de Beauclair 1971). He also drew on acknowledged scholars such as Kubary, Alkire, Lingenfelter, Friedman, Hezel and Lessa in a comprehensive review of relevant recorded oral traditions, traveller and trader accounts and the work of recognised predominantly socio-cultural anthropologists. Fitzpatrick returned to the oral histories and ethnographic accounts in his analysis of Yapese-Palauan interactions, and concluded that (2003:96):

> According to oral traditions and ethnographic accounts, the most extreme example of subservience within the three groups (Palauans-Yapese-Outer Islanders) of these exchange networks appear to have been the Yapese in their dealings with the Palauans. As noted previously, Palauan oral traditions state that the Yapese were subservient to the Palauans and worked building stone pathways, foundations, and other infrastructure projects in return for quarrying rights.

This is somewhat misleading, in that the accounts he referred to of the Yapese (and Outer Islanders) working on infrastructure projects in Palau were based on quotations from Kubary's late 19th century and Müller's early 20th century observations, not on the oral traditions. Returning to the oral histories, he then described more equal exchange relationships and cognate place names and titles from the two island groups, which he next discussed. Overall, Fitzpatrick used oral traditions to provide a descriptive introduction to frame his study.

My one concern in reading the thesis was that in the oral traditions section, the quoted oral histories were excerpted from an early version of my research paper on the Yap-Palau early quarrying relationships without seeking my permission, the normal academic protocol for using lengthy quotations. Nor in his thesis did he acknowledge working with any of the Yapese elders, which raised concerns about whether the Yapese were aware of and approved of the use of the materials, although the excerpts were drawn from a paper approved by the Council of Pilung and left with the Yap and Palau Historic Preservation Offices. In the absence of any communication from Fitzpatrick, I made arrangements to meet with my Yapese colleagues and appropriate elders and was happy to confirm that the Yapese elders were aware of and supported the use of the materials in support of subsequent proposals under the relevant Palau and Yap offices.

On further reflection, I appreciated that Fitzpatrick did not attempt to personally collect the oral histories. Especially at a doctoral level, it is difficult enough to master and demonstrate the appropriate level of archaeological theoretical and methodological expertise, much less that of a second discipline such as oral history, with its own protocols, research methods and analytical techniques. Any true integration of the epistemologies and methods of archaeological and oral historical expertise does not appear feasible for an individual's doctoral research. Nevertheless, normal academic and indigenous protocols must be identified and followed. I suggest that scholars take care in using written excerpts of oral histories and check these where possible with the collector of the histories and the oral historians who speak for the information.

Lessons from recent and current collaborative work in Palau

The work of archaeologists and oral historians differ epistemologically and in disciplinary preparation. The two fields both require long training periods and include specialist techniques and theoretical understandings. Both are site specific, although the time needed on site may significantly differ. Data collected by archaeologists generally requires some laboratory analysis. This is followed by analysis by the archaeologist and interpretation and preparation of the data. Information from oral historical accounts, collected in sequential interviews over months and sometimes years, must be reviewed, transcribed and often translated into a common language such as English. These accounts require verification by the persons/titles with the original source and appropriate local experts.

Recent studies recognising the importance of working with oral historians contribute to work between our sub-disciplines, reducing theoretical, methodological and terminological differences. Our success as we further refine their theoretical frameworks and methodologies will depend on our relationships with oral historians. With regard to oral histories, we must foreground the living knowledge of the oral historians as that passed on to future generations; it is the living tradition rather than any written portions of such knowledge that are authoritative. While recognising that oral histories will be recorded, transcribed, translated and written, we must acknowledge the effects of each transition. While hoping for greater insight through collaboration, we cannot expect that the knowledge collected through such different approaches will necessarily support, refute or provide mutually recognised value to the research. Finding ways to join the separate paths to knowledge that are followed by oral historians and archaeologists has been difficult in the past. Forging a shared path will involve constant negotiation and engagement with different types of knowledge.

One model of successful collaborative research was the incorporation of oral historical documentation by the Pacific Resource Institute (Tellei et al. 2005) in the Palau Compact Road cultural resource management investigations.[11] The Palau Historic Preservation Office began in the 1990s to ensure the active collaboration of oral historical and archaeological research in Palau. The collaboration was written into the Compact Road project from the outset to provide significant data and to ensure both the intangible and tangible cultural remains were appropriately mitigated. This supported frequent consultation, joint analyses and co-publication by archaeologists and oral historians. Following this model, rather than trying to bridge very different epistemological and methodological approaches, a team approach with active work towards interdisciplinary publications that highlight each other's strengths and the issues encountered will move us forward.

Notes

1. In this section, those definitions in quotations have been taken from the *Oxford Dictionary of English*, 2nd edition.

2. During my five years residence in Palau, I also worked closely with the Belau National Museum, the Palau Bureau of Arts and Culture (once named the Historic Preservation Office) and the Palau Society of Historians. Two families welcomed me as their '*ngalek*' or child, and have provided invaluable guidance and support throughout the years.

3. The male and female titles and councils have complementary responsibilities in managing village production and political relationships. Women's work centres on the customary symbolic and economic support of the male titles/councils by managing the feasts required to confirm the taking of a title or other major events. The male titleholders and councils present the political voice of the clan/village. Both types of councils are supported by age-graded and gendered *cheldebechel* (clubs). Through participating in this dispersed system of governance, members learn the structured relationships between clans and villages through practice. At most events, men and women, and often boys and girls, perform appropriate chants and dances commemorating major historical events, again ensuring wide distribution of historical knowledge.

4. I was permitted to use some of these materials as part of my doctoral thesis.

5. Under US trust territorial administration, the former district villages were recognised as municipalities which, in 1981, were replaced by state governments. In Koror, the traditional male chiefs generally held the highest municipal or state positions. During the Koror Constitutional Convention (1983–84), half the representatives were drawn from traditional leaders, and the remaining were elected (in many cases those elected would be likely to hold titles in the future). In recent years, both in amended constitutions and in daily practices, there are increasing separations between traditional and elected leadership, and the election of government officials.

6. An earlier offer to record the Koror histories was not accepted.

7. Beads and ring pieces made of *Tridacna* were used in many parts of the Pacific.

8. In Palau the name was changed to the Palau Bureau of Arts and Culture (BAC).

9. It appears Fitzpatrick was following Vansina's (1985) early nomenclature of oral traditions as accounts of events not personally witnessed.

10. Including traveller and trader accounts as ethnographic accounts stretches the usual requirements of scientific observation and analysis for an account to so qualify.

11. Compact Road cultural resource management work was conducted by International Archaeological Research Institute, Inc. out of Honolulu under contract to the US Army Corps of Engineers, Pacific Ocean Division.

Acknowledgements

Over the past two decades, support for this research has been received from a number of sources, including the University of California, Berkeley Institute of Social Change, the National Institute of Mental Health, Koror State Government, the Robert F. Gumbiner Fund of the University of California, Irvine and the National Science Foundation. Recent research trips were funded by the University of Auckland and the University of Canterbury in New Zealand.

I especially acknowledge the present and former Palau Ministers of Community and Cultural Affairs Faustina Rehuher and Senator Alexander Merep; oral historian Fermina Brel Murray; anthropologist Katharine Kesolei; archaeologists Rufino Mauricio, the late Rita Olsudong and Jolie Liston; the Palau and Yap Historic Preservation Offices; the Palau Society of Historians and the male and female elders of Palau and Yap who have patiently shared their knowledge with us and provided training in the protocols of local historical research. I also thank the support of the Koror State Government staff members.

References

Biersack, A. 1991. *Clio in Oceania: Toward a historical anthropology*. Smithsonian Institution Press, Washington.

Burley, D.V. 1998. Tongan archaeology and the Tongan past, 2850–150 B.P. *Journal of World Prehistory* 12(3):337–392.

Chaves, K.K. 2008. Ethnohistory: From inception to postmodernism and beyond. *Historian* 70(3):486–513.

Clark, G., Anderson, A. and Wright, D. 2006. Human colonization of the Palau Islands, western Micronesia. *The Journal of Island and Coastal Archaeology* 1(2):215–232.

Comaroff, J. and Comoroff, J. 1992. Ethnography and the historical imagination. In: Comaroff, J., Bourdieu, P. and Bloch, M. (eds), *Studies in the ethnographic imagination*, pp. 3–48. Westview Press, Boulder.

de Beauclair, I. 1971. Studies on Botel Tobago, and Yap. In: Tsuk'uang, L. (ed), *Asian folklore and social life monographs*, pp. 183–203. Orient Cultural Service, Taipei.

Dening, G. 1966. Ethnohistory in Polynesia: The value of ethnohistorical evidence. *Journal of Pacific History* 1:23–42.

Dening, G. 1980. *Islands and beaches: Discourse on a silent land: Marquesas 1774–1880*. The Dorsey Press, Chicago.

Dening, G. 1991. A poetic for histories: Transformations that present the past. In: Biersack, A. (ed), *Clio in Oceania*, pp. 347–380. Smithsonian Institution Press, Honolulu.

Descantes, C. 2005. *Integrating archaeology and ethnohistory: The development of exchange between Yap and Ulithi, Western Caroline Islands*. British Archaeological Reports International, Volume 1344. Archaeopress, Oxford.

Earle, T. 1991. The evolution of chiefdoms. In: Earle, T. (ed), *Chiefdoms: Power, economy and ideology*, pp. 1–15. Cambridge University Press, Cambridge.

Ericsson, K.A., Charness, N., Feltovich, P. and Hoffman, R.R. 2006. *The Cambridge handbook of expertise and expert performance*. Cambridge University Press, Cambridge.

Fitzpatrick, S.M. 2001. Archaeological investigations of Omis Cave: A Yapese stone money quarry in Palau. *Archaeology in Oceania* 36(3):153–162.

Fitzpatrick, S.M. 2002. A radiocarbon chronology of Yapese stone money quarries in Palau. *Micronesica* 34(2):227–242.

Fitzpatrick, S.M. 2003. Stones of the butterfly: An archaeological investigation of Yapese stone money quarries in Palau, Micronesia. Unpublished PhD thesis, Department of Anthropology, University of Oregon, Eugene.

Gilliland, C.L.C. 1975. *The stoney money of Yap: A numismatic survey*. Washington, DC. Smithsonian Institution Press.

Gosden, C. 1996. Transformations: History and prehistory in Hawaii. *Archaeology in Oceania* 31(3):165–172.

Gumerman, G.J., Snyder, D. and Masse, W.B. 1981. *An archaeological reconnaissance in the Palau Archipelago, Western Caroline Islands, Micronesia*. Center for Archaeological Investigations, Southern Illinois University, Carbondale.

Hambruch, P. 1932. *Ergebnisse der Südsee expedition, 1908–1910*, II, B, 7. In: Thilenius, G. (ed), Ponape, Volume 1. Friederichsen, De Gruyter, Hamburg.

Hambruch, P. 1936. *Ergebnisse der Südsee expedition, 1908–1910*, II, B, 7. In: Thilenius, G. (ed), Ponape, Vol. 2. Friederichsen, De Gruyter, Hamburg.

Hanlon, D. 1988. *Upon a stone altar: A history of the island of Pohnpei to 1890*. University of Hawai'i Press, Honolulu.

Hunter-Anderson, R.L. 1983. *Yapese settlement patterns: An ethnoarchaeological approach*. Pacific Studies Institute. Series 3.

Johannes, R.E. 1981. *Words of the lagoon: Fishing and marine lore in the Palau district of Micronesia.* University of California Press, Berkeley.

Kesolei, K. 1977. Cultural conservation: Restrictions to freedom of inquiry: Palauan strains. Paper presented at the Association of Social Anthropology in Oceania, Workshop on The Role of Anthropology in Contemporary Micronesia. Trust Territory of the Pacific Islands.

Kirch, P.V. 1984. *The evolution of the Polynesian chiefdoms.* Cambridge University Press, Cambridge.

Liston, J. [1999] 2007. *Archaeological data recovery for the Compact Road, Babeldaob island, Republic of Palau. Historic preservation investigations, Phase II. Volume V: Lab analyses, syntheses, recommendations.* Prepared for the US Army Corps of Engineers, Pacific Ocean Division, Hawai'i. International Archaeological Research Institute, Inc., Honolulu.

Liston, J. 2009. Cultural chronology of earthworks in Palau, western Micronesia. *Archaeology in Oceania* 44(2):56–73.

Liston, J. 2010. *Archaeological monitoring and emergency data recovery for the Compact Road, Babeldaob island, Republic of Palau. Historic preservation investigations, Phase III. Volume XII: Lab analyses, discussion, syntheses.* Draft report prepared for US Army Corps of Engineers, Pacific Ocean Division, Hawai'i. International Archaeological Research Institute, Inc., Honolulu.

Mason, R.J. 2000. Archaeology and native North American oral traditions. *American Aniquity* 65(2):239–266.

Masse, W.B. 1984. Rock Island village settlement systems: A preliminary report on the analysis of archaeological remains in the coralline limestone ('rock') islands, Republic of Palau. Centre for Archaeological Investigations, Southern Illinois University, Carbondale.

Masse, W.B., Liston, J., Carucci, J. and Athens, J.S. 2006. Evaluating the effects of climate change on environment, resource depletion, and culture in the Palau Islands between AD 1200 and 1600. *Quaternary International* 151:106–132.

Masse, W.B, Snyder, D. and Gumerman, G.J. 1984. Prehistoric and historic settlement in the Palau Islands, Micronesia. *New Zealand Journal of Archaeology* 6: 107–127.

Mauricio, R. 1992. A history of Pohnpei history or Poadoapoad: Description and explanation in recorded oral traditions. In: Rubinstein, D. (ed), *Pacific History: Papers from the 8th Pacific History Association Conference*, pp. 351–380. University of Guam Press and Micronesian Area Research Center, Mangilao.

Meleisea, M. 1987. *The making of modern Samoa: Traditional authority and colonial administration in the modern history of Western Samoa.* Institute of Pacific Studies of the University of the South Pacific, Suva.

Merwick, D. 1994. *Dangerous liaisons: Essays in honour of Greg Dening.* In: Mayne, A (ed), *Melbourne Monographs.* University of Melbourne, Melbourne.

Morphy, H. 1991. *Ancestral connections: Art and an aboriginal system of knowledge.* University of Chicago Press, Chicago.

Morphy, H. 1995. Landscape and the reproduction of the ancestral past. In: Hirsch, E. and O'Hanlon, M. (eds), *The anthropology of landscape*, pp. 184–209. Clarendon Press, Oxford.

Müller, W. 1918. *Ergebnisse der Südsee expedition, 1908–1910*, II, B, 2. In: Thilenius, G. (ed), Yap, Vol. 2. Friederichsen, De Gruyter, Hamburg.

Nero, K.L. 1987. A *cherechar a lokelii*: Beads of history of Koror, Palau, 1783–1983. Unpublished PhD dissertation, Department of Anthropology, University of California, Berkeley.

Nero, K.L. 1990. Linkages betwen Yap and Palau: Towards regional histories. Paper presented at 8th Pacific History Association Conference, Guam.

Nero, K.L. 2002. Keate's *Account of the Pelew Islands*: A view of Koror and Palau. In: Nero, K.L. and Thomas, N. (eds), *An account of the Pelew Islands: George Keate*, pp. 7–25. Leicester University Press, London.

Ohnuki-Tierney, E. (ed), 1990. *Culture through time: Anthropological approaches.* Stanford University Press, Stanford.

Palau National Committee on Population and Children (CoPopChi). 1997. *Population and development: Toward a Palau national policy for sustainable human development.* Office of the President: Republic of Palau, Koror.

Parmentier, R.J. 1987. *The sacred remains: Myth, history, and polity in Belau.* University of Chicago Press, Chicago.

Petersen, G. 1990. *Lost in the weeds: Theme and variation in Pohnpei political mythology.* Occasional Paper, Center for Pacific Islands Studies, University of Hawai'i, Honolulu.

Petersen, G. 1994. Kanengamah and Pohnpei's politics of concealment. *American Anthropologist* 95(2):334–352.

Ritzenthaler, R.E. 1954. *Native money of Palau,* Publications in Anthropology. Milwaukee Public Museum, Milwaukee.

Rubinstein, D.H. 1992. *Pacific History: Papers from the 8th Pacific History Association Conference.* University of Guam Press and Micronesian Area Research Center, Mangilao.

Sahlins, M. 1983. Other times, other customs: The anthropology of history. *American Anthropologist* 85(3):517–544.

Sahlins, M. 1985. *Islands of history.* University of Chicago Press, Chicago.

Sahlins, M. 2004. *Apologies to Thucydides: Understanding history as culture and vica versa.* University of Chicago Press, Chicago.

Schwarz, M.T. 1997. *Molded in the image of changing woman: Navajo views on the human body and personhood.* The University of Arizona Press, Tucson.

Sheppard, P., Walter, R. and Aswani, S. 2004. Oral tradition and the creation of late prehistory in Roviana Lagoon, Solomon Islands. *Records of the Australian Museum* Supplement 29:123–132.

Tellei, J., Basilius, U. and Rehuher, F.K. 2005. *Palau Compact Road archaeological investigations, Babeldaob island, Republic of Palau. Historic preservation investigations Phase I. Volume III: Oral history documentation.* Prepared for the US Army Corps of Engineers, Pacific Ocean Division, Hawai'i. Tomonari-Tuggle, M.J. (ed), International Archaeological Research Institute, Inc., Honolulu.

Vansina, J. 1985. *Oral tradition as history.* University of Wisconsin Press, Madison.

Voss, J.F. and Wiley, J. 2006. *Expertise in history.* In: Ericsson, K.A., Charness, N., Feltovich, P. and Hoffman, R.R. (eds), *The Cambridge handbook of expertise and expert performance*, pp. 569–584. Cambridge University Press, Cambridge.

Wickler, S.K., Addison, D.J., Kaschko, M.W. and Dye, T.S. [1997] 2005a. *Intensive archaeological survey for the Palau Compact Road, Babeldaob island, Palau. Historic preservation investigations Phase I. Volume II: Area survey reports.* Prepared for the US Army Corps of Engineers, Pacific Ocean Division, Hawai'i. International Archaeological Research Institute, Inc., Honolulu.

Wickler, S.K., Welch, D.J., Tomonari-Tuggle, M.J., Liston, J., Tuggle, H.D. and Grant, D. [1998] 2005b. *Intensive archaeological survey for the Palau Compact Road, Babeldaob island, Palau. Historic preservation investigations Phase I. Volume I. Scope, background, results, excavation, and recommendations.* Prepared for the US Army Corps of Engineers, Pacific Ocean Division, Hawai'i. International Archaeological Research Institute, Inc., Honolulu.

Wilding, J.R. and Valentine, E.R. 2006. *Exceptional memory.* In: Ericsson, K.A., Charness, N., Feltovich, P. and Hoffman, R.R. (eds), *The Cambridge handbook of expertise and expert performance*, pp. 539–552. Cambridge University Press, Cambridge.

11

Dynamic settlement, landscape modification, resource utilisation and the value of oral traditions in Palauan archaeology

David M. Snyder[1], W. Bruce Masse[2] and James Carucci[3]

1. Ohio Historic Preservation Office, Columbus, Ohio, USA
2. Environmental Stewardship Group (ENV-ES), Los Alamos National Laboratory, New Mexico, USA
3. James Carucci, Cultural Resources Section, Vandenberg Air Force Base, California, USA

Introduction

In their landmark analysis of Palauan kinship, Force and Force (1972) use the symbolic metaphor of 'Just One House' to capture the integration of kinship in traditional Palauan culture. They realised that then-current general anthropological concepts of kinship were not consistently isomorphic with the evidence from Palau, and additionally that kinship was dynamic, both with respect to the age of individuals as they grew older, and also as a product of outside influences brought on by colonisation and assimilation. They were able to focus on the time dynamic due to the good fortune of being able to conduct research in Palau over two widely separated periods of time (1954–1956 and 1971). Using an analogy with archaeology, Force and Force (1972:vi–vii) described the mosaic historic, social and political patterns as 'cultural stratigraphy', with their goal to excavate the various historical layers in order to expose underlying, earlier, presumably more traditional social patterns.

The research framework used by the Forces is a particularly apt model for our own interest in the historical and archaeological record of Palauan settlement. This paper provides the opportunity for its authors to revisit archaeological research initiated in Palau 30 years ago (e.g. Gumerman et al. 1981; Masse et al. 1984), and also allows us to consider and evaluate conceptual changes in archaeological thinking regarding Palauan settlement that have come about through recent intensive and innovative research programs by various colleagues during the past 15 years. This review also focuses our attention on aspects of the dynamic character of Palauan settlement.

We use the concept of settlement system in this paper to mean an integrated cultural pattern for the procuring, processing, use and discard of materials. The structure and organisation of the settlement system are integrated with the environment and with the ideational. That is, the environment does not determine the settlement system; rather, the settlement system is a part of the environment. And, at the same time, the settlement system is not uniquely determined by ideas, but cultural patterns, symbols and ideas actively impose on shaping the settlement system.

In all settlement systems, we expect to see responses to environmental variability. We expect to see over-exploitation of certain resources from time to time. Even under similar environmental conditions, we expect there will be different cultural responses that will come out of different settlement systems because of differences in belief and custom. At the same time, we also expect that different cultures will try similar approaches to solving different environmental challenges.

Previous and current models of warfare, climate forcing, population stress, sea-level change, anthropogenic subsistence over-harvesting, and historic contact social and demographic patterns all contribute to a general model for integrated Palauan settlement behaviour. A particular focus is on Palauan oral history, in which we discuss the general nature and reliability of oral traditions by analogy with recent chronometric studies of Hawaiian myth and oral tradition, and then present oral traditions relating to settlement behaviour in the Rock Islands and differences between the Rock Islands and elsewhere in the archipelago. We conclude that landscape and resource diversity led to an inherent dynamic plasticity for settlement in traditional Palau, with potential lessons for sustainability (and the related concepts of resilience and flexibility) in the face of modern economic and climate change.

Physical environment

The Palau archipelago contains more than 350 islands in a 150 km long north-to-southwest trending arc in the Caroline Islands of western Micronesia (Figure 1). The islands are part of the Palau ridge crest, one of several arcuate volcanic ridges separating the basin of the Pacific Ocean from that of the Philippine Sea. The approximate centre of equatorial Palau is 7° N and 134° E, about 870 km east of Mindanao in the Philippines and 900 km north of Irian Jaya. The following summary is largely extracted from a recent review of Palauan archaeology and physical environment (Masse et al. 2006; see also Mason 1955; US Army 1956; Vessel and Simonson 1958). Not included in this discussion are the isolated southwest islands of Palau, Sonsorol, Tobi, Pulo Ana and Merir, which are more than 280 km southwest of Angaur, and do not appear to have played a significant role in Palauan settlement-system history for the occupants of the main body of the archipelago between Angaur and Kayangel to the north (Osborne 1966; Intoh 2008).

Palau has a maritime tropical climate with little seasonal variation. The mean annual temperature is around 27°C, humidity 82%, and annual rainfall averaging around 3800 mm. February through April tends to be slightly drier than the other months. The most notable seasonal climatic difference is in the nature and direction of prevailing surface winds, affecting rainfall, humidity, tides, currents, sea swells and marine life. The winds are largely bimodal; during June to September west or southwest trade winds predominate, while during October through April they reverse and come from the northeast. Strong winds and associated large swells and breakers make fishing difficult and boat travel hazardous, with the eastern side of the larger islands being more protected during westerlies, and the western side being more favourable during north easterlies. Johannes (1981) noted that many reef fish species take advantage of the relative calm during the seasonal change in wind patterns for peak spawning periods.

Palau is located within the boundaries of the Indo-Pacific Warm Pool (Gagan et al. 2004).

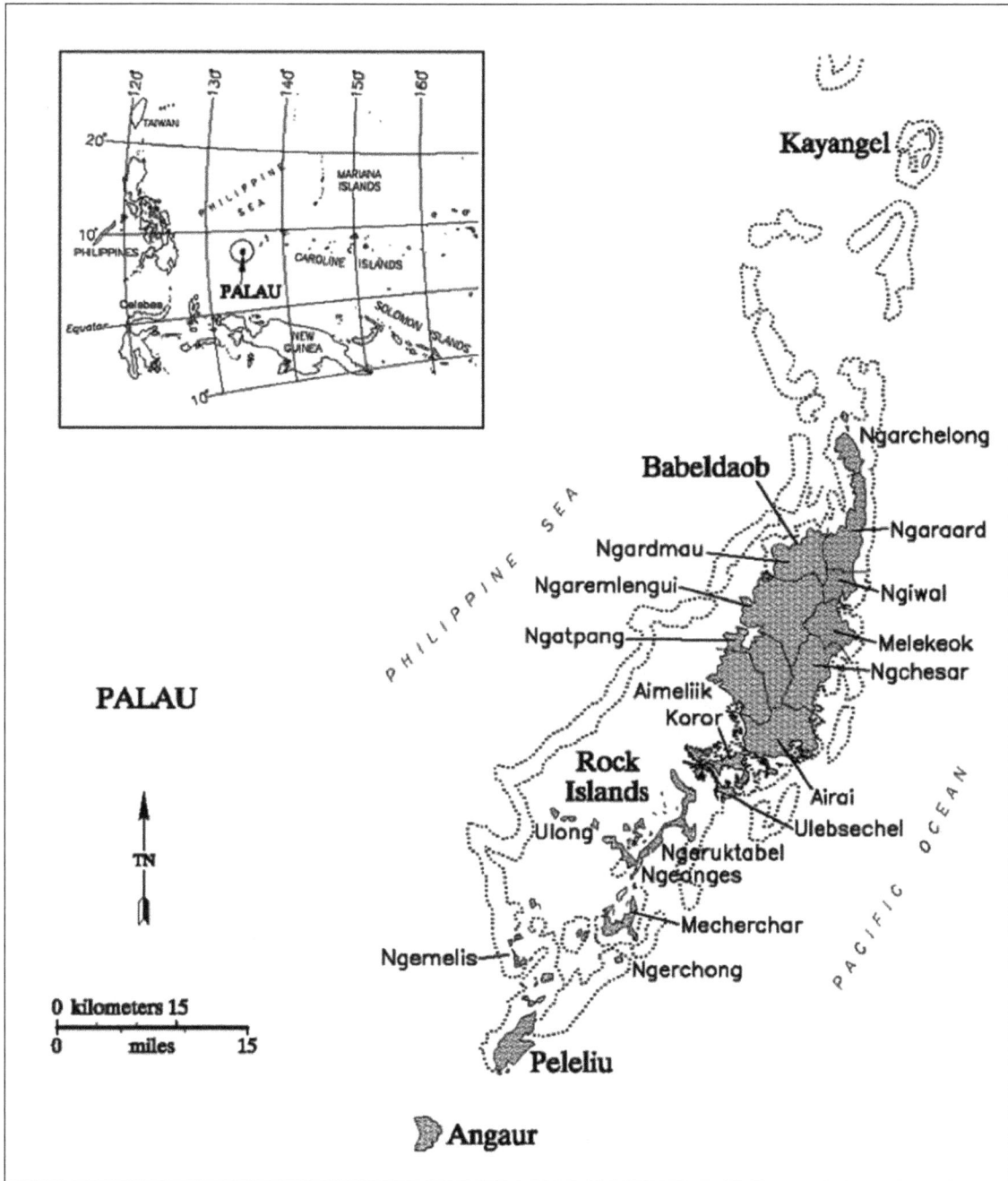

Figure 1. Map of Palau.

This is one of the wettest tropical ocean regions of the world and the largest expanse in the world of water whose annual temperatures exceed 28°C. As such, Palau is subject to dramatic potential effects from the El Niño-Southern Oscillation (ENSO). Historically, during moderate to strong El Niño events, Palau is in the area experiencing the greatest deficit of annual rainfall, more than 200 mm (Gagan et al. 2004:Figure 5). While this is a relatively minor percentage of overall rainfall for Palau, rare instances of significant increases in the frequency and severity of El Niño events possibly have had disruptive impacts on Palauan settlement systems (Masse et al. 2006). The fact that Palau is at the southern margin of the western Pacific typhoon corridor indicates that occasional severe cyclones could devastate the archipelago and its reefs, as exemplified elsewhere in western Micronesia (Yamaguchi 1975; Ogg and Koslow 1978).

Volcanic Babeldaob island, at 333 km², comprises nearly three-quarters of the land mass of the archipelago and is the second largest island in Micronesia, behind Guam. Five other primarily volcanic islands are also present in the northern portion of the archipelago near Babeldaob, the largest of which is Koror, at less than 9 km², with Ngerkelau being the smallest, at 0.08 km². Babeldaob, Koror and Malakal also contain remnants of uplifted karstic limestone reef in addition to the volcanic materials. The maximum elevation above mean sea level in Palau is 242 m on Babeldaob. Babeldaob's interior uplands are formed by three ridge systems aligned parallel to the island's north-south axis. The eroded and rounded peaks on the volcanic islands are from breccias and interbedded tuffs formed during the Eocene, and create an undulating terrain containing a series of small, narrow and steep-sided valleys. The coastal plains surrounding the uplands are formed by thick clay deposits of weathered andesite, basalt and dacite.

Of the two true atolls at the northern tip of the archipelago, only Kayangel has substantive land mass, at slightly less than 2 km², with an overall size of about 20 km², including the barrier reef and lagoon. Kayangel is about 35 km north of Babeldaob, but only 3 km north of Babeldaob's barrier reef. The other atoll, Ngaruangel, is about 9 km northwest of Kayangel, and is approximately one-third the size of Kayangel. The only appreciable land mass within Ngaruangel consists of a barren islet of chunks of reef rock and small patches of sand only about 0.015 km² in size. Intriguing is the fact that Palauan oral history indicates that a substantial population once thrived on Ngaruangel.

The great majority of the islands in the archipelago are tectonically uplifted coralline limestone islands, referred to locally as Rock Islands, and primarily distributed between Koror and Peleliu. The higher Rock Islands are uplifted ancient reefs dating from the mid Miocene to late Pliocene. The majority are steep, rugged and sinuous karstic islands averaging in elevation between 10 m and 100 m above mean sea level, with a maximum elevation of 210 m on large Ngeruktabel. A series of low coralline islands, including the Ngemelis group, is situated primarily along the southwestern barrier reef. These are formed from less-well-consolidated reef material dating to the Pleistocene and Holocene, and in the case of the Ngemelis group, are slightly uplifted portions of the present living reef system. Although three of the Rock Islands are quite sizeable (Ngeruktabel at greater than 18 km², Mercherchar at around 8 km², Ulebsechel at slightly more than 4 m²), the remainder are all less than 1.2 km² in size, typically less than 0.1 km².

At the southern tip of the archipelago are two sizeable platform-like reef islands, Peleliu at nearly 15 km² and Angaur at slightly more than 8 km². Both islands contain high limestone ridges, like the Rock Islands, but also contain extensive areas of low flat uplifted reefs that form broad platforms of land.

Table 1 lists the 22 largest islands in the archipelago, noting area, soil types and shoreline lengths. About 75% of the soils on the volcanic islands are highly acidic and severely leached latosols, with the remainder consisting of poorly weathered and shallow lithosols, alluvial deposits, bog soils (muck and peat) and unconsolidated calcareous sands (Shioya sand). Babeldaob exhibits the greatest diversity of soils and landforms. The Rock Islands are dominated by limestone outcrops and Shioya sand, while the two platform islands are notable for the presence of bog soils and other soils on limestone. Peleliu is also notable for extensive stands of mangrove forest.

Most of the islands in the archipelago are covered with thick stands of dense mixed tropical forest, with the remainder including savanna (on the volcanic islands), agroforest, or secondary vegetation. Forest vegetation types include upland, swamp, mangrove, plantation, and limestone forests. The upland forests of the volcanic islands are the most species diverse in Micronesia.

Table 1. Land area, shoreline length and soil types of the largest islands and island groups in the Palau archipelago, from north to south.

Island name and geological type	Total area (km²)	Shoreline length (km)	Mangrove forest (km²)	Soil on volcanics (km²)	Alluvial soils (km²)	Bog soils (km²)	Shioya sand (km²)	Soils on limestone (km²)	Limestone outcrop (km²)
Atoll									
Kayangel atoll	1.72	10.61				0.21	1.14	0.42	
Volcanic									
Ngerechur	0.31	3.06		0.26			0.05		
Ngerkelau	0.08	1.29		trace			0.08		
Babeldaob	366.48	157.52	33.67	313.36	11.19	5.85	1.35		1.06
Koror	8.89	26.55	1.55	4.56	0.08	0.03			2.67
Ngerekebesang	2.28	9.81	0.13	2.05					
Malakal	0.47	4.18		0.44					0.03
Rock Islands									
Ngerchol	0.65	8.21							0.65
Ulebsechel	4.33	20.60		trace			0.03		4.30
Ngeruktabel	18.62	91.55					0.05		18.57
Bungetiou	1.19	10.94							1.19
Ulong	0.59	4.67					0.05		0.54
Ngerukuid	0.47	6.92					0.03		0.44
Ngeanges	0.13	1.80					0.06		0.07
Mercherchar	8.03	43.44					0.03		8.00
Ngerchang	0.44	3.22	trace				0.34	0.10	trace
Babelomekang	0.21	3.38							0.21
Ngemelis group	1.18	14.32	trace				0.30		0.88
Uchuangelokel	1.14	5.95					0.13		1.01
Ngedebus	1.04	6.28					0.88	0.03	0.13
Platform									
Peleliu	14.84	39.90	2.46			0.70	1.53	1.76	8.39
Angaur	8.08	13.35	trace			0.65	0.31	4.09	3.03

Food plants observed at historic European contact in AD 1783 were the dry taro, 'giant swamp' (wetland) taro, coconut palm, breadfruit, tropical apple, Malay apple, banana, greater yam and tropical almond. Other significant plants included turmeric, the betel-nut palm and bamboo. The only economically significant quadruped in the archaeological record is the pig. Quite remarkably and of some consequence for our discussion of Palauan settlement, pigs had been extirpated throughout the archipelago sometime before AD 1783 (Masse et al. 2006), with only cats and ubiquitous rats being present. A variety of birds, the giant fruit bat and land crabs were among the few edible terrestrial fauna that contributed to human subsistence at contact.

A barrier and fringing reef complex surrounds all but Angaur and Kayangel, encompassing more than 1200 km² of variable lagoon with a maximum depth of about 50 m. A diversity of marine environments reflects an equal diversity of marine species available for human exploitation and consumption (Johannes 1981; Masse 1986, 1989; Carucci 1992; Fitzpatrick and Kataoka 2005; Fitzpatrick and Donaldson 2007). Mangrove swamps, estuaries, sandflats, seagrass beds and extensive reef systems occur variously throughout the archipelago, providing a much greater diversity of marine sources than anywhere else in Micronesia. Along with numerous economically important finfish and shellfish species were sea worms, sea cucumbers, sea urchins, starfish, octopus, squid, spiny lobsters, shrimp and crabs. Dugong, hawksbill turtle and green turtle played an important food-distribution social-status role, as did, probably, sharks and whales, based on archaeological evidence. About 80 marine lakes exist in the Rock Islands, connected to the ocean by fissures and solution cavities and responsive to tidal changes. Although these marine lakes are notable for their many unique characteristics and organisms, it is unclear to us what, if any, economic uses these lakes would have had for the occupants of the Rock Islands.

Not all villages and districts would have had equal access to land or marine resources. Clay deposits for making pottery vessels are confined to the volcanic islands. The volcanic islands would have also better supported large-scale horticulture and would have provided more varied plant resources than the limestone islands. Horticulture in the Rock Islands would have been largely limited to soil pockets in limestone pits and sinks and occasional patches of Shioya sand. Shioya sand consists of raised beaches and coastal terraces just above normal wave action, which appear to have developed primarily in the past 3000–4000 years. Coves containing deposits of Shioya sand suitable as canoe landings are present on only some of the Rock Islands. Fresh water is a particularly valuable and varied resource throughout the archipelago. Babeldaob contains perennial streams, a pond and a small lake. The moderate porosity and high permeability of the carbonate soils of the Rock Islands inhibit the development of potable water sources, being limited to a few fresh-water seeps and pockets of Shioya sand suitable for the development of Ghyben-Herzberg fresh-water lenses that can be tapped by shallow wells. Angaur and Peleliu support larger fresh-water lenses, although during periods of drought, even these may become brackish or disappear completely. We suspect that the dense stands of coconut palms on deposits of Shioya sand throughout the limestone islands were deliberately planted, in part to provide a source of nourishing liquid in areas normally lacking potable water and during periods of drought.

Past and current models of Palauan settlement

Palau has been continuously occupied since ca. 3100–2900 cal. BP (Fitzpatrick 2003; Liston 2005; Clark et al. 2006; Masse et al. 2006), although paleoenvironmental data from Babeldaob is suggestive of human occupation as early as 4300 cal. BP (Liston 1999; Athens and Ward 2001). The present data supports a date for initial colonisation at around 3400–3100 BP, as suggested by Clark et al. (2006), but the absence of intensive testing throughout the Rock Islands and portions of the volcanic islands leaves the door open both to push back this date and to provide data for a more comprehensive understanding of early Palauan settlement before 500 BC.

At initial sustained European contact in AD 1783 (Parmentier 1981, 1987; Keate 2002; Nero 2002), Palau housed a number of autonomous villages (*beluu*) that were politically organised into various village districts or federations (*renged*). Krämer (1919) provides a population estimate of 25,000 for Palau at initial sustained European contact in 1783, while Semper (1982) gives a population estimate of perhaps as many as 40,000–50,000. These values are problematic, but provide a starting point for much-needed population studies for Palau. Fifteen federations (*renged*) existed in Palau at European contact, corresponding to the 10 modern states depicted on Babeldaob Island in Figure 1. An 11th federation on Babeldaob, Ngersuul south of Melekeok, has since become extinct. At European contact, two federations were in the process of expansion, Koror and Melekeok, attempting to subjugate other *renged*. It is clear from historic contact-period observations and from Palauan oral history that the pattern of competing federations extended several hundred years back in time before European contact. Liston and Tuggle (2006) suggest that earlier earthwork village federations (discussed below) may have been roughly equivalent to the anthropological concept of small chiefdoms (e.g. Service 1962; Carneiro 1981:45), although they caution that political centralisation is not always the necessary product of such competition. We think it premature to define levels of early Palauan social complexity without more additional archaeological field study.

Palauan villages at European contact (with their notable absence in the Rock Islands, as discussed below) were nucleated, in contrast to the isolated hamlets and dispersed homesteads of many other Pacific Islands. Residences, club houses and village meeting houses (*bai*) were constructed on well-built stone platforms around a central paved square, with all being linked by stone pathways (Masse and Snyder 1982; Liston and Tuggle 2006). These platforms, along with burial, resting and cooking platforms, were constructed from multiple layers of basalt stones around an earthen core. Other stone features included docks, boathouses, shrines, wells and bathing places.

Monumental earthwork terrace complexes comprise a prominent class of archaeological features on the volcanic islands. However, as discussed below, they played an earlier role in Palauan settlement-system history, before the stonework villages. Villages did not exist on the Rock Islands at the time of European contact, but there is ample evidence for such earlier stonework villages. At contact, the Rock Islands were subject to what were probably frequent periodic visits to glean marine resources (e.g. Keate 2002:74).

The idea of a settlement system, that at any one time during a particular period the material-culture remains were created and subsequently discarded within an integrated culture, may seem almost taken for granted today. However, the concepts of settlement pattern and settlement system were still in their infancy in 1953–1954 when pioneering Palauan archaeologist Douglas Osborne (1958, 1966) first began archaeological survey of Palau.

Osborne, while not being formally trained in settlement-system archaeology, clearly understood that because of the considerable geographic diversity of landscapes within the Palau archipelago, it would be necessary to visit as many of the larger islands and districts as possible. To this end, Osborne visited Kayangel Atoll; he identified 55 stonework villages and earthwork terrace complexes on volcanic Babeldaob Island through both survey and aerial photographic interpretation, and visited most of them; he visited all five of the smaller volcanic islands, identifying another 33 or so villages and earthwork features; he visited and identified 42 sites on Peliliu and Angaur; and he visited several of the larger Rock Islands. Although Osborne's visits generally were quite brief, he recognised that resources were not uniformly scattered throughout the archipelago. For example, the clay for making pottery was restricted to the volcanic islands, and water was a scarce commodity on many of the coralline limestone islands. Osborne likewise soon realised that Palauan elders and some of his guides had oral traditions relating to a significant number of the sites that he visited. To Osborne's credit, he recorded and published lengthy synopses of most or all of these traditions.

Intensive test excavations conducted by Osborne in 1968–1969 at a few locations defined during his initial survey in the archipelago yielded only limited information of value for our interests in Palauan settlement systems (Osborne 1979). In a similar vein, work conducted and preliminarily reported on by Jun Takayama (1979; Takayama and Takasugi 1978) from the

Rock Island of Ulsbachel yielded only minor insights into the settlement history of the Rock Islands. And investigations by Laurie Lucking (1984) on Babeldaob's earthwork terraces were limited by the inability to employ mechanised equipment (e.g. backhoes and front-end loaders) to study monumental earthworks.

The Southern Illinois University at Carbondale Palau Archaeological Project (SIUPAP) began in 1979 (Gumerman et al. 1981). The settlement model that we developed during the 1980s (e.g. Masse and Snyder 1982; Masse et al. 1984; Masse 1989; Snyder 1989; Snyder and Butler 1997; see Table 2) was derived from settlement and land-use models developed in the American southwest and southeast (e.g. Masse 1991) and was too rigidly applied to Palau. The model centred on the geographical spacing of 'traditional' stonework villages on the volcanic islands (Masse and Snyder 1982; Snyder and Butler 1997), and saw the Rock Islands and the slew of smaller islands in and around the main volcanic islands as special resource-procurement zones. The volcanic island villages were seen as pie-shaped wedges. Beginning with the lagoon, where the wedge was the widest, and continuously narrowing to the higher ground near the centre of the island, the volcanic island village model gave maximum access to vital lagoon and mangrove swamp resources, allowed for village placement on the lower coastal ground where there were soils for a variety of different gardens. Within each pie-shaped wedge there would have been a primary village and several smaller associated villages.

Masse's work in the Rock Islands validated and amplified the assumptions by Osborne regarding the presence of substantial and permanent stonework villages scattered throughout the limestone islands of the central archipelago (Masse et al. 1984; Masse 1989). Despite the absence of volcanic stone building materials and the local peculiarities of the limestone terrain, the Rock Island stonework villages contain a suite of features functionally equivalent to features of volcanic island stonework villages (Figure 2) except that they were constructed from chunks of coralline limestone rather than basalt (Masse 1989; Masse et al. 2006). These Rock Island villages would have been heavily dependent on the resources of the lagoon (Masse 1989; Carucci 1992), although there also would have been important resources on the Rock Islands. Two chronological questions regarding the Rock Island stonework villages are of obvious importance for understanding settlement-system history. When were the stonework villages built and how long were they occupied? Our tentative answer was AD 1200 through 1450.

To accommodate the presence of Rock Island villages we first thought to incorporate ideas of population growth. As the population of Palau grew over a span of somewhat more than two millennia, new villages were added to fill existing space. When SIUPAP radiocarbon dating provided earlier dates for Rock Island stonework-village associations (ca. AD 1200–1450) than for volcanic island stonework-village associations (ca. AD 1500+), we viewed the Rock Islands as filling up earlier, with overflow expanding across the volcanic islands. As population continued to expand, resources were over-exploited. First, in the Rock Islands in the 14th and 15th centuries AD, and later in the volcanic islands, we see a rapid decrease in the population.

By the time of Krämer's (1919) research at the beginning of the 20th century, the population of Palau had declined to about 4000, not too different from Kubary's (1873) estimate of 3000 people a generation before. Krämer recorded volcanic-island villages that he described as abandoned. This pattern is likely to reflect disease, assimilation and conflict, similar to other populations following initial European contact (Stannard 1989; Reff 1991).

Archaeological research during the past 20 years does not support much of this model of the traditional Palauan settlement system, particularly Masse's (1990) estimated initial colonisation at around 2000 cal. BP (see Table 2). Our failure was, in part, due to the age-old archaeological nemesis of sampling – our limited sample of excavated sites and chronometric dates masked the

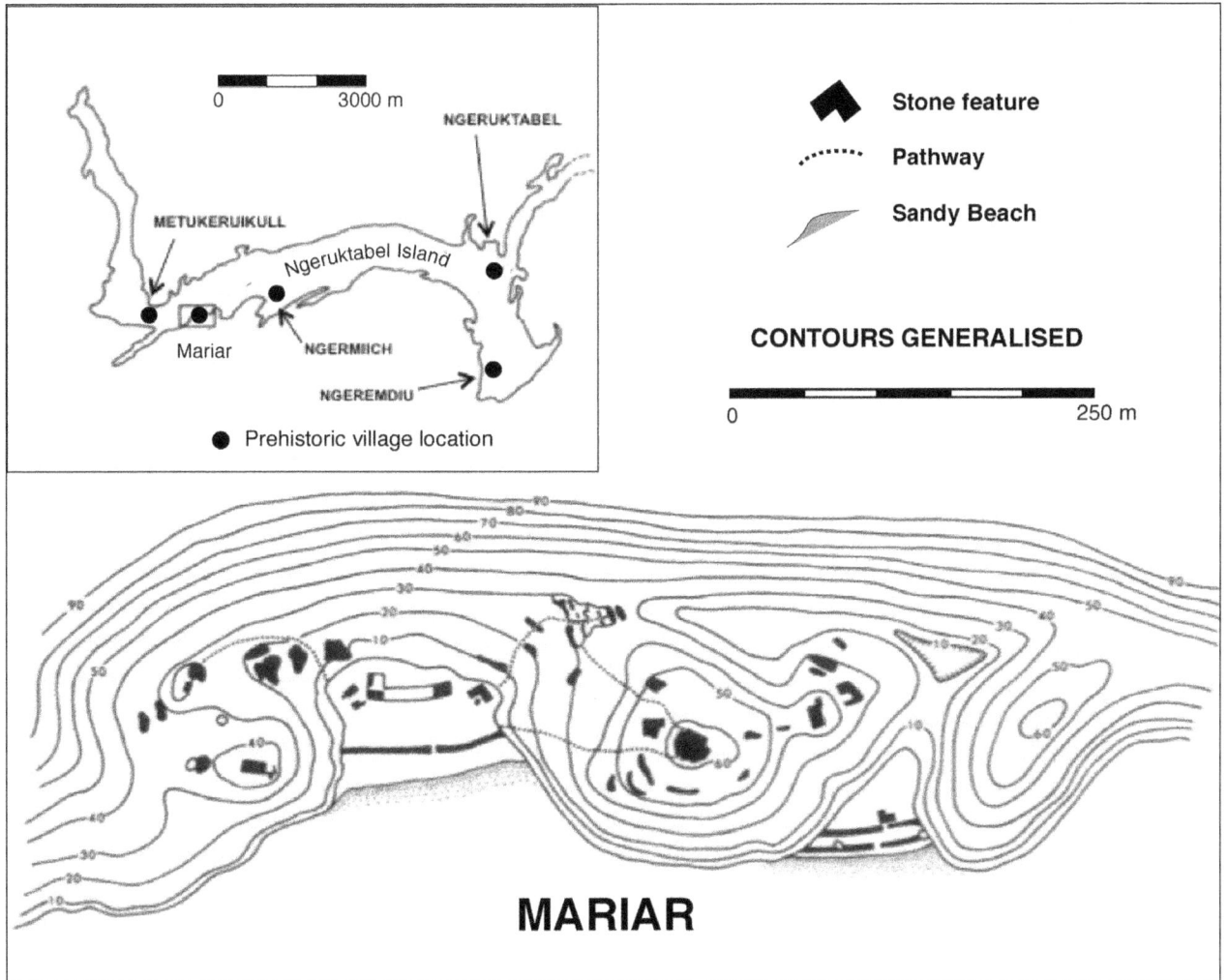

Figure 2. Map of the Rock Island stonework village of Mariar, along with the locations of five stonework villages on the island of Ngeruktabel.

overall complexity and longevity of Palauan settlement, but equally important are differences between our initial and current perceptions of the nature of culture change, a topic we return to at the end of this paper.

Our understanding of Palauan settlement patterns and systems has greatly accelerated due to the 1996–2003 monitoring investigations, survey and data recovery associated with the construction of the 85 km long road system encircling Babeldaob Island (Wickler et al. 2005). In addition to adding hundreds of radiocarbon dates from well-dated features and site complexes (Liston 2005), the work has given us an exciting new perspective on the monumental earthwork terraces (Liston and Tuggle 2006; Liston 2009).

Jolie Liston and her colleagues (Wickler 2002; Liston and Tuggle 2006; Phear 2008; Liston 2009) have now provided the first detailed overviews of the construction and use history of earthwork complexes in Palau, particularly from the northern Babeldaob districts of Ngiwal and Ngaraard (Table 2). Palauan earthworks are created by both cut-and-fill and sculpting of ridges and hilltops. The dominant features are step terraces of great variety, which occur with or in occasional isolation from high points termed 'crowns' and ditches. Together, these features cover at least 20% of the total landmass of Babeldaob. More than 100 crowns are present throughout the Babeldaob earthworks. They have nearly vertical sides and rise 3–10 m above the

Table 2. A comparison of Palauan archaeological periods and phases with respect to the 1980s Southern Illinois University Palau Archaeological Project (SIUPAP) model with the current 'Liston' model developed from data collected by International Archaeological Research Institute, Inc. Also depicted are major climatic phases and events.

Date	Siupap model (e.g. Masse 1989)	Liston model (e.g. Liston 2009)	Climatic events (e.g. Nunn 2007)
AD 1800	TRADITIONAL–historic		
1700	TRADITIONAL–initial contact		
1600	TRADITIONAL–protohistoric		MAUNDER MINIMUM
1500	TRANSITIONAL		
1400	ROCK ISLAND VILLAGE		
1300		STONEWORK ERA	AD 1300 EVENT
1200	ROCK ISLAND VILLAGE		LITTLE ICE AGE BEGINS
1100			
1000			
900	late		
800		TRANSITIONAL ERA	
700	early		
600	RESOURCE INTENSIFICATION		MEDIEVAL WARM PERIOD
500	COLONISATION	late	AD 536 EVENT
400			
300			
200			
100			
AD 1/1 BC	COLONISATION		
100 BC			
200		middle	
300			
400		early	
500		EARTHWORK ERA	
600			
700			
800			
900			
1000			
1100			
1200			
1300			
1400		SETTLEMENT AND EXPANSION ERA	
1500		[LATE COLONISATION]	
1600			
1700			
1800			
1900			
2000			
2100			
2200			
2300			
2400 BC		[EARLY COLONISATION]	

surrounding landscape. Nearly all crowns have an associated ring ditch up to 5 m deep, with the few excavated examples also containing palisades; additional ditches are present on ridgelines and between crowns.

Earthwork villages are located on low hillsides or along narrow ridgelines inland and upland from historic stonework settlements. They are characterised by earth platforms containing evidence for wooden structures, occasional stone features (e.g. pathways and facings for the earth platforms), and dense midden deposits. At least four, and perhaps as many as seven, such villages have been identified in association with the Ngaraard earthwork terraces. The initial construction of earthwork terrace complexes began as early as 500 BC, with the most intense period of terrace/village construction and use being between about 150 BC and AD 500. Terrace construction thereafter significantly declines until about AD 800, after which the earthwork terraces cease being focal points of activity. By around AD 1000–1200, the transition to coastal stonework villages on Babeldaob begins.

Liston and Tuggle (2006) suggest that the earthwork terrace complexes served as small fortified polities in which villages were defensively protected by the crown and ditch/palisade features noted above. The crowns served as fortified outposts, lookouts and brief refuges, and were visible symbols of power. What is still very unclear is the degree to which, if at all, some of the step terraces may have served as dryland agricultural field plots or for arboriculture. If the step terraces did not have a horticultural/arboriculture function, this raises a critical question as to where such activities took place on the landscape.

In addition to the recent work on the volcanic-island earthwork terraces, great strides have been made in the identification of early pre-earthwork terrace habitation sites on Ulong along the western barrier reef by Geoffrey Clark and his colleagues (e.g. Clark 2005; Clark, et al. 2006) and at Chelchol Ra Orrak near Babeldaob by Scott Fitzpatrick (2003). Burials and midden deposits have been found dating back to 3100–2900 cal. BP, with a reasonable assumption of colonisation in Palau at least by 3400 cal. BP.

As part of the dating of their excavated midden materials, Clark and his colleagues (2005; Clark et al. 2006) were able to obtain food shell collected and eaten in AD 1783 by the shipwrecked survivors of the British East India packet *Antelope* which had run aground on a reef adjacent to Ulong. This permitted them to obtain data for local reservoir correction (ΔR) for use with the radiocarbon dating of marine shell. While not absolutely convincing, they built a reasonable argument for ΔR=0 for at least some marine-shell species, rather than the ΔR=-250 year recently proposed by Masse and his colleagues (Masse et al. 2006). While the primary intention of Clark and his colleagues was to be able to generate a more accurate date for their model of Palau colonisation, this also calls into question the presumed dating of stonework villages at around AD 1200–1450/1500 in the Rock Islands (e.g. Mariar on Ngeruktabel island, Ngeanges and the Ngemelis group), previously excavated as part of the SIUPAP effort (Masse et al. 1984; Masse 1989; Masse et al. 2006). Using the suggested ΔR=0, the Rock Island stonework villages would date at around AD 1450–1750 (as depicted in Masse et al. 2006:Figure 7). Oral traditions collected during the SIUPAP fieldwork in 1981 and discussed below provide support for the revised AD 1450–1750 dating for most or all of the Rock Island stonework villages.

This dating also affects interpretation of the potential effects of the Little Ice Age (ca. AD 1300–1800) on stonework villages in the Rock Islands (Masse et al. 2006), and plays an important role in understanding Palauan settlement behaviour during the Little Ice Age (Table 2). We originally believed that the beginnings of the Little Ice Age and Patrick Nunn's (2000, 2007) related so-called 'AD 1300 Event' (a pan-Pacific environmental catastrophe) was a catalyst leading to the over-harvesting of inshore marine resources during the occupation of the Rock Island stonework villages (Masse 1989; Carucci 1992; Masse et al. 2006). It now appears that this apparent period of over-harvesting would have taken place about the time of the Maunder Minimum (ca. AD 1645–1715), which was the coldest portion of the Little Ice Age. While more data are needed, it is now not unreasonable to hypothesise that the Maunder Minimum had a direct role in the proposed over-harvesting of inshore marine resources, the extirpation of pig in Palau (Intoh 1986; Masse et al. 2006), and the apparent instability in Rock Island stonework-village settlement noted below in oral traditions, which led to the apparent abandonment of the last occupied Rock Island stonework settlements shortly before the wreck of the *Antelope* in AD 1783.

The traditional Palauan settlement system was likely to have been much more resilient than in our early SIUPAP program thinking. This is particularly evident in the calamitous, nearly catastrophic, social collapse precipitated by forced and heavy-handed colonial administrations during the 19th and early 20th centuries. We see changes occurring in Palau over millennia. Some of these changes required resource balancing necessary for sustainability, while other changes led to permanent, irreversible cultural change. The more that we learn about the dynamics of traditional Palauan culture, the better our understanding will be of the environmental conditions needed for sustainability and the cultural changes that occur when environmental variability exceeds the limits of human systems.

The nature and value of oral tradition, myths and legends

We when first began research in Palau 30 years ago, we had a nebulous understanding of Palauan oral traditions, and of the value of oral traditions to archaeological research, ranging from very sceptical (Masse) to sympathetic (Snyder). Like most American archaeologists at that time, we were schooled in the four-field approach to anthropology, combining cultural/social anthropology, linguistics and physical anthropology, along with our archaeological specialisations. However, as material-culture-oriented archaeologists, we had been trained to treat oral traditions with reserved scepticism beyond the passage of a few generations. The general view was that as historical information passed through the filter of oral transmission, each succeeding generation added both to the propensity to distort the information and the cultural introspection of beliefs, values, customs, traditions and history, so that after a handful of generations (100–150 years) the information could no longer be trusted.

We had likewise been taught that myths, i.e. tales of culture heroes and demigods imbued with supernatural powers and existing in a remote time before the present age, were primarily of psychological importance and overwhelmed historical content, despite being viewed as true by the cultures in which they are told. A similar scholarly contempt existed for legends, such as comprise many of the traditional stories in Palau. Legends are typically viewed as 'semi-historical' stories (of unknown or dubious meaningful historical content) that serve to establish local customs, recount the migrations of people, and account for the deeds of heroes. Legends typically combine realism with supernatural and mythic elements. In the discussion that follows, the terms myth and legend are largely viewed as synonymous.

Our Palau fieldwork experiences challenged these preset notions about oral tradition and myth/legend. We rapidly became aware that despite a lack of formal scientific training, Palauans are gifted observers of the natural environment. For example, the observations of Palauan master fishermen are of such detail and quality that they have been proven to aid marine biologists in documenting and understanding many previously unknown aspects of the biology and behaviour of fishes and other marine species (e.g. Johannes 1981; Masse 1985, 1989; McPherson et al.

2010). Such observational powers were not confined to fishermen, but also included both men and women who had spent their lives gleaning resources from Palau's forests and reefs.

Even more remarkable to us was the richness and detail preserved in oral traditions regarding specific villages in the volcanic islands and the Rock Islands (e.g. Osborne 1966:401–404, 424–425). For example, in 1981 we were privileged to interview noted historian Joseph Tellei, *Oukerdeu* of the Idid clan in Koror and a former police chief in the Japanese colonial administration, regarding his knowledge of villages and chiefly confederations in the Rock Islands. While intrigued by these stories, we nevertheless continued to view such information with caution:

> The stories … recorded from Tellei are sketchy because of … lack of time to pursue further details (both from Tellei and other informants) and because of the several hundred years of retelling these stories which had undoubtedly altered the original details. Nevertheless, these stories do provide an interesting perspective on this period of Belauan prehistory, and seem to indicate that Belauan social organisation during the rock island village period was perhaps as complex as that observed at historic contact. At the very least, these stories, when combined with the archaeological record, indicate that during A.D. 1200–1450 the rock islands witnessed a degree of intensive utilization not seen before or afterwards (Masse 1989:76).

Similar scepticism was expressed by Osborne (1966:300) about the story regarding the sizable population once said to be on Ngeruangel atoll, its ability to conquer neighbouring polities, and the subsequent complete destruction of the atoll by a cyclonic storm. Osborne was convinced the story was a fabrication.

Such scepticism regarding the worth of oral tradition and the nature of the myths and legends has been more recently challenged due to a chance encounter by one of the authors with the myths and oral traditions surrounding the eruption of a Hawaiian volcano (Holcomb 1987; Masse et al. 1991; see also Swanson 2008). Because Hawaiian mythology and oral tradition are directly tied into royal chiefly genealogies (i.e. specific myth storylines are stated to have taken place during the reigns of named genealogical chiefs), and because some historically recorded or reconstructible spectacular natural events (e.g. volcanic eruptions, total solar eclipses, the passage of unique long-visible comets) are demonstrably captured and preserved in myth storylines, it is possible to achieve a chronological perspective on the pervasive multifaceted role of myth and oral tradition in traditional Hawaiian culture (Masse 1995, 2010; Masse et al. n.d.). These data suggest there is a powerful historical core to at least some myths and legends that can be objectively retrieved and studied (Masse et al. 2007; Piccardi and Masse 2007; Cashman and Giordano 2008).

At the very least, Hawai'i well illustrates the basic conservative nature of traditional oral myth transmission (Vansina 1985; Rubin 1995; Masse et al. n.d.). Gifted narrators were sought out or occupied inherited positions, and were continuously trained. Myth transmission itself was performance driven (song, dance, chant and appropriate imagery), serving to reinforce the storyline, as did the use of repetition. Myths typically were the property of chiefs/priests and were publicly performed on an annual or more frequent basis, such as during annual solstice ceremonies, the births of royal chiefs and ceremonies surrounding the periodic visits of royal chiefs travelling among islands in the Hawaiian chain. Myth also served to link chiefs with the supernatural powers of *mana* (supernatural forces believed to dwell in certain persons and sacred objects) as manifested in remarkable natural events. Not only can it be demonstrated that some of the myth storylines match historic natural events, but also that the observational details being preserved in the myths often add new scientific or scholarly information to the original historic records. That such detail can be preserved and transmitted within the context of myth storylines across dozens of generations is strong testimony to the potential accuracy and effectiveness of oral transmission.

It would be unwise, though, to entirely dismiss scepticism when dealing with myths and oral traditions. There are many documented processes that serve to garble or destroy the original historic content of myth (Barber and Barber 2004). And there are many other complexly layered structural, cognitive and symbolic aspects to myth. The power of myth, in part, derives from the creation and manipulation of evocative symbols within and between cultural groups. The challenge for archaeology and any historical approach to myth and oral tradition is to meaningfully separate the elements of history and chronology from the diverse structural, symbolic and social aspects of myths.

Rock Island oral traditions

It is not our purpose here to directly apply this Hawaiian-derived natural-science approach to Palauan oral traditions, nor to demonstrate that an absolute chronology can be derived for Palauan oral tradition, as is the case for Hawai'i. There seemingly are significant differences between how myth/legend and oral tradition are used in Palau versus Hawai'i. The Hawaiian examples serve primarily to emphasise the general value of oral tradition and to suggest that previously collected Palauan traditions have the potential to be mined for additional information regarding Palauan culture history, including settlement, and also that the continued collecting of oral traditions should be an important endeavour.

A number of researchers have commented on the general value of Palauan oral traditions relating to the Stonework Village Era on the volcanic islands reaching back several centuries before European contact (e.g. Kubary 1873; Krämer 1919; Osborne 1966; Parmentier 1981, 1987; Nero 1987, 2002; Masse 1989; Snyder 1989; Lucking and Parmentier 1990; Snyder and Butler 1997; Wickler 2002; Liston 2009). Our aim is to briefly discuss Rock Island oral traditions as they relate to issues of settlement and with relations between the Rock Islands and the volcanic and platform islands of the archipelago. These oral traditions suggest that previously published (e.g. Masse 1989; Masse et al. 2006) assessments of the nature and dating of Rock Island stonework villages require modest revision.

As previously noted, during the 1981 SIUPAP excavations in the Ngemelis group, we (Masse) had the opportunity to discuss Rock Islands oral traditions with Joseph Tellei, with the assistance of then Historic Preservation Office historian Moses Mekoll, with Walter R. Metes as translator (Masse does not speak Palauan). Tellei was then a vigorous 80 years old, and held the chiefly title of *Oukerdeu* in the highest ranked clan (*Idid* clan*)* of Koror. Tellei indicated that he had heard the stories (presumably as a teenager or young man) from Koror and Babeldaob's high chiefs *Ibedul* Louch (who died in 1917) and *Ibedul* Tem (who became *Ibedul* in 1926). The brief notes (Masse 1981) from Tellei regarding the Ngemelis group and other Rock Islands are presented below.

> Around AD 1700 [… a date that Tellei took time to confirm with an original copy of Kubary 1873 that he had in a trunk] Ngeruangel atoll was destroyed by a storm. At that time no one was living on the Ngemelis group. Some of the Ngeruangel survivors, the *Ngerbuuch* clan, fled to Ngemelis, later moving to Angaur. Their house/stone platform name is *Ngerburech*. The modern Aimeliik clan and house/stone platform *Selau* also originally came from Ngeruangel.

Tellei knew of two stories about what happened to these particular residents of Ngemelis. The first was that they were attacked (or assisted in warfare) by Terebkul, a warrior from Peleliu. The second is that starvation forced them to leave Ngemelis for Babeldaob. Both of these events took place before the time of Captain Wilson, that is before AD 1783 when the British East India packet *Antelope* was shipwrecked on nearby Ulong Island (see Keate 2002; Clark 2005). Uchelmelis was the chief of Ngemelis at the time of Terebkul's attack, and he lived at Rois village (on Uchularois Island). Uchelmelis eventually moved to Aimeliik, where one of the chiefly titles (but not that of the high chief) is now *Uchelmelis*.

A famous Palauan love story is that Uchelmelis had a daughter who was courted by Terebkul, when Terebkul was living at Ngerengchol (next to volcanic Malakal Island). One evening they were on the western shore of Ngemelis Island at full moon when the daughter of Uchelmelis lost her grass skirt. Fifteen days later, the turtle that stole her skirt brought it back to the shore (an act that describes the egg-laying cycle of turtles).

Also bearing on this discussion are fuller versions of the Terebkul story published by Osborne (1966:401–404) and Parmentier (1987:288–289) regarding the abandonment of Ulong Island. Apparently Ulong chief Osilek was in control of several Rock Island groups and villages including Ngemelis. Food, artefacts and weapons were constantly being taken from the subject populations to the benefit of Ulong. Finally, the chief of Ngemelis, Uchelmelis, asked Terekbul, a powerful warrior from Peleliu and lover of the daughter of Uchelmelis, to come to the aid of Ngemelis. Uchelmelis and Terebkul painted their normally red war canoes white, and planned to attack Ulong at sunset when their canoes would be hidden by the sunlight behind them. The attack was successful and the population of Ulong fled to volcanic Ngerekebesang, where Osilek had forged a recent alliance with Ngerekebesang chief Uchelkebesadel. Other Ulong groups split up, some going to the Babeldaob village of Ngeburech near Melekeok, and others to Ngeremlengui. After a number of years, the Ngeremlengui refugees from Ulong decided to join those of Ngeburech. Because they did not have a sufficiently large money bead to repay their Ngeremlengui hosts for their past hospitality, they made payment by repaving the stone paths and platforms of Imiong village prior to leaving for Ngeburech.

Ulong was never again reoccupied before the *Antelope* shipwreck, and a number of years after its defeat by Terekbul and Uchelmelis, the people of Ngemelis moved to Babeldaob. Tellei noted that shortly after this migration, another group of survivors from the Ngeruangel storm may have moved into recently abandoned Ngemelis. These refugees had been living temporarily in Ngerchemai village in eastern Koror. They arrived in Ngemelis and several other Rock Islands at the time *Ibedul* Kereel was the high chief of Koror, some time before *Ibedul* Esuch, who ruled Koror at the time of the AD 1783 *Antelope* shipwreck. The final abandonment of Ngemelis appears to have taken place shortly after Koror made war with some of the villages on Ngeruktabel (discussed below).

Tellei also noted that at the time of the final abandonment of Ngemelis, a boatload of refugees on the way to Koror had to stop at an unnamed location because a woman was pregnant and needed to deliver a baby. The baby girl was named Tmanges because the journey was 'moving up' to the north. Another canoe with refugees passed by the stopped canoe, and invited everyone to come with them to Koror. At this time another woman became pregnant. When they reached Ngerchemai (earlier called Ngeding) in Koror the second pregnant woman delivered a baby who was called Leudii, because the trip was finishing or ending. Leudii became *Ibedul* Esuch's second wife, and the mother of Lebuu. Lebuu is, of course, 'Prince Lee Boo' of *Antelope* shipwreck fame (Keate 2002; Nero 2002:Plates 5 and 6) who travelled to England with Captain Wilson. *Ibedul* Esuch is Wilson's 'Abba Thule' (Keate 2002:Plate 18), and Leudii is Wilson's 'Ludee' (Nero 2002:Plate 7), all three being sketched in AD 1783 by Arthur William Devis, a passenger on the shipwrecked *Antelope*.

Curiously, Captain John McCluer in AD 1791 during a return voyage to Palau indicated that Lebuu was the adopted son of *Ibedul* (Keate 2002:294–295). Other traditions have suggested that Ludee was Yapese (Keate 2002:389, no. 15). These traditions do not necessarily conflict with Tellei's observation that Leudii (or at least her mother) was from Ngemelis. Perhaps Lebuu's father (if not *Ibedul* Esuch) was Yapese. At the very least, the Leudii and Lebuu oral traditions provide a robust date for the final abandonment of Ngemelis. If we assume that Lebuu was approximately 16–18 years old at the time of the *Antelope* shipwreck, as suggested by his sketched appearances, then Ngemelis was abandoned around AD 1765.

Tellei also provided descriptions of two other sets of Rock Island polities, one concerning villages on the largest Rock Island of Ngeruktabel, and the other centered on and near the second largest Rock Island of Mercherchar. There were five widely spaced isolated villages on Ngeruktabel, including Mariar, Ngermiich, Metukeruikull, Ngeremdiu and namesake Ngeruktabel (Figure 2). Mariar was occupied at the same time as Ngemelis [presumably after the Ngeruangel storm], but there were also earlier village occupations at Mariar, Metukeruikull, and Ulong prior to the establishment of a village at Ngemelis.

The village of Ngeruktabel controlled Mariar just prior to a war in which Koror conquered Ngeruktabel. The war with Koror was caused by people from Ngeruktabel who went on a fishing expedition to Ngerengchol (Lee Marvin Beach on Ulebsechel Island). While there, they captured and killed *Ibedul* Kereel, putting his right hand with his dugong bracelet in a basket that was sent to the chiefs of Koror. The chiefs of Koror got together and discussed a plan for retaliation. The *Klotraol* (the chief of the fifth clan in charge of security during times of warfare) of Koror married a Ngeruktabel woman and went to live at Ngeruktabel for three months, carefully learning the layout of trails and passes. During a feast in which all the people of Ngeruktabel got drunk, possibly from drinking fermented coconut milk, *Klotraol* led warriors from Koror into Ngeruktabel and slaughtered all of its inhabitants. Immediately before the raid, the Koror chiefs had spread the word to Mariar and Metukruikull to temporarily leave the island so that they wouldn't get caught up in the war (Ngeremdiu and Ngermiich were already long abandoned by this time). The Mariar and Metukeruikull people decided to move out of the Rock Islands entirely, temporarily residing in Ngermid on Koror island. Chief Ngirachitei (from Metukeruikull/Mariar) talked to Chief Tuchermel of Ngerusar on Babeldaob about settling at Oikull. The Rock Island people had discovered that the food was better at Ngermid and the volcanic islands, so they decided to move permanently to Oikull. Chiefs and *bai* names at Oikull are all from the Rock Islands (for example, the present [1981] No. 1 chief at Oikull is named *Ngirachitei*).

When the people from Ngeremdiu abandoned Ngeruktabel Island before Koror's war with Ngeruktabel village, some went to live in Melekeok on Babeldaob. Some of the Ngermiich village people went to Ngerekebesang in Koror, where there is still a piece of land today [1981] called Ngermiich. Others from Ngermiich went to Oliuch (near Melekeok). The Ngeremdiu people in Melekeok began to fight with the Ngermiich people in Oliuch. The Oliuch people were forced to move to Ngerbekuu in Ngiwal. Ngerbekuu proved to be too far from the seashore and subsequently the people moved to more coastal Ngardmau. Ngardmau then started fighting with Koror and Ngeremlengui. The chief of Ngardmau felt that they needed more help in their wars and gave money to high chief *Reklai* of Melekeok. There were several wars between Ngardmau and Koror, until *Ibedul* sent bribe money to *Reklai* to end Melekeok's assistance to Ngardmau.

Tellei also indicated that Chief Osilek of Ulong was married to a Mariar woman (appropriately named Mariar). A Ngeanges chief was also married to a Mariar woman, but Tellei was unfamiliar with their stories. Ngeanges village was under the control of Metukeruikull. The No. 2 chief Aderdei of Metukeruikull lived on Ngeanges island, which served as a border for Metukeruikull.

Tellei provided a brief sketch for the Mecherchar and Ngerchong (Ngerchang) polity. High chief Iyechaderchemai lived in the principal village on Mecherchar (unnamed). No. 2 chief Obechad lived on Ngerchong, and also ruled the Ngerukuid and Ngemelis groups. Chief Uchercheuar (presumably ranked No. 3) lived at and controlled the Metukercheaus area of southern Mecherchar. Chief Eriu (presumably ranked No. 4) lived on Ngerchong and ruled the half of the island opposite from Obechad, along with the Babelomekang group. Because Ngemelis here is part of a different polity than that in the previously described stories of Uchelmelis and Terukbul, it is suggestive that this polity was active before 'uninhabited' Ngemelis was settled by the refugees from Ngeruangel atoll (thus sometime before ca. AD 1700).

Rethinking culture change and dynamic models of sustainable Palauan settlement

Palau has been continuously occupied for at least 3000 and perhaps more than 4000 years. During this time, impressive earthwork-terrace complexes come and go; stonework villages come and go, or at least go from the Rock Islands. We have stories of incessant warfare, periods of starvation and major cyclonic storms, such as that which apparently devastated Ngeruangel atoll. And we know of major rapid climatic shifts and events, such as the Little Ice Age with its Maunder Minimum, the so-called 'AD 1300 event', and perhaps related over-harvesting of marine resources in the Rock Islands; and the AD 536 climatic downturn and possibly related increases in El Niño activity. There are many other instances of environmental and cultural change in the Palauan archaeological record.

As with the often polarised debate on current global warming and its effects and causes, it is tempting for archaeologists to paint a very dark picture of environmental/cultural change and to emphasise the negative aspects of change. This is not to imply that global warming and other hallmarks of environmental change are not serious and worthy of debate. Rather, we are concerned with how one approaches the dialogue. For every set of changes, either environmental or social, there are choices and opportunities. Often it is language and perception that prevents us from more clearly seeing the relationship between cause and effect.

Just as memory and the rules of performance play an important role in the faithful transmission of oral traditions, memory and cultural rules hidden from the archaeologist can play a vital role in buffering the effects of environmental and social change. For example, from the snapshot picture that we have from descriptions in the late 19th and early 20th centuries, it appears that many of the villages in the Rock Islands were abandoned (e.g. Krämer 1919; Liston 2009). We suggest that the English word 'abandoned' is not correct or accurate. The villages that did not have occupied houses probably should not be considered abandoned, in the sense that this was island space available for resettlement by clan members or through appropriate channels of exchange. Following the kinship model put forward by Force and Force (1972), perhaps not all, but certainly most, of these villages could be more constructively interpreted as idle or dormant social space. Temporarily, there were no occupied houses, and for the most part no actively tended gardens, but over a span of several generations, it is likely these villages would again have become places of settlement, with tended gardens. In anthropological parlance, at least into the mid-19th century, the usufruct rights were clearly established and maintained in the Palauan kinship system.

From an archaeological perspective, as part of a settlement pattern, these idled villages provided flexibility and sustainability. They allowed people to shift from areas where soils and lagoon resources were becoming depleted or over-exploited to areas that been allowed to regenerate during an extended, and culturally sanctioned, period of dormancy.

Even in the mid-to-late 20th century, we find ethnographic and archaeological evidence supporting an interpretation of idled villages rather than abandoned villages. At Ngatpang Village in the early 1950s, Douglas Osborne interviewed an elderly woman (Osborne 1966:Figure 3) about pottery making in the only occupied residence in this village. In the early 1980s when we (Snyder) revisited this village to collect a sample of clay, there was no evidence of occupation. However, a little more than 10 years later, when we (Snyder) returned to Ngatpang Village to map it (Snyder and Butler 1997), there was a family living there and beginning the construction of a house. They identified themselves as one of the grandchildren of the elderly woman interviewed by Osborne, though they had not met him because their parents were living at the time in villages in other parts of Babeldaob Island. Many cultural factors enter into our behaviour, including kinship, rights to land, politics, religion and subsistence. There is no doubt much more to these stories than we gathered from brief interviews. But time and time again, we were struck by the depth of knowledge of these so-called abandoned villages and the capability for people to shift the distribution of relatively compact villages across the Palauan landscape.

One of the themes of the *Pacific Island archaeology in the 21st century* conference was sustainability, exploring how Pacific peoples can sustain their livelihoods and cultures into the future. The concept of sustainability when coupled with the related concepts of resilience and flexibility is useful for our ideas on traditional Palauan settlement. Archaeological theory is too often rooted in structures such as phases or types that resist efforts to explain change. With the concept of the archaeological phase, one assumes a stasis throughout a region during a period of time. We hope that in this paper, we are successful in conveying the idea that traditional Palauan culture was dynamic. Its ability to change and adapt to changing environmental conditions and the introduction of new ideas, concepts and material culture allows traditional Palauan culture to achieve sustainability.

Our strategy in developing settlement-system models is to begin with the delineation of a pattern. A settlement pattern brings together procurement, processing, use and discard, from contemporaneous activities, integrating activities throughout the archipelago. A pattern brings together contemporaneous activities, but also extends across time because this is a cultural pattern. And, with its extent across time and space, the pattern will exhibit a range of variability. Within the pattern, we seek to analyse the relationships among many different activities. A sustainable pattern should allow for reinforcement of different activities through the range of variability. Different patterns are recognised when analysis indicates that activities are no longer integrated and no longer reinforcing. Primarily, the analysis is accomplished through comparisons. This strategy allows us to propose and analyse different perspectives before delineating a settlement system. In this regard, our strategy contrasts with other approaches that begin by delineating a classificatory system of periods and phases that further requires the delineation of a separate settlement system within each period.

The settlement pattern in Palau during the period of around AD 1300 to the present has focused on somewhat compact villages. These villages are nucleated settlements with houses and community centres clustered in a central area. In many, if not most, of the larger village areas there were several nucleated villages in close proximity. For example, in Melekeok there is a series of villages along the coastline. Not readily obvious to an outsider is that the villages are clearly named and delineated. In the 1980s, we observed people living in some of these villages while other villages were idle. Within this nucleated settlement pattern, the distance between villages, or clusters of villages, was much greater than the distances between houses within the cluster. Rock Island villages at Mariar, Ngeanges and the Ngemelis group mirror the nucleated pattern to the degree possible within the karstic terrain.

We also have begun to discern nucleated villages as part of the Earthwork Era between about 500 BC and AD 600–800 (e.g. Liston 2009). It is the roughly 600–800-year period between about AD 600 and AD 800 (the end of the Earthwork villages) and AD 1300 (the beginning of the Stonework Village Era) that we find particularly interesting. What explains this lengthy period of a seeming absence of nucleated villages in Palau? Is this due to sampling and the placement of archaeological investigations? Is this due to our inability to archaeologically recognise older components that are inter-mixed with the traditional villages that we currently understand to date to the past 400 years? Or is this because the settlement pattern in Palau was different at that time?

There are several factors that lead us to think that we should carefully consider the likelihood of a distinct dispersed settlement pattern in Palau between the Earthwork and Stonework Village eras. In the Rock Islands, Masse (Masse 1989; Masse et al. 2006) has demonstrated that midden deposits are present, lying below Stonework Village Era components, with these deposits being particularly rich and diverse in Uchularois Cave around AD 800–900, based on radiocarbon dating of charcoal. This led Masse to propose a period of smaller dispersed settlements in the Rock Islands coinciding with the large-scale abandonment of Earthwork Era villages and terraces and forest expansion in the interior of at least portions of Babeldaob (Liston 2009).

There are many different possible scenarios that could account for the current findings. It isn't our intention to be categorical about a final answer, but rather to propose a testable hypothesis. With testing of several hypotheses, we can move towards a robust interpretation. Embedded in our models are the concepts of 'nucleated' and 'dispersed', which we use to organise and describe our observations, keeping in mind that nucleated and dispersed are not mutually exclusive states. We view these as continuous – that is, we seek to measure the degree of nucleation and the degree of dispersal in the settlement pattern.

We offer as a hypothesis that the settlement pattern in Palau before 500 BC and between AD 800 and AD 1300 was characterised by a dispersed pattern. In contrast to the nucleated pattern of villages, in the dispersed pattern individual households were surrounded by a variety of kitchen gardens. There was relatively greater emphasis on the exploitation of resources associated with terraces. Individual households were relatively evenly distributed around the margins of the islands. Individual households may have included several buildings associated with resource-processing locations. It seems likely that households were integrated into alliances, perhaps based on kinship. It is possible that the population in Palau has been roughly the same (25,000–50,000) since before 500 BC. We lack sufficient data to allow even speculation on population trends. However, there is no reason to assume that population is a major driver in shifts between dispersed and nucleated settlement patterns. A dispersed settlement pattern would have resulted in equal and sustained pressure on resources in the lagoon and on the land. Masse and Carucci both found evidence of sustained pressure on lagoon resources over a span of several centuries at the end of the first millennium AD.

Shifting settlement patterns from dispersed to nucleated, perhaps several times over a span of several millennia, would have provided Palauans a basis of sustainability. It is apparent from oral traditions that even during periods of intense nucleation, such as during the period of stonework villages, there were often shifts in settlement as a response to changing environmental and social conditions. In the lagoon, a dispersed settlement pattern allows exploitation to be spread out, but in general the total yield would be less than obtained by more focused patterns. On the land, a dispersed settlement pattern minimises environmental degradation, but may make intensification of exploitation of a resource and social networking more difficult than with a nucleated settlement pattern.

The terraces functioned in a number of different ways. Comparing Palauan terraces with terraces in many other places, it seems likely that in addition to their use for villages and defensive posturing, an important function would be to control and manage water flow. The terraces slowed water flow during periods of high rainfall and thus lessened erosion, and they also slowed water flow during periods of low rainfall to conserve soil moisture and extend resource availability. As the soil on the terraces wore out, emphasis would have shifted to other kinds of resources, especially resources of the lagoon. But with less management of the terraces, there would have been greater erosion. Together, the erosion and the increasing exploitation of the lagoon resources would have diminished the resources of the lagoon. Shifting to a nucleated settlement pattern with a number of idle villages would have allowed the intensive exploitation of taro swamp gardens and other resources at the now nutrient-rich zone where the land meets the mangroves, and would have allowed regeneration of both land and lagoon areas around idle villages.

It is also important to point out the likelihood that at no time were the Rock Islands considered 'uninhabitable' by ancient Palauans. Limestone islands and coral atolls are a ubiquitous feature in Micronesia and island Southeast Asia. Although such environments require a fair amount of intervention by their human occupants (Kirch 2000:181–182) to provide some of the necessities for basic sustenance (e.g. fresh water or coconut milk, suitable areas for gardens, shells for tools and containers), these are well known to western Pacific Islanders and have been for thousands of years. In addition, the Rock Islands, even when not occupied for semi-permanent or permanent habitation, such as during the stonework village period, were well known to the people in the surrounding volcanic and platform islands. Memory and oral traditions of the Rock Islands and associated reefs would have provided many choices for settlement and resource-collection options. The other thing to remember about the Rock Islands is that based on the presence of ceramics as early as the 3100–2900 BP midden deposits on Ulong, the Rock Islands were never completely isolated from the volcanic islands. In fact, one of the notable aspects of the stonework village period in the Rock Islands is the fact that sherds are a major component of all midden deposits. Hundreds of ceramic vessels were probably brought to each Rock Island village every year. There is much still to understand about trade and exchange between the Rock Islands and the volcanic and platform islands.

In summary, shifts between dispersed and nucleated settlement patterns would have allowed Palauans to maintain sustainable ecological relationships over long periods of time. It is admittedly easy to postulate a settlement pattern in the absence of data. We believe that the models of Palauan settlement systems we outline in this paper offer testable hypotheses. Archaeological testing needs to be extended to lowland sites and locations between villages and at the end of villages, with sufficient sensitivity in the archaeological testing techniques to detect traces of activity areas and residences, if any exist, that are not as clearly demarcated as activity areas around stone platforms. Archaeological testing on terraces needs to expand to expose sufficient area with sufficient sensitivity in the archaeological testing techniques to expose activity areas and additional functional information. Additional archaeological survey and testing is also needed in the Rock Islands, especially at sites not immediately associated with large Rock Island stonework villages. In particular, we need to provide comparative data from analysis of shell middens, from both Rock Island and volcanic island sites, to test models of lagoon-resource exploitation and models of resource exchange.

Archaeology, sustainability and the future of Palau

Too often, archaeologists forget that our research has applied as well as scientific values and results. If anything, the *Pacific Island archaeology in the 21st century* conference should remind us that living Pacific Islanders and not just fellow archaeologists should be the primary beneficiaries of our work. Certainly, the validation of oral traditions is one important applied finding. No traditional cultural-knowledge keeper should feel anything other than respect and gratitude from anthropologists, archaeologists and historians for the gift of their precious oral traditions. And we scientists and scholars should never forget that the gift of precious and sacred oral tradition is usually only forthcoming when we have earned the trust and at least the tacit permission to use this gift appropriately and wisely.

In a similar vein, it is now our task to rethink the sterile or often unsettling archaeological concept of settlement system in order to put it into a context that better serves modern Palauans (Figure 3). Perhaps the easiest way to describe our model of the traditional Palauan settlement system is by noting that Palauans did not put all their settlement 'eggs' in one basket. The traditional Palauan settlement system had the inbuilt flexibility to achieve a new formation when environmental and/or social conditions changed. The system was sustainable, flexible and resilient because the overall diversity and variability of resources in the Palau archipelago buffered and facilitated changes in the settlement system.

Figure 3. Palauan children on a stonework village path.

Even with global warming and the potential of rapidly rising sea levels, there is no reason to think that contemporary and future Palauans will be any less successful with coping and adapting their settlement systems than was the case for their ancestors, described above. It is comforting to know that although people had not yet arrived in Palau at the end of the last ice age some 14,000 years ago, Palau and its incredible reefs survived a rise in sea level much more rapid and potentially catastrophic than anything that is likely to result from the present global warming (Kayanne et al. 2002).

Acknowledgements

Joni L. Manson helped much with drafting the conceptual ideas for this paper. George Gumerman and Brian Butler provided collegial encouragement and support for our Palau research. Moses Sam, Vicki Kanai, Moses Mekoll and the late Rita Olsudong provided critical assistance for our research and fieldwork from the Palau Historic Preservation Office. Vince Blaiyok and Water Metes served as crew chiefs for our 1981 surveys and test excavations, and have since served in numerous capacities to aid our work. Colleagues Jolie Liston, Geoffrey Clark, Scott Fitzpatrick and Steve Athens furnished us with copies of their recent publications. We are particularly grateful to the many Palauans, young and old, who took the time to share with us their love for and lore of Palau. The past, present and future of Palau remains as a gift and a promise for future generations. The authors of this paper are pleased and thankful to have played a small role in this evolving drama.

References

Athens, J.S. and Ward, J.V. 2001. Paleoenvironmental evidence for early human settlement in Palau: The Ngerchau core. In: Stevenson, C.M. and Morin, F.J. (eds), *Pacific 2000: Proceedings of the Fifth International Conference on Easter Island and the Pacific*, pp. 165–78. Easter Island Foundation, Los Osos.

Barber, E.W. and Barber, P.T. 2004. *When they severed earth from sky: How the human mind shapes myth.* Princeton University Press, Princeton, NJ.

Cashman, K.V. and Giordano, G. 2008. Volcanoes and human history. *Journal of Volcanology and Geothermal Research* 176:325–329.

Carneiro, R.L. 1981. The chiefdom: Precursor of the state. In: Jones, G.D. and Kautz, R. (eds), *The transition to statehood in the New World*, pp. 37–79. Cambridge University Press, Cambridge.

Carucci, J. 1992. Cultural and natural patterning in prehistoric marine foodshell from Palau, Micronesia. Unpublished PhD thesis, Southern Illinois University, Carbondale (Ann Arbor, MI, University Microfilms International).

Clark, G. 2005. A 3000-year culture sequence from Palau, western Micronesia. *Asian Perspectives* 44:349–380.

Clark, G., Anderson, A. and Wright, D. 2006. Human colonisation of the Palau Islands, western Micronesia. *Journal of Island and Coastal Archaeology* 1:215–232.

Fitzpatrick, S.M. 2003. Early human burials in the western Pacific: Evidence for a ca. 3000 year old occupation on Palau. *Antiquity* 77(298):719–731.

Fitzpatrick, S.M. and Kataoka, O. 2005. Prehistoric fishing in Palau, Micronesia: Evidence from the northern Rock Islands. *Archaeology in Oceania* 40:1–13.

Fitzpatrick, S.M. and Donaldson, T.J. 2007. Anthropogenic impacts to coral reefs in Palau, western Micronesia during the Late Holocene. *Coral Reefs* 26:916–930.

Force, R.W. and Force, M. 1972. *Just one house: A description and analysis of kinship in the Palau Islands.* Bernice P. Bishop Museum Bulletin 235, Bishop Museum Press, Honolulu.

Gagan, M.K., Hendy, E.J., Haberle, S.G. and Hantoro, W.S. 2004. Postglacial evolution of the Indo-Pacific Warm Pool and El Niño-Southern Oscillation. *Quaternary International* 118–119:127–143.

Gumerman, G.J., Snyder, D. and Masse, W.B. 1981. *An archaeological reconnaissance in the Palau Archipelago, Western Caroline Islands, Micronesia.* Southern Illinois Center for Archaeological Investigations Research Paper 23, Carbondale.

Holcomb, R.T. 1987. Eruptive history and long-term behaviour of Kilauea Volcano. In: Decker, R.W., Wright, T.L. and Stauffer, P.H. (eds), *Volcanism in Hawaii, Volume 1.* US Geological Survey Professional Paper 1350, pp. 261–350. Washington, DC.

Intoh, M. 1986. Pigs in Micronesia: Introduction or re-introduction by the Europeans. *Man and Culture in Oceania* 2:1–26.

Intoh, M. 2008. *Historical significance of the Southwest Islands Palau.* In: Clark, G., Leach, F.L. and O'Connor, S. (eds), *Islands of inquiry: Colonisation, seafaring and the archaeology of maritime landscapes*, pp. 325–338. Terra Australis 29, ANU EPress.

Johannes, R. 1981. *Words of the lagoon; Fishing and marine lore in the Palau district of Micronesia.* University of California Press, Berkeley.

Kayanne, H., Yamono, H. and Randall, R. 2002. Holocene sea-level changes and barrier reef formation on an oceanic island. Palau Islands, western Pacific. *Sedimentary Geology* 150:47–60.

Keate, G. 2002. *An account of the Pelew Islands.* In: Nero, K.L. and Thomas, N. (eds), Leicester University Press, London.

Kirch, P.V. 2000. *On the road of the winds: An archaeological history of the Pacific Islands before European contact.* University of California Press, Berkeley.

Krämer, A. 1919. In: Thilenius, G. (ed), *Ergebnisse der Südsee-Expedition 1908–1910.* II. Ethnographie; B. Mikronesien. Band 3, Teilband 2. Friederichsen, Hamburg (Human Relations Area file typescript, anonymous translation).

Kubary, J.S. 1873. Die Palau-Inseln in der Sudsee. *Journal des Museum Godeffroy* 1:181–238 (Human Relations Area File typescript, translated by Anonymous).

Liston, J. 1999. P*alau Compact Road, archaeological investigations, Babeldaob Island, Republic of Palau. Phase II: Data recovery. Volume V: Laboratory analysis, synthesis, and recommendations.* Draft report prepared for the U.S. Army Engineer District, Honolulu, Ft. Shafter, Hawai'i. International Archaeological Research Institute, Inc., Honolulu.

Liston, J. 2005. An assessment of radiocarbon dates from Palau, western Micronesia. *Radiocarbon* 47:295–354.

Liston, J. 2009. Cultural chronology of earthworks in Palau, western Micronesia. *Archaeology of Oceania* 44:56–73.

Liston, J. and Tuggle, H.D. 2006. Prehistoric warfare in Palau. In: Arkush, E. and Allen, M.W. (eds), *The archaeology of warfare: Prehistories of raiding and conquest*, pp. 148–183. University Press of Florida, Gainesville.

Lucking, L. 1984. An archaeological investigation of prehistoric Palauan terraces. Unpublished PhD thesis, Department of Anthropology, University of Minnesota.

Lucking, L J. and Parmentier, R.J. 1990. Terraces and traditions of Uluang: Ethnographic and archaeological perspectives on a prehistoric Belauan site. In: Hunter-Anderson, R. (ed), *Recent advances in Micronesian archaeology.* Micronesica Supplement 2:125–136.

Mason, A.C. 1955. *Geology of the limestone Islands, Palau, Western Caroline Islands.* Unpublished PhD thesis, Department of Geology, University of Illinois. University Microfilms, Ann Arbor.

Masse, W.B. 1981. Field notes on file at the Center for Archaeological Investigations, Southern Illinois University, Carbondale.

Masse, W.B. 1985. Review of 'Words of the Lagoon: Fishing and marine lore in the Palau District of Micronesia' by Johannes, R.E. (1981 – University of California Press, Berkeley). *Copeia* 1985:797–798.

Masse, W.B. 1986. A millennium of fishing in the Palau Islands, Micronesia. In: Anderson, A. (ed), T*raditional fishing in the Pacific: Ethnographic and archaeological papers from the 15th Pacific Science Congress.* Pacific Anthropological Records 37, pp. 85–117. Bernice Pauahi Bishop Museum, Honolulu.

Masse, W.B. 1989. *The archaeology and ecology of fishing in the Belau Islands, Micronesia.* Unpublished PhD thesis, Southern Illinois University, Carbondale (Ann Arbor, MI, University Microfilms International).

Masse, W.B. 1990. Radiocarbon dating, sea-level change, and the peopling of Belau. In: Hunter-Anderson, R. (ed), *Recent advances in Micronesian archaeology.* Micronesica Supplement 2:213–230.

Masse, W.B. 1991. The quest for subsistence sufficiency and civilization in the Sonoran Desert. In: Crown, P.L. and Judge, W.J. (eds), *Chaco and Hohokam: Prehistoric regional systems in the American Southwest*, pp. 195–223. School of American Research Press, Santa Fe.

Masse, W.B. 1995. The celestial basis of civilization. *Vistas in Astronomy* 39:463–477.

Masse, W.B. 2010. The celestial engine at the heart of traditional Hawaiian culture. Paper prepared for 'Astronomy and power: How worlds are structured', the European Society for Astronomy and Culture 18th Annual Meeting, Gilching, Germany, August 30–September 4, 2010.

Masse, W.B., Carter, L.A. and Somers, G.M. 1991. Waha'ula heiau, the regional and symbolic context of Hawai'i Island's "Red Mouth" temple. *Asian Perspectives* 30:19–56.

Masse, W.B. and Snyder, D. 1982. The final report of the 1981 field season of the Southern Illinois University Palau Archaeological Project. Report prepared for Historic Preservation Office, US Trust Territory of the Pacific Islands, Saipan. Center for Archaeological Investigations, Southern Illinois University, Carbondale.

Masse, W.B., Snyder, D. and Gumerman, G.J. 1984. Prehistoric and historic settlement in the Palau Islands, Micronesia. *New Zealand Journal of Archaeology* 6:107–127.

Masse, W.B., Liston, J., Carucci, J. and Athens, J.S. 2006. Evaluating the effects of climate change on environment, resource depletion, and culture in the Palau Islands between AD 1200 and 160. *Quaternary International* 151:106–132.

Masse, W.B., Barber, E.W., Piccardi, L. and Barber, P.T. 2007. Exploring the nature of myth and its role in science. In: Piccardi, L. and Masse, W.B. (eds), *Myth and geology*. Geological Society of London Special Publication 273.

McPherson, D.L., Blaiyok, V.K. and Masse, W.B. 2010. Unusual predatory and aggressive behaviors of Black-tip reef sharks (*Carcharhinus melanopterus*) and Jacks (Carangidae) in the Palau Islands, Micronesia. Submitted to *Environmental Biology of Fishes*.

Masse, W.B., Johnson, R.K. and Tuggle, H.D. n.d. *Islands in the sky: Traditional astronomy and the role of celestial phenomena in Hawaiian myth, language, religion, and chiefly power*. University of Hawai'i Press, Honolulu [Manuscript in preparation].

Nero, K.L. 1987. *A Cherechar a Lokelii: Beads of history of Koror, Palau, 1783–1983*. Unpublished PhD thesis, University of California, Berkeley (Ann Arbor, MI, University Microfilms International).

Nero, K.L. 2002. In: Nero, K.L. and Thomas, N. (eds), *An Account of the Pelew Islands –George Keate*, pp. 1–25. Leicester University Press, London.

Nunn, P.D. 2000. Environmental catastrophe in the Pacific Islands around A.D. 1300. *Geoarchaeology* 15(7):715–740.

Nunn. P.D. 2007. *Climate, environment, and society in the Pacific during the last millennium*. Elsevier Science, New York.

Ogg, J.G. and Koslow, J.A. 1978. The impact of typhoon Pamela (1976) on Guam's coral reef communities. *Environmental Biology of Fishes* 3:49–63.

Osborne, D. 1958. The Palau Islands: Stepping stones into the Pacific. *Archaeology* 11:162–171.

Osborne, D. 1966. *The archaeology of the Palau Islands, an intensive survey*. BP Bishop Museum Bulletin 230, Bishop Museum Press, Honolulu.

Osborne, D. 1979. *Archaeological test excavations, Palau Islands, 1968–1969*. Micronesia Supplement 1.

Parmentier, R.J. 1981. T*he sacred remains: An historical ethnography of Ngeremlengui, Palau*. Unpublished PhD thesis, University of Chicago (Ann Arbor, MI: University Microfilms International).

Parmentier, R.J. 1987. *The sacred remains: Myth, history, and polity in Belau*. University of Chicago Press, Chicago.

Phear, S. 2008. *Subsistence and inland landscape transformations: Investigating monumental earthworks in Ngaraard State, Republic of Palau, Micronesia: A landscape perspective*. In: Clark, G., Leach, F.L. and O'Connor, S. (eds), *Islands of inquiry: Colonisation, seafaring and the archaeology of maritime landscapes*, pp. 301–324. Terra Australis 29, ANU EPress.

Piccardi, L. and Masse, W.B. (eds), 2007. *Myth and geology*. Geological Society of London Special Publication 273.

Reff, D. 1991. *Disease, depopulation, and culture change in Northwestern New Spain, 1518–1754*. University of Utah Press, Salt Lake City.

Rubin, D.C. 1995. *Memory in oral traditions*. Oxford University Press, Oxford.

Semper, K. 1982. *The Palau Islands in the Pacific Ocean* (Translated by M Berg). Micronesian Area Research Center, University of Guam (Original German edition, 1873).

Service, E.R. 1962. *Primitive social organization*. Random House, New York.

Snyder, D. 1989. Towards chronometric models for Palauan prehistory: Ceramic attributes. Unpublished PhD thesis, Southern Illinois University, Carbondale (Ann Arbor, MI, University Microfilms International).

Snyder, D. and Butler, B.M. 1997. *Palau archaeology: Archaeology and historic preservation in Palau*. Micronesian Resources Study, Anthropology, Research Series 2. Micronesian Endowment for Historic Preservation Republic of Palau. U.S. National Park Service, San Francisco.

Stannard, D. 1989. *Before the horror: The population of Hawaii on the eve of Western contact*. University of Hawai'i Press, Honolulu.

Swanson, D.A. 2008. Hawaiian oral tradition describes 400 years of volcanic activity at Kilauea Volcano. *Journal of Volcanism and Geothermal Research* 176:427–431.

Takayama, J. 1979. Archaeological investigation of PAAT-2 in the Palaus: an interim report. In: Kusakabe, F. (ed), *Cultural anthropological research on the folk culture in the Western Caroline Islands of Micronesia in 1977*, pp. 81–103. Tokyo University of Foreign Studies, Tokyo.

Takayama, J. and Takasugi, H. 1978. Preliminary report of the archaeological excavation of PAAT-2, in Palau. Overseas Scientific Research, Ministry of Education, Japan. Tokyo University of Foreign Studies, Tokyo. Manuscript on file, Historic Preservation Office, Republic of Palau, Koror.

U.S. Army, 1956. *Military geology of Palau Islands, Caroline Islands.* U.S. Geological Survey, Washington, D.C.

Vansina, J. 1985. *Oral tradition as history.* University of Wisconsin Press, Madison.

Vessel, A.J. and Simonson, R.W. 1958. Soils and agriculture of the Palau Islands. *Pacific Science* 12:281–298.

Wickler, S. 2002. Oral traditions and archaeology: Modeling village settlement in Palau, Micronesia. *Micronesian: Journal of the Humanities and Social Sciences* 1:39–47.

Wickler, S.K., Welch, D.J., Tomonari-Tuggle, M.J., Liston, J., Tuggle, H.D. and Grant, D.M. 2005. *Palau Compact Road archaeological investigations, Babeldaob Island, Republic of Palau. Phase I: Intensive archaeological survey. Volume I: Scope, background, results, evaluation, and recommendations.* Prepared for U.S. Army Corps of Engineers, Pacific Ocean Division, Ft. Shafter, Hawai'i. IARII, Honolulu, Hawai'i (Report ID 566).

Yamaguchi, M. 1975. Sea level fluctuations and mass mortalities of reef animals in Guam, Mariana Islands. *Micronesica* 11:227–243.

12

Oral tradition and archaeology
Palau's earth architecture

Jolie Liston[1] and Melson Miko[2]

1. Archaeology and Natural History, College of Asia and the Pacific, The Australian National University, Australia
2. Palau Visitor's Authority, Palau

Introduction

The islands of Palau in the Western Carolines of Micronesia have a rich body of myths, stories and legends that are woven into every aspect of daily life. These oral traditions educate, mediate, amuse, guide and resolve issues of protocol and proprietorship to define, bond and embody Palauan heritage. They promote a continuation of norms, ideas and values from past to present, enabling members of modern communities to identify with their ancestors. Integration of these traditional narratives into archaeological history has the potential to reveal the complexities inherent to Palau's cultural landscape to form a more comprehensive depiction of the past.

Oral traditions are an alternative data set for interpreting archaeological expressions of social organisation, distinguishing temporal relationships and associating a location, feature or artefact with historical or legendary figures (see Vansina 1985). They can provide a social context for material remains that is unobtainable in archaeological investigations by identifying symbolic, social and ideological values. As an independent source of evidence, traditional narratives can correct or challenge archaeological interpretations and provide an interpretive framework for developing models to be tested against the material-culture record.

As oral traditions are used to process and comprehend cultural practices and traditional history and construct identity and social order, they can orient archaeological studies to focus on issues relevant to local communities (David et al. 2004). The act of collecting oral traditions associated with material remains engages the public in building archaeological knowledge and brings local values into cultural heritage interpretation and site assessment (Tellei et al. 1998a:93; Cachola-Abad 2000).

Despite the contributions traditional narratives can make to a broader understanding of archaeological data, there are limitations to their use. Their poetic aspects and abbreviation of long-term processes into single explanatory events require judicious interpretation. As in other societies, Palau's oral traditions can be largely shaped by or a reflection of those segments and aspects of society that are considered significant and beneficial to the dominant group (Hobsbawm and Ranger 1983; Parmentier 1987; Olsudong 1995). Only a selected piece of the whole may be relayed down through the generations and even this may be subject to vagaries in memory (see Rubin 1995). Considering the potential for subjectivity and issues about accuracy of memory, traditional narratives must be critically evaluated when used as a data source in archaeological investigations. Oral sources cannot be discounted as evidence in reconstructing the past as it is exactly the phenomena that is recalled when compared with the physical remains that can illuminate cultural transformations and significance.

Despite its encompassing realm, Palau's oral sources are conspicuously devoid of direct reference to the extensive clusters of earth architecture that dominate the topography of Babeldaob, the largest island in the archipelago (Figure 1). Although an association with intangible heritage does not ensure the protection of a cultural property, those sites that are not within the purview of the narratives or not considered to be anthropogenic remain largely external to Palauan cultural identity. Without ties to the living population, terrace sites are unlikely to be preserved for their informational value or preserved for future generations.

This paper explores the place of Palau's monumental earthworks in traditional narratives through an examination of the archaeological record in conjunction with ethnohistorical documents and oral-history collections. The aim is to ascertain the actual extent of their presence in the narratives and examine why such massive architectural complexes are largely excluded from Palau's traditional body of knowledge. We are not attempting to reconcile the oral historical and archaeological evidence to establish a single historical 'truth'.

Oral traditions and archaeology in Palau

In Palau's highly structured hierarchical society, access to information, particularly pertaining to social relations and their associated contexts, is culturally sanctioned. Even though an individual may know a story, if he or she is not from a specific location, clan or rank, he or she cannot claim aspects or segments of cultural knowledge. Furthermore, many histories are only transmitted to the legitimate heir to the information (Kesolei 1977; Nero 1987). As Tellei et al. (2005:14) explain:

> Knowledge, especially of history or the social sciences, is both a source of power and a commodity. It is a bargaining chip in cultural negotiations, with rules that limit access.

Accurate information can only be collected from legitimate knowledgeable informants and is generally divulged only to specific individuals. In some cases, others may know the story but they are not entitled to transfer the information. Hence, the authenticity of the information has to be verified. Interviews must be carefully planned since the specific question asked asserts a strong influence on the answer and the character of the information provided. Despite this restriction of information, oral historians can still generate valid histories by following proper protocol through appropriate channels (Tellai et al. 2005:11–15). Regardless, much information is not disclosed and is eventually lost when no one with the authority to retain that history survives.

In Palau, archaeological use of narratives requires not only careful evaluation but also an awareness of the process of acquiring information so that it can be filtered appropriately. Before integrating oral historical data into archaeological interpretations, Tellei et al. (2005:15) state that the information 'must be interpreted in terms of who the informant is, the source of his or her knowledge, and the context of the interview itself (what was the specific question that was asked)'. In the complex layering of Palau's social structure, foreign archaeologists often do not have the tools needed to ascertain the legitimacy of a story.

Palau's traditional narratives have been used to augment the interpretation of material

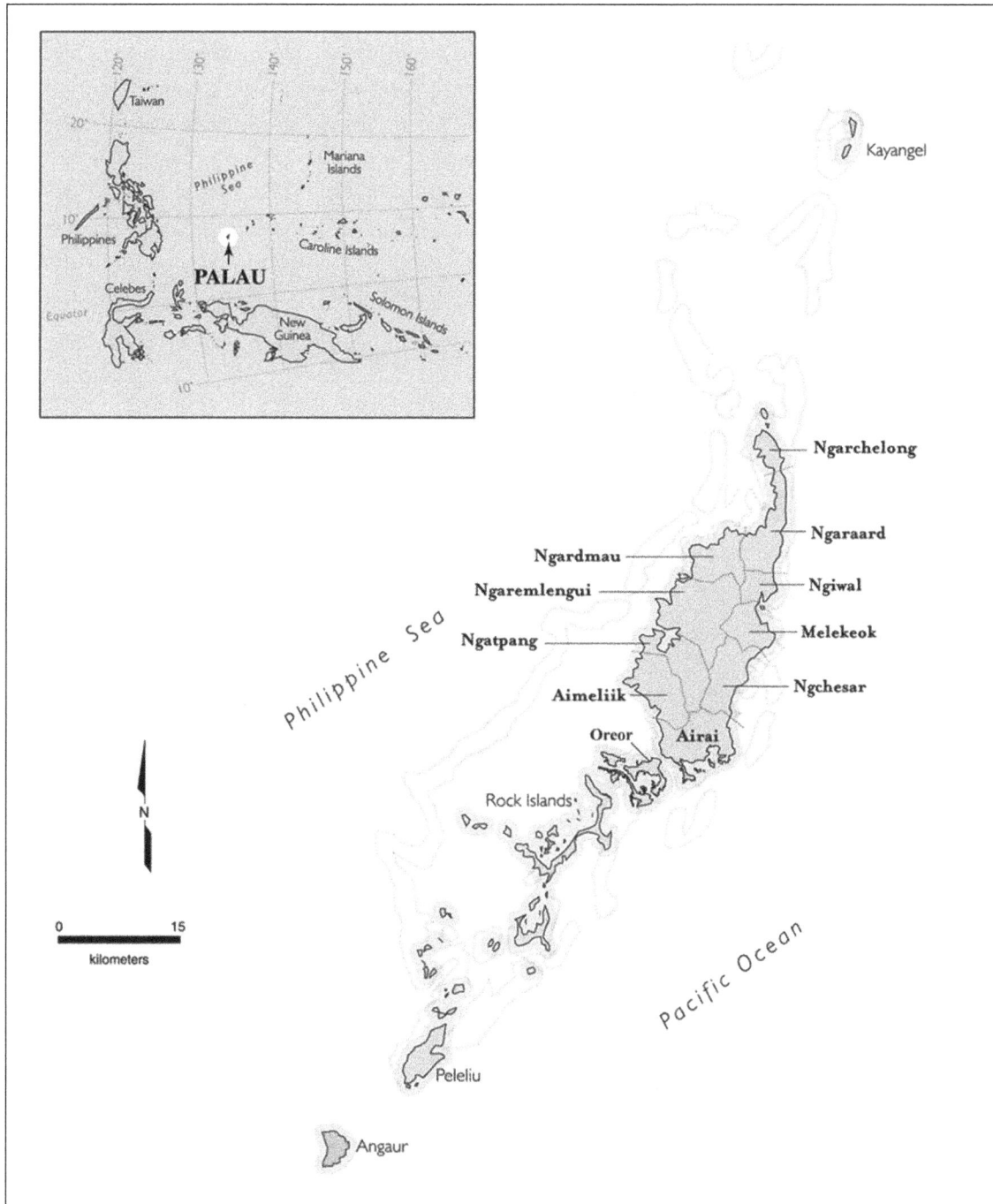

Figure 1. Map of Palau in the Western Caroline Islands of Micronesia.

remains (Beardsley and Basilius 2002; Liston and Rieth 2010), to locate cultural properties and identify temporal sequences (Lucking and Parmentier 1990), to identify cultural beliefs and ideology in the archaeological record (Olsudong 2002), and to correlate idealised traditional social, organisational and developmental models with archaeological evidence (Butler 1986; Olsudong 1995; Wickler 2002). These somewhat successful collaborations emphasised the need for considerable caution when combining the separate lines of inquiry. Olsudong (2002:158), finding discordance in the two data sets, concluded that although traditional history is a significant source of information for archaeological research, multiple factors must be considered in merging the two methodologies.

In the past 15 years, Palau has made considerable progress in its approach to and method for melding the documentation and interpretation of its intangible and tangible resources. Palau adopted a slightly modified version of Section 106 of the US National Historic Preservation Act of 1966, as amended, as its regulatory framework for cultural resources. One alteration to Section 106 is the recognition of a fundamental connection between tangible and intangible cultural properties. In archaeological site evaluations, either cultural or natural properties, the latter displaying no anthropogenic constructions or modifications, can be assessed as significant if they are 'associated with lyrics, folklore and traditions in Palauan culture'. This addition of a fifth significance criteria compels merging oral historical and archaeological interpretations to assign site designations.

This comprehensive Historical and Cultural Preservation Act (Title 19 PNC 103) is administered within the Bureau of Arts and Culture (BAC), a part of the Ministry of Community and Cultural Affairs. BAC receives funding from the US National Park Service and operates much like a US state historic preservation office. Three of BAC's five sections are pertinent to material-cultural resources: Oral History and Ethnography, Survey and Inventory/Archaeology, and the Register of Historic Places. These sections work closely with the Society of Historians *(Klobak er a lbetel a Cherechar)* – representatives from each state who are recognised as being particularly knowledgeable about the traditions and narratives of their region. As a body, these groups are tasked with documenting, protecting and fostering Palau's intangible and tangible cultural properties including, but not limited to, oral histories, customary practices, music, skills in applied arts and archaeological sites. The BAC's Oral History and the Archaeology sections collaborate by conducting annual joint surveys of cultural properties and determining historic clearances needed to obtain earthmoving permits.

To augment the archaeological evaluation of traditional sites, Palau's cultural resource management (CRM) projects are required to gather oral history related to the proposed construction parcel.[1] Collected and written by a Palauan oral historian, the oral history records are an appendix to the CRM report. This documentation is not an afterthought to the main body of 'scientific' data, but is intentionally retained as a separate work so that traditional history is presented from a Palauan perspective. The information is then incorporated into the body of the report by the generally non-Palauan archaeologist. It is the responsibility of the oral historian to provide legitimate, pertinent and comprehensive narratives and traditional histories concerning the property. The archaeologist must critically evaluate the data from a scientific perspective, provide coherence and integrate culture and the site, feature or artefact (Smith 1997:37). In conjunction with large-scale development projects, such as construction of the US funded Compact Road circling Babeldaob, a substantial amount of oral history has been collected in the past 15 years.

Palauan cosmology and time

Palau's origin myths pivot around political, demographic, economic and cultural transformations (Umetaro 1974; Aoyagi 1982; Nero 1987; Parmentier 1987). In Palauan cosmology, Latmikaik, a giant clam, arises from the sea to give birth to half-fish and half-human creatures that populate the islands. The first political institution is created on Angaur to control community affairs that were becoming too 'fierce and wicked' (Umetaro 1974:13). The chiefly councils (*klobak*) and appointed titleholders spread to eight villages on Peleliu, Oreor and Babeldaob.[2] These villages of the demi-god Chuab, one of Latmikaik's children, form a peaceful political federation. But the federation dissolves over an affront to the dignity and respect of Chuab's ranked hierarchy resulting from the removal of the gatekeeper to heaven's eye (Umetaro 1974:38–40). Other versions of the story refer to this defiance of the proper code of conduct by the violation of a food distribution convention (Parmentier 1981:245).

The lawlessness and improper behaviour dismays and angers the high god, Uchelianged. He sends messenger gods (Ruchel) to impose new laws, although they also fail to establish a stable political structure. The goddess Dirrauchulabkau befriends the Ruchel by preparing a dish of taro stuffed with fish. In frustration at the chaos that reigns throughout Palau, Uchelianged destroys the inhabitants of the lower world with a great flood to begin a new era of political stability. Dirrauchulabkau is reborn as the goddess Milad and gives birth to four children (Ngaremlengui, Melekeok, Aimeliik and Oreor) who represent four ranked political districts. This institutes a new political, social and ideological order that is still in effect today.

The cosmology above is conveyed with a Western sense of history, as a sequence of events with a logical progression. This use of a Western-style text to present Palau's oral histories freezes their structures without recognising that they are constructs in a constant state of flux (Tellei 1998a). Palauan society conceptualises time as a dynamic process, with the past, present and future being interrelated perspectives that feed off one another (Nero 1987:32–44). Nero (1987:36) describes Palauan history as:

> ... sets of relationships among corporate groups which form the basis of the present order. Their time is past and future at the same time, and actions of the individual titleholder are understood as representations of the collective title in which is embodied all past, present, and future titleholders.

As elements in a dynamic process establishing and legitimising relationships, the flexibility intrinsic to Palau's historical narratives prohibits their insertion into a Western linear chronology (Nero 1987; Tellei et al. 2005). Nero (1987:38) notes that when recounting histories, 'eras' are used as linguistic markers to frame the story; but these must be understood as 'duration, continued existence, and the nature of this existence', not as forming a chronological sequence. For example, *Er a Ititiumd* refers to 'the Mossy Past' or 'Time of the Gods' – an era outside of the foundation of time, and hence not clearly seen or understood. *Er a Rechuodel* is 'the Olden Times' and embodies the traditional ways of the ancestors before the changes brought about by Western contact or World War II. In a general sense, as Palau's cosmology is in 'the Mossy Past', specific events related to the demi-gods and associated archaeological remains cannot be assigned to fixed points in time. As Nero (1987:73) states, in Palau the critical dimension is not time but sedimentation – 'those markers left by the gods and the relationships they established which have remained from the past to form the basis of the present'.

Earthworks in archaeological and traditional history

Morphologically diverse and visually impressive earth architecture covers at least 20% of Babeldaob's volcanic landscape (Liston 2007a, 2009, 2010a) (Figure 2).[3] Earth structures are generally found in up to 27 km² clusters of modified terrain extending from the coastal lowlands to the central ridgeline. Earthworks are often massive in scale, with step-terraces and ditches descending up to 6 m and steep-sided and flat-topped hills called 'crowns' rising as much as 10 m (Figure 3).

Evolving in form, size and power, extensive clusters of earth architecture supported the majority of community activities and defined sociopolitical districts for more than 1200 years of Palau's history (Liston and Tuggle 1998, 2006; Liston 2007a, 2009). Archaeological evidence shows individual earthwork components supported burial grounds, habitation sites and, probably, cultivated fields; were used for water management, paths and other community infrastructure; had defensive elements; and played ceremonial and ritual roles. However, the distributional

Figure 2. Aerial photo of Ngermelkii crown complex in the Ngatpang Earthwork District (V1-VAP-61-USN-28-111—2 June 1969).

patterning, size and morphology of the complexes indicate that, although serving these practical uses, the earthworks as a whole were symbolic in nature. They primarily functioned as symbols to display individual chiefly or polity power, to legitimise corporate claims of land and other resources, and to create defensible terrain (Liston and Tuggle 1998, 2006; Liston 2007a). By functioning as land and resource markers, they delineated space to define polities.

Earth structures were built throughout most of Palau's cultural sequence (Liston 2009, 2010a). Construction probably began soon after colonisation because of the limited coastal margin bounded by a steeply sloped bench. The majority of earthworks were formed during the development, zenith and fall of the earthwork polities during the Earthwork Era (ca. 2400–1200 cal. BP).[4] At this time, there was probably a reliance on agroforestry and dryland crops and a largely interior-based settlement pattern, although where viable, the shoreline and Rock Islands remained integral to resource procurement and habitation. Individual earth structures and the extent of modified terrain reached monumental proportions between ca. 2000 and 1700 cal. BP, several centuries before monumental architecture appeared in other Pacific Island societies.

There was a dramatic decline in earthwork district use and a period of little cultural activity throughout the archipelago during the Transitional Era (ca. 1200–700 cal. BP). In the Stonework Era (ca. 700–150 cal. BP), the population relocated to coastal and Rock Island settlements identified by large and elaborate stone architecture and a subsistence economy based on pondfield cultivation (Wickler 2005; Masse et al. 2006). Earthwork construction may have been mostly confined to near-coastal, low step-terraces that functioned as structural foundations

Figure 3. Roisingang crown complex in the Ngaraard Earthwork District.

for stonework village features and associated dryland cultivation. Where earthworks once symbolically defined polity status, stone structures, including burial and foundation platforms, paths, docks and forts, now functioned as markers of clan and village prestige and rank (Liston and Tuggle 2006).

Despite their size and scale, earthworks are reported to be largely absent from Palau's traditional narratives. A few stories recount a mystical time where terraces are depicted as steps linking the gods to heaven and earth. Ethnohistoric accounts describe an unoccupied interior whose desolate terraced hills were said to have been either formed by receding floodwaters or built by an earlier population, unrelated to the island's current inhabitants.

A review of the relationship between Palau's terraced landscape and traditional history was called for due to the recent realisation of the actual extent of modified terrain. Additional interviews were conducted that asked specifically about earthworks. The ethnohistorical records and recent oral history collections were reviewed to identify places now known to be sculpted hills. The purpose of the inquiry was not to validate either traditional or archaeological history. Rather, the aims were to 1) verify past claims that earthworks are not in Palau's traditional narratives by taking into account newly acquired data, and 2) attempt to understand why such huge and extensive anthropogenic constructs do not play a role in such a rich corpus of oral traditions.

Oral history interviews

Miko conducted interviews that focused on Babeldaob's interior earthwork landscape with 10 elders from Ngaremlengui state.[5] Imiungs (Ngaremlengui's ancient name) is the eldest of Milad's four children and the state contains what is probably Palau's largest earthwork district. It was expected that the current interviews would mimic the ethnohistoric sources and previously collected oral histories by producing limited information on terraces. Surprisingly, seven of the 10 informants recalled that in their youth they were taught by their elders that terraces were built by humans for ritual, ceremonial and sacred purposes. The remaining three elders said the terraces were natural – not built by anyone, and had no additional information.

The Ngaremlengui elders relate that stories of the interior terraces were passed on through elders from generation to generation. They were told terraces were sacred and *mekull* (places not to go) because of their association with the ancient world. Hence, they possess power and must be revered. In the archaic world, before the flood of Milad, gods and goddesses travelled freely between the upper and the lower worlds. Within this context, the elders said that terraces are the remnants of ancient villages, altars and sentry posts.

Villages were built on stair-shaped hills to allow the gods and goddesses to easily travel between the upper and lower worlds. The access was needed for the deities to be able to stay in contact with one another. The elders said there are many oral histories of stairways to the upper world and remnants of these stairs are seen in the terraces and the piles of large stones on high peaks and savannas. Oral histories also tell of gods, such as Orachel, coming down to the lower world by descending from high peaks.

Altars were built on top of modified hills as humans attempted to be closer to the gods of the upper world. The story of Chuab describes how the inhabitants of the lower world elevated the ground with soil from the chief god to make a ladder to the upper world. Without this soil, the humans would not have been able to reach and hence feed the giant Chuab. The inhabitants of the lower world were always looking for ways to gap the two worlds.

It was also believed that great things would come to those who built their villages in elevated areas, closer to the upper world, the world of gods and goddesses. This upper world was rich in knowledge, skills and money. This, as the elders related, was one of the many reasons that villages were built on terraces.

It is said that when the flood of Milad came, the lower world was destroyed. After the water receded, debris and sedimentation covered the villages on the interior earthworks, suffocating and killing all life forms. This is why the archaic villages on the terraces are deeply buried in soil. Soon no one remembered how to build the old settlements and eventually their existence was forgotten.

After the flood, the demi-gods were saddened about the destruction of the lower world and therefore came down to give new life. This was the beginning of the Era of Milad. Again, people felt the need to be close to the gods who gave them new life, and the new settlements were built on the high places. Gods and goddesses continued to live among men, teaching and instructing them about the skills and knowledge lost during the flood. Among the many important aspects of life that were taught by the gods were the roles and responsibilities of the chiefs, how to tend taro patches, arts and crafts, the skills for building the *bai* (chiefly and community meeting house), and natural childbirth.

As time passed, people began to depend on the gods less and less. The gods who lived among them realised they were no longer needed and started to return to the upper world. As their spirits rose, the earthly bodies they left behind turned into stone. The many stone faces (*klidm*) scattered throughout Palau are the bodies of these gods. They are reminders that gods and goddesses continue to watch and monitor the people below.

After the flood, plants began to sprout on the rich soil in the coastal areas, birds were abundant and water from the high peaks trickled down to the coastal area, settling in the swamplands that are good for taro patches. Because people rely on the fertile soil to provide food, settlements began to abandon the higher land and relocate to the more fertile coastal areas.

The inhabitants of the lower world continued to try to please and show their gratitude to the gods by making offerings and sending praises to them. It is because of this reverence to the gods and goddesses that terraces and high peaks, remnants of the ancient world, are sacred and *mekull*.

Ethnohistorical records

Palau's earliest ethnographic accounts do not mention the earthworks in the largely deserted interior (Keate 1788; Hockin 1803). Cheyne, an English trader in Palau in the mid 1800s, is the first to document terraces, noting that Palauans did not recognise them as their own constructs (in Parmentier 1987:30):

> All the hills of the Pelew Islands that are clear of timber are terraced and crowned with a square fort, having a deep and wide ditch round it, evidently done by the hands of another race – probably Chinese – long ago exterminated by the savage invaders who now occupy the soil. The Pelew Islanders when questioned about the terraced hills and forts say it was either done by the gods or by the sea at the flood.

When the German ethnographer Krämer (1919:238–239) asked about terraces, the local population he spoke with denied that 'the shape of the mountain is the result of artificial construction', instead saying that the terraces were 'what remained after the great flood'. Many elders still consider the flood, referring to Palau's creation myth, to have formed the terraced hills. Tellei et al. (1998b:106) write that:

> Uodelchad, the female counterpart of Esbangel, the chief of Ngerkebesang, recounted the story of the terraces which she heard long ago from her elders. There was a great flood during which time everything was overwhelmed by water. When the flood receded, the water and the pressure to flow down shaped the terraces such as they are today, like large steps down the slopes of the hills.

Other contemporary elders claim the earthworks are the remains of 'those who came before' (*tirkel di mla chad*), the first wave of migrants who have no relationship to them and either left the islands before their own ancestors arrived or were annihilated in the great flood (Tellei et al. 1998a:240). Many contemporary Palauans are incredulous that their ancestors were capable of building such monumental structures (see Parmentier 1987:33). This scepticism about their ancestors' ability is the almost universal response Liston receives when asking Palauans whether they built the terraces.

Earthworks are not among the legends, historic events and significant symbols decorating the beams of each village's *bai era rubak* (chiefly meeting hall) that were meticulously copied by Elizabeth Krämer (1929) in 1909 and Hijikata (1996) in the late 1920s. Although wooden *bai* are rarely constructed today, visual representation of oral history continues through the medium of carved, mobile wooden planks (storyboards). A single known storyboard, carved before 1983, contains a representation of an earthwork (Figure 4). The crown and step-terrace complex is in the background behind the story's actors.

The Palauan term for earthwork, *oublallang el bukl* (stepped hills), is a recent and little used addition to the language (Olsudong pers. com.), while names for ditches, both transverse (*klaidebangel* 'hole dug as a trap') and lateral (*chomedoilmach, omdok uach* 'to catch a foot') appear to have long been used (Osborne 1966:232; Basilius 2002:143). During Krämer's (1917:261) visit, Palauans referred to the shaped mountains as *deleuechel* (steps cut into a coconut tree) and the hilltops as *telongeklel* (the heights). The words commonly used in describing Babeldaob's topography – *rois* (mountain), *bukl* (hill) and *ked* (savanna) – are not references to artificial constructs.

Place names

Traditional place names given to hills, savannas, bedrock outcrops and other prominent features on the Palauan landscape capture the significance of a location at a moment in time or identify a piece of its history. Some of the stories associated with place name refer to earthwork components.

A ring-ditch encircling a Melekeok crown is known as Meldobechbuuch 'felled betel nut tree' due to the impression left when a huge betel nut tree (*Areca catechu*) toppled over (Tellei 1998b:124). The 'hill in Aimeliik that overlooks Ngerchemai' is said to have been shaped when Ngesisech's giant betel nut tree landed on it (Holyoak et al. 1998:13). It is not clear which

Figure 4. Storyboard carved before 1983 with earthwork complex in background ('Elbebai' carved by B. Rdulaol, Belau National Museum collection).

hill this is, although it is most certainly one of the impressive crowns in Aimeliik's earthwork district. The depression in Ngchesar's Ultil Oeang ('footprints') crown was formed by warriors dancing atop the hill to celebrate their victory over a rival village (Hijikata 1996:144; Miko et al. 2001:85).

Aimeliik's Ngeruudes stonework village is on an earthwork complex named after the Uudes clan which migrated there from Ngaremlengui's Uluang village after being defeated in battle (Tellei et al. 1998a:182).[6] The defeat of Uluang village, also built on a pre-existing crown earthwork complex, is calculated to have been in the mid 1600s (Lucking and Parmentier 1990:126).

The place names of a few crowns (e.g. Meklechel a Beab 'taro swamp of the rats') suggest horticulture, which, in such a restricted space, probably had a ceremonial intent. A depression in a Ngardmau crown is said to hold a continuously producing taro patch. Its name, Ngkisikikl era ReDioll, derives from the story of a pregnant woman who climbed to the top, fell and scraped (*mle kisokl*) herself (Tellei et al. 2005:37). The surface of the former crown is about 50 cm lower than its bermed edges, hence it holds water during wetter periods. The top of the latter crown displays no signs of a depression. However, recent archaeological excavations revealed that in the ancient past some crown depressions were intentionally infilled to level the surface.

Origin and construction

There are no known oral traditions providing a generic explanation of how or by whom earthworks were constructed. Instead, specific locations or individual features on an earth structure are associated with creation stories. Krämer (1929:Legend 3) found some hills (e.g. Ngerunguikl, Ngeanges and Tukur, all in Oreor) to have been created by the spirits, while a Ngaremlengui chief is said to have pulled all the terraces in the north to the south below Melekeok (Lucking 1984:29–30).[7] A set of footprints on a rock slab atop Ngerekebesang's Roisngermesianged crown was made by Uchelkebesadel, one of the Ruchel (messenger gods), and his son when they left for the heavens (Basilius 2010:83).

Some Ngarchelong step-terraces were constructed as ladders for the gods travelling to and from heaven (Tellei et al. 1998a:228). A grooved stone on the Bischerad crown complex is identified as 'a 'ladder to heaven', *bischerad*, and the area is a holy place' (Osborne 1966:22). The ladder was used by the gods when journeying to heaven and back while they constructed Palau's only megalithic complex – Badrulchau (Tellei et al. 2005:210; Tuggle 2007:101). The boulders on the Ouballang earthworks in Aimeliik are the ruins of a ladder built by inhabitants of the lower world so they could reach the sky (Olsudong et al. 1998:170). A stone on Ngaraard's Obichang crown complex is identified as a stepping stone for spirits passing between heaven and earth and, until this generation, was a taboo place that could cause illness or injury if touched (Liston and Rieth 2009:454).

Graveyards

Since the 1920s, when the Japanese government mandated burial of the dead in cemeteries rather than clan burial platforms (*odesongel*), many village graveyards have been located on ancient modified ridges or crowns.[8] Long before their use as historic cemeteries, archaeological investigations indicate earthworks were used for gravesites. Some upland step-terraces, modified ridges, crowns and their capping knobs contain small burial sets radiometrically dated to between 2000 and at least 1200 cal. BP (Tuggle 2007:352–356, 2010; Liston and Rieth 2009:381). These Earthwork Era interments, often structured and associated with burial furniture, were possibly restricted to high-status individuals.

Parmentier (1981:115, 240, 250) was told that terraced or hillside graves are named *debull*, a word that also refers to individual stone or concrete grave markers. Contemporary Palauans almost unanimously state all burials were in *odesongel* before the Japanese period. *Debull*, as a Palauan word rather than a Japanese adaptation, might suggest that hillside graves extend far back in time.

Oral history relates that an ancient high chief of Ngerkeai village is buried standing up in the knoll of the Oltangelmad crown, the same crown currently used as a public cemetery (Olsudong et al. 1998:118). In one version of the Milad cycle of stories, the mother of Dilmalk (one of Milad's reincarnations) is buried on Omsangel, a crown earthwork in Airai (Parmentier 1987:156; Liston 2007b). Chelebuul (poverty), a descendant of the giant clam Latmikaik, is buried on Tuker crown in Oreor (Krämer 1926:3).

The giant Ngalekdmeuang was laid to rest in Ngchesar's Ngerngesang terraces after Melekeok villagers poisoned him so that he would stop consuming their food supplies (Hijikata 1996:140; Tellei 1998b:243). Parmentier (1981:228–230) documents a version of this story in which Chuab's children, after burning the giant to death, wander Babeldaob eating all the fruits and leaves off the trees and leaving the villagers to starve. They are poisoned and buried in terraced hills in Ngaremlengui and Ngchesar named Debellelangalekdmeoang (Debellir ar Ngalektmeuang 'grave of the cursed children').[9]

The crown on Medong, a terrace system in Ollei, supports a coral platform in which Palau's only stone sarcophagus was partly buried (Osborne 1979:203–212; Hijikata 1995:130–137). The coffin contained the incomplete skeletal remains of an adult (possibly female) and the single bone of a child. Hijikata (1995:136) recounts an unconfirmed story that the tomb belongs to a Ngeruangel chief (Delengeli Ruangel) who led the survivors to Babeldaob when the island sank.

Sacred Areas

Some interior areas, such as the non-terraced lowland savanna of Malk in Ngaraard and the crowns of Roisang in Chelab and Rois Beketei in Ngardmau, are commonly considered sacred areas (*chedaol*) because they are the home of deities and/or are places of worship or ceremonies (*tungl*) (Hijikata 1995:42, 135).

Village elders would conduct ceremonial events to petition the gods from these interior sacred areas. Tellei (1998b:122) lists the situations in which these rituals were called for:

- decreasing wealth or resources

- deteriorating social conditions

- epidemics caused by plant diseases

- to get rid of animal and plant-eating birds such as *uek* (*Porphyrio porphyrio*, purple swamp hen)

- deteriorating health conditions or an unusual frequency of deaths

- other extraordinary conditions which would require appeasing the gods and asking for reconciliation

One such place for communicating with the ancestral gods and deities was Ngerulmud in Melekeok. At 180 m^2, the surface of Ngerulmud, now home of the country's capital building, was Palau's largest known crown (Liston et al. 1998). As Tellei explains (1998b:122):

> It is believed that there was once a time when Ngerulmud was used as a place where women came forth with their offerings of fermented *mud* (keyhole angelfish, *Pomacentrus* spp.), supposedly eating them as a group, keeping each other company while trying to appease the gods. This practice was a communal activity. Thus the name of the place Ngerulmud.

Access to Ollei's Medong crown was restricted to elders in times of famine to offer sacrifices for better harvests (Hijikata 1995:135). There are no stories relating this taboo to the sarcophagus buried in the crown's coral platform.

Habitation

Traditional history relates that during the time of Milad, individuals, clans and whole villages migrated from the smaller islands of the archipelago to, and then within, Babeldaob, due to warfare, political intrigues, mythical calamities and natural disasters. The new settlers moved into land already populated by people descended from mythical figures. To protect themselves from attack, the narratives say these new settlements were located in strategic locations behind a protective barrier of mangrove forest, on the low ridges beyond the coastal plains, or above major waterways, providing rapid access to the lagoon. The population progressively relocated downslope and closer to the coast until, by the late historic period when warfare was abolished, villages directly fronted the shore. Even then, with Babeldaob's limited sandy coastline, many of these villages remained hidden behind protective barriers, whether or not defensive in intent.

Through oral history and material remains, Krämer (1919) identified 253 villages, most (n=169) of which were abandoned. The majority of these villages in the migration stories are constructed on low step-terraces close to the shore or a river, granting access to the coast, and exhibit typical Stonework Era features. The few villages archaeologically dated to very early in Palau's cultural sequence are not part of the migration histories, are located on interior hillslopes and ridges, have no known names or associated oral traditions and display simpler stonework architecture to the Stonework Era villages (Liston 2008, 2010b; Tuggle 2010). Temporal markers have yet to be identified distinguishing those villages listed in the narrative as established in the Era of Chuab from the later traditional settlements. Rather than being far inland, as might be expected, three of the early archaic world's six villages (Imul, Ngersuul and Mengellang) are located on step-terraced ridgelines between 0.5 km and 1.0 km from the lagoon, while the remainder are closer to sea level and the coastline. There is thus little archaeological evidence to corroborate the status or temporal sequence of the villages of Chuab as depicted in the origin myths.

The feature types and architectural style of some stonework on interior earthwork complexes suggest they are a later addition to, or a reoccupation of, previously abandoned earth structures. Employing oral history and genealogy, Lucking and Parmentier (1990:126) calculate that the stonework village on Ngaremlengui's Uluang crown complex was conquered and destroyed in the mid 1600s, long after large-scale earthwork construction. Likewise, the high-status stone features on the massive Roisingang earthwork complex are probably associated with Chief Ngirairung who, in traditional narrative, crossed the hill while relocating stonework villages from Ngaraard's west to its east coast (Figure 3; Tuggle 2010). Regardless, some of the migration stories may reveal the initial occupation of the inland earthwork complexes.

Early ethnographic sources tell of crowns supporting high-status residences. An Uluang and the Desekel crowns served as foundations for the homes of the villages' high chiefs (Krämer 1919:153, 248). Magicians, priests or mediums (*kerong*) lived on the terraced mountains of Eleos in Ollei, Ngeraod in Airai, and Ngulitel in Ngaraard (Krämer 1917:46; Hijikata 1995:114). The latter crown supported the priest's home until 1907 (Krämer 1917:238).

Traditional history more commonly identifies crowns as the home of demi-gods (*chelid*).[10] Krämer (1919:11, 181) lists Eleos, Ngeraod, Ngulitel and Ngadeg (Ngarchelong) as places of magic where *chelib* live in the form of fish and humans. Their association with demi-gods may have been why the priests built their homes on these same hills. Beautiful female spirits (*turang*) who turn into fish at night sleep in the water-filled depression in Aimeliik's Roisebong crown, and bathe in the hollow of the nearby Disechir era Turang crown (Olsudong et al. 1998:118). Hijikata (1996:76–78) was told the deity Odalmelech lived on Melekeok's Roismelech crown after it was constructed by the gods. Tellei (1998b:203) relates that the six gods who were building a *delengobel* (closed area) atop Roismelech planned to live below in what is now Ngeremelech village.

Often malevolent *chelib* inhabit the high-terraced hills. The demons residing in a beautiful clubhouse on the Klbael terrace complex brought a famine to the village below. They then 'pulled the dead people out of the houses, so that the residents had to hang on to them from the inside' (Krämer 1929:Legend 127b). Cannibalistic demons (*tekeelmeleb*) inhabit the Ngeraod crown to 'carry on their mischievous life in the forest on the hill, hunt for souls to devour ...' (Krämer 1929:Legend 137).

In Krämer's (1929:Legend 19) version of the lengthy Milad myth, Ngaraard's Ngulitel crown is the location of the heavenly village where the high god, Uchelelchelid, resides and from where Terkelel (Milad's son) steals the eye of the guard to heaven (Temedokl).[11]

> The seven *ketord* [demi-gods] came one day to Ngulitel, the hill near Ngkeklau in Ngerard [Ngaraard] out of heaven sent by Uchelelchelid, the 'first god', to visit the stone of Temedokl, which served as a watchman at the head of the path at Ngulitel and always inhaled loudly through compressed lips to warn the residents of heaven whenever strangers arrived.

Ngulitel, located at the south end of Ngaraard's extensive earthwork district, is one of Palau's largest and most impressive crown complexes. In addition to supporting a heavenly village and a priest's home, this massive forested earthwork is one of the 12 stops on Palau's rain path.[12] The mountain also figures in a version of the legend concerning the origin of dryland taro. In the narrative, the goddess Iluochel (Milad) travels the length and breadth of Palau creating taro patches. The patches are all in wetland locations (*mesei*) except for the one she cultivated on the slopes of Ngulitel (McKnight and Obak 1960:7).

Warfare

Ethnographically, warfare was an institutionalised component of traditional Palauan culture and 'dominates historical traditions as recorded in stories, chants, songs, proverbial expressions and pictorial carvings' (Parmentier 1987:90; Liston and Tuggle 2006). Construction of earthworks for defensive purposes is related in Palau's traditional history. A reference to *klaidebangel* (ditch cross-cutting a ridgeline) is found in the story of the battle between two Ngchesar villages (Tellei et al. 2005:70):

> … *klaidebangel* were dug and lined with spears with their points pointing up, and then covered. On the day of the battle, the villagers of Ngerkesou baited the men of Ngemingel by holding a festive dance at the other side of the trenches. The men of Ngemingel were offended by this behavior since they felt that an inferior village should not hold a festive dance in their sight. The men of the village rushed to attack them whereupon some of them fell into the trenches and were killed.

Palauan children still play the game '*klaidebangel*', in which, after digging a shallow hole in the beach and disguising it with twigs and leaves, they contrive to have someone fall into it through cunning and devious means (Basilius 2002:150). A post, a component of a palisade or possibly a lethal pointed stick, radiocarbon dated to 1420–1290 cal. BP, was revealed in the inner base of the ring-ditch around Ngatpang's Ngebar crown (Liston 2010b). Often the ridges leading to crowns are dissected by multiple *klaidebangel*. Defensive ditches also cut the ancient trail systems that crisscross Babeldaob on flattened ridgelines, elevated paths bounded by steep descents and tracks eroded below the surrounding topography by centuries of use (Liston et al. 2002:44; Olsudong et al. 2008).

One narrative tells how trench defensive features originated. A demi-god from Koror is said to have assisted Melekeok in destroying its enemy, Oliuch, by directing the war party to construct wide, deep ditches perpendicular to terrace tiers (*chomedoiluach* 'foot-catchers') to hinder the advance of their advisories (Lucking 1984:29–30). These ditch features may have also functioned to channel water for drainage and to water crops.

The ditches ringing some levelled hilltops are also described as defensive in traditional history. Ngerbeluud villagers dug the deep ditch circling Ngaraard's Obichang crown to trap the oppressive Ngeriteet warriors (Olsudong et al. 2000:158). At the ring-ditch around Ngchesar's Roisersuul crown:

> … warriors from Ngeremlengui, whooping their war cries, ran forward to intercept the warriors from Ngersuul and immediately fell into the trench. They were set upon by the warriors of Ngersuul and were beaten or speared to death (Basilius 2002:149–150).

Oral histories refer to the use of prominent hilltops, not all of which are shaped into crown earthworks, as signal towers (*klekat*) (Krämer 1929:95; Parmentier 1987:272–273; Tellei et al. 2005:72, 81). The allied villages of Oikull and Melekeok warned one another of impending attacks via smoke signals sent from high crowns, and Ngaremlengui signalled Oreor of approaching adversaries by building a fire on top of Etiruir. Ollei's Eleos crown and Ngaremlengui's Ngermengot crown also functioned as *klekat* (Olsudong et al. 1998:102).

Hills strategically located around villages, district borders and agricultural fields served as sentry posts. Sentries stationed on outposts along the Ngchesar Trail – crossing the terraced hills of Demailei, Roisersuul, Bluurois and parts of Mesiual – protected Ngersuul village by warning of imminent danger with signal fires (Basilius 2002:149). The Ngchesar trail is dissected by at least seven *klaidebangel*.

Locating earthworks in traditional history

In the majority of cases, Palau's oral traditions do not explicitly identify earthworks in themselves as anthropogenic, as imbued with meaning or as serving a function. However, the substantial reference to hills that are terraced can be interpreted as an implicit inclusion of the structures in the narratives. The lack of narratives connecting the contemporary community with the creators of the massive earthwork districts does not necessarily equate to a cultural discontinuity. Although new groups of settlers continuously landed on Palau's shores, there is no archaeological, linguistic or genetic evidence suggesting that today's population is not directly descended from the archipelago's earliest inhabitants. The question remains of why such monumental constructs are not an overt component of Palau's traditional body of knowledge.

The limitations of oral history collection in Palau probably contributed to the exclusion of terraces in the early ethnohistoric accounts. Restricted information would have been kept from early 20th century ethnographers due to their status as foreigners without clan ties and the unwillingness of Palauans to make knowledge public. The massive earth structures of the interior were long abandoned by the time Kubary, Krämer and others began collecting data, and these researchers, working and living in coastal stonework villages, may not have realised the actual extent of the inland earth construction. Hence, not only were they unlikely to have put much effort into asking about and understanding earthworks, but it is doubtful information on deserted terraces as anthropogenic features would have been spontaneously elicited. Furthermore, the bias of non-participant observation probably created gaps in the ethnohistorical record due to incomplete understanding or miscomprehension of Palauan society, although how far this extended into the role of monumental earthworks is not known.

The omission of earthworks in Palau's traditional history might relate to the lengthy period since their abandonment (Masse et al.1984:119; Lucking and Parmentier 1990:135). It has been some 1300 years (52 generations, assuming a 25-year span) since earthworks were the defining components of sociopolitical entities. Not just the length of time but also the events impacting a culture over time have a strong influence on what is retained in the oral histories. As stated by Clark and Martinsson-Wallin (2007:31):

> … given a tendency for such structures [monumental architecture] to achieve their final dimensions from multiple construction events, and the extensive rearrangement of indigenous societies due to warfare, the impact of introduced disease, and changes to native belief systems from missionary and colonial influence (Green 2002; Sand 2002), neither the origin nor the function(s) of monumental architecture should be expected to be fully documented in oral and textual accounts (Graves and Sweeny 1993:108).

Although these factors probably play a part, they are not seen as the key factor in the conundrum. The loss or change in value of particular aspects of traditional history, such as the earthworks, in Palau's collective consciousness is more likely linked to the dramatic alteration in the political order that is codified in the cosmology (Nero 1987, 1992; Parmentier 1987). An interpretative theme of Palau's creation myths is the attempt to establish harmony in the face of instability. The great flood that ushered in the current Era of Milad was in response to the chaos and lawlessness that erupted from the failure of political institutions in the time of Chuab. This shift between sociopolitical structures became 'embedded in the past through these founding legends' of symbolic transformations (Nero 1992:242).[13]

The 'Invention of Tradition' to validate contemporary hierarchical relationships, establish group identity and endorse innovation is a cultural universal used to invoke a legitimacy and authority for the current sociopolitical structure in terms of the past (Hobsbawm and Ranger 1983; see Nero 1987:32–44, 75–80). In the Pacific, Firth (1961) demonstrated how traditional stories validate Tikopia's social order, while Alkire (1984) showed that central Carolinian oral traditions pertaining to migration are structured to conform to the ruling hierarchy.[14] Ancient traditions and practices are adapted and re-used to establish continuity with the past. Once the transformations are established, grounded or 'sedimented' (Parmentier 1981:50; Sahlins 1981) into place, a culture will retain the body of traditional history that promotes its wellbeing and is relevant to its concerns.

In Palau's cosmology, the contemporary sociopolitical order did not develop through a historical process of succession through warfare and political alliances (Parmentier 1987:183). Rather, the ruling hierarchy in the time of Chuab was washed away by the flood to provide a fresh canvas for Milad's new world order. This provides an inherent supremacy to legitimise the current ideology. Hence, by providing a traditional explanation for the current hierarchical relationships, Palauan mythology supplies a vehicle to legitimise the new system and render the old obsolete (Nero 1987; Parmentier 1987:54, 138).

The creation myths could metaphorically reflect the relocation of the political economy from the more centralised authority of the interior earthwork polities (represented by Chuab) to the hierarchically structured alliances of autonomous stonework villages (represented by Milad). Palau's tangible cultural remains illustrate the dramatic transformations in the subsistence economy, settlement patterns and political organisation between these two eras, with the Earthwork Era referring to the former and the Stonework Era to the latter. The societal upheaval and instability described in the cosmology that invoked an inundation (Milad's flood) could relate to the period of transition, recognisable although not clearly defined in the archaeological record as the Transitional Era, between the Earthwork and Stonework eras. The flood annihilated the former population and with it any who could claim descent to its hierarchical structure, to give priority of rank to Milad's offspring. In a broad sense, the archaeological record mirrors the chronological framework provided by traditional history.

Though not directly linking the long-abandoned interior earthwork polities to Palauan historical narratives, this conceptual context may explain their relative absence. The massive terrace complexes' primary purpose as symbols of chiefly or polity power and prestige was no longer relevant to the inhabitants of the stonework villages. Their practical uses as cultivated fields, habitation foundations, community infrastructure, ceremonial space, defensive features and burial grounds continued in very limited and specific contexts. However, the majority of the massive structures were associated with a past obsolete lifestyle and of no value to the Stonework Era political structure. The exclusion of earthworks from overt reference in the oral accounts may be the strongest testament we have to their prehistoric importance.

Discussion

A review of the ethnohistoric literature, recent oral history documentation and newly collected oral history that focused on Babeldaob's interior landscape found that, contrary to historic perceptions, earthworks are a strong implicit component of Palau's historical narratives. In traditional history, terraces were used by humans and demi-gods alike for settlements, burial grounds, ceremonial events, transportation routes, cultivation and defence. A group of Palau's elders say the interior earthworks allowed humans to be closer to the heavens and gave gods and goddesses easy access between the upper and lower worlds. Many interior areas continue to be sacred and *mekull* (places not to go) due to their antiquity and association with the demi-gods.

In the 1930s, Hijikata (1995:70) observed that, despite not being part of daily life and found in impractical locations removed from the then inhabited villages, earthworks:

> ... do not seem to be treated irrelevantly either. Rather, it [earthworks] was taken care of and treated with consideration. Therefore, this was something reserved for religious beliefs ...

The altered interpretation of past and current ethnohistorical works and traditional history can be understood within its historic context. In the past decade, Palau's archaeological history has been largely rewritten due to archaeological mitigation for the Compact Road (Athens and Ward 2005; Wickler et al. 2005; Liston 2007a, 2010a; Tuggle 2010) and academic research (Fitzpatrick 2003; Clark 2005; Clark et al. 2006). These recent investigations on Babeldaob recognised the vast extent of modified terrain, identified a large number of previously undocumented earthworks, and radiometrically dated the era of significant terrace construction and use to ca. 2400–1200 cal. BP (Liston and Tuggle 1998, 2006; Liston 2007a, 2009, 2010a; Olsudong et al. 2008).

Many locations identified in Palau's oral narratives are only now being recognised as humanly modified or constructed earthwork sites. This archaeological information equipped contemporary oral historians with data useful for framing and guiding their inquiries towards specific earth structures as well as inland cultural properties in general. Currently, archaeological excavations in earthwork sites are open to public visitation and the new findings are widely publicised, taught and discussed to raise community consciousness of historic properties and assist in retaining cultural identity in a rapidly globalising Micronesia. Hence, the recent affiliation with, and the disclosure of information about, earthworks by some Palauans may be due to their exposure in archaeological work rather than a departure from indigenous knowledge.

An encompassing or interrelated causal factor to explain by whom, when or why earthworks were constructed is not presented in the narratives. Rather, individual structures appear as isolates in the larger landscape. The creation of specific structures is attributed to spirits and to humans for use by, or under the direction of, the gods. Only in the case of ditch defensive features is there an overt declaration of earthwork construction and only when described as a ladder is their shape distinguished from the surrounding topography. In the stories, the morphology of the earthworked hills is an inadvertent result of an activity (e.g. dancing, felled trees, leaping to heaven), seemingly unrelated to any conceivable ancient use.

The archaeological interpretation of earthworks defining ancient polities is not substantiated in traditional history. Terraced hills are not identified as boundary markers. Ethnohistoric and contemporary territory delineation refers to rivers, rock outcrops, boulders, stone paths, unmodified hills and tiny islands off Babeldaob's shores. Further investigation may reveal the use of crowns and modified ridges as marking political borders. Regardless, each of Babeldaob's 10 states roughly corresponds to the distributional patterning of an earthwork polity and its surrounding buffer zone.

A topographic setting could be included in a narrative due to its distinctive appearance, its strategic location or its religious or ancestral association. With at least 20% of Babeldaob formed into earthworks and many of these structures on the most prominent peaks and ridges, terraced hills are sure to be included in Palau's oral traditions regardless of their role in traditional history. A terrace as an anthropogenic construct with its own life history may have no relation to an accompanying traditional narrative. Even if acknowledging the constructed topography, the story may allude to re-use of the structure long after its construction and use as an earthwork district component.

Archaeological investigations of those ancient villages on interior earthworks that are associated with traditional migration histories (e.g. Ngermeskang, Rois) have the potential to disclose a timeframe for the transition from interior earthwork polities to stonework village districts. Careful consideration of the full range of these terrace complexes' archaeological histories can tie earthworks directly to both oral traditions and to significant unresolved issues such as the relationship between monumental architecture and increasing sociocomplexity, the variables underlying the transformation in Palau's settlement pattern and subsistence economy, and the structure of interior political organisation.

Conclusion

In a recent oral history collection, a group of Ngaremlengui elders provided a strong connection between the earthworks, deities and humans. Contrary to historic perceptions about the role of terraces in traditional history, they said that long ago humans constructed terraces for ritual, ceremonial and sacred purposes. Because of their association with the ancient times when the gods and goddesses of the upper world interacted with humans, these earthworks are sacred areas with forbidden access. The elders stated that interior villages built on terraces were covered by sediment during Milad's flood. These settlements were thus forgotten and would not necessarily be included in the corpus of contemporary oral traditions.

A review of the ethnohistoric records identified a substantial though indirect reference to terrace complexes. Traditional history relates that earthworks were ladders for the *chelib* to travel between the upper and lower worlds, burial grounds for human chiefs and mythological figures and the homes of demons, spirits, high-status individuals and heavenly villages. Interior areas, not all terraces, were sacred and used for worship or ceremonies to petition the gods for better harvests, to end epidemics, to increase wealth and for other matters pertinent to village welfare. Cultivation of dryland taro is said to have begun on a crown earthwork complex. Oral histories tell of the defensive element of some ditches and high crowns constructed as traps for advancing adversaries and serving as lookouts, smoke signal towers and sentry posts.

The lack of overt references to terraces in traditional narratives may be due to a combination of the lengthy period since their abandonment and the nature of oral history in general, and in Palau specifically. The main mitigating factor is likely the transformation in sociopolitical regimes that is expressed in both archaeological and traditional history. This change is associated with the transplantation of the subsistence economy and settlement pattern from the interior to the coastal margins. Mythology provided a traditional explanation to legitimise the new political, social and ideological order and establish social cohesion after this dramatic cultural transformation. When the lowlands and shoreline became the socioeconomic focus, individual inland earth structures were no longer valuable or relevant to societal functions and traditional history relegated the earthwork polities to an obsolete past. The interior earthwork complexes became ancient relics and were forgotten. Incorporation of oral sources of information extends and illuminates the archaeological knowledge of Palau's Earthwork Era by locating it within a long-term sociopolitical context of change.

Archaeological research reveals information relevant to Palau's cultural identity that, due to its antiquity and transformations in the sociopolitical structure, has been lost from traditional history. Recent archaeological investigations have led to a greater public awareness of the deep timeframe of Palau's past, to identification of Babeldaob as an anthropogenic landscape, and to a broader more inclusive framework for oral history interviews. Simultaneously, traditional narratives have provided archaeological history with a better understanding of the complexities inherent to Palau's cultural system by assisting in identifying the symbolic, social and ideological value of the material remains. Cultural dynamics are expressed in the transformations of traditional histories and leave traces in the material culture and landscape. The collaboration of archaeologists and oral historians allows for a multi-layered and holistic interpretation of the cultural journey.

Acknowledgments

We are deeply indebted to oral historians Julita Tellei, Umai Basilius, Maura Gordon and Faustina K. Rehuher from the Palau Resource Institute for their immense contributions to the preservation of Palau's traditional history. We acknowledge and thank Karen Nero for her equally important work documenting Oreor's oral histories and for her thoughts on Palau's cultural transformations which were adopted here in an archaeological context. Thank you to Kelly Marsh and Karen Nero for their comments and suggestions for refining and improving our text. We dedicate this paper to our friend Rita Olsudong who spent many hours with us discussing the relationship between Palau's traditional and archaeological histories.

Notes

1. This collaboration has been most successful between the now defunct Palau Resource Institute composed of Julita Tellei, Umai Basilius, Faustina K. Rehuher and Maura Gordon and archaeologists Felicia Beardsley, Myra Tomanari-Tuggle, Steve Wickler and Jolie Liston of the International Archaeological Resource Institute, Inc. (e.g. Basilius and Tellei 1996; Tellei et al. 1998a, 2005).
2. On Babeldaob the villages of Chuab are Imul, Ngerusar, Ngersuul, Ngeruikl, Ulimang and Mengellang.
3. Earthworks are also found in volcanic portions of the three smaller islands of Oreor, Ngerekebesang and Malakal that are close to Babeldaob's southern end.
4. These 'eras' are archaeological labels used in organising long time periods and have no inherent meaning to Palauans.
5. Miko was the oral historian for the Bureau of Arts and Culture for almost a decade until moving to the Palau Visitors Authority to incorporate heritage tourism into Palau's travel industry. He also has strong ancestral ties to Ngaremlengui.
6. Later the Uudes clan left Aimeliik to settle in Melekeok where it became the first ranking clan.
7. Titled Obakrailames, he actually lived in Blissang, a village in Melekeok.
8. Some of the historic graveyards located on crowns include Techobei (Melekeok), Chisau (Ngaremlengui), Bisecherad (Ngarchelong), Ngertacherudel (Airai) and Oltangelmad (Aimeliik), while ridgeline cemeteries are found at Terull (Ngaraard), and in ridges whose names are not known in Ngkeklau (Ngaraard) and Ngiwal.
9. This terraced legendary gravesite in Ngaremlengui, just east of Ngermetengel village, has been destroyed by construction of a landing strip, dump site and road (Lucking 1984:76; Olsudong et al 1998:35).
10. There is no overall Palauan god. Each clan has its own spirits, with the village adopting the most powerful clan's deity, and the most important of these worshipped by a group of villages or an entire polity (see Kubary 1888; PCAA 1976:78). The *chelid* (demi-gods) often communicated through the priest (*kerong*).
11. Other versions of the story list this heavenly village as located on Ngeraod, a hill in Airai.

12. The interconnected paths the wind and the rain follow as they cross Palau run generally north to south with villages or hills listed as points Rak, Chuab's brother, stopped at while traveling with the moon (Klee 1973; Aoyagi 1982; Tellei et al. 2005:21–22). The significant concept of paths (*rael*) in Palauan culture is explained by Parmentier (1987:108–137).

13. Within a grander theme of oral history, Nero (1992:237) aptly demonstrates how works of art 'not only reflects political and structural transformations of Palauan society but are in themselves active agents through which Palauans negotiate such changes'.

14. Alkire (1984:7) concludes that this tailoring of the narratives renders them of limited use for reconstructing cultural chronologies.

References

Alkire, W. 1984. Central Carolinian oral narratives: Indigenous migration theories and principles of order and rank. *Pacific Studies* 1:1–14.

Aoyagi, M. 1982. The geographical recognition of Palauan people with special reference to the four directions. In: Aoyagi, M. (ed), *Islanders and their outside world: A report of the cultural anthropological research in the Caroline Islands of Micronesia in 1980–1981*, pp. 3–33. Committee for Micronesian Research, Tokyo University of Foreign Studies, Tokyo.

Athens, J.S. and Ward, J.V. 2005. *Compact Road archaeological investigations, Babeldaob Island, Palau. Volume IV: The Holocene paleoenvironment of Palau*. Prepared for U.S. Army Corps of Engineers, Pacific Ocean Division, Hawai'i. International Archaeological Research Institute, Inc., Honolulu.

Basilius, U. 2002. Ngchesar oral history. In: Liston, J., Tellei, J., Basilius, U. and Rehuher, F.K., *Archaeological survey, monitoring, oral history of bore holes, rock quarries and coral dredging locations for the Compact Road, Babeldaob Island, Republic of Palau*, pp. 141–151. Prepared for U.S. Army Corps of Engineers, Pacific Ocean Division, Hawai'i. International Archaeological Research Institute, Inc., Honolulu.

Basilius, U. 2010. Oral history documentation. In: O'Day, P. and Liston, J., *Phase I Archaeological Intensive Survey Report for Palau Resort, Ngerekebesang, Republic of Palau*, pp. 83–86. Prepared for Sea World Marine Company. Garcia and Associates, Kailua, Hawai'i.

Basilius, U. and Tellei, J. 1996. Oral history documentation, a part of the archaeological survey for the rural water system project, Ngaraard, Republic of Palau. Appendix A. In: Beardsley, F.R., *Fragments of paradise: Archaeological investigations in the Republic of Palau rural water system survey and testing*. Prepared for Winzler and Kelly, Consulting Engineers, Agana Guam and Koror, Palau. International Archaeological Research Institute, Inc., Honolulu.

Beardsley, F.R. and Basilius, U. 2002. Sengall Ridge, Belau: Burials, spirit walks and painted pottery. In: *The Melaka papers: Proceedings of the 16th Congress of the Indo-Pacific Prehistory Association, Melaka, Malaysia, 1 to 7 July 1998*, pp. 147–151. Bulletin of the Indo-Pacific Prehistory Association, Volume 22.

Butler, B.M. 1986. Archaeological correlates of village rank in Palau. Paper presented at the 51st Annual Meeting of the Society for American Archaeology, New Orleans, Louisiana.

Cachola-Abad, C.K. 2000. The evolution of Hawaiian socio-political complexity: An analysis of Hawaiian oral traditions. Unpublished PhD thesis, University of Hawai'i, Manoa.

Clark, G. 2005. A 3000-year culture sequence from Palau, Western Micronesia. *Asian Perspectives* 44(2):349–380.

Clark, G., Anderson, A. and Wright, D. 2006. Human colonization of the Palau islands, Western Micronesia. *Journal of Island and Coastal Archaeology* 1:215–232.

Clark, G. and Martinsson-Wallin, H. 2007. Monumental architecture in West Polynesia: Origins, chiefs and archaeological approaches. *Archaeology in Oceania* 42:28–40.

David, B., McNiven, I., Manas, L., Manas, J., Savage, S., Crouch, J., Neliman, G. and Brady, L. 2004. Goba of Mua: Archaeology working with oral tradition. *Antiquity* 78(299):158–172.

Firth, R. 1961. *History and traditions of Tikopia*. Polynesian Society Memoir No. 32. The Polynesian Society, Wellington.

Fitzpatrick, S.M. 2003. Early human burials in the western Pacific: Evidence for a c.3000 year old occupation on Palau. *Antiquity* 77(298):719–731.

Hijikata, H. 1995. *Collective works of Hijikata Hisakatsu: Gods and religion in Palau*. Translated by H. Endo. Originally published 1940, Kagaku Nanyo. The Sasakawa Peace Foundation, Tokyo.

Hijikata, H. 1996. *Collective works of Hijikata Hisakatsu: Myths and legends of Palau*. Translated by H. Endo. Originally published 1940, Kagaku Nanyo. The Sasakawa Peace Foundation, Tokyo.

Hobsbawm, E.J. and Ranger, T. (eds). 1983. *The invention of tradition*. Cambridge University Press, Cambridge.

Hockin, J.P. 1803. *A supplement to the account of the Peleu Islands; Compiled from the journals of the*

Panther and Endeavor, two vessels sent by the Honourable East India Company to those islands in the year 1790 and from the oral communications of Captain H. Wilson. Bulmer and Co., London.

Holyoak, L., Miko, M. and Gibbons, F. 1998. *Inventory of cultural sites and oral history in Ngeremlengui and Imeliik states, Volume II: Oral history.* Division of Cultural Affairs, Historic Preservation Office, Ministry of Community and Cultural Affairs, Republic of Palau.

Kesolei, K. 1977. Restrictions to freedom of inquiry: Palauan strains. Paper presented at the Workshop on the Role of Anthropology in Contemporary Micronesia, Koror, Palau.

Keate, G. 1788. *An account of the Pelew Islands, situated in the western part of the Pacific Ocean. Composed from the journals and communications of Captain Henry Wilson, and some of his officers, who, in August 1783, were there shipwrecked, in the Antelope, a packet belonging to the Honourable East India Company.* G. Nicol, London.

Klee, G.A. 1973. The cyclic realities of man and nature in a Palauan village. Unpublished PhD thesis, Department of Anthropology, University of Oregon.

Krämer, A. 1917. In: Thilenius, G. (ed), *Die Seidelungen Ergebnisse der Sudsee-Expedition 1908–1910. Volume I.* L. Friedrichsen and Co, Hamburg.

Krämer, A. 1919. In: Thilenius, G. (ed), *Die Seidelungen Ergebnisse der Sudsee-Expedition 1908–1910. Volume II.* L. Friedrichsen and Co, Hamburg.

Krämer, A. 1926. In: Thilenius, G. (ed), *Die Seidelungen Ergebnisse der Sudsee-Expedition 1908–1910. Volume III.* L. Friedrichsen and Co, Hamburg.

Krämer, A. 1929. In: Thilenius, G. (ed), *Die Seidelungen Ergebnisse der Sudsee-Expedition 1908–1910, Volume IV.* L. Friedrichsen and Co, Hamburg.

Kubary, J.S. 1888. Die religion der Palauer In: Bastian, A. (ed), *Allelei Aus Volks, Vol. 1*, pp. 1–69. Verlag von A. Ashec, Berlin.

Liston, J. 2007a. *Archaeological data recovery for the Compact Road, Babeldaob Island, Republic of Palau. Historic preservation investigations, Phase II. Volume V: Lab analyses, syntheses, recommendations.* Prepared for the U.S. Army Corps of Engineers, Pacific Ocean Division, Hawai'i. International Archaeological Research Institute, Inc., Honolulu.

Liston, J. 2007b. *Archaeological data recovery investigations at Site IR-1:14, Omsangel Hill, Airai state, Republic of Palau.* Prepared for TRB Architects, Republic of Palau. Garcia and Associates, Kailua, Hawai'i.

Liston, J. 2008. *Archaeological data recovery at Tabelmeduu, Ngaraard earthwork district, Republic of Palau.* Prepared for Ngaraard State, Republic of Palau. Garcia and Associates, Kailua, Hawai'i.

Liston, J. 2009. Cultural chronology of earthworks in Palau, western Micronesia. *Archaeology in Oceania* 44(2):56–73.

Liston, J. 2010a. *Archaeological monitoring and emergency data recovery for the Compact Road, Babeldaob Island, Republic of Palau. Historic preservation investigations, Phase III. Volume XII: Lab analyses, discussion, syntheses.* Draft prepared for the U.S. Army Corps of Engineers, Pacific Ocean Division, Hawai'i. International Archaeological Research Institute, Inc., Honolulu.

Liston, J. 2010b. *Archaeological monitoring and emergency data recovery for the Compact Road, Babeldaob Island, Republic of Palau. Historic preservation investigations, Phase III. Volume XI: Monitoring field reports.* Draft prepared for the U.S. Army Corps of Engineers, Pacific Ocean Division, Hawai'i. International Archaeological Research Institute, Inc., Honolulu.

Liston, J., Kaschko, M.W. and Welch, D.J. 1998. *Archaeological inventory survey of the capitol relocation project, Melekeok, Republic of Palau.* Prepared for Architects Hawai'i, Inc., Honolulu. International Archaeological Research Institute, Inc., Honolulu.

Liston, J. and Rieth, T.M. 2009. *Archaeological monitoring and emergency data recovery for the Compact Road, Babeldaob Island, Republic of Palau. Historic preservation investigations, Phase III. Volume X: Monitoring field reports.* Draft prepared for the U.S. Army Corps of Engineers, Pacific Ocean Division, Hawai'i. International Archaeological Research Institute, Inc., Honolulu.

Liston, J. and Rieth, T.M. 2010. Palau's petroglyphs: Archaeology, oral history and iconography. *Journal of the Polynesian Society* 119(4).

Liston, J., Tellei, J., Basilius, U. and Rehuher, F.K. 2002. *Archaeological survey, monitoring, oral history of bore holes, rock quarries and coral dredging locations for the Compact Road, Babeldaob Island, Republic of Palau.* Prepared for U.S. Army Corps of Engineers, Pacific Ocean Division, Hawai'i. International Archaeological Research Institute, Inc., Honolulu.

Liston, J. and Tuggle, H.D. 1998. The terraces of Palau: New information on function and age. Paper presented at the 63rd Meeting of the Society for American Archaeology, Seattle, Washington.

Liston, J. and Tuggle, H.D. 2006. Prehistoric warfare in Palau. In: Arkush, E. and Allen, M.W. (eds), *The archaeology of warfare: Prehistories of raiding and conquest*, pp. 148–183. University Press of Florida, Gainesville.

Lucking, L.J. 1984. An archaeological investigation of prehistoric Palauan terraces. Unpublished PhD thesis, Department of Anthropology, University of Minnesota.

Lucking, L.J. and Parmentier, R.J. 1990. Terraces and traditions of Uluang: Ethnographic and archaeological perspectives on a prehistoric Belauan site. *Micronesica Supplement* 2:125–136.

Masse, W.B., Liston, J., Carucci, J. and Athens, J.S. 2006. Evaluating the effects of climate change on environment, resource depletion and culture in the Palau Islands between A.D. 1200 and 1600. *Quaternary International* 151(1):106–132.

Masse, W.B., Snyder, D. and Gumerman, G.J. 1984. Prehistoric and historic settlement in the Palau Islands, Micronesia, *New Zealand Journal of Archaeology* 6:107–127.

McKnight, R.K. and Obak, A. 1960. *Taro cultivation in Palau.* Trust Territory of the Pacific Islands, Guam.

Miko, M., Besebes, M. and Petrosian-Husa, C.C.H. 2001. *Inventory of cultural and historical sites and collection of oral history: Ngiwal and Ngchesar States. Volume II: Collection of oral history.* Draft prepared by the Bureau of Arts and Culture, Ministry of Community and Cultural Affairs, Republic of Palau.

Nero, K.L. 1987. *A cherechar a lokelii: Beads of history of Koror, Palau, 1783–1983.* Unpublished PhD thesis, Department of Anthropology, University of California, Berkeley.

Nero, K.L. 1992. The breadfruit tree story: Mythological transformations in Palauan politics. *Pacific Studies* 15(4):235–260.

Olsudong, R. 1995. Reconstructing the indigenous political structure in the recent prehistory of Belau, Micronesia. Unpublished MA thesis, Department of Anthropology, La Trobe University.

Olsudong, R. 2002. Oral traditions and archaeology in Micronesia: An attempt to study past ideology in a built environment. In: *The Melaka Papers: Proceedings of the 16th Congress of the Indo-Pacific Prehistory Association, Melaka, Malaysia 1 to 7 July 1998*, pp. 153–160. Bulletin of the Indo Pacific Prehistory Association, Volume 22.

Olsudong, R., Emesiochel, C.T. and Kloulechad, E.T. 1998. *Inventory of cultural sites and oral history in Ngaremlengui and Imeliik states, Volume I: Inventory of cultural sites.* Draft prepared by the Bureau of Arts and Culture, Ministry of Community and Cultural Affairs, Republic of Palau.

Olsudong, R., Emesiochel, C.T. and Kloulechad, E.T. 2000. *Inventory of cultural and historical sites and collection of oral history in Ngaraard State, Volume I: Inventory of cultural and historical sites.* Draft prepared by the Bureau of Arts and Culture, Ministry of Community and Cultural Affairs, Republic of Palau.

Olsudong, R., Emesiochel, C.T. and Kloulechad, E.T. 2008. *Inventory of historic properties in Ngiwal State, Republic of Palau (Final).* Bureau of Arts and Culture, Ministry of Community and Cultural Affairs, Republic of Palau.

Osborne, D. 1966. *The archaeology of the Palau Islands, an intensive survey.* Bernice P. Bishop Museum Bulletin 230. Bishop Museum Press, Honolulu.

Osborne, D. 1979. Archaeological test excavations, Palau Islands, 1968–1969. *Micronesia Supplement 1.*

Palau Community Action Agency (PCAA). 1976. *Traditional Palau, the first Europeans.* Ministry of Education, Koror, Republic of Palau.

Parmentier, R.J. 1981. The sacred remains: An historical ethnography of Ngeremlengui, Palau. Unpublished PhD thesis, Department of Anthropology, University of Chicago.

Parmentier, R.J. 1987. *The sacred remains: Myth, history, and polity in Belau.* University of Chicago Press, Chicago.

Rubin, D.C. 1995. *Memory in oral traditions.* Oxford University Press, Oxford.

Sahlins, M. 1981. *Historical metaphors and mythical realities: Structure in the early history of the Sandwich Island Kingdom.* Association for Social Anthropology in Oceania Special Publication, No. 1. University of Michigan Press, Ann Arbor.

Smith, D.R. 1997. *Palau ethnography: Recommendations for the preservation of historic and cultural resources in Palau.* Anthropology Research Series No. 3, Division of Cultural Affairs, Republic of Palau. U.S. National Park Service.

Tellei, J. 1998a. Oral history in Palau: A local perspective. Paper prepared for Settlement, Oral History, and Archaeology in Micronesia Session at the 16th Congress of the Indo-Pacific Prehistory Association. Melaka, Malaysia.

Tellei, J. 1998b. Oral history documentation. In: Liston, J., Kaschko, M.W. and Welch, D.J., *Archaeological inventory survey of the Capitol Relocation Project, Melekeok, Republic of Palau.* Prepared for Architects Hawai'i, Inc., Honolulu. International Archaeological Research Institute, Inc., Honolulu.

Tellei, J., Basilius, U. and Rehuher, F.K. 1998a. *Oral history documentation of specific features within archaeological sites to be affected by the PNCC underground telecommunications system.* Prepared for the Palau National Communication Corporation. International Archaeological Research Institute, Inc., Honolulu.

Tellei, J., Basilius, U. and Rehuher, F.K. 1998b. Oral history documentation. In: Magnuson, C.M. and Liston, J., *Archaeological inventory survey, Palau Peninsula Resort, Ngerekebesang Island, Koror, Republic of Palau*, pp. 91–109. Prepared for Haas and Haynie, San Francisco, California. International Archaeological Research Institute, Inc., Honolulu.

Tellei, J., Basilius, U. and Rehuher, F.K. 2005. *Palau Compact Road archaeological investigations, Babeldaob Island, Republic of Palau, Phase I: Intensive archaeological survey. Volume III: Oral history documentation.* Prepared for the U.S. Army Corps of Engineers, Pacific Ocean Division, Hawai'i. International Archaeological Research Institute, Inc., Honolulu.

Tuggle, H.D. 2007. Ngarchelong and Ngaraard field reports. In: Liston, J., Tuggle, H.D., Mangieri, T.M., Kaschko, M.W. and Desilets, M., *Archaeological Data Recovery for the Compact Road, Babeldaob Island, Republic of Palau. Historic Preservation Investigations Phase II. Volume I: Fieldwork Reports.* Report prepared for the U.S. Army Corps of Engineers, Pacific Ocean Division, Hawai'i. International Archaeological Research Institute, Inc., Honolulu. pp. 81–129, 150–197, 314–424.

Tuggle, H.D. 2010. Ngaraard ridgeline field report. In: Tuggle, H.D., Mangieri, T.M. and Liston, J., *Archaeological monitoring and emergency data recovery for the Compact Road, Babeldaob Island, Republic of Palau. Historic preservation investigations, Phase III. Volume IX: Planned data recovery field reports.* Draft report prepared for the U.S. Army Corps of Engineers, Pacific Ocean Division, Hawai'i. International Archaeological Research Institute, Inc., Honolulu.

Umetaro, S. 1974. *Belau: The beginning of Belau from Uab to Miladeldil.* Department of Education, Koror, Republic of Palau.

Vansina, J. 1985. *Oral tradition as history.* University of Wisconsin Press, Madison.

Wickler, S.K. 2002. Oral traditions and archaeology: Modeling village settlement in Palau, Micronesia. *Micronesian Journal of the Humanities and Social Sciences* 1(1/2):39–47.

Wickler, S.K. 2005. Survey area B report, part II. In: Wickler, S.K., Addison, D.J., Kaschko, M.W. and Dye, T.S., *Intensive archaeological survey for the Palau Compact Road, Babeldaob Island, Palau. Volume II: Area survey reports*, pp. 99–328. Prepared for the U.S. Army Corps of Engineers, Pacific Ocean Division, Hawai'i. International Archaeological Research Institute, Inc., Honolulu.

Wickler, S.K., Welch, D.J., Tomonari-Tuggle, M.J., Liston, J. and Tuggle, H.D. 2005. *Intensive archaeological survey for the Palau Compact Road, Babeldaob Island, Palau. Historic preservation investigations Phase I, Volume I: Scope, background, results, evaluation and recommendations.* Prepared for the U.S. Army Corps of Engineers, Pacific Ocean Division, Hawai'i. International Archaeological Research Institute, Inc., Honolulu.